THE SOLUTION?

Daniel 11:20-45

A Historical Interpretation

ROBERT

KNUTSON

Olympus Story House

CONTENTS

The Solution?: Daniel 11:20-45 – A Historical Interpretation is a breakdown of some verses in the book of Daniel. Author Robert Knutson clearly expounded 25 verses; Daniel 11:20-45, analyzing and giving as much information as he could on each verse.

Verse 20 says 'And in his estate shall stand up a raiser of taxes in the glory of the kingdom; but within a few days, he shall be destroyed neither in anger nor in battle.' Robert Knutson spells out every single word in that verse to enable the reader to deeply understand what the words mean. To put this into perspective, the author highlighted 'And in his estate', and explained that it refers to the estate of the late Roman Republic (168–30BC), 'shall stand up' to mean the beginning of the early Roman Empire (30 BC–AD 14), 'a raiser of taxes' to mean Caesar Augustus, and so forth.

The author wrote so well that even young readers can comprehend the context of his text. Apart from his excellent narration, Robert Knutson included Bible verses from other books. This is commendable as the reader is enlightened on the relationship between the texts and other stories in the Bible. I would not know that 'but within a few days' referred to the relatively short three-and-a-half-year ministry of Jesus Christ. This book is more than enlightening. By reading *The Solution?: Daniel 11:20-45 – A Historical Interpretation* you are able to comprehend why some phrases are used in the Bible, and why some words carry more weight than others.

History lovers will have a wonderful experience reading about Catholicism in France, Julius Caesar, and religion in the 18th century. Reading about dechristianization and how it had forced religious observance into the privacy of the home was intriguing. I enjoyed reading about the effects of the French revolution, Napoleone 1 and his influence in the French society back then, the dynamics in the Catholic church in the 1700s, and how things gradually changed for the masses. The inclusion of the history of the church was a perfect addition as the author discussed Daniell 11: 40.

This book can be described as the best guide for anyone who does not understand the Bible, shifts in religion over the years, and other historical references in the book of Daniel and the entire Bible by extension. The simplicity of the author's words, his enthusiasm when writing and his style of narrating events are some of the things that make this book outstanding.

I highly recommend *The Solution?: Daniel 11:20-45 – A Historical Interpretation* to every reader who wants to read about Christian church history and the impact of religion. If there is one thing the author focused on when writing this book was the details in the text. The decoding of bible verses and technical Christian terms are what I found to be most profound.

-PACIFIC BOOK REVIEW

"It is perceived that individuals who support certain views, in this case theological, become soldiers of that cause."

In an age of religious unrest, wars between different ideologies begin to unravel "in conjunction with the glorious incarnation of Christ." These wars started as wars of words between churches and civil states, ultimately leading to many separations from the Roman Catholic church and the transition to schools of thought. Knuston analyzes these historical occurrences in relation to the prophecies of Daniel 11:20-45.

The book's organizational style is phenomenally well done. The author takes a passage he is analyzing, such as Daniel 11:20, and then puts that scriptural passage in boldface in the first lines of the chapter, a technique that lets readers know it is the subject of the analysis. He then proceeds to compare and explore every single word of that passage in relation to historical events. Knuston goes as far as redefining words that would have a different context in history through the use of the *Macropaedia of the Encyclopedia Britannica* and other sources. He also uses multiple translations of the Bible to determine any similarities or contrasting evidence between languages and printings. This process is essential in an interpretation because of the personal beliefs he is imposing. Without historical references and research, the presentation would possibly not come across as valid.

Knutson analyzes the prophecies of Daniel from the viewpoint that the "wars between the north and south are understood as 'wars of words.'" These prophecies are argued by the author to be the "persecution" of the Middle Ages and the move from religious faith to philosophical reason. This title is an excellent read for anyone who enjoys theological interpretations as well as history.

-US REVIEW OF BOOKS

A debut treatise that aims to find new meaning in the biblical Book of Daniel.

Knutson takes readers on a deep dive into a short biblical passage: Daniel 11:20–45. It's clear that the author is well versed in Scripture, church history, and linguistic critiques of the Bible. Unfortunately, his inelegant prose serves as an impenetrable barrier to reader understanding. His work apparently builds on the history of the Great Disappointment, when Baptist preacher William Miller's prediction that Jesus would return on October 22, 1844, didn't materialize. Miller's prophecy was reworked by his followers, and soon, the Seventh Day Adventist movement was born. As the author explains it, "It would be discovered that Christ had come in the fulfillment of the prophecy, but not to the earth as expected. He had come to the Day of Atonement, Investigative Judgemnt [sic] phase of the parable of the heavenly sanctuary." A strong knowledge of Millerite/Adventist theology might give a reader a bit more clarity, but for lay readers, Knudson's conclusions are far too vague. Aside from a confusing, two-paragraph foreword, the author provides no explanation of the intent of his work. Some sentences are nonsensical, such as, "An inner and outer man manifestation since the incarnation the estate referred to also has both realities." In other cases, the author's use of metaphors is simply mysterious: "In the meat of the apple, or walnut meat, being analogy, between the core of stiffer substance of faith and the skin which also confessed faith in God, or walnut nut [sic] meat, under the hard outer shell of faith— Lucifer unexplainably chose to breakfaith [sic] in God." Also, his intolerance of Catholicism, which he refers to in such terms as "the religio-politico vile person system of Roman Catholicism," may put off many readers. Throughout, Knutson uses the Book of Daniel to refer to various eras in church history, displaying a definitive depth of knowledge in that area.

A series of religious reflections by a well-versed author, hampered by opaque prose.

-KIRKUS REVIEW

FOREWORD

Set in the Old Testament prophetic fulfillment, historical, reality of the incarnation, the unfolding of this prophecy continues through the end of time, which is marked off by the end of the 2,300-day prophecy, of Daniel 8:14, October 22, 1844. Just as joy filled the hearts of those living in expectation of Messiah occurred as they listened to His teaching, so joy would fill the believers' heart down through history as they witnessed prophecy predicted by Christ, and other prophets, fulfilled.

The wars between the north and south are understood as "wars of words" regarding the nature of Christ between the bishoprics of Rome, the north, and Alexandria, Egypt, the south. After Daniel 11:31 the arguments over words, following the interlude Dan. 11:32–35 which accounts for the persecution of the Middle Ages move from theological faith to philosophical reason culminating in events after the close of the 2,300-day prophecy prior to the second coming of Christ.

DANIEL 11:20

20. And in his estate shall stand up a raiser of taxes in the glory of the kingdom; but within few days, he shall be destroyed neither in anger nor in battle.

And in his estate refers to the estate of the late Roman Republic (168–30 BC)[1] **shall stand up** the beginning of the early Roman Empire (30 BC–AD 14)[2] in which **a raiser of taxes** Caesar Augustus (Luke 2:1) **in the glory** (#1925 heder) at this juncture in the prophetic flow takes on a dual interpretation from the word (#4515 mo'-shel Dan.11:4) namely (1) empire and (2) parallel dominion, like **of the kingdom** which is the "sinful kingdom" Amos 9:8 of human nature on this earth.

#1925 heh'-der; from1921; honour; used (fig) for the capital (Jerusalem:- glory *Strongs*, 1979)

#1925 heder n. m. splendor; "the royal splendor" may refer to the land of Israel, with the focus that this land is a valued ornament of the king:- glory *Strongs*, 2001

The aspect of the definition which seems to fit the historical-prophetic context for the word 'glory' refers to the land of Israel during the life and ministry of Christ specifically highlighting his journey's to and from Jerusalem. While he lived in the land of Israel which was part of the Roman empire, which was also part of the 'sinful kingdom" (Amos 9:8) of human nature, his kingdom was 'not of this world.' (John 18:36). It was a kingdom of the "inner man." (Ephesians 3:16) which was instructed by the parables of Jesus in conjunction with the Old Testament teaching.

It is perceived prophetically and historically that this "glory" does refer to Israel and Jerusalem in the statement of Simeon regarding the baby Jesus—"a light to the Gentiles, and the glory of thy people Israel" (Luke 2:32) coupled to Anna, a prophetess testimony who "spake of him to all them that looked for redemption in Jerusalem" (Luke 2:38).

1

Sources indicate that Caeser Augustus was a "ruler whose program they glorified" and that he lived in "the glory of Italy"[3] enjoying political/civil empire "glory" during his reign as Roman emperor. He is perceived to be the historical fulfillment of this prophecy because he is the only ruler associated with God becoming man in the person of Jesus Christ. As the incarnation of Jesus Christ, the second person of the Godhead simultaneously occurred, that "parallel dominion, like" "glory" was literally proclaimed by the angels to the shepherds (Luke 2:14), Simeon (Luke 2:25–32) in the temple, prophetically announced by the prophet Haggai as "glory coming to the temple" (Haggai 2:9), and in "figure" (#3850 par-bo-lay) (Hebrews 9:9) which is the same word Jesus used when "he began to speak unto them in parables (#3850 par-ab-ol-ay.)" (Mark 12:1). Thus, when God had given the command recorded in Exodus 25:8, "Let them make me a sanctuary that I may dwell among them," he proclaimed in their literal deliverance from Egyptian bondage through the blood of the slain lamb or goat applied to the doorposts of their dwellings, i.e., at the future incarnation of himself. As the second person of the Godhead, he would become "the lamb of God, which taketh away the sin of the world" (John 1:29). He would was also represented as a more elaborate tent (the tabernacle surrounded by the sanctuary) than that which the Israelites dwelt in after coming out of Egypt/sin. Into that tabernacle only priests were to enter, while all Israel, symbolizing the world were invited to enter with appropriate sacrifices. These behaviors were an anticipation of the future calvary figurative/spiritual deliverance from the enslaving bondage of sin at the upcoming sacrifice at the cross he would make. Historically, Moses' reception from God of instructions as how to build the sanctuary occurred in the fourth, fifth, and sixth month after the Exodus from Egypt/sin. In this time frame, Moses experienced two forty days' stay on Mt. Sinai preceded by three days of preparation to hear the Ten Commandments spoken, followed by seven days, equaling ninety days from arrival at Mt. Sinai, totaling 180 days, or six months from the Exodus. In a similar manner, so the coming of the incarnate redeemer would occur sometime after the fall of Adam and Eve. The construction of the sanctuary and tabernacle portrayed descriptively how God, in the second person of the Godhead, would accomplish reconciliation of fallen man to Himself and eternal banishment and obliteration of Satan and his angels from the universe. Thus, the body (Hebrews 10:5) literally prepared for Christ at His incarnation was figuratively portrayed years earlier as the tabernacle

2

in the wilderness sanctuary into which all Jewish, and for that matter humanity, was to enter and find reconciling fellowship to God. A year after the Exodus, the glory of the Lord filled the wilderness tabernacle. In like manner, so after the fall of Adam and Eve years later, at his baptism, A.D. 27 concluding the sixty-nine-week prophecy (Daniel 9:25), he would be filled by the Holy Spirit and ignited for three-and-a-half years of ministry, even as the glory of the Lord filled the first tabernacle, one year after the Exodus (Exodus 40:34, 35) and filled Solomon's temple (1 Kings 8;11, 2 Chronicles 7:1, 2). Thus when Christ said, "Destroy this temple and three days I will raise it up," speaking of His body, when the dove symbol of the Holy Spirit descended upon Him at His baptism, the plant-based wick spirits of humanity in the seven-branch candlestick was ignited as "the light of the world" (John 8:12) and lamb of God who would "take away the sin of the world" (John 1:29). Thus Christ's life was the "temple of the tabernacle" (Rev. 15:5). He proclaimed that His kingdom was a "parallel dominion like," in the inner man (Ephesians 3:16), soliciting heartfelt response to, the parables he taught. That kingdom was "not of this world, but from another place" (John 18:36). That other place was the inner man's (Ephesians 3:16) capacity to respond in allegiance to God in "a kingdom that was within you" (Luke 17:21). While the first definition "empire" would continue, it would be joined by a second "parallel dominion, like" kingdom in Christ's ministry in which the parables he taught would solicit the "inner man," hearer response of allegiance to God.

Glory of the kingdom

The glory of the kingdom, the Amos 9:8, sinful kingdom of fallen humanity occurs between the sixty-ninth week of the prophecy of Daniel 9:24 of the seventy week prophecy and the seventieth week, the beginning of which was A.D. 27 with the baptism of Jesus, which extended one week, or seven years to A.D. 34 when Stephen was stoned resulting in the gospel going to the Gentiles which ends the Daniel 9:24 seventy week prophecy.

Prior to that glorious week, which extended from A.D. 27 to A.D. 34, the last week of the Daniel 9:24 prophecy, there were many old Testament prophesies that predicted Christ's coming. Among them are: the Genesis 3:15 promise given to Eve; Deuteronomy 18:18 given to Moses; Isaiah 53 given to Isaiah; Haggai 2:9 of the latter glory would exceed the earlier glory, that is Christ woud enter the temple. Even before the great week and glorious week of the prophecy, angels announced to the shepherds

3

that he was born in Bethlehem and the wise men from the east followed the star to the place that Jesus was living. When Christ was eight days old, his parents took him to the temple to be circumcised and blest. Even in the temple, the prophetess Anna spoke of the glory that had come to Jerusalem in the birth of Jesus. At age twelve, his parents took him to the temple where he had discussions with the priests, Pharisees, and other temple teachers, telling his inquiring parents that he must be about his Fathers business. Of Christ it is said, "He increased in wisdom and statue and in favor with God and man."

At his baptism, A.D. 27, began the prophetic week "of the glory of the kingdom," the last week of the seventy week prophecy of Daniel 9:24, when the dove of the Holy Spirit lite on his shoulder after his baptism. Later John would write, "And we beheld his glory, the glory as of the only begotten of the Father, full of grace and truth. In John 2:11, John said that the miracle of Cana, changing water into wine that Christ manifested his glory. At the resurrection of Lazarus recorded in John 11:40, after Lazarus had been dead for four days, and the stone had been rolled away from the tomb, Jesus said to Martha, "If thou shouldest believe, thou shouldest see the glory of God." Then Christ raised Lazarus from the dead, who had been dead four days.

In Luke 9:32 on the Mount of Transfiguration, three disciples got a taste of Christ's glory that would be experienced at the second coming, when he would come to this earth a second time. When Christ rose from the dead, the disciples would see and acknowledge that God the Father according to Romans 6:4 the glory of the Father forgiving sins as he accepted the atoning sacrifice of Christ. This reality would enable every believer like Paul to exclaim down through the ages, the forgiveness of sin through Christ's substitute sacrifice, saying "God forbid that I should glory, save in the cross of our Lord Jesus Christ by whom the world is cruficifed to me and I to the world." (Galations 6:14)

When that ongoing experience occurs the believer can say with Christ, following his example, I have overcome the world that is the outside faith atmosphere of the world by faith even as Christ did. That glory of living as an overcomer of sin by faith in Christ's substitute sacrifice for sin, by faith in Christ by overcoming according to the messages to the seven churches in Revelation 2-3, living in his forgiveness would be the believers experience in the "glory of the kingdom" until the second coming of Christ.

But within few days refers to the relatively short three-and-a-half-year ministry of Christ.

He would be destroyed refers predictively to the upcoming crucifixion of Christ which would literally occur in Dan. 11:26 identified in the prophetic words, "Those who eat from a portion of his meat shall destroy him" and prophetically refer to the destruction of Arianism ([AD 320] heretical belief advocated by Arius of Alexandria, Egypt) that Christ was the first creation of God by the Council of Constantinople I (A.D. 381).

Neither in anger or battle literally refers predictively in the upcoming crucifixion of Christ that no one could kill him in anger or battle, but that his death was a result of him laying down his life in atonement for sin, only to take it up again (John 10:17) in a triumphal resurrection. In Christs' day these battles were fought over "who do you say I am?" (see Luke 9:20) Prophetically this passage refers to the "war of words" in the AD 325.

Council of Nicea and the AD 787 Second Ecumenical of Nicea. This standing for belief, was not in anger, but for the promotion of what was the right, orthodox, view of the nature of Christ contrasted initially to the wrong, heretical, view of Arianism advocated in A.D. 320 by Arius of Alexandria. These were not physical but argument battles.

DANIEL 11:21

21. And in his estate shall stand up a vile person, to whom they shall not give the honour of the kingdom: but he shall come in peaceably, and obtain the kingdom by flatteries.

And his estate

An inner and outer man manifestation since the incarnation the estate referred to also has both realities. On the one hand, according to the image of Daniel 2, Rome rules over the world. On the other hand, since the beginning of Christ's ministry, an antitypical inner man allegiance to God potential in the presence of Christ was simultaneously observable. Thus Christ would say,

"My kingdom is not of this world: if my kingdom were of this world, then would my servants fight, that that I should not be delivered to the Jews: but now is my kingdom not from hence." Pilate therefore said unto Him, "Art thou a king then?" Jesus answered, "Thou sayest that I am a king. To this end was I born, and for this cause came I into the world, that I should bear witness to the truth. Every one that is of the truth heareth my voice." (John 18:36, 37)

Christ prayed,

"I pray not that thou shouldest take them out of the world, but that thou shouldest keep them from the evil. They are not of the world, even as I am not of the world. (John 17:15, 16)

In his estate, i.e., the estate of sinful human nature, which according to Amos 9:8 is a sinful kingdom, the incarnation of Christ Jesus, the second person of the Godhead, enclosed with His righteousness. This enclosure of humanity was symbolized/depicted in the linen curtain that surrounded the Hebraic sanctuary.

Initially, the estate of sinful human nature, i.e., Adam and Eve after the fall, the Israelites enslaved by Egyptian bondage could only experience a covering of their nakedness by the blood of the slain

6

(presumed) lamb whose skin provided clothing, release from Egyptian-sin enslavement by the blood on their doorposts would after a year from the exodus entitle them to walk as priests clothed in linen under the tabernacle coverings of goat's hair, ram's skins dyed red which symbolized the blood on their doorposts in Egypt, and hides of sea cows or badger skins, despite nine months earlier at Mt. Sinai where they discovered what they were redeemed from Egypt-sin to be. They were to become a kingdom of priests. Alongside discovering what they were redeemed from Egypt to be, they discovered the behavioral boundaries of the Ten Commandments which would be a fence witness to the world of the love of God demonstrating to the world what a life of allegiance to God looked like.

For three months after the Exodus from Egypt/sin until that nation/believer came to Mt. Sinai where they not only discovered what they were to become, a kingdom of priests, but also how a priestly nation was to live, by the same "law of faith" (see Rom. 1:17) in the command of Moses to "slay the lamb, apply its blood to the doorposts of their dwellings, and enter in, and be saved from Egyptian bondage/sin's enslavement, now in their experience of "growth in grace" were commanded to live a life of faith according to the Ten Commandments

Like the Israelites who came out of Egypt, living in tents on their journey from Egypt/sin to Canaan/heaven living in tents, so Christ—depicted as a tabernacle in the sanctuary who came out of heaven to dwell among humanity—would eventually dwell among Israel/sinful human nature in a more elaborate dwelling. All Christ invited all human nature who were apart of the sinful kingdom (Amos 9:8) to come into a relationship to Himself.

The Israelites entered the Hebraic sanctuary in the wilderness with appropriate lamb and cow sacrifices. They sacrificed them in the midst of the outer court. The priests lay the slain sacrifice on the altar, entitling the penitent believer to receive a "type" of forgiveness of his sin. So Christ, as the lamb of God would lay down His life, providing atonement for all humanity. Those who believed in his substitute sacrifice for sin would be "antitypically" forgiven of their sins. Thus, the reality of "for God so loved the world that he gave his only begotten son that whosoever believeth in him should not perish but have everlasting life" (Jn. 3:16) could be antitypically claimed in the experience of the believer.

The sacrifices were symbols of Christ at the incarnation who became the lamb of God. The Israelite laid their hands on the sacrifice confessing

7

their sins, receiving a "type" forgiveness of sin. So the believer continues to bring "type" sacrifices to the altar of burnt offering. After Christ's resurrection, and ascension, the believer would figuratively bring Christ, the antitypical Lamb of God, to the "antitypical" cross of Calvary. This was the "type" in the altar of burnt offering, laying his hands figuratively on Christ, transferring his guilt from himself to the lamb of God, and receiving "antitypical" forgiveness (see Leviticus 4:20, 26, 31, 35) for sins committed.

Before that antitypical Calvary event would occur portrayed as the fourteenth day (see Exodus 12:6) of the first month after the incarnation, Christ lived at home for the first twelve years of his life. There he "increased in wisdom and stature and in favor with God and man" (Luke 2:52). At twelve years of age, the age of accountability, he knowledgeably went to the temple, although shortly after birth he had gone unknowingly with his influential parents to the temple. After this first encounter with the temple, although it is presumed that his parents had previously told him of it, he returned to Nazareth and worked with his father Joseph as a carpenter. In the antitypical clock of salvation history, on the tenth day (see Exodus 12:3) of the first month, which was the sixty-ninth week of the prophecy in Daniel 9, Christ began His public ministry for three-and-a-half years, in AD 27 with his baptism by John, after which the dove symbol of the Holy Spirit flew to his shoulder and the voice of the Father was heard, "This is my beloved Son in whom I am well pleased" (Matthew 3:17). From his baptism, Christ was driven by the Holy Spirit into the wilderness where he was tested for forty days. Those forty days are perceived to parallel the first forty days (see Numbers 14:34) that the twelve Israelite spies explored the promised land of Canaan, with ten not believing God could give them the promised land while only Caleb and Joshua believed God was able. After forty days in the wilderness, the devil came to Christ and tempted him to break "the law of faith" (Romans 3:27) in God, on the head's side of the love coin, which Eve broke by taking and eating the forbidden fruit, which Adam also later ate, as it were, growing from "faith unto faith" (Romans 1:17) and his spoken (see Exodus 20) and later written (see Exodus 32:19) Ten Commandments word. While God had promised the land of Canaan to the Israelite nation, if they only believed his promises, with ten manifesting doubt and two manifesting belief, Christ manifested belief that humanity, even in their degenerate since the fall condition, if their heart was shielded by faith in God could live victorious over Satan and his temptations to doubt God, taking situations into their own outside faith hands rather than maintaining trust and faith in God that He would supply all their needs, they could be victorious over the temptations of Satan by quoting the promises of Scripture which says, "It is written."

In antitypical reality with His inner plant-based wick spirit on the oil symbol of the Holy Spirit inside the seven-branch golden candlesticks, the gold symbolizing faith, Christ was the light of the world. He was touched by fallen human nature's mineral-based bronze humanity, which is symbolically birthed from the brass/bronze loin region of the image of Daniel 2. He possessed a bronze censor attitude which did the will of his father in heaven. That will was contained inside his bronze censor mind which was different from fallen humanity, who originally before the fall of human nature possessed a gold, symbol of faith (see 1 Peter 1:7), censor mind. Christ took upon himself a body [see Hebrew 10:5] common to fallen mankind, with its physical degeneracy, nevertheless possessing a right inner spirit at the incarnation. Of that experience, the Pen of Inspiration writes about Christ:

"He left His royalty, laid aside His glory, sacrifice His riches, and clothed His divinity with humanity, that he might reach men where they were. His example shows that He laid down His life for sinners."[4]

"Christ spoke with the authority of a king, and in His appearance, and in the tones of His voice, there was that which they had no power to resist. At the word of command they realized, as they had never realized before, there true position as hypocrites and robbers. When divinity flashed through humanity, not only did they see indignation on Christ's countenance; they realized the import of His words. They felt as if before the throne of the eternal Judge, with their sentence passed on them for time and eternity. For a time they were convinced that Christ was a prophet; and many believed Him to be the Messiah. The Holy Spirit flashed into their minds the utterances of the prophets concerning Christ. Would they yield to this conviction?"[5]

Prior to that experience on earth, the second person of the Godhead hypostasis plant-based incense divinity in heaven was in fellowship with the hypostasis heat, first person of the Godhead Father and third person of the Godhead Holy Spirit, who possessed a dual hypostasis essence of plant-based oil and elemental atmosphere like air. All three members of the Trinity. They united together in a consuming fire fellowship within the golden censor which was replicated as golden censor minds to all free thinking creatures throughout the universe of God's love.

9

Now at the incarnation, which occurred after the fall of humanity, still maintaining his plant based hypostasis essence, he extended it to a plant based wick spirit in the golden cup of faith. This extension is like a caterpillar extending itself through metamorphosis to a butterfly. Christ's extension was like a reverse metamorphosis from a butterfly, as it were in heaven, to fallen mankind on earth, typified as a caterpillar, unable because of sin to fly. That plant based wick spirit was enough like fallen humanities plant based wood spirit which was the fuel for the fire on the altar of burnt offering to be their savior. It was enough ullike fallen humanities spirit that it could be one day, in the gold cup of faith [see 1 Peter 1:7], be eventually baptized into the oil symbol of the Holy Spirit contained in the golden seven-branch candelabra. because his inner plant-based wick spirit was inside the gold cups of faith in the seven-branch candelabra.

As such, Christ dwelt among fallen creatures, whose bronze censor mind is like his human bronze censor mind. However, Christ's plant-based spirit wick-Roman world. was unlike fallen human nature's wood spirit. Those fallen human nature spirits could only be used for fuel in the fire on the altar of burnt offering in the midst of the outer court of the Hebraic sanctuary to support and sustain the lamb or other sacrifices. While plant-based wood spirits will be saved because they support and are surrendered to upholding the lamb or other sacrifice, the invitation will be extended to all to grow in the grace, being transformed from plant-based wood spirits used on the altar of burnt offering symbol of the cross of Calvary to plant-based wick spirits fit to burn on the oil symbol of the Holy Spirit inside the gold cup symbol of faith in the seven-branch candelabra as witnesses to the world. It t is true "to everyone is given a measure of faith" (Rom. 12:3). It is also perceived to be reasonable that it is easier for a plant-based wick spirit in the oil of the Holy Spirit surrounded by the gold cup of faith to live a life victorious over sin than for a plant-based wood spirit with "a measure of faith" (Rom. 12:3) to be able to use the "shield of faith" (Eph. 6:16).

Christ knew while on earth that— He possessed the same degenerate body common to man. His inner-man spirit—being a plant-based wick in the oil of the candelabra. . was unlike theirs which was wood. This reality was designed from eternity so that all fallen, human beings through His upcoming provisional atonement on Calvary could be antitypically transformed from plant-based wood spirits to plant-based wick spirits like himself. These light were to be witnesses with the oil

10

of the Holy Spirit within the gold cups of faith., ignited in a witness of allegiance to God by the hypostasis heat, first person of the Godhead, Father.

shall stand up (#5975 aw-mad lit. and fig. trans. and intrans.)

#5927 aw-mad: a prim root: to stand, in various relations lit. and fig., intrans. and trans): abide (behind), appoint, arise, cease, confirm, continue, dwell, be employed, endure establish, leave, make, ordain be [over], place, (be) present, (self, raise up, remain, remain, repair, + serve, set (forth, over, - tle, up, remain, repair, + serve, set (forth, over, -tle, up), (make to, make to be at a, with-) stand (by, fast, firm, still, up), (be at a) stay (up), tarry. <u>Strongs</u>, 1979

#5975 a-la v. [Q] to go up, ascend, rise,; [N] to be lifted up, withdraw, be exalted; [H] to take up, set up, offer a sacrifice; [Ho] to be offered up, be carried away, be recorded; [Ht] to raise oneself up; from the base meaning of rise in elevation comes the fig. extension "to exalt, honor, "as the lifting up of a person in status. <u>Strongs</u>, 2001

The aspect of the definition which seems to fit the historical-prophetic context for the word "stand up" refers to the literal influencial power of the Roman Catholic church over the figurative/spiritual belief system of Christian believers.

In the perspective of this prophetic interpretation, it is perceived that the historic/prophetic flow of

shall stand up a vile person (#959 baw-zaw)

#959 ; baw-zaw; a prim. root; to disesteem;- dispise, disdain, contemn (- ptible). + think to scorn, vile person. *Strongs,* 2010

#959 ba-za v. [Q] to despise, scorn, ridicule, show contempt for; [Op] to be despised; [N] to be despised, be contemptible; [H] cause to despise. *Strongs,* 2001. refers to the development of the Roman Catholic church.

The aspect of the definition which seems to fit the historial-prophetic context for the word "vile person," has to do with the contempt that the system of Roman Catholicism held against beliefs which were specifically Jewish, namely the seventh-day Sabbath.

I. Polycarp c.. AD 69–155

    A. Links together the apostolic age and nascent Catholicism

    B. Is a link between the apostolic age and the first of the catholic fathers,

    C. Is a living link between the apostolic age and the great writers who flo at the end of the second century. [6]

II. Ignatius of Antioch (d. 107, or 108 Foundations for dogmas that would be formulated in succeeding generations was laid by Ignatius of

Antioch[7] Christian religion in transition from Jewish origins to it assimilation into the Greco-Roman world.[8]

A. Basic tenants of belief promoted by Ignatius

  1. "Side with bishop."

  2. On this earth, the bishop represents to his church the true bishop, Christ

  3. Union with the bishop in belief and worship means union with Christ.

    a. Those who in a spirit of pride break away from the bishop destroy union.

  4. The unity of the church with its monarchial structure is a concrete realization of future life in Christ.

    a. Authority within the church has not yet become for him a principled institutional discipline.

  5. He uses, for the first time in Christian literature, the expression Catholic Church.

  6. He speaks of the Roman Christians in a letter to the church of Rome in of special distinction.

    a. The Roman church holds first place in the whole Christian "community of love" (agape).[9]

The "standing up" of the religio-politico "vile person," Roman Catholicism can be pictured in the following circlar historical stair step tower.

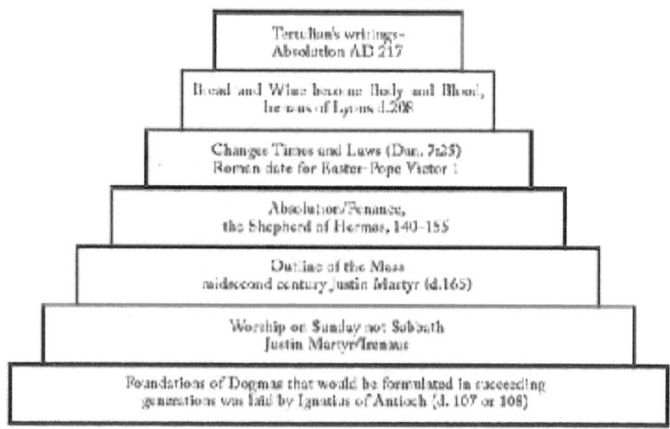

    Tertullian's writings–
    Absolution AD 217

    Bread and Wine become Body and Blood,
    Irenæus of Lyons d.208

    Changes Times and Laws (Dan. 7:25)
    Roman date for Easter–Pope Victor I

    Absolution/Penance,
    the Shepherd of Hermas, 140–155

    Outline of the Mass
    midsecond century, Justin Martyr (d.165)

    Worship on Sunday not Sabbath
    Justin Martyr/Irenæus

    Foundations of Dogmas that would be formulated in succeeding
    generations was laid by Ignatius of Antioch (d. 107 or 108)

The first and bottom step being the foundations for dogmas that would be formulated in succeeding generations laid by Ignatius of Antioch (d. 107 or 108).[10] The second ascending circular stair step in this tower is "worship on Sunday not Sabbath" as advocated by Justin Martyr (d. 165)[11] and Irenaus (d. 208). [Note: Mark 15:42ff] "The Sabbath began at sundown on Friday and ended at sundown on Saturday. Jesus died just a few hours before sundown on Friday. It was against Jewish law to do physical work or to travel on Sabbath. It was also against Jewish law to let a dead body remain exposed overnight (Deuteronmy 21:23). Joseph came to bury Jesus body before the Sabbath began. If Jesus had died on the Sabbath when Joseph was unavailable, his body would have been taken down by the Romans. Had the Romans taken Jesus'body, no Jews could have confirmed his death, and opponents could have disputed his resurrection." [Note: Luke 6:1, 2] "In Jewish legal tradition, there were 39 categories of activity forbidden on the Sabbath-and harvesting was one of them. The teachers of the law even went so far as to describe different methods of harvesting. One method was to rub the heads of grain between the hands, as the disciples were doing here. God's law said farmers were to leave the edges of their fields unplowed so travelers and the poor could eat from this bounty (Deuteronomy 23:25), so the disciples were not guilty of stealing grain. Neither were they breaking the Sabbath by doing their daily work on it. In fact, though they may have been violating the Pharisees' rules, they were not breaking any divine law."[6] The third ascending historical step is the outline of the Mass, by midsecond century Justin Martyr (d. 165). The fourth historical step is the absolution/penance advocated by the Shepherd of Hermas (140–155).[12] The fifth historical step begins the "thinking to change times and laws" (Dan. 7:25) when Pope Victor changed the Jewish date for Easter to the Roman date.[13] The fifth sixth step is the belief that the bread and wine become the body and blood of Christ as advocated by Ireanaeus of Lyons (d. 208). The seventh step is the writings on absolution AD 217 by Tertullian.[14]

I. The Quartodecimens or Asiatic churches manifested noncompliance with Roman date for Easter AD 196. [15]

II. Tertulian does not give the bishop of Rome exclusive jurisdictional rig absolve a penitent. [16]

III. Cyprian, Bishop of Carthage, opposed with resolution and success ambition of the Roman Pontiff. [17]

IV. Vigilantius of Toulouse of Gaul, criticized the basic principle of the c relics, declaring that it constituted nothing less than idolatry.[18]

A. He was an early Christian priest against who St. Jerome (347– 419) wrote a defense of monasticism in 406.[19]

but he shall come in peaceably,

I. Great external peace for the Roman church during the closing years of the reign of Commodus (180–192) and early years of Septimus Severus

(Roman emperor 193–211)[20] (from 193)[21] During the reign of pope Urban I (220–230) was also "a time of peace for the church."[22]

and obtain the kingdom by flatteries.

I. There are at least five flatteries by which Roman Catholicism obtained an influential supervisory role in governing the historical church.

    A. The bishop of Rome claimed to have exclusive jurisdictional right absolve the penitent.

        1. Baronidus (1538–1607) and the flatterers of the bishop of Rome triump in the passage of Tertullian (d. 220) in which he does not give the bisho of Rome exclusive jurisdictional right to absolve a penitent.[23]

    B. The "intrigue" (NIV) that the pope is always chosen by the Holy Ghost.

        1. Modern notion: Pope is always chosen by the Holy Ghost. The idea was first espoused at an assembly which elected Pope Fabianus (236–250 when a dove unexpectedly lite on his head, not being an inhabitant of Rome, a layman, he was not even considered a candidate.[24]

    C. Participating in pagan worship offering incense to Jupiter, Hercules, and Saturn.

        1. Pope Marcellinus (296–308) in the temple of Vesta he offers incense to Jupiter, Hercules, and Saturn. It flatters the ambition of the successors to Marcellinius. On the occasion of his fall, it exalts the see of Rome abov other sees. [25]

    D. Receive letters from the unorthodox.

        1. Pope Julius I (337–352) receives flattering letters 341 from Eusebian (proponents of Arianism). [26]

    E. Imitating the awful secrecy which reigned in the Eleusian mysteries.

        1. By imitating the awful secrecy which reigned in the Eleusinia mysteries, the Christians had flattered themselves that they should rende their sacred institutions more respectable in the eyes of the paga world.[27]

DANIEL 11:22

22. And with the arms of a flood shall they be overflown from before his, and shall be broken; yea, also the prince of the covenant.

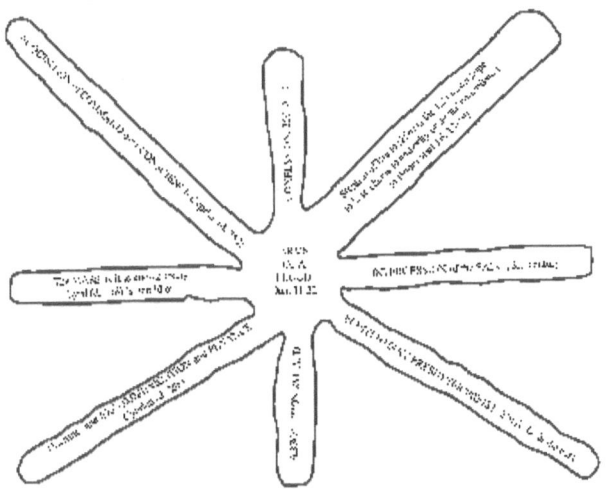

And with the arms of a flood

The word for "arms" (#2220 zer-o-ah) according to <u>Strongs Concordance</u>, 1979 is defined as "the arm (as stretched out) or (of animals) the foreleg: fig. force:-xcommunication arm + help, mighty, power, shoulder strength."

The word for "arms," (#2220 zer-o-ah) according to *Strongs Condance*, 1979, is defined as "the arm (as stretched out) or (of animals) the foreleg- (fig.) force: arm, to help, mighty, power, shoulder strength. The aspect of the definition which seems to fit the historical-prophetic context is the literal outer man and figurative-spiritual inner man [see Ephesians 3:16] belief force exercised first of all in ecclesiastical circles and systems which eventually influenced the civil realm. Those beliefs were based on faith or unbelief [see Romans 11:20].

For example, the third century teaching on excommunitation was rooted in the Scriptural account of Christ's parents who feared they would be thrown out of the synagogue by if they confessed that their son Jesus was the Christ. [see John 9:22]. Just a few verses later, after testifying that Christ had healed his blindness, he was "cast out" (word in Greek means excommunication) of the Pharisees fellowship. [see John 9:34]. Hence, the roots of the mid-third century doctrine of excommunication.[28]

Jesus taught the way to be reconciled if that person had been wronged by another individual in Matthew 18:15-18:

> "Moreover, if thy brother shall trespass against thee, go and tell him his fault between thee and him alone: if he shall hear thee, thou hast gained thy brother. But if he will not hear thee, then take with thee one or two more, that in the mouth of two or three witnesses every word may be established. And if he shall neglet to hear them, tell it unto the church: but if he neglect to hear the church, let him be unto thee as an heathen man and a publican. Verily I say unto you, Whatsoever ye shall bind on earth shall be bound in heaven: and whatsoever ye shall loose on earth shall be loosed in heaven."

"Note Matthew 18:15-17 (Josh 7:10-26). Some are Not to Be Retained.- "The names of those who sin and refuse to repent should not be retained on the church books, let the saints be held accountable for their evil deeds. Those who pursue a course of transgression should be visited and labored with, and if they then refuse to repent, they should be separated from church fellowship, in accordance with the rules laid down in the Word of God. . .

Those who refuse to hear the admonitions and writings given by God's faithful messengers are not to be retained in the church. They are to be disfellowshiped, for they will be as Achan in the camp of Israel-deceived and deceiving.

Who, after reading the record of Achan's sin and punishment, can think it according to the will of God that those who do wickedly, refusing to repent, are to be retained in the church? To retain them would be an insult to the God of heaven. (Letter 215, 1902)"[29]

"[see EGW on John 20:23.] [Note John 20:23] (Matthew 16:18, 19; 18:18). Man Cannot Remove One Stain of Sin.- Christ gave no ecclesiastical right to forgive sin, nor to sell indulgences, that man may sin without incurring the displeasure of God, nor did he give His servants

16

liberty to accept a gift or bribe for cloaking sin, that it may escape merited censure. Jesus charged his disciples to preach the remission of sin *in his name* among all nations; but they themselves were not empowered to remove one stain of sin from the children of Adam. . .Whoever would attract people to himself as one in whom is invested power to forgive sins, incurs the wrath of God, for he turns souls away from the heavenly Pardoner to a weak and erring mortal (3SP 222)."[30]

The third century belief arm of appealing to the state, in the A.D. 272 instance of Paul of Samosata,[31] is rooted in the events surrounding Calvary when a group of religious people, the the unbelieving Jewish leaders [see Acts 7:52], although they were offered forgiveness at Calvary appealed to Pilate, the civil state, [see John 19:15, 16] to have Christ crucified. Yet, even though many religious leaders initially held onto an attitude of unbelief in Christ, eventually many, including priests, eventually came around to believing in him. [see Acts 6:7] This all occurred prior to the stoning of Stephen A.D. 34 recorded in Luke 7 which marked the end of the seventy week prophecy of Daniel 9:24. That event marked the end of the gospel being exclusively with the Jewish nation. Now the gospel would go to the world.

The third century arm of forgiveness and absolution[32] is rooted in the event where the priests said "only God can forgive sins" coupled to Christ's cry on Calvary "father forgive them for they know not what they do" (Luke 23:34). From this "type" or "antitypical" grace taught in the Lord's prayer "forgive us our debts as we forgive our debtors," (Matthew 6:12) all believers are empowered to forgive others.

The third century arm of confession[33] is rooted in 1st John 1:9: "If we confess our sins he is faithful and just to forgive our sin."

The word for "flood" (#7857 shaw-taf) according to Strongs Concordance, 1979 is defined as "a primary root; to gush; by impl. to inundate, cleanse; by anal. To gallop, conquer, drown, (over-) flow (-whelm), rinse, run, rush (thoroughly) wash (away).

The aspect of the definition of the word for "flood" which seems to fit the historical-prophetic context is to "inundate." In the time of Christ, the mind/heart/garden plot, soil estate of Judaism was inundated by tradition:

"The Pharisees traditions and their interpretations and applications of the laws had become as important to them as God's law itself. Their laws were not all bad-some were beneficial. The problem arose when when the religious leaders (1) took manmade rules as seriously as God's law, (2) told the people to obey these rules but did not do so themselves, or (3) obeyed the rules not to honor God but make themselves look good. Usually Jesus did not condemn what the Pharisees taught but what they were hypocrites."[34]

"God's law said that crops should not be harveseted on the Sabbath (Exodus 34:21). The law prevented farmers from becoming greedy and ignoring God on the Sabbath. It also protected laborers from being overworked."

"The Pharisees interpreted the action of Jesus and his disciples-picking heads of grain and eating it as they walked through the fields- as harvesting, and so they judged Jesus as a lawbreaker. But Jesus and the disciples clearly were not harvesting the grain for personal gain: they were simply looking for something to eat. The Pharisees were so focused on the words of the rule that they missed the intent."[35]

"The Pharisees added hundreds of their own petty rules and regulations to God's holy laws, and they tried to force people to follow these rules. These men claimed to know God's will in every detail of life. There are still religious leaders today who add rules and regulations to God's Word, causing much confusion among believers. It is idolatry to claim that you interpretation of God's Word is as important as God's Word itself. It is especially dangerous to set up unbiblical standards for others to follow. Instead look to Christ for guidance about your own behavior, and let him lead others in the details of their lives."[36]

By Jesus's time, the Jews had accumulated hundreds of laws — 613 by one historian's count. Some religious leaders tried to distinguish between major and minor laws, and some taught that all laws were equally binding and that it was dangerous to make any distinctions. This teacher's question could have provided controversy among these groups, but Jesus' answer summarized all of God's laws.[37]

"According to the traditions of the religious leaders, no healing could be done on the Sabbbath. Healing they argued, was practicing medicine, and a person could not practice his or her profession on the Sabbath. It was more important for the religious leaders to protect their laws than to free a person from painful suffering."[38]

"According to the Pharisees, carrying a mat on the Sabbath was work and therefore unlawful. It did not break an Old Testament law, but the Pharisees' interpretation of God's command to "remember the Sabbath day by keeping it holy" (Exodus 20:8). This was just one of the hundreds of rules they had added to the Old Testament law."[39]

It is perceived that in the prophetic verse flow of Dan. 11:22, the arms referred to are the literal beliefs, initially advocated by religious thought leaders in Christianity that would have a literal- figurative/spiritual impact, or influence, upon followers in Christianity. These beliefs would flood the mind/heart, soil, garden plot estate of Christendom, inundating their views as they professed to follow Christ.

The arms of a flood state are as follows:

I. Arms

  1. Confession/penitentiary priests

    A. Confession/penitentiary priests were established in the East after January 250 edict of the Roman emperor requiring all citizen perform a religious sacrifice in the presence of commissioners.[40]

Flood

  1. Confession/penitentiary priests

    A. The flood stage of confession developed visibly by the Fourth La? Council of 1215 when confession becomes a sacrament.[41]

      a. The official Catholic doctrine on confession promulgate in 1 "sacrament of penance" established the necessity of auricular rejecting the 1215 opinion.[42]

      b. Canon 6 says, "If anyone denies that sacramental confession was by divine law or is necessary to salvation; or says that the confessing secretly to a priest alone, which the Catholic church observed from the beginning and still observes, is at varianc institution and command of Christ and is a human contrivance, anathema."[43]

Arms

  2. Absolution

    A. Rooted in the Shepherd of Hermas 140–155, Tertulian, popes Call and Hippolytus 217, this belief arm flexed with the 251, mid century consensus at Rome which held that bishops and presbyter their ordination were vested with the power to bind and loose 16:18–19), to excommunicate and absolve.[44] The influential beli extended with the 251 Council of Carthage right and power to r deadly sins.[45] This arm stretched with the Baptismal controversy regarding absolution given by imposition of hands in R Alexandria, and Palestine.)[46]

Flood

  2. Absolution

    a. The flood stage of absolution is historically viewable by replacement of the supplicatory (May the Lord absolve the authoritative form (May the Lord absolve thee and I also absolve t b. The Council of Trent

The following sections are lifted from *www.trosch.org/chu/trent-1html*

1' The Council of Trent Canon 9 states, "If any one says that the sacramental absolution of the priest is not a judicial act but a mere service of pronouncing and declaring to him who confesses that the sins are forgiven, provided only he believes himself to be absolved, even though the priest absolves not in earnest but only in jest; or says that the confession of the penitent is not necessary in order that the priest may be able to absolve him, let him be anathema."[48]

3. Current Roman Catholic stance on absolution

a. December 12, 1984, Los Angeles Times in the article, "No Forgi 'Directly from God,' Pope says."[49]

Arms

4. Penance

a. At the council of Carthage 251, Cyprian says, "No one should be excluded from penance."[50]

Flood

Penance

A. Council of Trent[51]

The following are lifted from *(http://www.trosch.org/chu/trent-1htm)*

a. Canon 1 reads, "If any one says, that man may be justified before God by his own works, whether done through the teaching of human nature, or that of the law, without the grace of God through Jesus Christ; let him be anathema."[52] Canon 4 reads, "If anyone denies for the full and perfect remission of sins, three acts are required part of the penitent, constituting as it were the matter of the sacrament of penance, namely, contrition, confession and satisfaction, which are called the three parts of penance; or says that there are only two parts of penance, namely, the terrors of a stricken by the realization of sin and the faith received from the Gospel or from absolution, by which believes that on his sins are forgiven him through Christ, let his anathema sit."[53]

Arms

5. Command over conscience

A. Cyprian (d. 258)

a. The acquisition of absolute command over the conscience

understand of the congregation began to develop at the time of Church (d. 258).[54]

Arms

6. Relics

A. Developed by midthird century[55]

Flood

6. Council of Nicaea III (787)

a. Its flood began in the East after the theological settlement or iconoclastic dispute at the Council of Nicaea III (787), when the church relics as well as images had a considerable development.[56]

Council of Trent

a. Twenty-fifth session made no reference to scripture, but appear apostolic tradition and the constant practice of the church.[57]

Arms

7. Intercession of saints –Third century[58]

Flood

7. Reformation

A. The Confession of Augsburg 1530 denied as prejudicial to mediatorship their role as intercessors.

B. The council of Trent 1563 appeals to apostolic tradition, teachings of Fathers and council. The faithful should be instructed that saints int men.[59]

Arm

8. Binding and loosing

A. The arm of authority based on Jesus's commission to Peter (16:18–19) is claimed by the pope for the first known occasion in 256

Flood

8. Binding and loosing

A. Council of Trent a. Canon 10 reads:

The following are lifted from *www.trosch.org/chu/trent-1htm*

(a) If anyone says that priests who are in mortal sin have not the power of binding and loosing, or that not only priests are only minsiters of absolution, but that to teach and all of the faithful of Christ: "Whatsoever you shall bind upon earth shall be bound in heaven, and whatsoever you shall loose upon earth, shall be loosed on earth. And "If you forgive the sins of any, they are forgiven them, sins you shall retain, they are retained," by virtue of these words everyone can absolve from sins, from public sins by merely by correction provided the one reproved

21

accept correction, and from secret ones by voluntary confession, let him be anathema.

b. Cannon 15

(a) If anyone says that the keys have been given to the church on 1715 and not also to bind, and that therefore priests, when imposing penances on those who confess, act contrary to the purpose of the keys institution of Christ, and that if is a fiction that there remaining temporal punishment to be discharged after the eternal punishment by virtue of the keys been removed, let him be anathema.

Arm

9. The Mass as it is known today

A. Heralded by Cyril (d. 258)[52]

Flood

9. Council of Trent

a. The Sacrifice of the Mass together with the decree on justification viewed by far the most important definitions of the entire Council.[53]

Arm

10. Appeal to secular power to enforce decisions AD 272

Flood

10. Synod of AD 445

A. Pope Leo I, the Great, obtained the support of the secular government and secure the enforcement of decisions made at a Roman synod of 445.[65]

Shall they be overflown

The word for "overflown" (#7857 shaw-taf) according to Strongs Concordance, 1979, is defined as "a prim. root; to gush; by imp. to inundate, cleanse; by anal. to gallop, conquer-drown, (over) flow (-whelm), rinse, run, rush (thoroughly) wash (away).

The aspect of the definition of the word for "flood" which seems to fit the historical-prophetic context is to "inundate." In the third century, the mind/heart/garden plot, soil estate of Christianity was inundated by professing "inner man' [see Ephesians 3:16:11] beliefs that would break their faith. With the arm of the "command over conscience" during the time of Cyprian (d. A. D. 258) conscience was broken when Lapsi Christians fell from faith in the persecution of Decius (A. D. 249-250). They were overflown in three ways: 1) "Sacrificati,"- those who offered sacrifices to pagan gods, 2) "thurificati,"- those who burned incense at pagan religious ceremonies, 3) "libellatici"- those who obtained certificates. At the time of the Decius persecution, when it began to be diminished, confessors, i.e. those who stood firm from their faith, reconciled the lapsed on easy terms, claiming that as friends of Christ, they had the right of granting pardon, even more than priests and bishops.

I. Cyprian

A.When Cyprian went into hiding in early 250, "thousands of Christians apostatized (rejected their faith) or obtained 'libelli pais' (certificates), by which they declared they had sacrificed to the pagan gods.

B. Lapsi

a. The Lapsi were Christians who fell from the faith in the persecution Decius (249–250). They were of three kinds: "Sacrificati," those offered sacrificed to the pagan gods; "thurificati" those who burn incense at pagan religious ceremony; and "libellatici," those obtained certificates.[67]

from before him

I. Fetal orthodox Catholicism

A. Decius persecution

(a) When the (Decius) persecution began to diminish the confessors, those who had stood firm from their faith—reconciled the lapsed on terms, claiming that as "friends of Christ" they had the right of gran pardon, even more than did priests and bishops.[68]

(b) While there had always been apostates, the "lapsi" formed a prob because of their great number and the desire most had of be readmitted to communion in the Church even while the persecuted continued.[69]

and shall be broken

broken (7665 shaw-bar) according to Strongs, 1979 is defined as "a prim. root; to burst (lit. or fig.): break (down, off, in pieces, up) broken ([-hearted]), bring to birth, crush, destroy, hurt, quench quite, tear, view. [by mistake for 7663]

The aspect of the definition of the word for "broken" which seems to fit the historical-prophetic context is to "break down," in both a literal outer man and figurative-spiritual inner man (see Ephesians 3:16). In the third century, the literal health of Christians like Origen, was broken by imprisonment and torture of the Decius persecution. Similtaneously the consciences of lapsi Christians were broken by being forced to sacrifice to pagan gods, burn incense to pagan gods, or obtain certificates.

Jerimiah 17:18 states, "Destroy (#7665 shaw-bar) with a double destruction." Thus, Christ in the future calvary experience, depicted in

Daniel 11:26 in the words "and those who eat from a portion of his meat shall destroy (#7665 shaw-bar) him would literally die an atoning death in which Christ's inner man comprised of a plant-based wick spirit in the oil symbol of the Holy Spirit and a censor mind containing his plant-based hypostasis essence incense divinity in the heat hypostasis essence Father and elemental atmosphere, like air, hypostasis essence Holy Spirit who also possessed the dual hypostasis essence of plant-based oil, all, the heat, oil, elemental atmosphere like air being withdrawn from the plant-based hypostasis essence incense divinity in the golden censor and plant-based wick spirit in the golden candlestick in the upcoming atonement for sin provision.

Jesus said, "And fear not them which kill (#615 ap-ok-ti'-no) the body, but are not able to kill (#615 op-ok-ti'-no) the soul: but rather fear him which is able to destroy (#622 ap-ol'-loo-mee) both soul and body in hell" (Mt. 10:28).

#615 ap-ok-ti'-no; from 575 and kteino (to slay; to kill outright; fig. to destroy:- put to death, kill, slay. Strongs Concordance, 1979

#622 ap-ol'-loo-mee; from 575 and the base of 3639; to destroy fully (reflex. To perish, or loose) lit. or fig.:-destroy, die, lose, mar, perish Strongs Concordance, 1979

"In Christ's antitypical life as 'the lamb of God who takes away the sin of the world" (Jn. 1:29), following the incarnation when Mary would conceive of the Holy Spirit, he would come to see and acknowledge that he, had by the incarnation, enclosed the fallen world as the antitypical laver/sea, in the reconciling heavenly sanctuary and all who dwelt therein with the linen of his righteousness. Christ proclaimed during his ministry, still under the "type" sanctuary service, what his followers were to expect after his future Calvary sacrifice in which he would be broken from a relationship to his Father in an atonement for sin, as the antitypical lamb, in the antitypical kingdom of God, following His death, resurrection, and ascension.

"But beware of men: for they will deliver you up to the councils and they will scourge you in their synagogues; And ye shall be brought before governors and kings for my name sake, for a testimony against them and the Gentiles. But when they deliver you up, take no thought how or what ye shall speak, for it will not be ye that speak, but the Spirit of the Father which speaketh in you. And brother shall deliver up the brother to death, and the father the child; the children shall rise up against their parents, and cause them to be put to death. And ye shall be hated

24

of all men for my name's sake: but he that endureth to the end shall be saved. But when they persecute you in this city, flee ye into another: for verily I say unto you. Ye shall not have gone over the cities of Israel, til the Son of man be come." (Mt. 10:18–23)

I. Midthird century movement from the original spiritual-subjective-adoration celebration of the Eucharistic Mass to the objective as it is known today.

   A. The Catholic Church broke away from the Apostolic tradition in the middle of the third century when it moved from the original spiritual subjective-adoration celebration of the Eucharistic Mass to the objective- adoration as it is known today.[70]

II. Health broken by imprisonment, torture, and persecution

   A. The health of Christians, like Origen, was broken by the imprisonment and torture of the Decius persecution c. 250[71]

III. Conscience broken

   A. The Libeliatici Christians conscience was broken when they obtained certificates which stated that they had sacrificed though they had not done so. [72]

IV. Church breaks away from private confession

   A. The church in the east breaks away from private confessions, utter abolishing it. AD 390[73]

V. Western Christianity vs. Eastern Christianity

   A. Egyptian Church Order. An early Christian liturgical document that substantially the "Apostolic Tradition" of Hippolytus of Rome c. 215).

Although in the West the "Apostolic Tradition" along with the other works of Hippolytus was forgotten, this earliest and most important of all Christian church orders came to be accepted as typical in the East, particularly in Egypt; and translations in Coptic, Ehiopic, and Arabic played an important role in forming the liturgy of the Oriental Churches as well as their Cannon Law.[74]

yea also the prince of the covenant.

I. Prince of the covenant

   A. Christ Jesus

      a. But ye denied the Hoy One and the Just, and desired a murderer to be unto you: And killed the Prince of life whom God had raised from whereof we are witnesses. (Acts 3:14, 15)

      b. The God of our fathers raised up Jesus, whom ye slew and hanged Him hath God exalted with his right hand to be a prince and a Savior give repentance to Israel, and forgiveness of sins. (Acts 5:30, 31)

B. Breaking the prince of the covenant

  a. Third century arm of intercession of dead saints on behalf of the breaks Christ's ascended role, "seeing he ever liveth to make intercession for them." (Hebrews 7:25) "And he that searcheth the hearts knoweth what is the mind of the Spirit, because he maketh intercession of the saints according to the will of God." (Romans 8:27). "He that spared not his own Son, but delivered him up for us all, how shall he not with him also freely give us all things? It is God that justifieth… It is Christ that died, yea rather, that is ris who is even at the right hand of God, who also maketh intercession." (Rom. 8:32-34.)

  b. Appeal to secular arm power to enforce decisions AD 272 would prince of the covenant, Christ, in His body, the church when they required by civil authorities to go against conscience.

Christ, to be an atonement for sin, was born with an inner man/ heart bent to uphold that golden censer mind of faith in his father. He had been separated at Calvary from the eternally existing relationship with the heat, hypostasis Father, first person of the Godhead and the third person of the Godhead Holy Spirit who possessed a dual hypostasis essence of elemental atmosphere. This Godhead manifested themselves in a consuming fire. As one God, he offered in the second person of the Godhead, Christ Jesus at Calvary for a provisional atonement for sin. Humanity would literally need "type" clothes until restoration would occur at the second coming of Christ, clothing them once again with the garment of light, perceived to be the linen of Christ's righteousness.

DANIEL 11:23

23. And after the league made with him, he shall work deceitfully: for he shall come up, and shall become strong with a small people.

And after the league (2266 khaw-bar lit. or fig.) made with him, he shall work (#6213 aw-sad) deceitfully (4820 meer-maw): and come up (5927 aw-law lit. and fig.), and become (NIH) strong (#6105 aw-tsam) with a small (#4592 meh-at or awt) people (1471 go'-ee).

league

2266 khaw-bar; a prim. root; to join (lit or fig.); spec. (by means of spells) to fascinate:-charm (-er), be compact, couple (together), have fellowship with, heap up, join (self, together), league. Strongs, 1979.

2266 ha-bar v. [Q] to join, unite, be attached, to be touching; to cast spells, to enchant; [Qp] to be joined [P] to fasten, be closed, compacted; [Ht] to make an alliance, become allies: [H] to make fine speeches: Strongs, 2001

The aspect of the definition of the word for "league" which seems to fit the historical-prophetic context is to "join together, or make an alliance, become allies" in both a literal outer man and figurative-spiritual inner man (see Ephesians 3:16) sence.

Literally Constantine (Roman Emperor A.D. 306-337) after his victory over Maxentius (Roman Emperor A.D. 306-312) at the Milvian Bridge, October 28, 312 immediately secured toleration for adherants to Catholic Christianity. He made an unwritten agreement (Edict of Milan) with Licinius (Roman Emperor A. D. 308-324) in Milan (February 313). This edict specified certain legal provisions for the Christians.

Figuratively/spiritually for the inner man believers in Catholic Christianity, Licinus' June 5, 313 edict granted toleration to the Christians and restored church property. Constantine intervenes in the Donatist controversy as early as A.D. 313. Constantine presides at the Council of Arles A.D. 314. A series of enactment, immunities, and privileges of various kinds were conferred on the Catholic church and clergy-heretics being specifically excluded.

After the league *made* (NIH) **with him**

The position is taken that the vile person system, Roman Catholicism, was not a real religio-politico force until it established statements of orthodoxy at the Council of Nicaea (325)[76]. In the the infancy of Catholic Christianity Constantine (Roman Emperor A.D. 306 to 337) secured toleration for its adherents immediately after his victory over Maxentius (Roman Emperor A.D. 306-312) (Milvian bridge, October 28, 312).[77] Constantine met with Licinius (Roman Emperor A.D. 308-324 in Milan (February 313) and made an unwritten agreement (Edict of Milan) on certain legal provisions in favor of the Christians.[78] Shortly thereafter, on June 5, 313, Licinus issues an edict granting toleration to the Christians and restoring church property.[79]

Constantine intervened in the Donatist controversy as early as 313[80] by instructing Pope Miltiades to hold a synod at Rome (October 2). On August 1, 314, Constantine presided at the Council of Arles which confirmed the decision of Rome. By a series of enactments, immunities, and privileges of various kinds were conferred on the Catholic church and clergy heretics being specifically excluded.[81]

In the childhood of Roman Catholicism, Constantine issued Sunday legislation in 321[82] which was in harmony with the embryonic values of Justin Martyr (d. 165 and Irenaeus. Another value espoused by Catholicism in that same year was that parties in dispute could by mutual agreement bring a matter before the bishop, even when it was already pending before a civil judge, and the latter was obliged to put into effect the decision of the bishop.[83]

The decision-making ability of Catholicism's adolescence was perceived in 324 by Constantine, who having become sole ruler of the empire, made full recognition of Christianity as the religion of the state.[84] Now the state discerned the possibility of relationship between itself and the church.

The position taken is that the league refers to an alliance made between the church and state. Only after Constantine became sole ruler of the empire (324) did he give full recognition to Christianity as the religion of the state.[85] Because of the literal-figurative/spiritual interpretation of the word "league" (2266 khaw-bar) and "come up" (5927 aw-law), the reader is to not only observe and acknowledge that this history occurred, but also inwardly advocate one or the other lifestyles. Every one would be required to agree or disagree with the church's or Scriptures teaching on the Sabbath. In this way all would potentially form a league with God or man in an influencial witness to the world. Figuratively/spiritually humanity would be individually called to go along with the tradition of the church, or follow Scripture. Each individual would be invited by religious leaders to figuratively/spiritually league up with religio religio-politico system of Roman Caholicism. They had changed the Sabbath from Saturday, the seventh day, to Sunday, the first day of the week. Or they would be faithful to God and worship on Saturday, the seventh day Sabbath. There is ample evidence in book of Acts after the resurrection and ascension of Christ, that the day had not been changed. The evidence includes "And Paul, as his manner was, went in unto them, and three Sabbath days reasoned with them out of the Scriptures (Act 17:2). And he reasoned in the synagogue, and persuaded the Jew and the Greeks (Acts 18:4).

he shall work

The position is taken or leaned toward, that the vile person system, Roman Catholicism, was not a real religio-politico force until it established statements of orthodoxy at the Council of Nicaea (325).[86] This is the first occasion in which the young adult phase of Catholicism began to work after having made an alliance with the state.

According to an imperial constitution of the year 331 the parties in dispute could, by mutual agreement, bring the matter before the bishop even when it was already pending before a civil judge, and the latter was obliged to put into effect the decision of the bishop.[87]

The Catholicism attitude had matured from its 321-child view of suits between parties to its 331 stance where in any stage of a suit anyone of the parties could appeal to the bishop even against the will of the others.[88]

The ecclesiastical jurisdiction of the Church was recognized by the civil (imperial) power when it became Christian. As long as Christianity was not recognized by the State, it was left to the conscience of the individual whether he would conform to the decision of the bishop or not.[89]

deceitfully

The Catholic church worked deceptively through violation of the Fourth Commandment (Ex. 20:8–11) which reads:

"Remember the Sabbath day to keep it holy. Six days shalt though labour, and do all thy work: But the seventh day is the Sabbath of the Lord thy God" in it thou shalt not do any work, thou, nor they daughter, thy manservant, nor thy maidservant, nor thy cattle nor thy stranger that is within thy gates: For in six days the Lord made heaven and earth, the sea, and all that in them is, and rested the seventh day; wherefore the Lord blessed the Sabbath day and hallowed it."

It must be noted that:

During the first three centuries practice and tradition had consecrated the Sunday to public worship of God by the hearing of Mass and resting from work. With the opening of the fourth century positive legislation, both ecclesiastical and civil, began to make these duties more definite. The council of Elvira (A.D. 300) decreed:

If anyone in the city neglects to come to church for three Sundays, let him be excommunicated for a short time so that he may be corrected. (xxi).[90]

In A.D. 321 Constantine passed Sunday legislation which is a direct violation of the Fourth Commandment.

Sunday laws are at least as old as an enactment ascribed to Constantine (A.D. 321). That statue curiously anticipates the pattern of modern legislation in its sweeping condemnation of work and labor on Sunday, except that which cannot practicably be interrupted. The measure, which appears in the 'Code Justinianus, Liber 3, Title 12, could be rendered in English: Let all judges, and city people, and all occupied in trades, rest on revered Sunday (venerabili die solis). But let those dwelling in the country freely and with full liberty attend to the culture of their fields since it frequently happens that no other day is so fit for the sowing of grain or the culture of vines; hence the favorable time should not be allowed to pass lest the provisions of heaven be lost.[91]

The intensity of this deception was augmented by the Council of Laodicea, c. A.D. 363 in which Christians were commanded not to Judaise by resting on the Sabbath, but must work on that day and instead honour the Lord's day.[93]

The convert's Catechism of Catholic Doctrine, by Rev. Peter Geiermann, says this: Question — Which is the Sabbath day? Answer — Saturday is the Sabbath day. Question — Why do we observe Sunday instead of Saturday? Answer — We observe Sunday instead of Saturday because the Catholic Church, in the Council of Laodicea (A.D. 336, 39 o), transferred the solemnity from Saturday to Sunday.[94]

The Church, after changing the day of rest from the Jewish Sabbath, or seventh day of the week, to the first, made the third commandment

30

refer to Sunday as the day to be kept holy as the Lord's day.[95]

Of course, the Catholic Church claims that the change was her act. And the act is a mark of her authority in religious matters.[96]

But since Saturday, not Sunday, is specified in the Bible, isn't it curious that non-Catholics who profess to take their religion directly from the Bible and not from the Church, observe Sunday instead of Saturday? Yes of course it is inconsistent; but this change was made about fifteen centuries before Protestantism was born, and by that time the custom was universally observed. They have continued the custom, even though it rests upon the authority of the Catholic Church and not upon an explicit text in the Bible. The observance remains as a reminder of the Mother Church from which the non-Catholic sect broke away - like a boy running away from home but still carrying in his pocket a picture of his mother of a lock of her hair.[97]

The worship of saints and relics—a violation of the First and Second Commandments (Ex. 20:3–6) and the State-of-the-Dead message in Ecclesiastes 9:5—corrupted the pure and perfect simplicity of the Christian model in the twelve hundred years which elapsed between the reign of Constantine and the reformation of Luther. In the Synod of Tyre 335, many well-meaning bishops were deceived into condemning Athanasius.[98]

When Athanasius believed in pope Liberius' A.D. 357 formula of Sirmium fall when he was hiding, he was apparently deceived for a moment by the rumors spread by the Arians.[100]

Catholics deceived into a false and fatal security by the January 16, A.D. 356 treaty between the civil powers of Egypt and popular leaders of Alexandria.[101]

for he shall come up

5927 aw-law: a prim. root: to ascend, intrans. (be high) or act. (mount): used in a great variety of senses, primary and secondary, lit and fig. (as follows): arise (up), cause to ascend up, at once, break (the day) (up), bring (up), cause to) burn, carry up, cast up + shew, climb (up), (cause to make to, come (up), cut off, dawn, depart, exalt, excel, fall, fetch up, get up, (make to) go (away, up), grow (over), increase, lay, leap, levy, lift (self) up, light (make) up, x mention, mount up, offer, make to pay, + perfect, prefer, put (on), raise, recover, restore, (make to) rise (up), scale, set (up) shoot forth (up), (begin to) spring (up), stir up, take away (up), work. Strongs, 1979 5927 ala v. [Q] to go up, ascend, rise; [N] to be lifted up, withdraw, be exalted; [H] to take up, set up, offer a sacrifice; [Ho]

31

to be offered up, be carried away, be recorded; [Ht] to raise oneself up; from the based meaning of rise in elevation comes the fig. extension" to exalt, honor," as the lifting up of a person in status. Strongs, 2001 The aspect of the definition of the word for "come up" which seems to fit the historical-prophetic context regarding the religio-political, influencial system of Roman Catholicism is to "literally rise influentially in ecclesiastical power." That power would cause the individual believer, in their inner man [see Ephesians 3:16] to figuratively-spiritually believe or not believe what the church taught based on their study of Scripture.

The precedent was established at Nicea A.D. 325 that Catholicism would henceforth issue statements of orthodoxy through ecumenical councils.[102]

Pope Sylvester (A.D. 314–335) was accorded a preeminent role in the Arian crisis. Although invited, he did not attend the Council of Nicaea personally but was represented by two legates, who were treated with great honour and respect yet did not preside at the debates.[103]

Concerning the inner life of the Roman Church during the pontificate of Julius (pope 337–352), we have no exact information, however, that there was a rapid increase in the number of the faithful in Rome.[104]

and become strong

The Council of Sardica 342/343 acknowledged the pope's supreme authority, enhancing his power in ecclesiastical affairs by granting him the right to judge cases of legal possession of episcopal sees.[105]

In 362 pope Liberius renewed his authority and received some Eastern bishops and had them profess the Nicene faith.[106]

Pope Damasus I (366–384) is the first pope to 1) refer to Rome as the apostolic see; 2) distinguish Rome as established by the Apostle St. Peter, founder of the church; 3) officially pronounce Rome's primacy in a synod 282; 4) introduce Latin as the language of the Mass.[107]

In 380, the emperors Gratian in the West and Theodosius in the East declared

1.) Christianity as preached by Peter to be the religion of the Roman Empire;

2.) Defined orthodoxy as the doctrines proclaimed by the bishops of Rome and Alexandria.[108]

Pope Siricius (384–399) asserts his primacy over the universal church with the consciousness of his supreme ecclesiastical authority.[109] He view himself as the sovereign of the whole western church, for which he makes laws. [110]

with a small people.

The Christians (at the time of emperor Constantine 306–337) formed only a small portion of the population, being a fifth part in the west and the half of the population in a large section of the east.[111]

Christianity by the end of the Third century was spreading throughout the empire, and despite attempts during the reign of Diocletian to suppress it, by the middle of the Fourth century Egypt seems to have become predominantly Christian, and the religion had penetrated throughout the native population... The granting of tolerance in 313 to the Christians by the emperor Constantine I (306–337) gave impetus to the development of a formal Egyptian church that soon vied with that of Constantinople. The orthodox Alexandrian patriarchs were often at odds with large segments of the Egyptian population, which tended to favor heterodox Christian teaching (e.g., Arianism and Monophysitism)[112]

By the second century Ignatius, of Antioch d. A.D. 107 or 108 leaned toward honoring Sunday instead of Saturday as the Sabbath. This belief did away with the Sabbath which was uniquely Jewish. That influence was at least one seed, which grew into the blade of Irenaeus, d. A.D. 208 and Justin Martyr d.

A.D. 165 who advocated worship on Sunday not Saturday the Sabbath.[113] By the time of Constantine, the civil state, in relationship to the ear form of Christianity, was developing intothe full corn in the ear. Coupled with A.D. 312 league with with Maxentius at the Milvian bridge, now Constantine was influenced deceptively to league up with the vile, contemptible, religious beliefs of Roman Catholicism, in passing of the A.D. 321 Sunday legislation. Further deceptive beliefs included the mid-second century intercession of the saints, and relics- akin to idolatry. All these beliefs yielded a powerful influence throughout the Roman Empire and world, so that the the Roman Catholic church became an influential, religio-politico vile person. Early Christianity was influenced by the thought leader imagination of Ignatius of Antioch, Irenaeus of Lyons, and Justin Martyr who advocated the worship on Sunday, the first day of the week instead of Saturday, the Sabbath, seventh day of the week.

Thus, the Sabbath after Constantine's A.D. 321 Sunday legislation would still be a test that God would provide for their needs. Israel was called to depend upon God for the food of manna and later Christians will be called to trust God and obey Him despite civil laws passed in opposition to God's law in their journey of faith to heaven in the wilderness of this world.

DANIEL 11:24

24. He shall enter peaceably even upon the fattest places of the province; and he shall do *that* which his fathers have not done, or his fathers' fathers; he shall scatter among them the prey, and spoil, and riches: yea, and he shall forecast his devices against the strong hold, even for a time.

He shall enter peaceably

The position espoused here is that Catholicism is born shortly after Constantine's battle of the Milvian Bridge (Oct. 28, 312).[114] For nine to ten years, this infant religio-politico power enjoyed the peace of Constantine prior to 321/322 when Licinius began to persecute the Christians.[115]

even upon the fattest places of the province

The geography of that time and place was divided into provinces. The sources quoted confirm that Constantine (A.D. 306–337) regarding himself as "pontifex maximus" had the supreme control of religious matters. It was his view that the regulation of Christianity fell within his province.[116] Constantius II (A.D. 337–361) divided the eastern provinces (Thrace, Macedonia. Greece, Asia, and Egypt for himself.[117] Pope Siricus (A.D. 384–directed that his decrees be made known to the neighboring provinces.[118] He made allusions to a decree of his predecessor Liberius (A.D. 352–366) which was supposedly to have been addressed to the provinces.[119] It is the position leaned toward that the "fattest places of the province" refer to major religio- theological centers such as Egypt, Alexandria, Constantinople, and Rome.

and he shall do

Catholicism would establish tests of orthodoxy for Christians in general through solemn ecclesiastical meetings, the first of which was the Council of Nicaea (A.D. 325)[120] Creedal statements were developed. The Roman church in particular regarded itself, and was regarded by many, as in a special appointed custodian and mouthpiece of the apostolic tradition.[121]

that which his fathers

The position leaned toward here is that the fathers of the religio-politico vile person identified as the Catholic church are historically sectioned off beginning with the death of Polycarp A.D. 156. Polycarp (A.D. 69–155), Bishop of Symrna, and one of the apostolic fathers 1) links together the apostolic age and nascent Catholicism, 2) is the link between the Apostolic age and the first of the catholic fathers, 3) is the living link between the apostolic age and the great writers who flourished at the end of the second century.[122]

The fathers of Catholicism are identified as the mid second–third century religio-theological thinkers.[123] The Catholic fathers include: Ignatius of Antioch d. A.D. 108, Justin Martyr d. A.D. 165, The Shepherd of Hermas A.D. 140–155, Pope Victor I, Irenaeus of Lyons d. A.D. 208, Pope Zephyrinus d. A.D. 217, Tertullian d. A.D. 220., Antipope Hippolytus, Pope Callistus d. A.D. 223, Pope Fabianus d. A. D. 250, Pope Stephen, Cyprian, bishop of Carthage d. A.D. 258, and Pope Marcellinus d. A.D. 308.

The following sections are lifted from "Fathers of the Church," *The Catholic Encyclopedia*, 1913, vol. 6, pages 1-2.

"Fathers of the Church." The word Father is used in the New Testament to mean a teacher of spiritual things, by whose means the soul of man is born again into the likeness of Christ. . . The first teachers of Christianity seem to be collectively spoken of as "the Fathers". . . A bishop is emphatically a 'father in Christ', both because it was he, in early times, who baptized all his flock, and because he is the chief teacher of his church ...

It follows that, as our own fathers are the predecessors who have taught us, so the Fathers of the whole Church are especially the earlier teachers, who instructed her in the teaching of the Apostles, during her infancy and first growth. It is difficult to define the first age of the Church, or the age of the Fathers...

The appeal to the Fathers. Thus, the use of the term fathers has been continuous, yet it could not at first be employed in precisely the modern sense of Fathers of the Church. In early days the expression referred to writers who were then quite recent... appeals to the Fathers are a subdivision to appeals to tradition. In the first half of the second century begin the appeals to the sub-apostolic age: papias appeals to the presbyters, and through them to the Apostles. Half a century later St. Irenaus supplements this method by an appeal to the tradition handed down in every Church by the succession of its bishops, and Tertullian clinches this argument by the observation that as all the Churches agree, their tradition is secure, for they could not all have strayed by chance into the same error. The appeal is thus to Churches and their bishops, none but bishops being the authoritative exponents of the doctrine of their Churches. . .

Eventually, it appeared that bishops as well as priests were fallible. In the second century the bishops were orthodox. In the third they were often found wanting. In the fourth, they were the leaders of schisms, and heresies. . . It came to be seen that the true Fathers of the Church are those Catholic teachers who have persevered in her communion, and whose teaching has been recognized as orthodox".[124]

or his fathers' fathers;

The following sections are lifted from "Fathers of the Church," *The Catholic Encyclopedia*, 1913, vol. 6, page 1.

"Thus Fathers have learnt from Fathers, and in the last resort from the Apostles, who are sometimes called fathers in this sense; 'they are your Fathers' says St. Leo, of the Princes of the apostles, speaking to the Romans; St Hilary of Arles calls them 'sancti patres'; Clement of Alexandria says that his teachers, from Greece, Ionia, Coele-Syria, Egypt, the Orient, Assyria, Palestine, respectively, had handed on to them the tradition of blessed teaching from Peter, and James, and John, and Paul, receiving it 'as son from Father.'"[125]

he shall scatter among them the prey,

The position is leaned toward that the "he" refers to the Nicean orthodox Catholic Christians, i.e., the vile person/king/army. They scatter their Nicean orthodox views to the people living throughout the Roman Empire. The prey upon which the Nicean orthodox Catholic Christians pounce, beginning with the establishment of orthodoxy (325) people who espouse heterodox Arian Christianity and pagan philosophies.

and spoil,

Sources indicate that upon the reading of Diocletian's will spoils-men came to see the spoils divided.[126] Another evidence of 'spoils' is when Constantine repeated the most dreadful menaces of fire and sword against the Borderers who dare 1) to desert their colors, 2) connive at the inroads of the barbarians, and 3) participate in the spoil.[127]

A second alternative is to view "confession" as a spoil of theological ideas which was kept up in the West. It (the institution of penitentiary priest) was universally received and maintained in the church till the year 390, when that office was suppressed, and the practice of private confession utterly abolished, first at Constantinople, by Nectarius, bishop (a most orthodox prelate) of that city, and afterward all over the east.128 Sources indicate that Clovis acquired wealth by the sword, and purchased soldiers with the fruits of conquest. After each successful battle or expedition the spoils were accumulated in one common mass; every warrior received his proportionable share, and the royal prerogative submitted to the equal regulations of military law.[129]

and riches:

The suggested historic chronological fulfillment of this segment of prophecy apparently begins following the Edict of Milan (313). Sources indicate that Constantine spilled upon the church great sums of silver and of gold from the imperial treasury. Not only did the church begin to acquire the riches of precious metals but also real estate. Constantine gave the church land by the acre, by the mile. He took temples and land from the pagan congregations and gave them to Christians.[130] In 391, the Sarapeum, a rich heritage of paganism was destroyed by Theophilus, a priest of Alexandria. The stones from that structure were used to build Christian churches.[131]

and he shall forecast against

2803 khaw-shab; a prim. root; prop. to plait or interpenetrate i. e. (lit.) to weave or (gen.) to fabricate. (fig.) to plot or contrive (usually in a malicious sense): hence (from the mental effort to think, regard, value, compute:- (make) account (of), conceive, consider, count, cunning (man, work, workman), devise, esteem, find out, forecast, hold, imagine, impute, invent, be like, mean, purpose, reckon (-ing be made), regard, think Strongs, 1979 2803 ha-sab v. [Q] to plan, plot, purpose, consider; to credit, account, impute; to be thought, considered, regarded; be reckoned, accounted; [P] to determine, plan, plot; to compute, account; [Ht] to consider oneself Strongs, 2001 The aspect of the definition of the word for "forecast" which seems to fit the historical-prophetic context regarding the religio-political, influencial system of Roman Catholicism is to literally weave together, fabricating mental thoughts regarding a certain issue. In this case, and for that matter, the next seven ecumenical councils, there would be "war of words" regarding the positional issues pertaining to nature of Christ. Figuratively-spiritually, in the "inner man" [See Ephesians 3:16] of ecclesiastical church leaders, their would be mental efforts resulting in plots or contrivances, usually in a malicious sense, to draw believers away or toward a particular point of view. His devices 4284 makh-ash-aw-baw or makh ash-eh-beth: from 2803, a contrivance, i.e. (concr.) a texture, machine, or (abstr.) intention, plan (whether bad: a plot; or good: advise): cunning (work), curious work, device (-sed), imagination, invented, means, purpose, thought Strongs, 1979 4284 mah saba n.f. thought, plan, scheme, plot, design Strongs, 2001 The aspect of the definition of the word for "devices" which seems to fit the historical-prophetic context regarding the religio-political, influencial system of Roman Catholicism is to "contrive, or form mentally an intentential plan or plot, which could be good or bad." This was done toward other people, or groups of people, who possessed an opposing view, in this case, regarding the nature of Christ.

These positional views regarding the nature of Christ were in thought the purposed, imagined, invented, devices of the Catholic church articulated in the seven ecumenical councils from A.D. 325-A.D. 787 The following sections are lifted from *http://en.wikipedia.org/wiki/ First_Seven_Ecumenical_Councils*

1. First Council of Nicaea (325)
2. First Council of Constantinople (381)
3. First Council of Ephesus (431)
4. Council of Chalcedon (451)
5. Second Council of Constantinople (553)
6. Third Council of Constantinople (680)
7. Second Council of Nicaea (787)[132]

against the strongholds

4013 mib-tsawr'; also (in plur.) fem. (Dan. 11:15) mib-tsaw-raw'; from1219; a fortification, castle, or fortified city; fig. a defender:-(de-, most) fenced, fortress, (most) strong (hold). Strongs, 1979 4013 mib-sar n. m. fortress, fortification, stronghold; ore. Strongs, 2001 The aspect of the definition of the word for "strongholds" which seems to fit the historical-prophetic context regarding the religio-political, influencial system of Roman Catholicism is literally the geographical cities of Rome in Italy, Alexandria in Egypt, and Constantinople in Turkey. These locations predominately advocated certain views regarding the nature of Christ. Initially the Roman Catholic church advocated the Nicene creed developed in A.D. 325 in Nicaea, Turkey. Alexandria, Egypt was the initial center which advocated Arianism taught by Arius.

Because of the figurative/spiritual nature of this word, the mind of a believer can become a fortified castle/city, fortress advocating certain views regarding the nature of Christ.

Ye are the light of the world. A city that is set (2749 ki-mahee) on (1883) an hill cannot be hid. Mt. 5:14

2749 ki-mahee; mid. of a prim. verb; to lie outstretched (lit. or fig.):-be (appointed, laid up, made, set), lay, lie Comp 5087. Strongs, 1979

2749 kei-mai v. to lay, lie, be laid, laid out; be destined, appointed: Strongs, 2001

The middle voice invites the reader to enter into the situation calling him to acknowledge the historical literal belief event, then coupled to its figurative/spiritual meaning, in his "inner man" (see Ephesians 3:16) witness to promote or deny the belief.

1883 ep-an-o; from 1909 and 507; up above, i. e. over or on (of place, amount, rank, etc.):-above, more than, (up-) on, over. Strongs, 1979 1883 ep- an-o adv. above, on, upon; more than. Strongs, 2001 The strongholds of religious belief are:

1. Arianism—Christ is the first creation of God.
2. Apollarianism—the teaching that there was no human mind or soul in Christ.
3. Nestorianism—teaching that there were two separate persons in the atonement of Christ.
4. Monophysitism—teaching that in the incarnate Christ there is one in human natures.
5. What belief? Condemned certain Nestorian writings and authors in an effort to co monophysite Christians. Resolve "three chapters" controversy.
6. Monothelitism—Christ has two natures (human and divine) but only one will.
7. What belief? Images of Jesus misrepresented Him and that images of Mary and th were idols. [133]

even for a time.

6256 ayth: from 5703; time. espec (adv. with prep.) now, when, etc.- + after, [al-] ways x certain, + continually, + evening, long, (due) season, so [long] as, [even-, evening, noon-] tide, ([meal-] what), time, when. Strongs, 1979 6256 'et n. f. time [in general]: a unit of time (of various lengths): season Strongs, 2001

The aspect of the definition of the word for "time" which seems to fit the historical-prophetic context regarding the religio-political, influencial system of Roman Catholicism is a long time of varying lengths. This fits the time span over which the seven ecumenical councils occurred.

A "time" in the strictest prophetic sense equals 360 days or prophetic years. The "time and times and the dividing of time" (Dan. 7:25) utilizing a different word (#5732 id-dawn) a set time; tech. a year (Strongs, 1979), like comparing apples with oranges] has historically been interpreted as 1260 days/years from 538 to 1798. It can be observed that God foretold that the Israelites would live in Egypt for four hundred years and in actuality it was four hundred and thirty years. It could be that this reference to a "time" could be not in the strictest sense 360 years. In God's promise to Abraham, He said, "I will certainly return unto thee according to the time, (6256 ayth) of life; and lo, Sarah thy wife shall have a son" (Gen. 18:10).

The embryonic and fetal religio-politico vile person, Roman Catholicism system, had developed its tower of ideas and beliefs upon which it stood literally/figuratively-spiritually during the latter part of first century to Tertullian A.D. 217. Having stood on those positions of belief referred to in Dan. 11:21, that belief system began to advocate the elemental influential views it exercised in the Dan. 11:22 "arms of a flood" in the-third century. By the fourth century after the league it made with Constantine, (A.D. 313 Milvian Bridge) in its mind, it started to think of ways it could be the most influential over the subjects of humanity within the Roman Empire. Like a baby in the womb takes some time to grow before it is born, although Roman Catholicism was born at the time of Constantine, nevertheless it took some time after birth, developing in its mind as to how it would attempt to influence the hearts of mankind, over which it desired, promoting certain ideas and values, to rule. That time of thought gestation would occur over some years, as to how they would prevent heresy, advance truth, even though at their heart, they honored Sunday instead of Saturday as the Sabbath in their roots. This time, or season of mental development would be the seven ecumenical councils [A.D. 325–787].

It is suggested that seven ecumenical councils (A.D. 325–787) span the "time" period when the devices were forecasted against the stronghold.

DANIEL 11:25

25. And he shall stir up his power and his courage against the king of the south with a great army; and the king of the south shall be stirred up to battle with a very great and mighty army; but he shall not stand: for they shall forecast devices against him.

And he shall stir up his power and courage

Against the king of the south with a great army;

The position leaned toward is that the two religio-politico kings, the vile king and the king of the south are respectively the bishop s of Rome and Alexandria. It is perceived that individuals who support certain views, in this case theological, become soldiers of that cause. The Scriptural support for this concept is seen in the writings of Paul when he admonished Timothy to be "a good soldier of Jesus Christ" and that God "hath chosen him to be a soldier" (2 Tim. 2:3, 4).

The battles are "war of words," i.e., arguments over words and word usage to describe and define theological philosophy and thought. This notion finds Scriptural support in the writings of Paul, for he says: "Avoid foolish questions, and genealogies, and contentions, and strivings about the law; for they are unprofitable and vain" (Titus 3:9). "That thou mightiest charge some that they teach no other doctrine, neither give heed to fables and endless genealogies, which minister questions, rather than godly edifying which is in faith: so do" (1 Tim. 1:3, 4). "But foolish and unlearned questions avoid, knowing that they do gender strifes" (2 Tim. 2:23). "And this I say, lest any man beguile you with enticing words" (Col. 2:4).

The historian Socatres (A.D. 380–450) writing some generations later has left a vivid description of the astonishing failure of the two sides to comprehend each other. "The situation," he remarked, "was exactly like a battle by night, for both parties seemed to be in the dark about the grounds on which they were hurling abuse at each other."[134]

Initially the "war of words," put Arianism in opposition to Nicene orthodoxy.

It then focused on Nestorianism verses Nicene orthodoxy. The "war of words" moved to Nicene orthodoxy opposing Monophysitism. Then to an off shoot of Monophysitism called Monothelism. Regarding this, history records: "It was not perceived by the ancients that this Monothelism, when it arose was no new heresy, but expressed the very essence of Monophysitism. This was because the war with the latter heresy had been a war of words. The Catholics, following St. Leo and the Council of Chalcedom, confessed two natures, (Greek word) in Christ, using the word nature to mean an essence without subject, i.e., as distinct from hypostasis, whereas the Monophysites, following St. Cyril, spoke of "one nature," understanding the word of subsistent nature or subject, and as equivalent to "hypostasis." They consequently accused the Catholics of Nestorianism, and of teaching two Persons in Christ; while the Catholics supposed the Monophysites to hold that the human nature in Christ was so swallowed up in the divine that it was nonexistent. It does not appear that the Monophysite leaders really went so far as this; but they did undoubtedly diminish the completeness of the human nature of Christ, by referring both will and operation to the one Person and not to the two distinct natures."[135]

The power and courage of the vile king, Roman Catholicism system, lay in its subscription to the advocation of the elementary, adolescent, Catholic orthodox ideas of the Council of Nicaea A.D. 325. The Nicene creed was developed to express the relationship between God the Father and God the Son. The word "Honoousion," meaning Christ identical in substance, or co-essential with the Father became the official orthodox vernacular. A particular Greek phrase comprised the most significant sword of division for decades after the council[136] "great army" of the vile king included the 300–318 members who supported the orthodox views of Nicaea (A.D. 325)[137] and the major party of [A.D. 343] Sardica.[138]

and the king of the south shall be stirred up to battle with a very great and mighty army;

The king of the south (A.D. 325–381) is identified as the religious philosophy of Arianism geographically located in the bishopric influence center of Alexandria Egypt. This philosophy battles against Nicaean orthodoxy. Although Athanasius (bishop of Alexandria A.D. 293–373) is Nicene orthodox, sources indicate that he was regarded as "prince bishop of Alexandria."[139]

The victorious Arian battlefields include the synod of Tyre A.D. 335, Jerusalem synod A.D. 335,[140] and Council of Milan, A.D. 355.[141] "Pope Liberius asked Constantius to call a general council to deal with the eastern bishops' doctrinal claims and their condemnation of Athanasius."[142]

Following the orthodox council of Sardica A.D. 343, Arian persecution against the orthodox party broke out.[143] Historical evidence to support this fact include: 1) In A.D. 354 pope Liberius was driven into exile 2) The orthodox bishop of Alexandria, Athanasius, was banished by the Arians on four occasions. Upon the return of the orthodox pope Liberius from exile A.

A.D. 357, the Arian emperor Constantius was stirred up to wishfully perceive that the influence of Arianism was so great evoking from him the response to decree in A.D. 358 that the Arian antipope Felix and the orthodox pope Liberius should co-rule.[144] By the Council of Ariminum A.D. 359, St. Jerome writes, "The whole world groaned and marveled to find itself Arian."[145]

The Arian army was "great and mighty" in the number of councils it held during these years and the world influence it held by A.D. 359. This is in stark contrast to the two, one major and one minor orthodox Council of Nicaea (A.D. 325) and Sardica (A.D. 343). The orthodox influence throughout the empire diminished markedly after Nicaea with Arianism dominating religious thought centers.

but he shall not stand:

The prophecy states that the king of the south "shall not stand." The anti-Nicene coalition thought that the A.D. 356 exile of orthodox Athanasius was an apparent triumph. In reality this exile caused its downfall. Although this coalition was united in the battle against Athanasius and the faith of Nicaea, its members fell out with each other when trying to impose a definitive substitute for the "Nicaenum."[146] Emperor Constantius A.D. 357 sees the failure of his Arian antipope to rule in Rome.[147] Upon the return of orthodox pope Liberius (A.D. 357) from exile, Constantius decreed (A.D. 358 that Felix and Liberius should co-rule the church of Rome. The people received their legitimate pope with great enthusiasm, but a great commotion arose against Felix, who was finally driven from the city.[148]

In A.D. 362 Athanasius presided at Alexandria over a gathering which united the orthodox semi-Arians with himself and the West. By A.D. 362 the Semi-Arians joined the orthodox ranks of Athanasius.[149] "However, the long battle was now turning decidedly in favor of Catholic tradition ... As an intellectual movement the heresy (Arianism) had spent its force ... Athanasius died in A.D. 373; but his cause triumphed at Constantinople, long an Arian city, first by the preaching of St. Gregory Nazianzen [c. A.D. 329-390[150]], then in the Second General Council (A.D. 381). The Council became ecumenical by the Pope and ever orthodox westerns. From this moment Arianism in all its forms lost its place with the Empire."[151]

for they shall forecast devices against him.

For they (the vile Nicene orthodox) shall forecast (to weave, to fabricate) devices (a contrivance, intention, invention) against (above, over, upon or against-yet always in the last relation with a downward aspect) him(the philosophy of Arianism practice in Egypt), In summary the orthodox Nicenes would weave together and fabricate an invented contrivance or intention against (i.e. considering themselves above, over,) elevating themselves (looking with a downward aspect) to the Arianism in Egypt.

The vile Nicene orthodox civil leaders of the cause against the Arianism in the south i.e. Egypt are E. Roman emp. Theodosius I (A.D. 379–395), called the great in Christian tradition, and emp. Gratianus. Theodosius forcasted, by weaving and fabricating a creed, without ecclesiastical authorities, that was binding on all subjects. It conveyed the idea that: Only persons who believed in the consubtantiality of God the Father, Son, and Holy Spirit were henceforth to be considered Catholic Christians, a designation that here appears for the first time in a document."[152]

The creed was against the religious philosophy of Arianism taught in Egypt. It elevated its adherents above individuals who practiced other religious persuasions. Possessing an exclusionary view of who was to be considered a Catholic Christian, it had the tendency to look at the value of other Christians with a downward aspect.

The council of Constantinople (A.D. 381) was yet another device by which the Nicean orthodox cunningly contrived their purposeful thoughts and imaginations against Arianism. It should be noted that councils were not inherently vile, for God ordained such gatherings to give direction to Christian church at the Jerusalem A.D. 50. At this Council of Constantinople (A.D. 381), the Nicene orthodox Catholics forcasted, i.e., fabricate and wove together word definitions in this "war of words" against Arians. From this moment Arianism in all its forms lost its place within the Empire.[153]

DANIEL 11:26

26. Yea, they that feed of the portion of his meat shall destroy him, and his army shall overflow: and many shall fall down slain.

Yea, they that feed

#398 aw-kal; a prim. word; to eat (lit. or fig.): x at all, burn up, consume, devour (-er, up), dine eater (-er, up) feed, (with), food, x freely, x in. . . wise (-deed, plenty (lay (meat), x quite. Strongs, 1890. #398 a-kal v. [Q] to eat; [N] to be eaten; [Pu] be consumned, be destroyed; to give to eat, feed; from the base meanint of eating food is the fig. Extension of consuming and destroying something. Strongs, 2001.

The aspect of the definition of the word for "feed" which seems to fit the historical-prophetic context regarding the religio-political, influencial system of Roman Catholicism is literally consuming, or devouring as one would eat food, the ideas of Arianism. Literally speaking in witness the ideas and beliefs of Araianism automatically means that in the inner man [see Ephesians 3:16] heart there has been a figurative-spiritual endorsement of that belief. For Scripture records, "out of the abundance of the heart the mouth speaketh." Matthew 12:34.

of the portion of his meat

#6598 path-bag; of pers. or; a dainty: portion (provision) of meat. Strongs, 1979 #6598 path-bag n. [m] (fine) food, choice provision: portion of meat [5] Dan. 1:8, 13, 15, 16. 11:26. meat [1] Dan. 1:5. Strongs, 2001 The aspect of the definition of the word for "portion of meat" is the belief, held in the inner man [see Ephesians 3:16] regarding the nature of Christ referred to as Arianism which espouses the notion that Christ is the first creation of God. The semi-arians known as Macedonians are the ones who have fed on and partook of Arian meat ideas and philosophy.

shall destroy him,

#7665 shaw-bar: a prim. root; to burst (lit. or fig.): break (down, off, in pieces, up), broken (-[hearted], bring to the birth, crush, destroy, hurt, quench x quite, tear, view [by mistake for 7663]

#7665 sa-bar v, [Q] to break, destroy, crush; [Qp] to be broken; [N] to be destroyed, smashed, be broken [P] to break, smash, shatter; [H] to break through (of birth); [Ho] to be crushed Strongs, 2001

The aspect of the definition of the word for "destroy" which seems to fit the historical-prophetic context regarding the religio-political, influencial system of Roman Catholicism is literally to break down or crush in a destroying sense the influence of Arianism.

The destruction of Arianism begins in A.D. 362 by the semiarians who were persuaded by the orthodox Athanasius to join the group of men or army supporting Nicene orthodoxy.[154]

and his army shall overflow:

The influence of the anti-Arians army began to overflow and flood the Roman Empire when Theodosius decreed an edict in 380 that "only persons who believed in the consubstantiality of God the Father, Son, and Holy Spirit were henceforth to be considered Catholic Christians, a designation that appears for the first time in a document.'[155] All subjects of the empires of Gracian and Theodosius were required to profess the faith of the Bishops of Rome and Alexandria. Theodosius began to expel the Arians from Constantinople. In January A.D. 381 the prefect had orders to close all Arian chapels in that city. The same severe measures were ordered through Theodosius's dominion although they were not carried out. In A.D. 380 and A.D. 381 Catholic orthodoxy was imposed on all Christians and the Arians were deprived of their offices and churches. In A.D. 381 the Council of Constantinople for the East and that of Aquileia for the West sealed the final adoption of the faith of Nicaea by the entire Church and completed it by proclaiming the full divinity of the Holy Spirit against the so-called Macedonians, or Semi-Arians as they were also known.[156]

and many shall fall down

#5307 naw-fal a prim. root: to fall, in a great variety of applications (intrans or causat. lit. or fig.): be accepted, cast (down, self, [lots] out), cease, die divide (by lot), (let) fall, (cause to, let, make ready to_ fall (away, down, -en, -), fugitive, have [inheritance], inferior, be judged [by mistake for 6419] lay (along), (cause to) lie down, light (down) be (x hast), lost, lying, overthrow, overwhelm, perish, present (-ed, ing), (make to) rot, slay, smite out x surely, thrown down. Strongs, 1979.

#5307 na-pal v. [Q] to fall, fail: [Piul] to fall [H] to cause to fall, cast down, drop:)used of casting lots) to allocate. Strongs, 2001

The aspect of the definition of the word for "fall down" which seems to fit the historical-prophetic context regarding the religio-political, influencial system of Roman Catholicism is literally that the influence of Arianism ceases to be dominate, being cast down.

slain.

#2491 khaw-lawl; from 2490: pierced (espec.to death); fig. polluted:- kill, profane, slain(man) x slew, (deadly) wounded. Strongs, 1979.

#2491 ha-lal n.m. & a. dead, slain, casualty; defiled, profane (moral or ceremonial failure): Strongs, 2001

The aspect of the definition of the word for "slain" which seems to fit the historical-prophetic context regarding the religio-political, influencial system of Roman Catholicism is literally that Emperor Theodosius would slay seven thousand citizens. the figurative-spiritual inner man [see Ephesians 3:16] believer would now endorse the belief in the co-eternalness of Christ and the Father. This is in stark contrast to heresy of Arianism which advocated that Christ was the first first creation.

Emperor Theodosius's worst crime, the massacre of at least seven thousand citizens of Thessalonica in revenge for a tumult (April 390); of St. Ambrose's refusal to allow him to enter the Church.[157]

The banner of the ancient gods fell near Aquileia on 6, Sept., 394, when the Christian Labarum triumphed allowing emp. Theodosius to enter Rome sole master of the now Christian empire.[158] Rome was sacked August 24–29, 410, by Alaric, a Visigoth chief, which symbolized to many of his contemporaries, the fall of the Western Roman Empire.[159]

DANIEL 11:27

27. And both these kings' hearts shall be to do mischief, and they shall speak lies at one table; but it shall not prosper: for yet the end shall be at the time appointed.

And both these kings'

I. Pope Celestine (A.D. 433–432) and Cyril, bishop of Alexandria (A.D. 412–444)

  A. Council of Ephesus – June 22, A.D. 431

    1. John, (bishop of Antioch refused to attend the Council of Ephesus because it was dominated by Cyril, who he viewed as an Egyptian "Pharaoh"[160]

      A. Although pope Celestine did not attach this label to Cyril, he did reg as the first prelate of the East and the inheritor of the tradi Athanasius. [161]

      B. Pope Leo, the great. 440–461) referred to Dioscorus (.4451) who su Cyril as bishop of Alexandria as the "second Pharaoh.

      1. Dioscorus was so elated with the extraordinary deference and respect governor (Theodorus, of Egypt) paid him, that blind with pride ambition, he began to look upon himself as sovereign of Alexandria, king of all Egypt.[162]

hearts

I. Condemnation of Nestorius and his "innovations."

  A. The hearts or purposes of orthodox pope Celestine and Cyril, bis Alexandria, were united on one issue. They were in favor of the Augustus 430 solemn condemnation of Nestorius and his 'innovations'[163]

  B. The principle fame of St. Cyril rests upon his defense of Catholic doctrine against Nestorius. When his writings are surveyed as a whole, it becomes certain that he always held the true view, that the one Christ has two and distinct natures, divine and human. He rightly

48

taught that the person suffered, in His human nature.[164]

II. Hearts wrestled with the following theological ideas with regard to the nature of Christ:

Nestorians: One person, two hypostasis, two natures.

Catholics: One person, one hypostasis, two natures.

Monophysites: One person, one hypostasis, one nature.[165]

shall be to do mischief,

I. Nestorianism and Monophysitism

A. Sources indicate that the theological bogus/mischief which tainted orthodox Catholicism of these times was the advocation of Nestorianis and Monophysitism.[166]

  1. Cyril's opponents misrepresented him as teaching that the Divine natur suffered. In spite of his own firm grasp of the truth, the whole of hi patriarch fell away a few years after his time, into a heres (monophysitism) based on his writings and could never be regained int the Catholic faith.[167]

B. The Monophysites always withstood the Catholic doctrine, declaring Nestorian, or half Nestorian, and that it divided Christ in two.[168]

C. Nestorianism as it was understood at the time, so insisted upon to humanity of Christ's human nature that it was believed to divide him in persons, one human and the other divine.[169]

  1. It was referred to as the doctrine of "two Sons."[170]

  2. II. After the Council of Chalcedon (A.D. 451)

A. After Chalcedon (A.D. 451) pope Leo waged a double war against enemies of the church, and wounded either foe with the darts adversary. Against Nestorians he seemed to introduce the term Monophysites. Against the Monophysites he appeared to countena term of the Nestorians.[171]

B. For Eudocia, widow of Theodosius II (E. Rom. Emp. A.D. 408–45 news that the council of Chalcedon had betrayed the cause of Cy reinstated 'Nestorianism' as the official theology of the Empire gave admirable opportunity for increasing the difficulties of the regime of M (E. Rom. Emp. A.D. 450–457).[172]

C. Nestorius pleads that his beliefs are identical with pope Leo and orthodoxy.

  1. Nestorius wrote a book late in his life entitled *Book of Heracleides* whe Monophysitism had become a bogy. In this prolix apology Nestorius pleads that his own beliefs are identical with those of Leo (pope A.D. 440–461) and the new orthodoxy.[173]

and they shall speak lies

I. Calumnies, false and malicious statements meant to hurt someone's
   reputation

  A. Historically, Cyril, bishop of Alexandria calumniates Nestorious,
     bisho of Constantinople, to pope Celestine in the following incident.

    1. Cyril accused Nestorius to pope Celestine of heresy, and the pope
       has replied on 11 August, 430, by charging St. Cyril to assume his
       authorit and give notice in his name to Nestorius that, unless he
       recanted withi ten days of receiving this ultimatum, he was to
       consider himsel excommunicated and deposed. The summons was
       served on Nestoriu on Sunday 30 November, or 7 December, by
       four bishops sent by Cyri But Nestorius was evidently well
       informed of what he was to expect. H regarded himself as having
       been culminated to the pope, and he did no choose to be given over
       into the hands of Cyril.[174]

  B. Pope Leo I, the great wrote letter of 455 which bore false witness
     again Hilarious, bishop of Ales.

    1. In this letter Leo intended to discredit Hilarious among the bishops
       of his own diocese, who looked upon Hilarious as a true pattern
       of Christia virtue. Leo gave an entire credit to every malicious
       report he had heard to the prejudice of that excellent prelate,
       Hilarious. Leo inveighs against Hilarious in the most bitter terms,
       as one who was a disgrace to the episcopal order, and therefore
       deserved to be deprived, not only of the power and jurisdiction,
       which he had wantonly abused, but of the dignity itself.[175]

at one table;

I. The definition of the word 'one' means 'unity."[176]

II. Council of Ephesus began June 22, 431

  A. At the council of Ephesus both pope Celestine and Cyril, bishop
     Alexandria were in unity with regard to the condemnation Nestorius. [177]

    1. Like the modern-day convention table, when the heads of two
       neg nations are not always present, so it was at the Council of
       Ephesus bishop of Alexandria, presided over the council, armed
       with the auth pope Celestine.[178]

    2. The legates from Rome represented the pope, like modern day
       amba would represent the president or king of a country. Pope
       Celestine' was heard, although not physically present, through
       letters which we by his legates.[179]

B. Evidence which shows the unity and oneness between Cyril and pope Celestine is demonstrated by the father's cry (July 10, 331).

This is a just judgment. To Celestine the new Paul! To the new Paul Cyril! To Celestine, the guardian of the Faith! To Celestine agreeing with the Synod! The synod gives thanks to Cyril. One Celestine, one Cyril!

III. Pope Leo I, the great (A. D. 440–461) continued adherring to the theological unity/oneness between the papacy and the see of Alexandria demonstrated at the Council of Ephesus (A. D. 431). The church fathers at the Council of Chalcedon (A. D. 451) said that Leo and Cyril taught the same thing.[181]

but it shall not prosper:

I. The Robber Council at Ephesus (A. D. 449)[182]

A. Wedge which began to split the unity which existed between Rome and Alexandria at the Council of Ephesus (A. D. 431).

B. Presided over by Dioscoros, Bishop of Alexandria

1. Presented unorthodox monophysite view.

II. Council of Chalcedon (A. D. 451)

A. Pope Leo I, in full agreement with Cyril and Celestine,183 used the hammer of orthodoxy in the condemnation of Dioscorus and oth monophysites.

a. The bogus/mischiefs do not prosper after Chalcedon (A. D. 451) as e in pope Leo's waging of a double war against the enemies of the wounding either foe with the darts of the adversary. Against Nest seemed to introduce the terms of the monophysites. Against Monophysites he appeared to countenance the terms of the Nestorian

b. Thus began the undesired severing of the "one table" unity of purpose experienced between the see of Rome and Alexandria which at the Council of Ephesus (A. D. 431).

III. It is also perceived that his passage points toward the future time when the orthodox Catholic succession of the Alexandrian see was interrupted for sixty years beginning with the exile of John Talaia in A. D. 482

for yet the end shall be at the time appointed.

I. In Daniel 11, the word for "time appointed," #1450 mo-ed occurs three times. Those occurrences are Daniel 11:27, 29, and 35. Thus it is perceived tha short-term prophetic time span and in a long prophetic time span, events will come to an end. The initial short term "mo-ed prophetic ti Daniel 11:29 span refers to Gaiseric's "ships of Chittim" in the prop "feast of trumpets" heralding the Daniel 11:31 belief "arm" of third ce "intercession of saints" which Clovis, king of the Franks, after the A.D battle of Voille, endorsed attributing that victory to St. Martin of Tours. This belief arm of "intercession of saints," which is the "foundation spiritualism" coupled to the might of military "arms," he would pave the for the little horn Roman Catholicism to begin their rulership for "a times, and a half."

II. Like Gaiseric's "ships of Chittim" in the 'feast of trumpets" announce beginning of the 1,260 days so the long term "mo-ed" prophetic tim Daniel 11:35 would point to close of the 2,300-day prophecy in Daniel which is synonymous with Daniel 11:40

DANIEL 11:28

28. Then shall he return into his land with great riches; and his heart shall be against the holy covenant; and he shall do exploits, and return to his own land.

Then shall he return into his land with great riches;

The position is leaned toward that the papacy in the person of Leo I, the great (A. D. 440–461) returns to his own land after the "one table" experience portrayed in Daniel 11:27. In this interpretation the riches are viewed to be the bishoprics of Gaul over which the religio-politico vile person, system, the papacy gained control. By definition the Hebrew meaning for the word "riches" is property.

#7399 rek-oosh'; from pass. part. of 7408; property (as gathered):- good, riches, substance. Strongs, 1979.

#7399 re-kus, n. m. possessions, property, goods, equipment. Strongs, 2001.

It is perceived that the bishoprics of Gaul are the religious property. In gaining control over the bishoprics the papacy exerted its influence over the minds of these various leaders. This was acquired by pope Leo upon application to the weak prince Valentinian III (A. D. 423–450)[186] who issued an edict July 8, A. D. 445. With this edict the primacy of the Bishop of Rome over the whole Church was solemnly recognized.[187]

A prophetic guide used in this interpretation is the Spirit of prophecy referred to in Revelation 19:10. The testimony of Jesus portrayed in the writings of Ellen G. White has brought Seventh-day Adventists to believe that she is an end-time fulfillment of the Spirit of Prophecy. She identifies influence as a talent in 2T[188] 243, 285. If pope Leo I the great, were placed in the parable of the talents Matt. 25: 14–30, one of the great riches he would be perceived as possessing is influence. The advocation of the primacy of the Roman Church in his letter (ep. ix)[189] of 21 July, 445, to Dioscorus, bishop of Alexandria is one example of influencing mind property.[190]

and his heart

The chief object and heart purpose of pope Leo I, the great (440–461) was the increase of his power, or the exaltation of his see. This was the point in which all his cares, all his thoughts and endeavors, finally centered. He had more at heart the advancement of his see, that is of his own power and authority, than either the purity of the faith or the welfare of the church.[191] His letters and sermons expound his precept of papal primacy in church jurisdiction.[192] He is regarded as the true inventor of the theory of an ecclesiastical monarchy under the headship of the pope. This theory hangs on two propositions; the first is that the primacy of Peter among the apostles, on account of which all pastors are subject to his supreme authority. The second is that in the transference of that primacy to his successors, the bishops of Rome, Peter himself speaks whenever a Pope speaks.[193]

shall be against the holy covenant;

A guide to understanding how the papacy was against the holy covenant must consider the Hebrew meaning of the word *against*. According to <u>Strongs Corcordance</u> 1979 the word means "above, over, upon, or against (yet always in this last relation with a downward aspect)." The historical events in this time period will show that the papal heart possesses an attitude of being against the holy covenant.

The exaltation of the see of Rome and establishing papal primacy is a manifestation of being against the holy covenant. Such action caused the papacy to look at other bishoprics with a downward aspect. When one organization views itself as being more important that another, it is in danger of violating the second greatest commandment, "love your neighbor as yourself" (Mt. 22:39).

Evidence which points to such an occurrence in the papacy is found in the relationship between pope Leo I, the great, and bishop Hilarius of Arles. Leo had resentment against Hilarius and tried to discredit him among the bishops of his own diocese. He wrote a letter (A. D. 445) in an attempt to excoriate Hilarius. In the letter he gives an entire credit to every malicious report he heard. He inveighs against Hilarius in the most bitter terms as one who is a disgrace to the episcopal order. With this view Leo thinks that Hilarius deserves to be deprived, not only of the power and jurisdiction, which he had wantonly abused, but of the dignity itself.[194] This bearing of false witness against your neighbor (Exodus 20:16), breaking the ninth commandment of the Decalogue is heart evidence that Leo was against the holy covenant.

Yet another manifestation of the papacy being against the holy covenant is identified by the historians Socrates (A. D. 425–450)[195] and Sozeman (A. D. 400–450).[196] They state that during these years Rome and Egypt no longer worshiped on the Sabbath,[197] thus breaking the fourth commandment (Exodus 20:8–11) of the Decalogue.

and he shall do *exploits,*

Although the word *exploits'* meaning "his pleasure" is supplied, the passage is perceived to mean that the papacy would do things to exalt the primacy of its see.

The chief object and heart purpose of pope Leo I, the great (A. D. 440–461), was the increase of his power, or the exaltation of his see. This was the point in which all his cares, all his thoughts and endeavors, finally centered. He had more at heart the advancement of his see, that is of his own power and authority, than either the purity of the faith or the welfare of the church.[198] His letters and sermons expound his precept of papal primacy in church jurisdiction.[199]

He is regarded as the true inventor of the theory of an ecclesiastical monarchy under the headship of the pope. This theory hangs on two propositions; The first is that the primacy of Peter among the apostles, on account of which all pastors are subject to his supreme authority. The second is that in the transference of that primacy to his successors, the bishops of Rome, Peter himself speaks. . . the primacy of the Roman Church was thus manifested under this pope in the most various and distinct ways.[200]

Pope Leo I's ambition in pursuit of its own ends and designs, tended also to raise and promote the greatness of his see, that very crime became the cause of his sanctification, being more meritorious to Rome than all his virtues. Indeed, he was the principal founder of her exorbitant power. . . observe that such an ambition, in a Christian bishop, is a vice for which no virtue can we can atone.[201]

and return to his own land.

The primary historical event toward which this interpretation leans is Valentinian III, and his mother Galla Placedia visit to Rome in A. D. 450.

In 450 emperor Valentinian III visited Rome accompanied by his wife Eudoxia and his mother galla Placidia. On the feast of Cathedral Petri (22 February), the imperial family with their brilliant retinue took part in the solemn services at St. Peter's upon which occasion the pope delivered an impressive sermon.[202]

It is perceived that an additional historical event toward which this passage of prophecy could point, is in letter XLIV dated Oct. 13, A. D. 449 in which pope Leo I, the great, asks for a Council in Italy. The view is leaned toward that the papacy moves about throughout the land by letter and not through the physical presence of the pope. This letter indicates that pope Leo is leaning toward a heart desire to have a council in his own land.

DANIEL 11:29

29. At the time appointed he shall return, and come toward the south; but it shall not be as the former or latter.

At the time appointed

#4150 mo-ade; or mo-ade; or (fem.) (2 Chron. 8:13), mo-aw-daw; from 3259; prop. an appointment, i. e. a fixed time or season; spec. a festival; conventionally a year; by implication, an assembly (as convened for a specific purpose); technically the congregation; by extension, the place of meeting; also a signal (as appointed beforehand:-appointed (sign, time), (place of solemn) assembly, congregation, (set, solemn) feast, (appointed, due) season, solemn (-ity), synagogue, (set) time (appointed). Strongs, 1979 #4150 mo-ed n. m. [Tent of] Meeting; appointed time, designated time, season. Strongs, 2001 This interpretation leans toward the view that this passage refers to the second and third historical trumpets (Revelation 8:8–11) of Gaiseric[203] A. D. 428–468 and Attila the Hun A. D. 434–453 blowing simultaneously (See Numbers 10:1-2) in the prophetic clock of salvation. It is recognized that there is no word for "time" such as identified in Daniel 11:24. The word used is "appointed" meaning properly "an appointment," i.e., "a fixed time or season: spec. a festival" (Strongs). Hence, it is perceived that this refers to the feast of trumpets when both Gaiseric and Attila, the second and third trumpet, according to Gibbon were active simultaneously. A time relationship of 360 years could exist between the council of Jamnia A. D. 91[204] and the Council of Chalcedon A. D. 451. But this is not a primary consideration because the Hebrew word of 'appointed' is used instead of 'time.'

he shall return,

It is perceived that the papacy in the person of pope Leo I, the Great, returned to his land in A. D. 449 to write his Tome to Flavian which was to have been read at the Robbers Council of Ephesus in that same year. Dioscorus, the monophysite bishop of Alexandria,[205] who is referred to as the Second Pharaoh[206] and referred to himself as the 'king of all Egypt'[207] presided at that meeting. Leo's tome was laid aside, disregarded, and not read.

and come toward the south;

It is perceived that the papacy came toward the south at the Council of Chalcedon A. D. 451 because of the Christological quarrels regarding monophysitism.[208] Although the pope was not physically present at this council his words were heard through the reading of his tome which was not read at the Robbers Council of A. D. 449. This council was against the monophysitism of Dioscorus, the bishop of Alexandria whom Leo styles as the second pharaoh.

but it shall not be as the former,

The previous occasions in which the papacy and the see of Alexandria, the south, interacted is recorded in Daniel 11:25, 26, 27. The first occasion was the papacy vs. Arianism in which the papacy won the war of words as demonstrated in the synod of A. D. 362[209] and the Council of Constantinople A. D. 381.[210] The second occasion was at the Council of Ephesus A. D. 431[211] in which the papacy and see of Alexandria, the south, were at a 'one table' unity of mind against Nestorianism.[212] This unity between the two sees lasted in part through the papacy of Leo, for he believed the same as Cyril, previous bishop of Alexandria.[213] With the Monophysitism espoused by Dioscorus, bishop of Alexandria, the Egyptian see broke from the previously known unity.

The schism thus begun by Dioscorus and Timothy gave rise to two factions, the orthodox, or Catholic party, which maintained the faith of the two natures in Christ, as prescribed by the Council of Chalcedon (A. D. 451), and the Monophysites, who followed the heresy of Dioscorus.[214]

or as the latter.

The latter event is viewed to refer to the see of Alexandria's sixty-year monophysitic split off from orthodox Catholicism (A. D. 482–542) which began with John Talia.[215] It is perceived that this passage refers chronologically to the relationship between the see of Alexandria and Rome following the event of Daniel 11:30.

Another view could consider this "latter" to refer to some undisclosed future event at the close of the prophecy.

It should be noted that the primary perspective of this prophecy toward which this interpretation leans is a historical, chronological flow.

DANIEL 11:30

30. For the ships of Chittim shall come against him; therefore he shall be grieved, and return, and have indignation against the holy covenant: so shall he do; he shall even return, and have intelligence with them that forsake the holy covenant.

For the ships of Chittim shall come against him:

The country of Chittim,[216] by definition, refers to "Greek or Roman holdings on the shores opposite Palestine." The peninsula of Carthage is here considered as fulfilling the requirements of this definition. This interpretation agrees with Uriah Smith who quotes from *Clarke's Commentary*[217] in his book *Daniel and the Revelation*[218] substantiating this view.

The ships of Chittim refer to Gaiseric's fleet which after the Oct. 19, A. D. 459, capture of Carthage soon came to control much of the western Mediterranean. Gaiseric with his ships came against Rome, the papacy's capital, in June A. D. 455.[219] The Vandals under the leadership of Gaiseric entered Rome on the 15th of June A. D. 455 and continued there till the twenty-ninth of the same month. During this time, there was no house, no church, no public building, which they did not ransack, or strip of all their wealth, and valuable monuments.[220]

therefore he shall be grieved,

The primary reason Pope Leo I, the great, is grieved relating to the ships of Chittim is that the husbands of the wives of Rome were taken captive by Gaiseric. Not thinking that the husbands would return some wives remarried. The husbands were returned to Rome in A. D. 457. This caused Pope Leo's grief as to who was the rightful husband of the wives left behind."[221]

In lieu of Leo's successful mediation with Attilia (A. D. 452), Leo was saddened by his failure to prevent Gaiseric from entering Rome, ransacking churches and stripping them of wealth and valuable monuments.

59

Another source of grief for Leo unrelated to the ships of Chittim in these years was the A. D. 457 murder of Proterius, the new orthodox patriarch of Alexandria, by the monophysites of Egypt in the baptistry[222] [223] [224] [225] This event was the outgrowth of the A. D. 453 blood bath in Jerusalem by the monophysites.

and return

The interpretation of this passage leans toward the view that the vile person, Roman Catholicism in the person of Pope Leo I, the great (A. D. 440–461), returned to his letter writing on monophysitism and primacy of the Holy See.

From his first letter on this subject (monophysitism), written to Eutyches on 1 June, [A. D.] 448 (ep. Xx) to his last letter written to the new orthodox patriarch of Alexandria, Timotheus Salophaciolus, on 18 August, [A. D.]460 (ep. Clxxi), we cannot but admire the clear, positive, and systematic manner in which Leo, fortified by the primacy of the Holy See, took part in this entanglement.[226]

and have indignation

In the chronological historical flow of this prophecy, it is perceived that this passage refers to an indignant attitude manifested toward the twenty-eighth Canon of Chalcedon by the leader of the vile person, Roman Catholicism, pope Leo I, the great. History records:

In writing to the emperor (footnote dates letter May 22, [A. D.] 452 to Marcian, Eastern Roman emperor [A. D.] 450–457) he (Leo) stated that he was overjoyed at the unanimity with which the council vindicated the truth, yet he took no pains to conceal his indignation regarding the twenty-eighth canon for which, in his view, Anatolius (bishop of Constantinople who succeeded Flavian after the Robbers Council [A. D.] 449) was personally responsible.[227]

Leo shows himself especially indignant that a council which, as he says, was assembled for the express purpose of confirming the Catholic Faith should be diverted to serve the lusts of ambition, as though it were possible to undo what was once appointed by the canons of Nicaea. No mere boast as to the size of the council which has supported his claims can avail Anatolius anything.[228]

Last of all was a personal letter addressed to Julian. The note to which it was a reply appears to have urged Leo to daily no longer in sending his formal approval of the decisions of the council. The pope was highly indignant at Julian's suggestion that the required assent would be a personal favor to himself and asserted that neither persuasion nor pleading would procure his endorsement of proposals which he held to be destructive of order in the Church. To grant such a request, he says, would mean that both Julian and himself would be involved in responsibility for an illicit act.

In spite of Leo's evident indignation at the use which had been made of the council to obtain approval for the enlarged jurisdiction of the see of Constantinople there is a remarkable tone of restraint in these letters, not the least in those addressed to Anatolius and Julian.[229]

Yet another event toward which pope Leo I, the great (A. D. 440–461) directed his indignation were the acts of violence by monophysites which had resulted in the deaths of priests and bishops. History records:

> The first of these (letters) is addressed to the Empress Eudocia (footnote June 15th, A. D. 453) at Jerusalem... The second letter is directed to the monks themselves. . . Referring to the strong feeling of opposition to the Christological doctrine of the "Tome". . . Finally he expressed his deep indignation at acts of violence which had resulted in the deaths of priests and bishops, pointing out that such conduct was totally inconsistent with the peace of the religious life. He concluded with an earnest appeal to the monks to abandon their errors.[230]

against

The understanding of the prophetic historical chronology of this passage leans toward the view that the indignation of pope Leo I, the Great, against the 28th Cannon are evidence of downward aspect toward the geographical see which the cannon sought to elevate. Leo was disturbed and indignant that the see of Constantinople by the jurisdiction of Cannon 28 was granted equal power and authority as the see of Rome. It is perceived that Leo felt that this cannon was a threat to his attempt to exalt the primacy of the see of Rome.

the holy covenant:

The holy covenant is the new covenant (Jeremiah 31:31) which God makes with his people, writing His law, the Ten Commandments (Deuteronomy 4:13), upon their hearts (Hebrews 8:10 as originally designed (Deuteronomy 6:6). It was a covenant of love (Deuteronomy 7:12 NIV) given at Horeb (Deuteronomy 5:2) written on the tablets of stone, the tablets of the covenant (Deuteronomy 9:9). This was to place the awe and fear of God within them (Exodus 20:20). Outward manifestation of this inward (Ephesians 3:16) working covenantial relationship to God would be visible in obedience to the second greatest commandment, "Love your neighbor as yourself" (Matthew 22:39). In this covenantial relationship, there is no provision for viewing of himself "higher than he ought to think" (1 Samuel 15:17). The words "Whoever exalts himself shall be humbled and whoever humbles himself shall be exalted" (Matthew 23:12; Luke 14:11, 18:14) should have been heeded Scriptural warning to Leo not to exalt the primacy of the see of Rome. The real challenge is "walk humbly with God" (Micah 6:8). Only then can one "love your neighbor as yourself" from the heart.

The primary heart violation of the Ten Commandments (Exodus 20:3–17), comprising the thoughts of the holy covenant, which the leader of the religio-politico vile person, Roman Catholicism, Leo I, the great, was the tenth commandment. Leo coveted the jurisdictional power and authority given to the neighboring see of Constantinople by Cannon 28. In pursuit of his objective to elevate the primacy of the see of Rome, the outward manifestation of his indignation was due to a cherished attitude of covetousness, against which the tenth commandment warns.

so shall he do;

Scripture records: "for whosoever shall keep the whole law, and yet offend in one point, he is guilty of all" (James 2:10).

The view is leaned toward that in the historic/prophetic narrative this passage refers to the vile person, Roman Catholicism, reiteration that it in fact has made void the law of God in Sabbath keeping, the fourth commandment (Exodus 20:8–11). They had and continue to "teach for doctrines the commandments of men" (Matthew 15:9). Socatres and Sozemen give evidence to this fact by stating that Rome and Egypt no longer worship on Sabbath.[231]

he shall even return

The position is leaned toward that this passage of prophecy refers historically to Pope Leo (A. D. 440–461) letter CLIX to Nicaetas, Bishop of Aquileia dated 21st March, in the consulship of Majorian Augustus (A. D. 458) regarding the eating of food offered to idols.

> About captives, who were compelled to eat of sacrificial food. Concerning those Christians who are asserted to have been polluted with sacrificial food, have thought it right to make this reply to your enquiry, dear brother, that they be purged by a satisfactory penitence which is to be measured not so much by the duration of the process as by the intensity of the feeling. And whether their compliance was wrung

from them by terror or hunger, there need be no hesitation at acquitting them, since the food was taken from fear or want, not from superstitious reverence.[232]

and have intelligence with them that forsake the holy covenant.

This prophetic passage refers to Pope Hilary (A. D. 461–468) and Pope Gelasius (A. D. 494–496) preaching and communicating with idolaters.

Yet some suspicious appearances are found to sully the theological fame of Anthemius (W Rom. Emp. A. D. 467–472). From the conversion of Philiotheus, a Macedonian secretary, he had imbibed the spirit of religious toleration; and the Heretics of Rome would have assembled with impunity, if the bold and vehement censure which Pope Hilary pronounced in the church of St. Peter, had not obliged him to abjure the unpopular indulgence. Even the Pagans, a feeble and obscure remnant, conceived some vain hopes, from the indifference, or partiality of Anthemius; and his singular friendship for the philosopher Severus, whom he promoted to the consulship, was ascribed to a secret project of reviving the ancient worship of the gods. These idols were crumbled into dust: and the mythology which had once been the creed of nations, was so universally disbelieved, that it might be employed without scandal, or at least without suspicion, by Christian poets. Yet the vestiges of superstition were not absolutely obliterated, and the festival of the Lupercalia, whose origin had preceded the foundation of Rome, was still celebrated under the reign of Anthemius. The savage and simple rites were expressive of an early state of society before the invention of arts and agriculture. The rustic deities who presided over the toils and pleasures of the pastoral life, Pan, Faunus, and their train of satyrs, were such as the fancy of shepherds might create, Sportive, petulant, and lascivious; whose power was limited, and whose malice was inoffensive. A goat was the offering the best adapted to their character and attributes; the flesh of the victim was roasted on willow spits; and the riotous youths, who crowed to the feast, ran naked about the fields, with leather thongs in their hands, communicating, as it was supposed, the blessing of fecundity to the women whom they touched. The altar of Pan was erected, perhaps by Evander the Arcadian, in a dark recess in the side of the Palatine hill, watered by a perpetual fountain, and shaded by a hanging grove. A tradition, that, in the same place, Romulus and Remus were suckled by the wolf, rendered it still more sacred and venerable in the eyes of the Romans; and the sylvan spot was gradually surrounded by the stately edifices of the Forum. After the conversion of the imperial city, the Christians still continued, in the month of February, at the annual celebration of the Lupercalia; to which there ascribed a secret and mysterious influence on the genial powers of the animal and vegetable world. The bishops of Rome were solicitous to abolish a profane custom, so repugnant to the spirit of Christianity; but their zeal was not supported by the authority of the civil magistrate: the inveterate abuse subsisted till the end of the fifth century, and Pope Gelasius, who purifies the capital from the last slain of idolatry, appeased, by a formal apology, the murmurs of the senate and people.[233]

Lupercalia, in Roman religion, ancient festival under the superintendence of a corporation of priests called Luperci. The festival, held on February 15, began with the sacrifice of goats and a dog. Later there was a sacrificial feast, after which the Luperci cut thongs from the skins of the victims and ran in two bands around the walls of the old Palatine city. A blow from the thong was supposed to cure sterility. The ritual is apparently in honour of no god; Lupercus, whom authorities sometimes name, seems a mere invention Fanunus is a guess of the moderns. The celebration of the festival went until AD 494, when it was changed by Pope Gelasius I into the Feast of Purification.[234]

DANIEL 11:31

31. And arms shall stand on his part, and they shall pollute the sanctuary of strength, and take away the daily sacrifice, and they shall place the abomination that maketh desolate.

And arms

The word or "arms" (#2220 zer-o-ah) according to is defined as "the arm (as stretched out), or (of animals) the foreleg; fig. force:- arm + help, mighty, power, shoulder strength." Strongs Concordance, 1979. The ete (2220 zeroa) arm, forearm, shoulder; power, strength, force. Strongs Concordance, 2001.

The word for "arms," (#2220 zer-o-ah) according to *Strongs Condance*, 1979, continues to be defined as as it was in Daniel 11:22 as "the arm (as stretched out) or (of animals) the foreleg-(fig.) force: arm, to help, mighty, power, shoulder strength. The aspect of the definition which seems to fit the historical-prophetic context is the literal outer man and figurative-spiritual inner man [see Ephesians 3:16] belief force exercised first of all in ecclesiastical circles and systems which eventually influenced the civil realm has now grown or matured. Those beliefs continue to be based on faith or unbelief [see Romans 11:20].

With the spirit of unbelief in the Scriptures which says "the dead know not anything," Ecclesiastes 9:5 the religio-politico vile person system of Roman Catholicism believes in the intercession of saints as advocated by Clovis in his A. D. 507 victory at Voille to Saint Martin of Tours. Clovis, originally being a pagan, advocated the Roman Catholic belief arm, of intercession of saints, adopted by that belief system from paganism in the third century. This belief in his the inner man (see Ephesians 3:16), was probably greatly influenced by his Roman Catholic wife Clotida. Advocating this belief arm would take away the daily mediatorial work of Christ in the heavenly sanctuary, who always intercedes for us, focusing on a lie, of creature rather than Creator worship, which is the foundation of spiritualism.

Another arm of belief and practice was for the religio-politico vile person system of Roman Catholicism was to literally appeal to the civil state to enforce her figurative-spiritual beliefs.

shall stand

#5975 aw-mad: a prim. root: to stand in various relations (lit. and fig., intrans. and trans.):- (abide (behind) appoint, arise, cease, confirm, continue, dwell, be employed, endure, establish, leave, make, ordain, be [over], place, be present (self), raise up remnant, repair, + serve, set (forth, over, -tle, up) (make to, make to be at, with) stand (by, fast, firm, still up, *Strongs*, 1979.

#5975 a-mad v. [Q] to stand, stand up, stand still; [H] to cause to stand, present; to appoint, assign; [Ho] to be presented, be caused to stand. *Strongs*, 2001

on his part

#4480 min; or min-nee; or (constr. plur.), min-nay' (Isaiah 30:11); prop/a part of; hence (prep), from or out of in many senses (as follows):- above, after, among, at, because of, by (reason of), from (among), in, x neither, x nor, (out) of, over, since, x then, through, x whether, with. *Strongs*, 1979.

#4480 min. or minni pp. marker of a source or extension from a source: from, out of, of; temporary: since, after; logically: because of; of degree: more than. *Strongs*, 2001

The aspect of the definition of the word for "stand on his part" which seems to fit the historical-prophetic context regarding the religio-political, influencial system of Roman Catholicism is literally to take an inner man [see Ephesians 3:16] belief positional figurative-spiritual stand on issues. Then literally promote those ideas in ecclesiastical teaching which literally could and would eventually influence the arising of civil law to reflect those views.

While Scripture advocates and promotes church government of "first apostles then prophets etc." [see I Corinthians 12:28], it also advocates civil government in the "giving to Caesar that which is Ceasars"[see Matthew 22;21]. Yet in the promotion of ecclesiastical beliefs by the government of the religious church or civil state, one is cautioned and counciled by the response of the disciples," we aught to obey God rather than man"[see Acts 5:29]. Their stand is echoed in "to the law and to the testimony, if they speak not according to this word, it is because there isno light in them" [see Isaiah 8:20].

It is perceived that the religio-politico arms which stand on the part of the Roman Catholic Church in the latter fifth, early sixth century include the following:

I. Belief arms
  A. Intercessions of saints

Clovis ascribes AD 507 victory at Vouille over Arian Visigoths at Vouille, The battle of Vouille was fought in the northern marches of Visigothic territory, at Vouille, Vienna, near Poitiers, (Gaul) in the spring of 507 between the Franks commanded by Clovis and the Visigoths of Alaric II (d. AD 507), the Conqueror of Spain.[235] near Poitiers, to St. Martin of Tours, greatest of the Gallo-Roman saints. "In 506 Clovis was still active in the Rhineland against both the Alamanni and the Thuringians. In 507 he finally turned against the powerful Visigoths of Gaul south of the Loire. But first he sought the patronage of St. Martin of Tours, greatest of the Gallo-Roman saints. His subsequent victory over the Arian Visigoths at Vouille, near Poitiers, was attributed by him to that patronage. His family had acquired a spiritual patron revered by all his Gallo-Roman subjects."[236]

The underlying doctrine of patrons is that of communion of saints, or bond of spiritual union existing between God's servants on earth, in heaven, or in purgatory. The saints are thereby regarded as the advocates and intercessors of those who are making their earthly pilgrimage.[237]

The "belief" arm "of intercession of the saints" entered into by Clovis in 507, the sixth century, ascribing his victory at Vouille to St. Martin of Tours is rooted in one of the third century "arms of a flood," escribed in Daniel 11:22.[238]

A saint or angel designated (by individuals, groups, or the church) as the heavenly protector of individuals, institutions, or specialized activities. The example of the saints life is proposed to those under his care (see 1 Cor. 14:12), and it is customary that his intercession be specially invoked.

The practice of choosing patrons dates from the early church. In the early 4th century Christians were already being named for apostles and martyrs. Dedication of churches to saints soon followed. It is not known when angels were first chosen as patrons, but in 545 a church in Ravenna was dedicated to St. Michael, the arch angel. Patrons found their greatest popularity in the Middle Ages.[239] This appealing to dead saints who "know not anything"

(Eccl. 9:5) is an advocation of the vile person system of the Roman Catholicisms false, devil devised doctrine of the immortality of the soul.

According to the Pen of Inspiration, the endorsement of the idea of the immortality of the soul is the very foundation of spiritualism.[240] Civil arm ecclesiastical arms

Pope Gelasius (A.D. 492–496) wrote a letter to Zeno's successor, the Eastern emperor Anastasius, in which he declared 'there are. . . two by whom principally the world is ruled! The sacred authority of the Pontiffs and the royal power. Of these the importance of the priests is so much greater, as even for kings of men they will have to give account in the divine judgement."[241]

B. Ecclesiastical arms
    1. The pope becomes the Vicar of Christ, AD 495.[242]
    2. In 502 Bishop Ennodius of Pavia urged that the pope can be judge alone.[243]
    3. Roman Catholic Church was, and is, only paganism baptized.
    a. From the time when these success were fully accomplished, in AD 5, the papacy was triumphant so far as paganism was concerned; for thou the latter doubtless retarded the progress of the Catholic faith, yet it h not the power, if it had the disposition, to suppress the faith, and hin the encroachments of the Roman pontiff. When the prominent powers Europe gave up their attachment to paganism, it was only to perpetual its abominations in another form; for Christianity as exhibited in Roman Catholic Church was, and is only paganism baptized.

The status of the see of Rome was also peculiar at this time. In 498, Symmachus ascended the pontifical throne as a recent convert from paganism. He found his way to the papal chair by striving with his competitor even unto blood. He received adulation as the successor of St. Peter and struck the keynote of papal assumption by presuming to excommunicate the Emperor Anastasius.[244]

The Ostrogothic Papacy was a period from 493 to 537 where the papacy was strongly influenced by the Ostrogothic Kingdom, if the pope was not outright appointed by the Ostrogothic King.[245]

C. Civil arms
    1. The Ostrogothic king, Theodoric the Great, known as a friend of being himself a Catholic who was religiously bent toward Aria heresy advocated by Arius c. 320, was called to mediate the dispute

pope Symmachus and the antipope Lawrence (A.D. 498–506) vaci then supported Symmachus.[246]

2. Clovis, he alone in the Christian world deserved the name and prero a Catholic king.[247]

Clovis's conversion to orthodox Catholicism rather than Arianism was of great importance.[248]

a. The original lateral "belief arm" mentioned in Dan. 11:22 of the "church appealing to the state" at the time of Paul of Samatosa A. D. 272[249] finds a bilateral extension with Clovis, the leader of the "civil state" the Franks in Gaul, latter known as France, "appealing to the church" the "mid-third century belief of "intercession of saint"[250] "in the ascri of the victory of Voille to St. Martin of Tours."

3. In 508, the E. Emp. Anastasis I conferred on him (Clovis) the title "proconsul."[251]

In 508, Clovis received at Tours the insignia of the consulship from the Eastern emperor Anastasis, but the title was purely honorific.[252] Clovis gave the domain of Micy, near Orleans at the confluence of the Loire and Loiret for a monastery (508).[253]

Clovis gave Euspicius and his nephew Mesmin the domain of Micy near Orleans an the confluence of the Loire and Loiret for a monastery in 508.[254]

With the Roman Catholics mid-third century endorsement of the arm of "intercession of the saints," which "takes away the daily" mediatorial work of Christ in the heavenly sanctuary, "who always liveth to make intercession for us," and in the early sixth century Clovis, at the encouragement of his wife, Clotilda, joins orthodox Catholicism not Arian Catholicism, following the belief (in his 'inner man' belief) of "intercession of saints" by attributing his AD 507 spring of that year victory at Voille to St. Martin of Tours, by the time E.emp. Anastasis confers on him the civil title of "proconsul" in 508, Clovis becomes the vessel, in his inner man belief being, to not only "take away the daily" ministry of Christ by focusing on, or praying to, dead saints, rather than the living Christ, "who ever liveth to make intercession" (Hebrew 7:25) but also sets up the civil/ state force that will ultimately sanction and enforce that ecclesiastically religious belief which is "the foundation of spiritualism."[255]

and they shall pollute

#2490 khaw-lal. A prim. root [comp.] 2470] prop. To bore, i. e. (by impl) to wound, to dissolve; to profane (a person, place, or thing), to break (one's word), to begin (as if by "an opening wedge"): denom. (From 2485) to play (the flute);- begin (x men began) defile, x break, defile, x eat (as common things) x first, x gather the grape thereof, x take inheritance, pipe, player on instruments, pollute, (cast as) profane (self), prostitute, slay (slain), sorrow, stain, wound. Strongs, 1979.

#2490 ha-lal v.[Q] to be wounded; to play the flute; [N] to defile oneself, be profaned, be desecrated; [P] to pierce, wound; to defile, profane, desecrate; to enjoy; to play the flute; [Pu} to be killed; to be defiled; [Pol] to pierce, wound; [Polal] to be wounded ; [H} to begin, to proceed, to launch; [Ho] to begin. Strongs, 2001

The aspect of the definition of the word for "pollute" which seems to fit the historical-prophetic context regarding the religio-political, influencial system of Roman Catholicism is literally to take an inner man [see Ephesians 3:16] positional stand to neglect God's ten commandments.

The good Catholics are historically perceived to be the ones polluting by their lives the sanctuary of strength according to Salvian, a Christian writer of the fifth century. He seems to have been still living at Marseiles when Gennadius wrote under the papacy of Gelasius (492–496).

He declares in book iii. That the misery of the Roman world is all due to the neglect of God's commandments and the terrible sins of every class of society.[256]

"What the Romans," that is the natives called Romans, "have polluted with fornication," says Salvianus, "the barbarians have purified with their chastity. We, who are good Catholics, love uncleanness; they, who are heretics, abhor and detest it; we hate purity, and avoid it; they admire and embrace it," A mortifying comparison to the Catholics of those days; the rather, as it was made by a Catholic bishop.[257]

The Pen of Inspiration, although not referring to the above historical fact, indicates that the human heart is sinful and polluted, cleansed only by Christ's efficacy.

Like Peter and his brethren, we too have been washed in the blood of Christ, yet often through contact with evil the heart's purity is soiled. We must come to Christ for His cleansing grace. Peter shrank from bringing his soiled feet in contact with the hands of his Lord and Master; but how often we bring our sinful polluted hearts in contact with the heart of Christ! How grievous to Him is our evil temper, our vanity and pride! Ye all our infirmity and defilement we must bring to Him. He alone can wash us clean. We are not prepared for communion with Him unless cleansed by His efficacy.[258]

the sanctuary (#4720 mik-dash)

#4720 mik-dawsh or (Exodus 15:17) mik-ked-awsh; from 6942; a consecrated thing or place, espec. a palace, sanctuary (whether of Jehovah or idols) or asylum:-chapel, hallowed part, holy place, sanctuary. *Strong*s, 1979.

#4720 miq-das. n. m. holy place, sanctuary, shine. Strongs, 2001 The aspect of the definition of the word for "sanctuary" which seems to fit the historical-prophetic context regarding the religio-political, influencial system of Roman Catholicism at this time, five to six centuries after Christ, is an abiding, holy place, relationship to the risen Christ.

"Therefore say, Thus saith the Lord God; Although I have cast them for off among the heathen, and although I have scattered them among the countries, yet will I be to them as a little sanctuary (#4720 mik-dawsh) in the countries where they shall come" Ezekiel 11:16.

"Sanctify the Lord of hosts himself; and let him be your fear;, and let him be your dread. And he shall be for a sanctuary (#4720 mik-dawsh); but for a stone of stumbling and for a rock of offence to both houses of Israel, for a gin and for a snare to the inhabitants of Jerusalem." Isaiah 8:13-14.

"Then the first covenant had also ordinances of divine service, and a worldly (#2886 kos-mee-kos lit. or fig.) sanctuary (#40 hag-i-os)" Hebrews 9:1.

2886 kos-mee-kos; from 2989 (in its second sense): terr3ne ("cosmic"). lit. (mundane) or fig. (corrupt; worldly. Strongs, 2010 2886 kos-mi-kos a. earthly, worldly Strongs, 2001

40 hag-ee-os; from ha-gos (an aw-ful thing) [comp 53, 2282] sacred (phys. pure, mor. blameless or religious, cer. Consecrated):- (most) holy (one, thing), saint. *Strongs,* 1979.

40 hag-i-os a. (moral quality), consecrated [ceremonially] acceptable to God): holy person/people+saints), holy place = sanctuary Strongs, 2001 When declaring that Israel's house, was left unto them desolate [see Matthew 23:38, Luke 13:35], Christ was referring to himself as the fulfillment of the temple. The Jewish nation, although not necessarily individuals within that nation, had rejected a relationship to him, their creator. This temple had grown out of the tabernacle in the wilderness sanctuary. Hence Revelation would record a "temple of the tabernacle of the testimony" [see Revelation 15:5]. Since Christ spoke of his body as being the temple [see John 2:21], he would be the antitypical fulfillment of the "temple of the tabernacle of the testimony [see Revelation 15:5]."

Originally God had said "Let them make me a sanctuary that I may dwell among them." Exodus 25:8. It would be in the future tent-tabernacle within the sanctuary curtain arms of his righteousness that Christ would dwell among fallen humanity. After the incarnation, fallen humanity can be depicted as fish followers of God in the laver/sea outer court of the heavenly sanctuary, subjected to outside faith waves of temptations to sin. Once they died to outside faith self, they were to ultimately rise and be transformed throough a process, called growth in grace [see 2 Peter 3:18], into priestly followers of God, ministering in the holy place of the wilderness depicting the heavenly sanctuary. The linen clothes the priests wore in the wilderness sanctuary symbolized the righteousness of Christ that post calvary-ressurrection-ascension believers were to spiritually put on as they ministered to others, in relationship to Christ, their heavenly high priest, who was also the holy place in the heavenly sanctuary. Like the priests in the wilderness sanctuary put on linen, priestly, robes before ministering in the wilderness sanctuary, so post-calvary believers were to put on Christ's righteousness to serve as priests in the heavenly sanctuary. Prior to becoming priests that would minister in a priestly relationship to Christ, the holy place, they like Abraham would "believe God and it would be counted to them as righteousness. [see Genesis 15:6, Revelation 6:7]" Like the Israelite believer brought his sacrifice to the altar of burnt offering, transferred his sin to it by laying his hand on the the victims head, then slayining it, finding the "type" forgiveness strength, the post-calvary would find anti-typical forgiveness strength in Christ.

Originally, the sanctuary with the tabernacle was to be made according to the pattern. [see Exodus 25:8, 9. This structure modeled, in type, through forms and figures how God would ultimately reconcile humanity to Himself. Following Christ's life, death, resurrection and ascension the anti-typical manifestation of this reconciliation which had occurred literally, "in type," in Israel were now to be understood in a figurative-spiritual [see Hebrews 9:24] disclosure of the heavenly sanctuary message. By Christ's incarnation the curtain enclosing the the earthly Hebraic sanctuary symbol of the heavenly had been antitypically fulfilled. By his death on calvary, the literal animal sacrifices had been antitypically fulfilled. With his ascension to heaven, Christ sat down at the right hand of God, as the bread of heaven which was on the north side of the tabernacle, on the table of shewbread throne. The first record of the ascended Christ being at the right hand of God is at the stoning of Stephen.

"But he being full of the Holy Ghost, looked up stedfastly into heaven, and saw the glory of God and Jesus standing on the right hand of God. And he said, "Behold, I see the heavens opened, and the Son of man standing on the right hand of God." Acts 8:55, 56.

Simultaneously, he antitypically took a high priestly position carrying out the priestly phase of the heavenly sanctuary ministry. Not only was Christ the ascended high priest teaching figurative-spiritual priestly believers how to live, but they were to imbibe, assimilate his teaching into their lives as food.

It is interesting to note that one stack of showbread symbolized himself, who left heaven to come to this earth as the bread of heaven, while the other stack of showbread symbolized his father who remained in heaven. The importance of noting that the table of shewbread is the throne of the holy is because, it is on the north side of the tabernacle. Consequently when the father arises from the throne at the close of the 2300 day prophecy of Daniel 8:14, and goes on a flaming chariot into the most holy place, he sits down on the ark which is at the west end of the sanctuary. Then the son arises from the same throne, also mounts a chariot, and goes into the most holy place.[259]

So it is important to note that after Christ's ascencion to heaven, he began his high priestly work in the holy place of the heavenly sanctuary. There he carried out the daily phase of the heavenly sanctuary ministry as fallen humanities high priest which lasted from A.D. 31 — October 22, 1844. Other scripture references which support the risen Christ at the right hand of God, other than the account of Stephen, include:

"Now the things which we have spoken this is the sum: We have such an high priest, who is set on the right hand of the throne of Majesty in the heavens: A minister of the sanctuary, and of the true tabernacle, which the Lord pitched and not man. . . Who serve unto the example and shawdow of heavenly things, as Moses was admonished of God when he was about to make the tabernacle: for "See," saith he, "that thou make all things according to the pattern shewed to thee in the mount." Hebrew 8:1-5.

"And verily the first covenant had also ordinances of divine service, and a worldly sanctuary. For there was a tabernacle made: the first, wherein was the candlestick, and the table, and the showbread; which is called the sanctuary. And after the second veil, the tabernacle which is called the Holiest of all." Hebrews 9:1-2.

"The Holy Ghost was signifying, that the way into the holiest of all was not made manifest, while the first tabernacle was yet standing.

Which was a figure for the time then present, I which were offered both gifts and sacrifices, that could not make him that did the service perfect, as pertaining to the conscience." Hebrews 9:8, 9.

"But Christ being come an high priest of good things to come, by a greater and more perfect tabernacle, not made with hands, that is to say, not of this building." Hebrews 9:11.

"How much more shall the blood of Christ, who through the eternal Spirit offered himself without spot to God, purge your consciences from dead works to serve the living God?" Hebrews 9:14.

"It was therefore necessary that the patterns of things in the heavens should be purified with these; but the heavenly things themselves with better sacrifices than these. For Christ is not entered into the holy places made with hands, which are figures of the true; but into heaven itself, now to appear in the presence of God for us." Hebrew 9:23, 24.

"So Christ was once offered to bear the sins of many; and unto them that look for him shall he appear the second time without sin unto salvation." Hebrew 9:28.

"By a new and living way, which he hath consecrated for us, through the veil, that is to say, his flesh; And having an high priest over the house of God; Let us draw near with a true heart in full assurance of faith, having our hearts sprinkled from an evil conscience, and our bodies wash with pure water." Hebrews 10:20-22.

"Thy way, O God, is in the sanctuary (#6944 ko-desh): who is so great a God as *our* God." Psalms 77:13.

#6944 ko-desh; from 6942: a sacred place or thing; rarely abstr., sanctity, consecrated (thing), dedicated (thing), hallowed holiness, (x most) holy (x day, portion, thing), saint, sanctuary. *The New Strong's Exhaustive Concordance of the Bible, 2010* #6944 qo-des n. m. holy or sacred thing, holy or sacred place, sanctuary; holiness, set apart as dedicated to God; the "holy of holies" is the most holy place, set apart exclusively for the Presence of God, with limited high priest access *The Strongest Strong's exhaustive Concordance Of the Bible* 2001 It is important to note that when God originally said to the Israelites in the wilderness "let them make me a sanctuary (#4720 mik-dash) that I may dwell among them" (see Exodus 25:8). they would discover that anyone could bring a sacrifice to the altar of burnt offering. Upon bringing the sacrifice to the altar, the believer was forgiven, [see Leviticus 4]. This forgiveness was the strength of the sanctuary. That altar in the outer court of the earthly sanctuary symbolized the future, sacrificing, calvary, experience of Christ, the lamb of God, in the outer court of the heavenly sanctuary.

When God said to Moses at the burning bush, "take off your shoes, for the place you are standing is holy (#6944 ko-desh) ground," he was stating that a person could only be in his presence if they met certain conditions. In the case of Moses that condition was to remove his shoes. Thus in the inner court of the Hebraic sanctuary, the area on which the tabernacle (4908 mish-kawn) was set up would be regarded as a holy (#6944 kodesh). The one hundred (#6944 qo-desh) silver bases [see Exodus 38:27], upon which the tabernacle (#4908 mish-kan) was constructed is evidence of this reality. Moses had to fulfill the condition of taking off his shoes to stand on the holy ground before the burning bush. In like manner, so only the priests fulfilling the condition of being clothed with white linen, a symbol of Christ's future righteousness, would be allowed to minister in the inner court tabernacle (#4908 mish-kawn) holy place.

While the sacrifice of Christ, the lamb of God, at calvary, symbolized in the sacrifices on the altar of burnt offering were antitypically complete, when Christ said "It is finished" John 19:30, there was still a work to be antitypically completed in post-calvary priestly followers. The word for "finished" (#5055 tel-eh-o[260]) used in John 19:30, indicating the antitypical fulfillment of the lamb sacrifice is related to the word (#2005 epi-tel-eh-o[261]) in Philipians 1:6 translated "perform" that now believers partaking of calvary's merits can now grow in grace as antitypical priests, in the "priesthood of believers." This work was to "put on Christ" Galations 3:27. Like the priests put on [see Exodus 29:8] linen priestly garments before ministering in the tabernacle/temple, so Christs followers were to put on his righteous before ministering in the heavenly sancturay.

As the death of Christ at calvary, fulfilling antitypically the type lamb or other sacrifices in the sacrificial system, so the power of God's grace shining from the empty tomb empoweredpost-calvary believers to put on Christ's righteousness, living as a priesthood of believers. While the whole nation of Israel was called at Mt. Sinai to be a priesthood of believers, three months into their journey from Egypt, a year after the Exodus from Egypt/sin, only the tribe of Levi were to function as priests. In like manner the whole post-calvary world is called to be priests, putting on the righteousness of Christ, only a few, like priests, ministers, rabbies etc. would function as religious leaders. According to the parable of the wedding feast [see Matthew 22:3-12], all are to "put on" the wedding garment symbol of Christ's righteousness. They are refered to in John 3:16 as the "whosoever." Everyone may not be a religious leader or teacher, but they all must have the wedding garment on.

Once the ascension occurred (see Acts 1:11) Christ ascended to heaven, evidenced by Stephen's exclaimation as he was being stoned, "Behold, I see the heavens opened, and the Son of man standing on the right hand of God" Acts 7:56.

This sanctuary was made according to a pattern of the heavenly as echoed in Hebrew 8:5. "Who serve unto the example and shadow of heavenly things, as Moses was admonished of God when he was about to make the tabernacle: for, See, saith he, that thou make all things according to the pattern shed to thee in the mount." Hebrews 8:5. "Then verily the first covenant had also ordinances of divine service, and a worldly sanctuary." Hebrews 9:1.

Originally God had said to Moses, "Let them make me a (type) sanctuary that I may dwell among them," (Exodus 25:8), saying to the nation of Israel years later, "yet will I be to them a little sanctuary in the countries they have come." Ezekiel 11:16 last part. Now after six hundred years since the life, death, resurrection and ascension of Christ, God would continue to be their (antitypical) sanctuary. In this heavenly sanctuary, Jesus Christ, our risen high priest, (see Hebrew 8:1). He would begin and continue this phase of ministry up to and shortly before the second coming. The "daily" phase of ministry which Christ, our high priest had begun after his ascension would continue till October 22, 1844, when similtaneously the day of atonement phase of ministry would begin.

The intercession of Christ in man's behalf in the sanctuary above is as essential to the plan of salvation as was His death on the cross. By His death He began that work which after His resurrection. He ascended to complete in heaven.[262]
Scripture records in Philippians1:5-6:

"For your fellowship in the gospel from the first day until now; Being confident of of this very thing, that he which hath begun a good work in you will perform it until the day of Jesus Christ."

While the antitypical reality of Christ's death on calvary was a fulfillment of all the animal, plant, and mineral sacrifices in the Old Testament portrayed in the words "It is finished,(#5055 tel–eh-o)[263]" John 19:30, there was still a work, an unfinished work, to be done. That work was portrayed in Philipians 1:6 which reads:" Being confident

76

of this very thing, that he which hath begun a good work in you will perform (#2005 ep-i-tel-eh-o)[264] it until the day of Jesus Christ." That is to say, once calvary's sacrifice, typically or antitypically occurred, there would still be a work for God's people, Jewish or Gentile, to do.

Once the work of God was complete at calvary in the taking away of sins as proclaimed by John "behold the lamb of God that taketh away the sin of the world," John 1:29, the antitypical reality fulfillment of the heavenly sanctuary was finished. That work is perceived to be the "very thing, that he which hath begun a good work" (Philippians 1:6), fulfilled in "type" for the Hebraic sanctuary at the altar of burnt offering. Not only was that sacrifice good for the Jews but also for all people participating in like sacrifices before a knowledge of the sanctuary occurred. Antitypically calvary's sacrifice did away with the earthly Hebraic sanctuary service, evidenced by "the veil of the temple was rentin twain from top to bottom" (see Matthew 27:51). This reality simultaneously inaugurated Christ antitypical fulfillment of the altar of burnt offering in the the heavenly sanctuary. Like the Israelites had lessons to learn about dependence upon God in all situations before they erected the Hebraic sanctuary one year after the Exodus, so post calvary believers could experience some time before they put on Christ's righteousness as priestly believers. While Christ's righteousness was credited, (Genesis 15:6) just like Abraham to their accounts just by believing in his sacrifice (#5055 tel-eh-o), there would be a more complete, or further fulfilment when believers began to allow Christ to perform (#2005 ep-pi-tel-eh-o), through his spirit, his works in them.

The writer of Hebrew says in Hebrew 8:1-5:

> "Now of the things which we have spoken this is the sum: We have such an high priest, who is set on the right hand of the throne of the Majesty in the heavens; A minister of the sanctuary[265], and of the true tabernacle, which the Lord pitched, and not man. For every high priest is ordained to offer gifts and sacrifices: wherefore it is of necessity that this man have somewhat also to offer. For if he were on earth, he should not be a priest, seeing that there are priests that offer gifts according to the law: Who serve unto the example and shadow of heavenly things, as Moses was admonished of God when he was about to make the tabernacle; for, "See," saith he, "that thou make all things according to the pattern shewd to thee in the mount."

Since one of the meanings of the word for sanctuary is "a saint," there would be many believers who would practice in their individual lives a "holy place," relationship to God. They would view themselves and be regarded by others as "lively stones," [see 1 Peter 2:5] on journey in the world of being fashioned as stones in the temple of God. Just as Solomon had timber and stones cut and quarried out of Lebanon, then conveyed[266] them to the land of Israel "by sea in floats." 1 Kings 5:9, so God would take (or quarry) people out of this world, spiritually, to form his temple [see 1 Corinthians 3:17].

For the post calvary, resurrection and ascension of Christ, it is perceived that the believer, in mystery, held on to the hope of Jesus returning to this earth, from the sanctuary in heaven like a kite flyer holds on to the string tethering him to the kite. While living on earth, in their inner man, spiritually, having put on the righteousness of Christ by faith, they were to live as a priesthood of believers. They were to regard themselves as "a chosen generation, a royal priesthood, an holy nation, a peculiar people," (1 Peter 2;9) who held the kite message of what Christ was doing for them in the heavenly sanctuary.

"The kite has been claimed as the invention of the fifth century BC Chinese philosophers Mozi (also Mo Di) and Lu Ban (also Gongshu Ban). By 549 AD, paper kites were certainly being flown, as it is recorded that in that year a paper kite was used as a message for a rescue mission."[267]

While most people at the time of the writing of Hebrew were probably not aware of kites, they were nevertheless in existence, so that it would be a mystery of Christ in the heavenly sanctuary.

Just like the Israelites dwelt in tents from Egypt to Canaan, so the future Messiah would be depicted as dwelling in the tabernacle/tent within the sanctuary among his chosen people on their 'type', and 'antitypical' journey to Canaan or heaven.

#4908 mish-kawn; from 7931: a residence (incl. a shepherd's hut, the lair of animals. fig. the grave; also the Temple); spec.the Tabernacle (prop. the wooden walls):- dwelleth, dwelling (place), habitation, tabernacle, tent. Strongs, 2010

#4908 mis-kan n. m. dwelling place, habitat, tent tabernacle, the tent used as the central place of worship before the temple. *Strongs,* 2001

The first occurrence of the word "sanctuary," occurs after the Israelites came out of Egypt, having slain the lamb or goat, a symbol of calvary in Exodus 15:17 on the other side of the Red Sea. For the Israelites sanctuary occurred after the baptism of the Red Sea, for in this

78

experience they declared that they desired to be dead to the enslaving bondage of Egypt/sin.

That slaying of the lamb or goat symbol of calvary is portrayed in Dan. 11:26 "And they that eat of a portion of his meat shall destroy him." Prior to eating the lamb or goat, the Israelite had slain the sacrifice, applied the blood to their doorposts, entered into that dwelling, ate roasted lamb or goat over the fire in that dwelling as they waited for the midnight judgment. After this experience they were led out of Egypt, a symbol of sin, to begin their journey to the promised land of Canaan, a symbol of heaven. While they were initially led out of Egypt, a symbol of sin, to Succoth where they could, and most probably did, proclaim 'all we needed to be released from Egyptian bondage, symbol of sin, was to follow the command of Moses by slaying the lamb/goat symbol of the future calvary, apply its blood to the doorposts of our dwellings,' a symbol of accepting the sacrifice as an entitlement, or personal savior, to leave Egypt, then be commanded to enter in to await the midnight judgment, after which they would be led out of Egypt, a symbol of sin, or post calvary to a place where they would proclaim, that ll we need to be released from sin was to accept calvary's sacrifice then enter into the new life free from sin, awaiting the midnight judgement, after which there is, and they would be led to, a new life free from the condemning guilt of sin, proclaiming all we need is Jesus.

Then being directed to turn back toward Egypt, encamping before the Red Sea, through which they were to cross in a baptism, it was not until after they were on the other side of the Red Sea, having passed through its baptism that they could sing about the the sanctuary even though they did not know what it was. In reality they would not know until five months after the exodus what the sanctuary type would be into which the priests were to enter and minister, one year after the Exodus.

Initially for Israel redeemed from Egyptian bondage/sin through the blood of the slain lamb or goat, whose blood was applied to their doorposts, the sanctuary they sang about on the other side of the Red Sea, was anyplace outside of Egypt/sin. They had no concept of the sanctuary which was to be set up in the wilderness after five months outside of Egypt/sin. For them sanctuary was in "type" anywhere outside the Egyptian enslaving bondage/ enslaving bondage to sin, which symbolized Christ's incarnation as the type tabernacle, which would occur in type, five plus months after the Exodus, and antitypically many years after sin had been on this earth.

79

Yet when he did come, selected humanity, the Jewish nation, would enter into a literal relationship to Him and after His death, resurrection and ascension all humanity would be invited, as spiritual Israel, after having accepted calvary's sacrifice to figuratively rise with Him, entering a priesthood of believers, where clothed with His righteousness, they would go in and out of Him, the tabernacle/temple, ministering to those fish, as it were, in the laver/sea/earth/world which was enclosed, in the outer court, with the linen of Christ's righteousness, like the linen curtain enclosed the wilderness courtyard, which contained the tabernacle symbol of the incarnate Christ, who would dwell among humanity.

While the Israelites after the exodus would know and experience a #4720 mik-dawsh sanctuary in an area outside Egypt, a symbol of sin and the domain of sin after passing through the baptism of the Red Sea, of which they sang about on the other side of the Red sea, there would still be a further manifestation of that sanctuary in their "type," growth in grace, from the lamb/goat slain in Egypt, whose blood was applied to their doorposts, and into which they had entered, demonstrating their acceptance of that sacrifice as their entitlement to leave Egypt/a life of sin. In the "type" growth in grace, which the Israelites would experience as they journeyed toward the promised land of Canaan, like the post calvary believer after accepting calvary's antitypical sacrifice would journey toward heaven in the genuine "antitypical" grace shining from Christ's victory over sin, they were to discover that a grace-filled life was not only a life outside Egypt, a symbol of sin, but five or more months after their exodus from Egypt/sin they would be asked to make a sanctuary so that God could dwell among them.

This illustrated that God would become one like them in fulfilment of the seed promised to Eve. While the Israelites left Egypt to dwell in tents on their journey from Egypt/sin to the promised land of Canaan/heaven, after God gave by speaking then writing the Ten Commandments, He, through the incarnation would come and dwell among them in a tent, like they were dwelling, but it was a more sophisticated tent called the Tabernacle. Surrounding that tabernacle symbol of the second person of the Godhead's future incarnate life would be the linen courtyard symbol of His righteousness which would surround all humanity, symbolized as fish in the laver/sea/earth/ world, although prior to that incarnation, they would live encamped outside that symbol, even though they were commanded to bring sacrifices into that #4720 mik-dawsh sanctuary. Some, the priests, who lived outside the sanctuary would be called, or set aside, to work within the sanctuary and would be entitled to enter the tabernacle symbol of the future incarnate second person of the Godhead, carrying out the sacrificial services on behalf of themselves and the Israelite community. It would be a #4720 mil-dawsh sanctuary into which all were invited to enter, receiving "type" forgiveness and fellowship with God, having left their tents which were encamped outside the #4720 mik-dawsh sanctuary. Only those priests clothed with linen, the future symbol of Christ's righteousness, could minister in the tabernacle on behalf of all the Israelite nation who were called to be priests, although only a select few, the Levites were to function as priests.

Even after the Israelites entered the promised land of Canaan, a "type" symbol of a little heaven on earth, depicted in the Lord's prayer by "thy kingdom come, thy will be done on earth as it is in heaven," for almost three hundred years after Israel entered Canaan, a symbol of heaven, the sanctuary services were carried out. It was not until the time of David that the idea arose to build a house/temple for God to replace the sanctuary. God came to Nathan, saying, "Go and tell David my servant, Thus saith the Lord, Thou shalt not build me an house to dwell in: For I have not dwelt in an house since the day that I brought up Israel unto this day; but have gone from tent to tent, and from one tabernacle to another. . . I will raise up thy seed after thee, which shall be of thy son: and I will establish his kingdom. He shall build an house, and I will stablish his throne for ever" (1 Chronicles 17:3–12). While David because of bloodshed (1 Chronicles 22:8) could not "build a house for the #4720 mik-dawsh sanctuary" (1 Chronicles 28:10) his son Solomon would be able to build it. During Isaiah's ministry 740–681 BC, when he announces Assyria as the Lord's instrument, he writes that "the Lord Almighty. . . he will be a #4720 mik-dawsh sanctuary" (Isaiah 8:14). At the time of Ezekiel 593–571 BC, he writes, "Therefore say, Thus saith the Lord God; Although I have cast them far off among the heathen, and although I have scattered them among the countries, yet will I be to them as a little sanctuary (#4720 miq-dawsh) in the countries where they shall come" (Ezekiel 11:16).

Thus when God through the prophet Isaiah proclaims that "the Lord Almighty will be a sanctuary" (Isaiah 8:14), it becomes plain to see in lieu of the original command, "Let them make me a sanctuary that I may dwell among them," (Exodus 25:8) that God desires to be the center of Israel's life and for that matter the lives of all in fallen human nature. Since the (#4720 mik- dawsh) sanctuary had been replaced by Solomon's temple, even though the wilderness tabernacle still remained in the land of Israel, it had now become the focal point of Israel's worship. [In Haggai 2:9,the prophet said that this "type" tabernacle/temple would be visited in the future by the "antitypical" fulfillment, namely the incarnate Lord, who would bring greater glory to that reconstructed temple than had been with the original Solonmonic temple.]

That's why Christ, the antitypical fulfillment center of Israel, and for that matter humanity, could say "Destroy this temple (speaking of his body temple) and in three days I will raise it up." With His death, he would do away with the old sacrificial system yet inaugurate a new sacrificial system in which humanity by accepting Him as their personal Savior from sin as the lamb of God would be able to rise with Him in his resurrection, putting on the righteousness of Christ, like the priests put on their linen garments before they ministered in the wilderness sanctuary or temple.

of strength

#4581 maw–oze, maw-ooz, or maw-oze, maw-ooz from 5810; a fortified place: fig. A defense:-force, fort (-ress), rock, strength (-eu) (x most) strong (hold) #4581 ma-oz n.m. refuge, stronghold. Fortress, place of protection; (used with "head") helmet. *Strongs, 2001*

The aspect of the definition of the word for "of strength" which seems to fit the historical-prophetic context regarding the religio-political, influencial system of Roman Catholicism at this time, five to six centuries after Christ, is a figurative-spiritual abiding, relationship to the risen Christ.

The strength of believers after Christ's life, death, resurrection, and ascension lay in the fact that even though Christ had left this earth, He was still with them in spirit. Stemming from Ezek. 11: 16, "I will be to them a little sanctuary to them in whatever countries I have scattered them," bolsters Christ's proclamation, "I am with you always even unto the end of the age." So in an antitypical sense, now instead of having to bring a lamb to sacrifice, believers could claim Christ's sacrifice as their substitute for sin. Even though He was not with them literally He was with them figuratively- spiritually through the promised gift of the Holy Spirit.

and take away

#5493 soor (Hos. 9:12) soor: a prim root: to turn off (lit. or fig.):- be [- head], bring, call back, decline, depart, eschew, get [you], go (aside). x grievous, lay away (by), leave undone, be past, pluck away, put (away, down), rebel, remove (to and fro), revolt, x be sour, take (away, off), turn (aside, away, in), withdraw, be without. Strongs, 1979.

#5493 sur v, [Q] to turn away, depart, leave, to saw; [Qp] to be rejected; [Pol] to drag from, turn aside; [H] to remove, get rid of, take off; [Ho] to be removed, be abolished; by extension: to forsake, reject. *Strongs, 2001.*

The aspect of the definition of the word for "take away" which seems to fit the historical-prophetic context regarding the religio-political, influencial system of Roman Catholicism at this time, is to literally advocate another way to God than through Christ Jesus. This was the result of the third century, inner man [see Ephesians 3:16] figurative-spiritual, adoption of the pagan belief of intercession of saints, i.e. deads saints on behalf to the living, which is the foundation of spiritualism. Clovis, the pagan king of the Franks followed the beliefs of his Catholic wife, Clotilde.

the daily *sacrifice*

#8548 taw-meed: from an unused root mean. To stretch: prop. continuance (as indef. extension) but usually only (attributively as adj.) constant (or adv. constantly): ellipt. the regular (daily) sacrifice:- alway (-s), continual (employment, -ly), daily ([–]) ever (-more) perpetual. Strongs, 1979.

#8548 ta-mid, n. m. (used as adv.). continually, constantly, regularly, daily. Strongs, 2001

"The word ("taw-meed") itself does not mean "daily," but simply "continual" or "regular." Of the 103 occurrences, it is translated "daily" only in Num. 4:16 and in the five occurrences of it in Daniel (chs. 8:11, 12, 13; 11:31; 12:11). The idea of "daily" was evidently derived, not from the word itself, but from that with which it was associated.

In ch. 8:11 *tamid* has the definite article and is therefore used adjectivally. Furthermore, it stands independently, without a substantive, and must either be understood subjectively as meaning "continuance" or be supplied with a substantive. In the Talmud, when *tamid* is used independently as here, the word consistently denotes the daily sacrifice. The translators of the KJV, who supplied the word "sacrifice," obviously believed that the daily burnt offering was the subject of the prophecy.

As to the meaning of *tamid* in this (Dan. 8:11) passage three main views have been held:

That the "daily" refers exclusively to the sacrifices offered in the Temple in Jerusalem. Some expositors holding to this view apply the taking away of the "daily" to the interruption of the Temple service Antiochus Epiphanes for a period of about three years from 167 to B.C ... (see on ch. 11:14). Others apply it to the desolation of Temple by the Romans in AD 70.

That the ""daily" stands for "paganism," in contrast with abomination that maketh desolate" (ch. 11:31), or the papacy; that terms identify persecuting powers; that the word for "daily," correct meaning "continual," refers to the long continuance of Sat opposition to the work of Christ through the medium of paganism; the taking away of the daily and the setting up of "the abomination maketh desolate" represents papal Rome replacing pagan Rome, and this event is the same as that described in 2 Thes. 2:7 and Rev. 13:2.

That the term "daily"—"continual"—refers to the continual prie ministry of Christ in the heavenly sanctuary (Hebrew 7:25; 1 John 2:1) to the true worship of Christ in the gospel age; that the taking away the "daily" represents the substitution by the papacy of compulsory unit in a visible church in place of the voluntary unity of all believer Christ, of the authority of a visible head-the pope-in place of that in Christ, the invisible head of the church, of a priestly hierarchy in place direct access to Christ by all believers, of a system of salvation by which ordained by the church in place of salvation by faith in Christ, and particularly, of the confessional and the sacrifice of the mass in plac the mediatiorial work of Christ as our great high priest in the court heaven; and that this system quite completely diverted men's atten from Christ and thus deprived them of the benefits of His ministry.

Further, in as much as this third view maintains that the little horn is a symbol of imperial Rome as well as of papal Rome (see on vs. 9, 13), predictions concerning its activities may also be understood as applying to pagan Rome, as well as to papal Rome. Thus the "daily" may also refer to the earthly Temple and its services, and the taking away of the "daily" to the desolation of the Temple by Roman legions in AD 70 and the consequent cessation of the sacrificial services. It was this aspect of the activity of "the abomination of desolation" to which Christ referred in His delineation of future events (see on Dan. 11:31; cf. Mt. 24:15–20; Luke 21:20).

In comment on these three views, it may be said that the Antiochus view must be ruled out for the reason that Antiochus does not fit the time periods or other specifications of the prophecy (see on Dan. 9:25).

Both the second and the third interpretations have been held by various able expositors within the Advent Movement. Some devout Bible students have considered that the "daily" refers to paganism, and other equally devout Bible students, that the "daily" refers to the priestly ministry of our Lord. Perhaps this is one of the passages of Scripture on which we must wait until a better day for a final answer. As with other difficult passages of Scripture, our salvation is not dependent upon our understanding fully the meaning of Dan. 8:11."[268]

Although we are presently discussing Daniel 11:31, it may be helpful for us to take another glance at Daniel 8:11. It reads:

Yea, he (a little horn) magnified himself even to the prince of the host, and by him (the little horn, identified in 11:9) the daily *sacrifice* was taken away, and the place of his sanctuary was cast down.

It is perceived that originally the "daily" or "continual" created faith bent of creatures originally belonged the prince of the host, namely the second person of the Godhead, Creator, who became the incarnate Jesus Christ. To him all freethinking creatures were created, as it were, on the heads side of the coin with a bent in freedom to give allegiance to their Creator.

Yet in that freedom there was the tails side of the coin, which although provided for, was not designed by God for freethinking creatures to experience. If that tails side of the coin was ever entered into rebellion in God's universe would originate, and the originator would become the father of sin. This is a window to see, in part, the nature of Lucifer's unexplainable, yet provided for in freedom, rebellion against God. With Lucifer's inner creature nature change from mineral-based bronze winged spirit overlaid by the gold of faith, depicted in the four wings covering the ark in the most holy place of Solomon's temple, symbolizing the Trinity-winged spirits plus the winged spirit of a creature, namely Lucifer, (in as it were a four-leaf clover threaded wing-nut which upheld the golden censer mind of God, meshed to the bolt of God's love comprised of braided strands of eros, agape, epithumia, phileo, and storge love), to plant-based wood, he was unable to stand in the consuming fire of God.

Originally with an inner mineral-based bronze winged spirit overlaid with the gold of faith, if the heat hypostasis essence of the first person of the Godhead, Father, became intense, or was elevated, the creature's spirit would only melt. Now with an inner spirit change from mineral-based bronze to plant-based wood, the spirit would be consumed to ash, hence the Father had to hide Himself in darkness, withdrawing from sinful creatures. From that position, on the tails side of the same love coin on which Lucifer was originally created to dwell on the heads side, he tempted the angels on the heads side of the coin of love to break faith in God and join him on the tails side of the love coin where their inner nature would be/ was changed from the originally created mineral-based bronze to plant-based wood. Originally the mineral-based bronze would only melt in the heat of God's love in contrast to plant-based wood which would be consumed. After one-third of the angels in heaven fell to Lucifer, He the originator of broken faith, called sin, would be in charge of those who had also broken faith in God, having their inner natures changed, like his, from mineral-based bronze to plant- based wood, unable to stand in the heat of God and not be consumed. Thus Lucifer, who became known as Satan, would become the ruler over those whose inner nature had changed from mineral-based bronze to plant-based wood, known as their "daily."

As "prince of the air" in the atmosphere on the tails side of the love coin, as it were, he, Lucifer who had, and would developmentally, become in his transformation known as "Satan," the devil, dragon would be allowed by God to exercise limited "daily" influence over all who had sinned. Like Christ said to Pilate, "You would have no power over me unless it was given to you from above," so Satan would "have no power" over humanity, on the tails side of the love coin "unless it was given to him from above." Even though Satan, the dragon, devil did, and would, have power over all who were on, as it were, the tails side of the love coin, God in the sacrificial system, begun in Eden, by taking an animal's life from which He extracted the skins to make clothing to cover Adam and Eve's nakedness, pointed to the a plan of restoration.

On that "tails side of the love coin," outside Eden, humanity would continue to acknowledge that God would one day send the antitypical promised "seed," to provide reconciliation and restoration to Himself. That "seed" was Christ Jesus, the Savior of the world. While He came, as it were, from heaven, symbolized as the heads side of the coin to fallen humanity on the tails side of the coin, by His death He provided the antitypical sacrifice whereby fallen humanity could live, as it were, figuratively on the heads side of the coin of God's love. Even though they might experience the sleep of death, they would have the assurance of redemption and life on the "heads side of the love coin of God in heaven, but also be able to experience a little heaven on earth, illustrated in the Lord's prayer "thy will be done on earth as it is in heaven."

By the time of the incarnation, the Israelites had already experienced "in type" being released from the enslaving Egyptian bondage, baptized in the Red Sea, realizing God's provision of water and food, the call to be priests with the Ten Commandment parameters they were to live by, and the construction of the sanctuary and tabernacle which pointed to the incarnation when God would dwell among them. Like the priests literally ministered "in type" within the sanctuary and tabernacle to those in the Israelite community who lived and worked outside the tabernacle, being called a kingdom of priests, themselves, living outside the tabernacle but working inside the sanctuary and tabernacle, so after Christ's life, death, resurrections, and ascension, the "antitypical priesthood of believers," would figuratively accept Calvary's sacrifice, then rise in newness of life and antitypically put on Christ's righteousness, like the priests put on their linen garments. Like the priests who "in type" put on their linen garments celebrating the life of "a kingdom of priests," to which they had been called, having previously one year before, put the blood of the slain lamb or goat on their doorposts, now celebrated what God had done, commemorating that event of being released from Egyptian, in calling them to be priests.

In support of that "type" event in Egypt, the priests "daily" brought their plant-based wood spirits to support the lamb sacrifice on the altar of burnt offering, commemorating supportingly, their deliverance.

Idolatry would surround Israel, in Egypt/sin, Ex. 12:12, and also by the nations that surrounded them as they journeyed through the wilderness (Ex. 34:15, 16) toward the promised land of Canaan. Once in Canaan (Judges 10:13), a symbol of heaven, the God of Israel, (symbolized by the slain lamb in Egypt) would be figuratively commemorated in the wilderness sacrificial system of the wilderness sanctuary. The shed blood applied to their doorposts back in Egypt was the only reason they were entitled to be in unbroken families, on their way to Canaan/heaven. With God's call to the Israelite nation to be a priesthood nation, three months after their Exodus from Egypt, was symbolized the new life they were designed to enter, later known as the "new birth."

While the entire nation of Israel was called to be a "kingdom of priests, a holy nation," only the tribe of Levi would literally function as priests in the wilderness sanctuary. The non-Levite Israelite symbolized the nation/world God had literally /figuratively called out of the enslaving Egyptian/sin bondage.

Israel, symbolizing the world was/is freed from the enslaving bondage to Egypt/sin by the slain lamb/goat and its acceptance would be demonstrated by an application to the doorposts/soul Symbolically they would be spiritually resurrected having applied His shed blood to the doorposts of their dwellings into which they were to enter on their way to Canaan/heaven. The Israelite/believers were to be continually reminded in the sanctuary service that it was the blood of the slain/ Calvary lamb/goat in Egypt, applied to their doorposts that demonstrated outwardly an inward acceptance of that sacrifice. An acceptance of that sacrifice gave them entitlement to leave Egypt/sin, no matter where they were in their journey/development/maturity "growth in grace" (2 Pet. 3:18), "first the blade then the ear, then the full corn in the ear" (Mk. 4:28) to the promised land/heaven. Thus Christ said, "No man cometh to the Father but by me," (Jn. 14:6) and "no man cometh to me except the Father draws him." (Jn. 6:44)

The coming of Christ at the incarnation is depicted as the coming of the construction of the sanctuary at God's command "Let them make me a sanctuary that I may dwell among them." Ex. 25:8 and the tabernacle, a little more than five months after their deliverance from Egypt/sin by the blood of the slain lamb/goat applied to their doorposts symbolizing acceptance of that sacrifice. With the establishment of the sanctuary after the Israelites had slain the lamb/goat, applying its blood to their doorposts, a symbol of calvary and acceptance of it, the Israelites/believers were called literally/figuratively to become a kingdom of priests.

With the birth of Christ, almost four millennium after the original sin of Adam and Eve at which time they and their descendants were placed, as it were, outside the Garden of Eden, having been originally created in Eden on the "heads side of the coin of God's love," where they experienced a "daily" taw-meed, face-to-face relationship with their Creator, now found themselves, after the broken faith of sin, outside Eden on the tails side of the coin of God's love, where they were no longer able to experience a face-to-face relationship with their Creator, but now were under the "daily" taw-meed of Satan on the tails side of the love coin, provided for in freedom but not designed to be experienced. That's in part, a window into understanding how the "daily" was taken away by the ultimate "little horn," Satan, uprooting the other Three, namely the Father, Son, and Holy Spirit and the "daily," on the tails side of the love coin, outside Eden, given over to it.

According to Dan. 8, the original "daily," (on the heads side of the love coin whose leader was "the prince of the host," namely the second person of the Godhead, who would become the incarnate Christ Jesus, our Savior and Lord,) was "taken away" by the ultimate, original, "little horn," Satan, the dragon, devil. And the "daily" on the tails side of the love coin "was given over to it.

It was the object of God, in part, to "take away" the "daily" rulership which Satan exercised over fallen humanity on the tails side of the love coin outside Eden, restoring them, as it were to the original, heads side, albeit they would not be like unfallen beings who had never sinned, for they had known sin and were now or could be redeemed. Also it was the object of God, in part, not to "take away" the "daily" rulership which Satan, "the prince of the air," on the tails side of the love coin, exercised over the fallen angel who had succumbed to the originator of sin, allowing them to experience, along with their leader, the consequences of the wrong choice in their God-given freedom, banishment from God. Thus there would be a demonstration of both God's love and justice. God could justly love and reconcile those who accepted His provision of reconciliation and also justly love, with tears in his voice, respecting the choice of those who had rebelled against Him by banishing them from Himself, in the consuming fire of hell.

While God called the entire Israelite community to literally and figuratively become "a kingdom of priests, a holy nation," in the world, only a subset of the Israelite nation, the tribe of Levi, would literally function as priests, and even within that tribe there would be subdivisions of priestly duties.

Thus life inside Eden, and for that matter in an unfallen heaven, is perceived to be a parallel equivalent to life on the heads side of the love coin, where mineral-based bronze creatures, on the rim universe, because they possess inner mineral-based bronze winged spirits overlaid with the gold of faith, on the God-sphere hub, participate in the created bent of faith, yielding allegiance to God.

Unexplainably Lucifer, who became Satan, the dragon, in freedom, because the love coin has two sides, even though God only designed for his creation to live on the heads side, chose to rebel against God. In so doing, his inner spirit was changed, or transformed from mineral-based bronze to plant- based wood, unable to stand in the heat of our consuming fire, one God, manifested in three persons as first person of the Godhead hypostasis heat Father, second person of the Godhead hypostasis plant-based incense/fuel Son, and third person of the Godhead, who possessed two hypostasis of plant-based oil and elemental atmosphere, like air

Holy Spirit, who in fellowship in the combustion of a consuming fire.

Unlike unfallen mineral-based creatures on the rim universe, possessing inner mineral-based winged spirits overlaid with the gold of faith which were able to uphold the consuming fire of our one God in the censer minds which they were created to possess, now their censer minds were changed from gold to bronze, still able to contain the consuming fire of our one God, but their inner spirits were changed from mineral-based bronze to plant-based wood, unable to stand in the presence of the hypostasis heat, first person of the Godhead, Father, without being consumed.

Life outside Eden or outside heaven is perceived to be a parallel equivalent to life on the tails side of the same love coin.

It would be Satan's (the ultimate vile being) purpose to do everything in his power to distract believers from acknowledging Christ's sufficiency as their mediator between them and the Father. Even in these times he would use the midthird century belief arm of intercession of the saints advocated by Clovis in his 507 victory at Voille, ascribing it, that victory, to Saint Martin of Tour, a dead saint, instead of Christ, the living, ascended, mediator between God and man.

Notes: Inasmuch as the taking away of the continual mediation of Christ is made the beginning of a prophetic period, there must be some definite act at some definite time which, in form and intent, takes from Christ His priestly work in the heavenly sanctuary.

This act was the official decree of the ecclesiastical council held at Rome in 503 A.D., by which it was declared "that the Pope was judge as God's Vicar, and could himself be judged by no one". . . The work of Clovis, king of the Franks, who earned for himself the title of 'the eldest son of the church' by his campaigns to subdue the kingdoms hostile to the Papacy, contributes much toward putting into practical effect this claim of the Papacy, which finally resulted in establishing the pope as the head of the Roman priesthood which has usurped the priestly work of Christ, and has established another system of mediation in its place. This work of Clovis came to its climax in the period 503–538, and this period therefore becomes the natural one from which to date the 1290 years of Dan. 12:11, which would accordingly end in the period 1793–98 at the same time as the 1260 years of Dan. 7:25.[269]

When a civil power, like the Franks, forerunner of France, i.e., under Clovis reaches out, at a state level, to the belief subscribed to by Roman Catholicism, at a church level, namely "intercession of saints," that is intercession of dead saints on behalf of the living, like as in the case of Clovis ascribing his victory at Voille to Saint Martin of Tours, then you have a perpetuation of the falsehood of Satan in Eden who said "you shall not surely die," confirmed latter in Solomon's writings of Eccl. 9:5, "The dead know not anything," then you have a "taking away of the daily, mediatorial work of the risen Christ who "ever liveth to make intercession for us."

Originally, the "daily" occurred after the wilderness sanctuary was set up, more than five months after the Exodus. It involved the Israelite encamped outside the sanctuary bringing sacrifices into the sanctuary to the altar of burnt offering in the midst of the outer court, slaying them, which commemorated the slaying of the lamb/goat, a symbol of calvaries' sacrifice, then taking some of the blood and applying it to the doorposts of their dwellings, into which they entered, eating roasted lamb or goat, over wood fires, until the midnight judgment, much like the priests, poured out before, or took some of the blood into the tabernacle, "daily" ministering therein until the day of atonement. In a similar. While the Israelite ate roasted lamb/goat within their dwelling which had the blood on the doorposts, the priests ate the sacrifices within the confines of the linen curtain, symbol of Christ's righteous, which enclosed the sanctuary. Originally the priests were to bring wood, according to Lev. 6:12, to the altar of burnt offering to keep it burning continually. Upon that wood fire was laid the various sacrifices. After the Gibionite deception, the Gibionites to be reconciled to the Israelites were made hewers of wood and carriers of water (Josh. 9:21–27). While plant-based wood is perceived to be the fuel reacting with the heat and air that forms a fire, it is also perceived to be the inner spirit of humankind to which they were transformed from mineral-based bronze after the fall (see Isaiah 60:17).

It is perceived that the "daily" experience of creatures in relationship to their Creator was to be a mineral-based bronze creature on the rim universe of Ezekiel's wheel connected by a silver spoke of the divine nature to the God-sphere hub. There they would with mineral-based bronze winged spirits-overlaid with the gold of faith-joined with the Trinity-winged spirits, forming a four-leaf clover. In this state they were to uphold in freedom a created bent of faith in the golden censor mind of God. That censer contained His presence of the first person of the Godhead hypostasis heat Father, second person of the Godhead hypostasis plant-based incense/fuel Son, and third person of the Godhead possessing a dual hypostasis essence of elemental atmosphere, like air, and plant-based oil/fuel., They united in the fellowship of a consuming fire of our one, united, God. To as many mineral-based bronze creatures throughout the rim universe, this experience was replicated in little pinholes on the hub's edge which were omnipresently identical to the axle of the wheel. Thus God would be omnipresent, omniscient, and omnipotent.

If a mineral-based creature on the rim universe unexplainably broke that faith bent in which they were created to uphold the golden censer mind of God, containing His consuming fire manifestation, then the second person of the Godhead, who was the omnipresent look-alike of the mineral-based bronze creature on the rim universe would come to that creature and plead with the rebellious creature to return to the faith in which they were originally created. If that rebellious, inner mineral-based bronze winged spirit originally overlaid with the gold of faith was persistent in their entertainment of rebellion against God, their inner spirit would be changed from mineral-based bronze to plant-based wood, unfit to stand in the hypostasis heat presence of the first person of the Godhead and not be consumed. That experience would be unlike their original mineral-based bronze winged spirit over laid with the gold of faith which would only melt in the presence of the hypostasis heat presence of the first person of the Godhead Father.

Hence the reconciling wilderness sanctuary would be instituted in which plant-based wood spirits, to which mineral-based bronze spirits were transformed after the fall of broken faith in God would be called to support the lamb or other animal sacrifices on the altar of burnt offering in the midst of the outer court. As Israel brought their sacrifices to the sanctuary, they commemorated that they were one year or more from the event of slaying the lamb/goat and applying its blood to their doorposts, symbolizing the future calvary sacrifice which had already occurred, beckoning them to accept and renew that acceptance that the antitypical substitute sacrifice was their only entitlement to heaven, experiencing now, even a little heaven on earth, highlighted in the Lord's prayer, "Thy kingdom come on earth as it is in heaven" (Mt. 6:10).

Living in that kingdom would mean acknowledging that the sins of the world, including their individual sins, were laid on Christ at calvary. Like the Israelites applied the blood to their doorposts as their entitlement to leave Egypt/sin, so the post-calvary believer would accept calvary's empowering grace entitlement to leave sin, entering into their new life in relationship to Christ., even though they still lived in this world of sin symbolized by Egypt's enslavement. While they would "eat the body and blood of Christ," Jn. 6:53 symbolized by the Israelites eating roasted lamb (Ex. 12:8) over the wood (Isaiah 60:17) (symbol of their inner spirits) fire in their dwelling before the midnight judgment, they would be led five months or more to later construct a sanctuary symbol of the future "seed" promised to Eve who would come and dwell among them at the incarnation.

To the altar of burnt offering in the midst of the outer court, the priests would, as part of the "daily" sacrifice put wood Lev. 1:7 (a symbol of the believing Israelite's spirit Isaiah 60:17) to support the slain lamb/ram/kid/goat/bull/pigeon sacrifice so that the fire would never go out.

After slaying the sacrifice for himself, other priests, or the Israelites encamped around the sanctuary, the priest would, symbolizing new, resurrected life, clothed with linen, a symbol of the future righteousness of Christ, rise and minister in the sanctuary or tabernacle therein, carrying out certain duties. While the non-Levite, or Levite not on duty, in the Israelite community, not dressed in the linen symbol of the future lamb of God, Christ Jesus's righteousness could not minister in the sanctuary or tabernacle, their ministry symbolized what the whole nation of Israel was to become, "a kingdom of priests, a holy nation." Not every Israelite could literally put on the linen symbol of the future Christ's righteousness. Yet they could figuratively in their mind put on that linen symbol of the future lamb of God's righteousness, because the whole nation was called to be a kingdom of priests. This literal linen symbol of the future Christ's righteousness, which the priests literally "put on" was to figuragively/spiritually be "put on" by all post-calvary believers. Then they were to figuratively/spiritually rise in newness of life and "put on" the robe of Christ's righteousness after they accepted Calvary's antitypical sacrifice on their behalf. Figuratively post calvary believers were go in and out of a relationship with Christ, the antitypical tabernacle/temple as they ministered to those in the world, symbolized by the laver. After the incarnation of Christ, the whole world was enclosed with the linen curtain of His righteousness like the linen curtain that enclosed the wilderness sanctuary.

The pre-calvary penitent Israelite brought from outside the wilderness sanctuary "type" animal sacrifices to the altar of burnt offering in the midst of the Hebraic outer court. Now in the post-calvary "antitype" humanity enclosed by the linen of Christ in the antitypical heavenly sanctuary would be called to acknowledge that Christ was the "lamb of God that taketh away the sin of the world" They would figuratively/spiritually come to the cross of calvary, placing their hands on Christ, confessing their sins, then "put on" the righteousness of Christ, like the priests literally put on linen, beginning a life known as the "new creation."

"Daily," with inner plant-based wood spirits supporting "the Lamb of God slain from the foundation of the earth," placed on their "inner man" wood spirits, they would be able to rise in newness of life and live as "a priesthood of believers." They would come figuratively/spiritually into a relationship with Christ symbolized by the tabernacle/temple, like the priests went into the tabernacle/temple then went out to minister to the Israelites/people of the world, being vessels through whom God could minister.

It is perceived that the precalvary priests who ministered in the "type" tabernacle/temple were to look at the light coming from the seven-branch candlesticks., and see through a glass darkly, what they were to become. Following the Pentecostal outpouring of the Holy Spirit, fifty days after the crucifixion, resurrection, and ascension of Christ, they were to become light witnesses in the seven-branch candelabra. This transformation from plant-based wood to plant-based wick spirit witnesses would occur as believers experienced being "brands plucked from the burning."

The "daily" experience of all humanity since the fall of Adam and Eve, in their inner soul spirits is to be plant based. There are three types of plant based spirits. The three are wood to support or not to support as fuel the sacrifice on the altar of burnt offering, or to be transformed from wood into a wick in the oil of the candelabra Whatever the "daily" experience of the believer as plantbased spirit, they would all be "lights of the world," in witness. Those who chose not to support with their wood spirits the sacrifice would be fuel for the fires of hell. Those who chose with their wood spirits the sacrifice would be given white robes. Those who chose to be transformed from wood spirits to wick spirits would not only be given white robes but would enjoy the witness in the oil of the Holy Spirit located in the seven-branch candelabra. All three groups would be lights. Two groups, the wood sprits supporting the sacrifice and the wick spirits in the seven-branch candelabra would acknowledge the justice and provisions of God to save them from sin. One group, the wood spirit that did not support the sacrifice would also acknowledge the justice of God in their destruction, for they had rejected the provision of salvation. it would be Satan's "daily" passion to do everything in his power to keep them from submitting their inner wood spirits to supporting calvary's lamb sacrifice and from being transformed into a wick light witness for God. Like the priest had to "daily" arrange firewood on the altar of burnt offering, so the priest had to "daily" make sure there was oil in the lamps to keep the light shining. As long as the Israelite/believer surrendered his inner wood/wick spirit to supporting a belief in the lamb sacrifice and what God would one day do in the candelabra experience, they would be safe from the fiery darts of the devil who bombarded their faith with his temptations to break faith in God.

By the mid-third century, many years after Calvary, Christianity adopted belief in the "intercession of saints." That belief is parallel to the Israelite experience of slaying the lamb/goat in Egypt, then three months latter, having received the law of God and forty days latter in the fifth month after the Exodus, worshiping the golden calf. Like the Israelites turned back to the gods of Egypt, forty days after receiving the spoken law of God, instead of remembering the slain lamb/goat in Egypt which had entitled them to leave Egypt, so Christianity by the third century turned to a belief form called "baptized paganism." Instead of worshiping many gods like the pagans, Christianity worshiped many saints in their "intercession of saints" belief. This belief conflicted with Scripture which says, "The dead know notanything" (Eccl. 9:5) refuting allegiance to Christ "who ever liveth to make intercession for us" (Heb. 7:25). By the sixth century, Roman Catholicism strongly believed this way as evidenced in the Roman Catholic wife of her pagan husband Clovis, who decided after the AD 507 battle at Voille to ascribe that victory to St. Martin of Tours instead of the pagan gods he had formerly served.

With E. emperor Anastasis conferring on Clovis in AD 508, the title of "proconsul" the civil arm of the state grasped hands with the religious belief arm of the church "intercession of the saints," taking away the focus on Christ, "who ever liveth to make intercession for us," distracting them to give glory to the "intercession of saints," thus taking away the "daily" mediatorial work of Christ in the heavenly sanctuary.

and they shall place

#5414 naw-than ; a prim. root; to give, used with a great latitude of application (put, make, etc.) ... Strongs, 1979

#5414 na-tan v. (also used with compound proper names) [Q] to give, put; [Qp] to be given, dedicated; [N] to be given ; [Ho or Qp] to be given. Strongs, 2001 the abomination #8251 shik-koots; from 8262; disgusting, i. e. filthy; espec. idolatrous or (conc.) an idol;-abominable filth (idol,

-ation), detestable (thing).

#8251 siq-qus n. m. detestable thing, vileness, abomination. <u>Strongs</u>, 2001

that maketh desolate.

#8074 shaw-mame; a prim. root; to stun (or intrans. grow numb) i. e. devastate or fig. stupify (both usually in a passive sense:-make amazed, be astonied (be, an) astonish (-ment), (be, bring into, unite, lay, lie, make) desolate (-ion, places), be destitute, destroy (self), (lay, lie, make) waste, wonder.

#8074 sa-mem v. [Q] to be desolate, be appalled; [N] to become desolate, be appalled; [Po] to cause desolation, be appalled; [H] to bring to devastation, caused to be appalled; [Ho] to lie desolate; [Htpol] to destroy oneself, be appalled. Strongs, 2001 The abomination is ascribing to a creature something that is only due to God. Even in Christ's day the religious leaders looked to the temple instead of the One who was the fulfillment of the temple. Thus Christ could say, "Your house is left unto you desolate" because they did not acknowledge Him as the antitypical fulfilment of the temple. When one ascribes a victory to a creature rather than the Creator, that is the foundation of spiritualism. From that ascribal of victory to Saint Martin of Tours, the religio-politico vile person system of Roman Catholicism would be empowered 30 years later to set up its rule for 1,260 days, 538–1798.

At this AD 538 juncture in the prophetict flow of Daniel 11, which was the beginning of the 1260 day prophecy Rev. 12:6, "Time, times, and dividing of times of (Daniel 7:25) it is pereceived that God is going to do something in history which will in the future counteract Roman Catholicism. Already the "daily" mediatorial work of Christ had been historically taken away in AD 508 by the pagan king of France, Clovis, who followed his Catholic wife's belief, adhered to since the mid-third century, of intercession of saints, in ascribal of his AD 507 victory at Voille to St. Martin of Tours. In AD 533 Emperor Justinian declares the Bishop of Rome as head of all churches, settling the controversy between the precedency between the seas of Rome and Constantinople. The armies of the Byzantine emperor Justinian drove out the Arian Ostrogoths from Italy in AD 538, thereby putting into effect Justinian's decree of 533 which recognized the primacy of the bishop of Rome over Christendom. Thus began the 1,260-year period (538–1798) when papal Rome hid the atoning power of Christ from the people of the covenant (Dan. 11:31 comp. 8:11) (p. 14, "An Outline of the book of Daniel, by Dr. Douglass Waterhouse, Professor of Religion, Andrews University Berrien Springs,

96

Michigan. Sunday Law—the Third council of Orleans AD 538).

Consistent with His character and method of doing things, it is perceived that God, like He did with the Israelites when they crossed over Jordan into the promised land, left the Philistines, Canaanites, Sidonians, and Hivites in the land to be his instruments to discipline/prove Israel, (Judges 3:3), so He would arrange kingdoms according to the image of Dan.2 to govern the earth including His chosen people down through the end of time. Within those kingdoms and sometimes outside those kingdoms, people would arise advocating in their inner man belief, systems of belief that would war against those who advocated other inner-man beliefs. While Jews and Judaism gave birth to Christianity, Christianity gave birth to Roman Catholicism which gave birth to Protestants.

At this historical juncture of AD 538 in the 2,300-day prophecy flow of Daniel 8:14, with the mediatorial work of Christ in the heavenly sanctuary taken away by Roman Catholics who had already adopted the midthird century pagan belief of intercession of saints. Clovis, a pagan king of the Franks was married to his Catholic wife and, following her belief, ascribed thereafter in 508 his AD 507 victory to St. Martin of Tours. When the civil state adhered to this religious philosophy, "the intercession of saints" which is the foundation of spiritualism, "the daily" is "taken away." In that historical event, "Papal Rome" historically brought forth the beginning of the 'time, times, and half a time' (Dan. 7:25, Rev. 12;14), 1,260 days. (Rev. 12:6) forty-two months (Rev. 13:5), 538–1798, in which it "hid the atoning power of Christ from the people of the covenant" (Dan. 11:31; compare 8:11).[270]

With the religo-political system of Roman Catholicism beginning in AD 538, it is perceived that God, to counteract the evils that would be accomplished, raised up Mohamedan, whose Islamic religion, different from Christianity, would be the belief force that waged war against Roman Catholicism in the Crusades.

It is perceived that God can view this world as a house. Scripture records: But in a great house (#3416 oy-lee-ah abstr. or concr. lit. or fig.) there are not only vessels of gold and of silver, but also of wood and of earth; and some to honour, and some to dishonor (2 Tim. 2:20).

#3416 oy-lee-ah from 3624. prop.residence (abstr.) but usually (concr.) an abode (lit. or fig.), by impl. a family (espec. domestics):- home, house (-hold) Strongs, 2010 #3416 oi-ki-a n. house, home, family. Strongs, 2001 And said unto them, It is written, My house (#3624 oy-kos lit. or fig) shall be called a house (#3624 oy-kos lit. or fig.) of prayer, but ye have made it a den of thieves (Mt. 21:13).

#3624 oy-kos of uncertain affin.: a dwelling (more or less extensive, lit. or fig.) by impl. a family (more or less related, lit. or fig.):- home, house (-hold), temple. Strongs, 1979 #3624 oi-kos n. house, home, a physical edifice; of royalty; palace; of deity: temple: by extension: family, lineage, people who live in, or originate in a particular house. Strongs, 2001

In Jerusalem, Jesus beheld a symbol of the world that had rejected and despised His grace. [271]

But now, O Lord, thou art our father; we are the clay, and thou our potter; and we all are the work of thy hand (Isa. 64:8).

Then I went down to the potter's house, and behold, he wrought a work on the wheels. And the vessel that he made of clay was marred in the hand of the potter: so he made it again another vessel, as seemed good to the potter to make it. Then the word of the Lord came to me, saying, O house of Israel, cannot I do with you as this potter? saith the Lord. As the clay in the potter's hand, so are ye in mine hand, O house of Israel. At what instant I shall speak concerning a nation, and concerning a kingdom, pluck up, and to pull down and to destroy it; If that nation, against whom I have pronounced, turn from their evil that I thought to do unto them. And at that instant I shall speak concerning a nation, and concerning a kingdom, to build and to plant it. If it do evil in my sight, that it obey not my voice, then I will repent of the good, wherewith I said I would benefit them (Jer. 18:3–10).

God chooses people to be vessels to accomplish his purposes. Some are chosen for honourable (2 Tim. 2:20) purposes, like Saul/Paul (Acts 9:15). Others, like Nebuchadnezzar, king of Babylon, God's servant (Jer. 25:9) was chosen to do the dishonourable work (2 Tim. 2:20) of taking Israel, God's chosen nation, captive into Babylon as a result of their disobedience to Him.

So now, AD 538, the vile/person/belief system, Roman Catholicism, having taken away the "daily" mediatorial work of Christ, our High Priest in the heavenly sanctuary, when the civil, pagan, King Clovis ascribes his AD 507 victory at Voille to St. Martin of Tours, following the religious belief from AD 508 f his Catholic wife, "the daily" was taken away. With the institution of Justinian's AD 533 laws in AD 538, the 1,260 day 538–1798 began.

Now at this time in salvation history, it is perceived that God brought forth in history Mohamed (570–632)[272] resulting in Islam to discipline/

prove the church during the future crusades eleventh–fifteenth century.[273] Like the Canaanites, Sidonians, Philistines, Canaanites, and Hivites or the people of Babylon, Medo-Persia, Greece, and Rome did not have the knowledge and law of God like the Israelites did in the Ten Commandment law and sanctuary service, they nevertheless had the law of God "written on their hearts" (Rom. 2:15.) enabling them to know right and wrong, known a sharia law, a "code of conduct."[274] The warfare of the crusades is seen in Daniel 11:33 "fall by the sword, by flame,…"

Because humanity since the Fall was living, as it were, on the tails side of the love coin, God could use other nations, or belief systems, to test the allegiance of those who subscribed to Christianity. That is why Islam was used to war against Christianity and Roman Catholicism.

Like Nebuchadnezzar, the king of Babylon, a servant of God, would do the works of God in taking Israel captive, yet there would be a prophecy against that nation (Jer. 50). In a similar manner there is a prophecy in Rev. 9:15 regarding "an hour, and a day, and a month, and a year" discussed in Dan. 11:40 "time of the end" which shows Islam surrendering to the four Christian nations, England, Russia, Austria, and Prussia on Aug. 11, 1840.

DANIEL 11:32

32. And such as do wickedly against the covenant shall he corrupt with flatteries: but the people who know their God shall be strong and do exploits.

And such as (NIH)
do wickedly (#7561 raw-shah)

#7561 raw-shah: a prim. root; to be (cause, do, or declare) wrong; by impl. to disturb, violate: condemn, make trouble, vex, be (commit, depart, do) wicked (-ly, ness). Strongs, 1987.

#7561 ra-sa. v. den. [Q] to do evil, act wickedly; be guilty; [H] to declare guilty, condemn, inflict punishment; to do wrong. <u>Strongs</u>, 2001.

   I. Papal Rome

     A. A power that takes away the daily sacrificial services and tramples to sanctuary (Dan. 11:31–39).

       1. The armies of the Byzantine emperor Justinian drove out the A Ostrogoths from Italy in 538 thereby putting into effect Justinian decree of 533 which recognized the primacy of the bishop of Rome Christendom. Thus began the 1,260-year period (538–1798) when p Rome hid the atoning power of Christ from the people of the coven (Dan. 11:31; compare 8:11).[275]

against (NIH)
the covenant (#1285)

#1285 ber-eeth: from 1262 (in the sense of cutting (like [1254]): a compact (because made by passing between two pieces of flesh):-confederacy, [con-] feder [-ate], covenant, league <u>Strongs</u>, 1979.

#1285 berit, n. f. covenant, treaty, compact, agreement, an association between two parties with various responsibilities, benefits and penalties; "to cut a covenant" is "make a covenant," a figure of the act of ceremonially cutting an animal into parts, with an implication of serious consequences for not fulfilling the covenant. <u>Strongs</u>, 2001

100

Historical evidence points to the Roman Catholics as being the people who do wickedly against the covenant. This covenant (Ex. 19:5, Deut. 4:13, 23. 5:2 is the Ten Commandments (Ex. 20:3–17. Deut. 5:7–21) which are to be written on the heart (Deut. 6:6, Jer. 31:31–33) of every human being.

shall he
corrupt (#2610 khaw-nafe)

#2610 khaw-nafe. a prim. root; to soil, espec. in a moral sense:-corrupt, defile, x greatly, pollute, profane. Strongs, 1979.

#2610 ha-nep v. [Q] to be desecrated, be defiled: [H] to corrupt, defile, pollute. Strongs 2001 In 538 at the Council of Orleans, the Roman Catholics made an assault against the fourth Commandment (Ex. 20:8–11, Deut. 5:13–15). This marked the beginning of the "time, times and the dividing of time" (Dan. 7:25), the "time, times and the dividing of time" (Dan. 12:7), and the "time, and times, and a half a time" (Rev. 12:14).

Sunday Law

The third Council of Orleans, AD 538 says in its twenty-ninth cannon: "The opinion is spreading amongst the people, that it is wrong to ride, drive, or cook food, or do anything to the house or person on the Sunday. But since such opinions are more Jewish than Christian that shall lawful in the future, which has been so to the present time. On the other hand agricultural labor ought to be laid aside, in order that the peop may not be prevented from attending church ...

Labor in the country (on Sunday) was not prohibited till the council of Orleans, A. D. 538. It was thus an institution of the church as Dr. Paley has remarked. The earlier Christians met in the morning of that day for prayer and singing of hymns in commemoration of Christ's resurrection, and then went about their usual duties."[276]

And he shall speak great words against the most High, and think to change times and laws: and they shall be given into his hands until a time and times and the dividing of times (Dan. 7:25).

And to the woman were given two wings of a great eagle, that she might fly into the wilderness, into her place, where she is nourished for a time and times, and half a time, from the face of the serpent (Rev. 12:14).

And there was given unto him a mouth speaking great things and blasphemies; and power was given unto him to continue forty and two months (Rev. 13:5).

Early Middle Ages, Dark Ages,
5th-10th century[277]

The AD 538 Sunday legislation at the Council of Orleans marks the moral corruption (see Strongs, #2610 c. 1979) which begins the 1260 day prophecy (538–1798) referred to as "a time and times, and the dividing of times" (Dan. 7:25), "time and times, and a half a time" (Rev. 12:14), and "forty and two months" (Rev. 13:5) empowered by Justinians AD 533 decree which was coupled to the pagan Clovis AD 508, endorsing the faith of his Catholic wife who endorsed the midthird century belief arm of intercession of saints, referred to in Dan. 11:22, in his ascribal of the 507 victory at Voille to St. Martin of Tours. Worshipping dead saints is the foundations of spiritualism.

Not only was the Sabbath changed from Saturday to Sunday worship against the fourth commandment of the covenant, whose parameters were delineated in the Ten Commandments, but also the first and second commandment prohibiting worship of other gods and images.

(They were) disputes over the use of religious images (icons) in the Byzantine Empire in the eighth and ninth centuries. The Iconoclasts (those who rejected images) objected to icon worship for several reasons, including the Old Testament prohibition against images in the Ten Commandments (Ex. 20:4) and the possibility of idolatry. The defenders of icon worship insisted on the symbolic nature of images and on the dignity of created matter.

In the early church, the making and veneration of portraits of Christ and the saints were consistently opposed. The use of icons, nevertheless, steadily gained in popularity, especially in the eastern provinces of the Roman Empire. Toward the end of the sixth century and in the seventh, icons became the object of an officially encouraged cult, often implying a superstitious belief in their animation. Opposition to such practices became particularly strong in Asia Minor. In 726 the Byzantine emperor Leo III took a public stand against icons; in 730 their use was officially prohibited. This opened a persecution of icon worshipers that reached great severity in the reign of Leo's successor, Constantine V (741–775).

In 787, however, the empress Irene convoked the seventh ecumenical council at Nicaea at which Iconoclasm was condemned and the use of images was reestablished. The Iconoclasts regained power in 914 after Leo V's accession, and the use of icons was again forbidden at a council (815). The second Iconoclast period ended with the death of the emperor Theophilus in 842. In 843 his widow finally restored icon veneration, an event still celebrated in the Eastern Orthodox Church as the Feast of Orthodoxy. [278]

The following historical events show the development of image worship in the system of the religio-politico vile person, Roman Catholicism.

The new emperor after Justinian II erected images.[279]

Despite all provocation, Gregory II (pope (715–731) never for a moment swerved in the loyalty to the iconoclastic emperor: but as in duty bound, he opposed his efforts to destroy an article of Catholic faith. By his letters sent in all directions, he warned the people against the teachings of the emperor, and in a council at Rome (727) proclaimed the true doctrine on the question of the worship of images.[280]

In the matter of iconoclasm, he (Pope Gregory III, 731–741) followed the policy of his predecessor. He sent legates and letters to remonstrate with the persecuting emperor, Leo III, and held two synods in Rome (731) in which the image-breaking heresy was condemned. By way of a practical protest against the emperor's action he made it a point of paying special honour to images and relics, giving particular attention to the subject in St. Peters.[281]

Soon after his (Pope Zachary, 741–752) elevation, he notified Constantinople of his election; it is noticeable that his "synodica" (letter) was not addressed to the iconoclastic patriarch Anastasius but to the church of Constantinople. .

In 744. . . still papal envoys do not seem to have come into close relations with the usurper at Constantinople, although the latter reestablished the worship of images. After Constantine V had overthrown his rival, the envoys of the pope presented to him the papal letter in which Zachary, exhorted the emperor to restore the worship of images.[282]

Stephen (pope 757–767) corresponded with the emperor Constantine on the subject of the restoration of the sacred images, and himself restored many of the ancient churches of the city.[283]

In 765. . . Paul's (pope 757–767) opposition to the scheme of emperor Constantine Copronymus had no real political basis. The pope's aim was to defend ecclesiastical orthodoxy regarding the doctrine of the Trinity and the veneration of images against the eastern emperor. Paul repeatedly dispatched legates and letters in regard to the veneration of images to the emperor at Byzantium … In 767 a Frankish synod was held at Gentilly, near Paris, at which the church doctrines concerning the Trinity and veneration of images were maintained … To this church and other churches of Rome, Paul transferred the bones of numerous martyrs from the decayed sanctuaries in the catacombs devastated by the Lombards in 756. He transferred the relics of St. Petronilla from the catacomb of St. Domitilia to a Chapel in St. Peter's erected by the predecessor for this purpose ... Paul also built an oratory of the blessed virgin in St. Peter's.[284]

His (pope Adrian I, 772–795) merits were equally great in the more spiritual concerns of the church. In cooperation with orthodox empress Irene, he laboured to repair the damages wrought by the Iconoclastic storms. In the year 787, he presided through his legates, over the seventh general council, held at Nicaea, in which the Catholic doctrines regarding the use and veneration of images was definitely expounded.[285]

The impetus of the whole movement was Charlemagne, who was impressed by the Byzantium and even had diplomatic relations with the Moslems. However, he allied himself to the papal throne in the accession of Adrian I in As a result of the iconoclastic struggle in the East. . . Charlemagne became concerned for the use of images in religious art and wrote to Adrian recommending pictures for their commemorative and decorative value.[286]

During the time of pope Eugene II (824–827) the following historical incidents regarding image worship are recorded.

Seemingly before Lothair left Rome, there arrived ambassadors from emperor Louis and from the Greeks concerning the image-question. At first the Greek emperor Michael II showed himself tolerant toward image-worshippers, and their champion, Theodore, the studite, wrote to him to exhort him "to unite us (the church of Constantinople) to the head of the churches of God, viz. Rome, and through it with the three patriarchs:" and in accordance with the ancient custom to refer doubtful points to the decision of old Rome. But Michael soon forgot his tolerance, bitterly persecuted image worshippers, and endeavored to secure the cooperation of Louis, The Pious. He also sent envoys to the pope (Eugene II, 824–827) to consult him on certain points connected with the worship of images. Before taking any steps to meet the wishes of Michael, Louis sent to ask the pope's permission for a number of his bishops to assemble and make a selection of passages from the fathers to elucidate the questions the Greeks had put before them. The leave was granted, but the bishops who met at Paris (825) were incompetent for their work. Their collection of extracts from the fathers was a mass of confused and ill-digested lore, and both their conclusions and the letters they wished the pope to forward to the Greeks was based on a complete misunderstanding of the decrees of the Second council of Nicaea (787) ... (their) labour did not accomplish much.[287]

Although Michael II (Byzantine emperor d. 829) was an iconoclast (a member of the party opposed to the use of religious images or icons), in practice he followed a policy of toleration. He even freed prisoners who had been jailed for their devotion to icons and recalled former patriarch Nicephorus, Theodore Studites, and other theologians who had been exiled for that reason.[288]

Owing to dissensions and attacks from without, the kingdom of the Franks was in disorder, and the church within its borders was oppressed. Benedict III (pope 855–858) wrote to the Frankish bishops, attributing much of the misery in the empire to their silence ... and to lessen its internal evils endeavoured to curb the powerful subdeacon Hubert. . . who was the brother-in-law of Lothaire II, king of Lorraine, and defied the laws of God and man till he was slain, in 864. . . He continued the work of repairing the damage done to the churches in Rome by the Saraceans of 846.[289]

with flatteries. (#2514 khal-ak-vaw)

#2514 khal-ak-vaw. fem. from 2505; flattery:- flattery. Strongs, 1979 #2514 ha laq qi n.f. smoothness, flattery:-flatteries [1] Dan. 11:32 Strongs, 2001 Yea, the time cometh, that whosoever killeth you will think that he doeth God service. (John 16:2, last part) It is perceived that his passage of prophecy identifies historically the dawning of the medieval religio-politico vile person system, Roman Catholicism. With Gregory I, the great (590–604 it is said that:

He is one of the most notable figures in Ecclesiastical history. He exercised in many respects a momentous influence on the doctrine, the organization, and the discipline of the Catholic Church. To him we must look for an explanation of the religious situation of the Middle Ages: indeed, if no account were taken of his work, the evolution of the form of medieval Christianity would be almost inexplicable. And further, insofar as the modern Catholic system is a legitimate development of medieval Catholicism, of this too Gregory may not unreasonably be termed the Father. Almost all the leading principles of the later Catholicism are found, at any rate in germ, in Gregory the Great.[290]

The medieval Catholicism began to corrupt Christianity with the flatteries of an augmented third century notion referred to as "intrigues" in Daniel 11:21 (NIV). This was the "modern notion that the pope is always chosen by the Holy Ghost,"[291] which arose from the following historical incident.

> At an assembly to elect the successor of pope Anterus, a dove expectantly lights on Fabianus (pope 236–250) head, not being an inhabitant of Rome, a layman, he was not even considered a candidate. [292]

Of this event it is said:

> In vain therefore, O eminent electors, are all your intrigues; the person on whose head the heavenly dove is pleased to perch, will in spite of them be chosen.[293]

The following incident in the life of pope Gregory the Great illustrates the continuation of this midthird century flattering notion:

> A dove is his special emblem, in allusion to the well-known story recorded by Peter the Deacon (Vita, xxvii), who tells that when the pope was dictating his homilies on Ezechiel a veil was drawn between the secretary and himself. As, however the pope remained silent for long periods at a time, the servant made a hole in the curtain and, looking through, beheld a dove seated upon Gregory's head with its beak between his lips. When the dove withdrew its beak the holy pontiff spoke and the secretary took down his words; but when he became silent the servant again applied his eye to the hole that the dove had replaced its beak between his lips.[294]

Another early medieval Catholic flattery, baptized paganism, seems to be related to a flatter used in the latter-third century. Originally Pope Marcellinus (296–308) offers incense to Jupiter, Hercules, and Saturn in the temple of Vesta. This incident flatters the ambition of the successors of Marcellinus. On the occasion of his fall, it exalts the see of Rome above other sees.[295] The use of a pagan temple for Christian services seems to be the medieval augmentation of this mid-third century flattery.

Boniface (IV 608–615) obtained leave from the emperor Phocas to convert the pantheon into a Christian church, and on 13 May, 609 (?) The temple erected by Agrippa to Jupitaer the Avenger, to Venus and to Mars was consecrated by the pope to the virgin Mary and all martyrs. It was the first instance at Rome of the transformation of a pagan temple into a place of Christian worship. Twenty-eight cartloads of sacred bones were said to have been removed from the catacombs and placed in the porphyry basis beneath the high altar.[296]

This seems to substantiate the claim that Catholicism is "baptized paganism."[297]

II. Waldenses

A. They declared the Church of Rome to be the apostate Babylon of the Apocalypse, and at the peril of their lives they stood up to resist the corruptions.[298]

but the people who know their God shall be strong and do *exploits.* In every age, there were witnesses for God-men who cherished faith in Christ as the only mediator between God and man, who held the Bible as the only rule of life, and who hallowed the true Sabbath.[299]

I. Early Middle Ages, Dark Ages (476–1000)300,5th–10th century[301]

A. Columba (521–597)

1. From Ireland came the pious Columba and his colaborers, w gathering about them the scattered believers on the lonely island of I made this the center of their missionary labors. Among these evange was an observer of the Bible Sabbath, and thus this truth was introdu among the people. A school was established at Iona, from w missionaries went out, not only to Scotland and England, bu Germany, Switzerland, and even Italy.[300]

The following sections are lifted from *http://www.sabbathtruth.com/ sabbath history/sabbath-through the centuries/id/1004/6th-century*

B. Sixth Century

1. Scottish Church

"In this latter instance they seemed to have followed a custom of which we find traces in the early monastic church of Ireland by which they held Saturday to be the Sabbath on which they rested from all their labors" (W. T. Skene, "Adamnan Life of St. Columba" 1874, p. 96).

2. Scotland, Ireland

"We seem to see here an allusion to the custom, observed in the early monastic Church of Ireland, of keeping the day of rest Saturday, or the Sabbath." "History of the Catholic Church in Scotland"(Vol. 1, p. 86 by Catholic historian Bellesheim).

3. Scotland-Columba

"Having continued his labours in Scotland thirty-four years, he clearly and openly foretold his death, and on Saturday, the month of June, said to his disciple Diermit "this day is called the Sabbath, that is, the rest day, and such will it truly be to me; for it will put an end to my labours" ("Butler's Lives of the Saints," Vol. 1, AD 597, art "St. Columba" p. 762). Columba (Regarding Dr. Butler's description of his death): The editor of the best biography of Columba says in a footnote: Our Saturday. The custom to call the Lord's day Sabbath did not commence until a thousand years later. "Adamnan's Life of Columba" (Dublin 1857)[303]

The following sections are lifted from*http://www.sabbathtruth.com/ sabbathhistory/sabbath-through* the centuries/id/1004/7th-century

7th century

Scotland and Ireland

Professor James C. Moffatt, DD, Professor of Church History at Princeton, says: "It seems to have been customary in the Celtic churches of early ties, in Ireland as well as Scotland, to keep Saturday, the Jewish Sabbath, as a day of rest from labour. The obeyed the fourth commandment Literally upon the seventh day of the week" ("The Church in Scotland," p. 140).

Scotland and Ireland

The Celts used a Latin Bible unlike the Vulgate (R.C.) And kept Saturday as a day of rest, with special religious services on Sunday. Flick, "The Rise of Medieval Church," p. 237

4. Rome

Gregory I (AD 590–640) wrote against "Roman citizens (who) forbid any work being done on the Sabbath day." "Nicene and Post- Nicene Fathers," Second series, Vol. XIII, p. 13, epist. 1

Rome (Pope Gregory I, AD 590 to 604)

"Gregory, bishop by the grace of God to his well-beloved sons, the Roman citizens: It has come to me that certain men of perverse spirit have disseminated among you things depraved and opposed to the holy faith, so that they forbid anything to be done on the day of the Sabbath. What shall I call them except preachers of anti-Christ" (Epistles, b. 13:1)

Rome (Pope Gregory I)

Declared that when anti-Christ should come he would keep Saturday as the Sabbath. "Epistles of Gregory I, "b 13, epist. 1 found in "Nicene and Post-Nicene Fathers."

"Moreover, this same Pope Gregory had issued an official pronouncement against a section of the city of Rome itself because the Christian believers there rested and worshiped on the Sabbath." Same reference[304]

The following sections are lifted from *http://www.sabbathtruth.com/ sabbathhistory/sabbath-through the centuries/id/1004/8th-century*

Eighth Century
Council of Friaul, Italy, AD 791 (Canon 13)

"We command all Christians to observe the Lord's day to be held not in honour of the past Sabbath but on account of that holy night of the first day of the week called the Lord's day. When speaking of that Sabbath, which the Jews observe, the last day of the week, and which also our peasants observe ..." (Mansi, 13,851).

Persia and Mesopotamia

The hills of Persia and the valleys of the Tigris and Euphrates reechoed their songs of praise. They reaped their harvests and paid their tithes. They repaired to their churches on the Sabbath day for the worship of God. ("Realencyclopaedia fur Protestatische and Krche," art. "Nestorianer," also Yule, "The book of ser Marco Polo," Vol. 2, p. 409).

India, China, Persia, etc.

"Widespread and enduring was the observance of the seventh-day Sabbath among the believers of the Church of the East and the St. Thomas Christians of India, who never were connected with Rome. It also was maintained among those bodies which broke off from Rome after the Council of Chalcedon namely, the Abyssinians, the Jacobites, the maronites, and the Armenians" (Schaff-Herzog, The New Encyclopedia Of Religious Knowledge," art. "Nestorians"; also Real encyclopaedie fur Protestantische Theologi and Kirche," art. "Nestorian"; also Real encyclopaedie fur Protestantische Theologie und Kirche.," art. "Nestorianer").

Council of Liftinae, Belgium - AD 745 (Attended By Boniface)

"The third allocution of this council warns against the observance of the Sabbath, referring to the decree of the council of Laodicea." Dr. Hefele, Counciliengfesch, 3, 512, sec. 362 China-AD781)

In AD 781, the famous China Monument was inscribed in marble to tell of the growth of Christianity in China at that time. The inscription, consisting of 763 words, was unearthed in 1625 near the city of Changan and now stands in the "Forest of Tablets," Changan. The following extract from the stone shows that the Sabbath was observed:

"On the seventh/day we offer sacrifices, after having purified our hearts, and received absolution for our sins. This religion, so perfect and so excellent, is difficult to name, but enlightens darkness by its brilliant precepts." Christianity in China, M. I'Abbe Huc. Vol. I, ch. 2, pp. 48, 49 The following sections are lifted from *http://www.sabbattruth.com/ sabbathhistory/sabbath-through the centuries/id/1004/9th-century*

9th Century

Bulgaria

"Bulgarian the early season of its evangelization had been taught that no work should be performed on the Sabbath" (Responsa Nicolai Papae I and Con-Consulta Bull 111garorum, Responssum 10, found in Mansi, Sacrorum Concilorum Nova et Amplissima Colectio, Vol 15; p 406; also Hefele, Conciliegeschicte, Vol. 4, sec 478).

(Pope Nicholas I, (Pope Apr. 24, 858–Nov. 13, 867) in answer to letter from Bogaris, ruling prince of Bulgaria.) "Ques. 6-Bathing is allowed on Sunday. Ques. 10-One is to cease from work on Sunday, but not also on the Sabbath." Hefele, 4,346-352, sec. 478.

The Bulgarians had been accustomed to rest on the Sabbath. Pope Nicholas writes against this practice.

Constantinople

(Photuus, Patriarch of Constantinople {in counter-synod that deposed Nicolas}, thus accused Papacy). Against the canons, they induced the Bulgarians to fast on the Sabbath. Photius, vonKard, Hergenrother, 1, 643 Note:

The papacy tried to bring the seventh-day Sabbath into disrepute by insisting that all should fast on that day. In this manner (she sought to turn people toward Sunday, the first day, the day that Rome had adopted.

Athingians

Cardinal Hergenrother says that they stood in intimate relations with Emperor Michael II (821–829) and testifies that they observed the Sabbath.

Kirchengeschichte, 1, 527.

India, Abyssinia "Widespread and enduring was the observance of the seventh-day Sabbath among the believers of the Church of the East and the St. Thomas Christians of India. It was also maintained by the Abyssinians."

Bulgaria

"Pope Nicolas I, in the ninth century, sent the ruling prince of Bulgaria a long document saying in it that one is to cease from work on Sunday, but not on Sabbath. The head of the Greek Church, offended at the interference of the Papacy, declared the Pope ex-communicated." (Truth Triumphant p. 223).[305]

The following sections are lifted from _http://www.sabbathtruth.com/ sabbathhistory/sabbath-throughthe centuries/id/1004/10th-century_

10th Century

Scotland"They worked on Sunday, but kept Saturday in a Sabbatical manner" (A history of Scotland from the Roman Occupation, Vol. I, p. 96. Andrew Lang).

Church of the East-Kurdistan

"The Nestorians eat no pork and keep the Sabbath. They believe in neither auricular confession nor purgatory" (Schaff-Herzog, *The New Encyclopaedia of Religious Knowledge*, art. "Nestorians.)"

Waldenses

"And because they observed no other day of rest but the Sabbath day, they called them Insabathas, as much as to say, as they observed no Sabbath." Luther's "Fore-Runners" (original spelling), PP. 7, 8.

Roman Catholic writers try to evade the apostolic origin of the Waldenses, so as to make it appear that the Roman is the only apostolic church, and that all others are later novelties. And for this reason they try to make out that the Waldenses originated with Peter Waldo of the twelfth century. Dr. Peter Allix says:

On the other hand, he "was called Valdus, or Waldo, because he received his religious notions from the inhabitants of the valleys" (History of the Christian Church, William Jones, Vol II, p. 2).[306]

High Middle Ages (c. 1001–1300)[307]

The following sections are lifted from *http://www.sabbathtruth.com/ sabbath history/sabbath-through the centuries/id/1004/11th-century*

11th Century

Scotland

They held that Saturday was properly the Sabbath on which they abstained from work. "Celtic Scotland," Vol. 2, p. 350.

"They worked on Sunday, but kept Saturday in a sabbatical manner … These things Margaret abolished." "A History of Scotland from the Roman Occupation" (Vol.1, p. 96).

"It was another custom of theirs to neglect the reverence due to the Lord's day, by devoting themselves to every kind of worldly business upon it, just as they did upon other days. That this was contrary to the law, she (Queen Margaret) proved to them as well by reason as by authority. "Let us venerate the Lord's day,' said she, 'because of the resurrection of our Lord, which happened upon that day, and let us no longer do servile works upon it; bearing in mind that upon this day we were redeemed from the slavery of the devil. The blessed Pope Gregory affirms the same'" (Life of Saint Margaret, Turgot, p. 49, British Museum Library).

(Historian Skene commenting upon the work of Queen Margaret) "Her next point was that they did not duly reverence the Lord's day, but in this latter instance they seemed to have followed a custom of which we find traces in the early Church of Ireland, by which they held Saturday to be the Sabbath on which they rested from all their labours." Skene, "Celtic Scotland," Vol.2, p. 349

Scotland And Ireland

"T. Ratcliffe Barnett, in his book on the fervent Catholic queen of Scotland who in 1060 was first to attempt the ruin of Columba's brethren, writes: "In this matter the Scots had perhaps kept up the traditional usage of the ancient Irish Church which observed Saturday instead of Sunday as the day of rest." (Barnett, "Margaret of Scotland: Queen and Saint," p. 97).

Council of Clermont

"During the first crusade, Pope Urban II decreed at the council of Clermont (AD 1095) that the Sabbath be set aside in honour of the Virgin Mary" (History of the Sabbath, p.672).

Constantinople

"Because you observe the Sabbath with the Jews and the Lord's Day with us, you seem to imitate with such observance the sect of Nazarenes" (Migne, "Patrologia Latina," Vol. 145, p.506; also Hergenroether, "Photius," Vol. 3, p.746. [The Nazarenes were a Christian denomination]).

Greek Church

"The observance of Saturday is, as everyone knows, the subject of a bitter dispute between the Greeks and the Latins" (Neale, "A History of the Holy Eastern Church," Vol. 1, p. 731. [Referring to the separation of the Greek Church from the Latin in 1054]).

The following sections are lifted from _http://www.sabbathtruth.com/ sabbath history/sabbath-through the centuries/id/1004/12th-century_

12th Century

Lombardy

"Traces of Sabbath-keepers are found in the times of Gregory I, Gregory VII, and in the twelfth century in Lombardy" (Strong's Cyclopaedia, 1, 660). Spain (Alphonse of Aragon)

"Alphonse, king of Aragon, etc., to all archbishops, bishops and to all others. We command you that heretics, to wit, Waldenses and Insabbathi, should be expelled away from the face of God and from all Catholics and ordered to depart from our kingdom" (Marianse, Praefatio in Lucam

Tudensem, found in "Macima Gibliotheca Veterum Patrum," Vol. 25, p. 190).
Hungary France, England, Italy, Germany

(Referring to the Sabbath-keeping Pasagini) "The spread of heresy at this time is almost incredible. From Gulgaria to the Ebro, from southern France to the Tiber, everywhere we meet them. Whole countries are infested, like Hungary and southern France, they abound in many other counties, in Germany, in Italy, in the Netherlands and even in England they put forth their efforts" (Dr. Hahn, "Gesch. Der Ketzer," 1, 13, 14).
Waldenses

"Among the documents. we have by the same peoples, an explanation of the Ten Commandments dated by Boyer 1120. Observance of the Sabbath by ceasing from worldly labours, is enjoined" (Blair, History of the Waldenses, Vol. 1, p. 220).

"Robinson gives an account of some of the Waldenses of the Alps, who were called Sabbati, Sabbatati, Insabbatati, but more frequently Inzabbatati. "One says they were so named from the Hebrew word Sabbath, because they kept the Saturday for the Lord's day" (General History of the Baptist Denomination, Vol II, p. 413).
Wales

"There is much evidence that the Sabbath prevailed in Wales university until A.D. 1115, when the first Roman bishop was seated at St. David's. The old Welsh Sabbath-keeping churches did not even then altogether bow the knee to Rome, but fled to their hiding places" (Lewis, "Seventh Day Baptists in Europe and America," Vol. 1, p. 29).
France

For twenty years, Peter de Bruys stirred southern France. He especially emphasized a day of worship that was recognized at that time among the Celtic Church of the British Isles, among the Paulicians, and in the great Church of the East namely, the seventh day of the fourth commandment
Pasagini

The papal author, Bonacursus, wrote the following against the "Pasagaini": "Not a few, but many know what are the errors of those who are called Pasaagini ... First, they teach that we should obey the Sabbath. Furthermore, to increase their error, they condemn and reject all the church Fathers, and the whole Roman Church" (D'Achery, Spicilegium I, f211–214; Muratory, antiq.med. aevi.5, f.153,Hahn,3,209).[308]

The following sections are lifted from *http://www.sabbathtruth.com/ sabbath history/sabbath-through the centuries/id/1004/13th-century*

13th Century

"The inquisitors…[declare] that the sign of a Vaudois (Waldenses of France), deemed worthy of death, was that he followed Christ and sought to obey the commandments of God" ("History of the Inquisition of the Middle Ages," H. C. Les, vol. 1).

Waldenses

"They say that the blessed Pope Sylvester was the Antichrist of whom mention is made in the Epistles of St. Paul as having been the son of perdition.[They also say] that keeping of the Sabbath ought to take place" ("Ecclesiastical History of the Ancient Churches of Piedmont" p. 169, by prominent Roman Catholic author writing about Waldenses).

France (Waldenses)

To destroy completely these heretics, Pope Innocent III sent Dominican inquisitors into France, and also crusaders, promising "a plenary remission of all sins, to those who took on them the crusade … against the Albigenses" (Catholic Encyclopaedia, Vol XII, art. "Raymond VI," p. 670).

France

Thousands of God's people were tortured to death by the Inquisitions, buried alive, burned to death, or hacked to pieces by the crusaders. While devastating the city of Biterre the soldiers asked the Catholic leaders how they should know who were heretics; "Slay them all, for the Lord knows who is His" (History of the Inquisition, pp. 96).

France-King Louis IX, 1229

Published the statute "Cupientes" in which he charges himself to clear southern France from heretics as the Sabbath-keepers were called.

Waldenses of France

"The heresy of the Vaudois, or poor people of Lyons, is of great antiquity, for some say that it has been continued down ever since the time of Pope Sylvester, and others, even since that of the apostles" (The Roman Inquisitor, Reinerus Sacho, writing about 1230).

France-Council Toulouse, 1229

Cannons against Sabbath-keepers: "Canon 3.-The lord of the different districts shall have the villas, houses and woods diligently search, and the hiding-places of the heretics destroyed. "Canon 14-Lay members are not allowed to possess the books of either the Old or the New Testaments" (Hefele, 5, 931, 962).

Europe

"The Paulicians, Petrobusinas, Passagianians, Waldenses, Insabbatati were great Sabbath—keeping bodies of Europe down to 1250 A.D."

Pasaginians

Dr. Hahn says that if the Pasaginians referred to the 4th commandment to support the Sabbath, the Roman priests answered, "The Sabbath symbolized the eternal rest of the saints."

Mongolia

"The Mongolian conquest did not injure the Church of the East. (Sabbath-keeping) On the contrary, a number of the Mongolian princes and a larger number of Mongolian queens were members of this church." The following sections are lifted from *http://www.sabbathtruth.com/sabbathhistory/sabbath-throughthecenturies/id/1004/14th-century*

14th Century

Late Middle Ages, period of European history

14th and 15th centuries (c. 1301–1500) Renaissance[309]

14th–17th century[310]

"Also the priests have caused the people to keep Saturdays as Sundays" (Evangelical Lutheran Church in Norway [See below], Vol.1, p.184 Oslo).

Waldenses

"That we are to worship one only God, who is able to help us, and not the Saints departed; that we ought to keep holy the Sabbath day" (Luther's Fore- runners, p. 38).

Insabbati

"For centuries evangelical bodies, especially the Waldenses, were called Insabbati because of Sabbath-keeping" (Gui, Manueld' Inquisiteur).

Bohemia, 1310 (Modern Czechoslovakia)

"In 1310, two hundred years before Luther's theses, the Bohemian brethren constituted one fourth of the population of Bohemia, and that they were in touch with the Waldenses who abounded in Austria, Lombardy,. Bohemia, north Germany, Thuringia, Brandenburg, and Moravia. Erasmus pointed out how strictly Bohemian Waldenses kept the seventh day Sabbath" (Armitage, "A History of the Baptists," p. 313; Cox, "The Literature of the Sabbath Question," vol. 2, pp. 201–202).

Norway

Then, too, in the "Catechism" that was used during the fourteenth century, the Sabbath commandment read thus; "Thou shalt not forget to keep the seventh day." This is quoted from "Documents and Studies Concerning the History of the Lutheran Catechism in the Nordish Churches," p. 89. Christiania 1893, "Also the priests have caused the people to keep Saturdays as Sundays," (Theological Periodicals for the Evangelical Lutheran Church in Norway, Vol. 1, p. 184 Oslo).

England, Holland, Bohemia

"We wrote of the Sabbatarians in Bohemia, Transylvania, England and Holland between 1250 and 1600 A.D. (Truth Triumphant, Wilkinson, p. 309).[311]

The following sections are lifted from *http://www.sabbathtruth.com/ sabbath history/sabbath-through the centuries/id/1004/15th-century*

15th Century

"The accused [Sabbath-keepers] were summoned; they openly acknowledged the new faith, and defended the same. The most eminent of them, the secretary of state, Kuritzn, Ivan Maximow, Kassian, archimandrite of the Fury Monastery of Vovgorod, were comdemned to death, and burned publicly in cages at Moscow; Dec. 17, 1503" ("Geschichte der Juden" [Leipsig, 1873], pp. 117–122).

Bohemia

"Erasmus testifies that even as late as about 1500 these Bohemians not only kept the seventh day scrupulously, but also were called Sabbatarians" (Cox, "The Literature of the Sabbath Question," Vol.2, pp. 201, 202 "Truth Triumphant," p. 264).

Norway

(Church Council held at Bergin, August 22, 1435)

"The first matter concerned a keeping holy of Saturday. It had come to the earth of the archbishop that people in different places of the kingdom had ventured the keeping holy of Saturday. It is strictly forbidden-it is stated-in the Church Law, for anyone to keep or to adopt holy-days, outside of those which the pope, archbishop, or bishops appoint" (The History of the Norwegian Church under Catholicism, R. Keyser, Vol. II, p. 488.Oslo: 1858). Norway, 1435 (Catholic Provincial Council at Bergin)

"We are informed that some people in different districts of the kingdom, have adopted and observed Saturday-keeping. It is severely forbidden-in holy church canon-one and all to observe days excepting those which the holy Pope archbishop, or the bishops command. Saturday—keeping must under no circumstances be permitted hereafter further than the church canon commands. Therefore we counsel all the

116

friends of God throughout all Norway who want to be obedient towards the holy church to let this evil of Saturday- keeping alone; and the rest we forbid under penalty of severe church punishment to keep Saturday holy" (Dip. Norveg., 7, 397 Norway, 1436).

(Church Conference at Oslo) "It is forbidden under the same penalty to keep Saturday holy by refraining from labour" (History of the Norwegian Church, p. 401).

Russia (Council, Moscow, 1490)

"The accused [Sabbath-keepers] were summoned; they openly acknowledged the new faith, and defended the same. The most eminent of them, the secretary of state, Kuritzyn, Ivan Maximow, Kassian, archimandrite of the Fury Monastery of Novgorod, were condemned to death, and burned publicly in cages, at Moscow; Dec. 17, 1503" (H. Sternberfi, "Geschichte der Juden" [Leipsig, 1873], pp.117–122).

France - Waldenses

"Louis XII, King of France (1498–1515), being informed by the enemies of the Waldensees inhabiting a part of the province that several heinous crimes were laid to their account, sent the Master of Requests, and a certain doctor of the Sorbonne, to make inquiry into this matter. On their return they reported that they had visited all the parishes, but could not discover any traces of those crimes with which they were charged. On the contrary, they kept the Sabbath day, observed the ordinance of baptism, according to the primitive church, instructed their children in the articles of the Christian faith, and the commandments of God. The King having heard the report of his commissioners, said with an oath that they were better men than himself or his people"(History of the Christian Church, Vol. II, pp. 71, 72, third edition. London: 1818).

India

Separated from the Western world for a thousand years, they were naturally ignorant of many novelties introduced by the councils and decrees of the Lateran. "We are Christians, and not idolaters," was their expressive reply when required to do homage to the image of the Virgin Mary.[312]

The following sections are lifted from _http://www.sabbathtruth.com/ sabbath history/sabbath-through the centuries/id/1004/16th-century_

16th Century

"The famous Jesuit, Francis Xavier, called for the Inquisition, which was set up in Goa, India in 1560, to check the 'Jewish wickedness' (Sabbath-keeping)" (Adeney, "The Greek and Eastern Churches." p. 527, 528).

England

"In the reign of Elizabeth, it occurred to many conscientious and independent thinkers (as it previously had done to some Protestants in Bohemia) that the fourth commandment required of them the observance, not of the first, but of the specified 'seventh' day of the week" (Chambers' Cyclopaedia, article "Sabbath," Vol. 8, p. 462, 1537).

Sweden

This zeal for Saturday—keeping continued for a long time: even little things which might strengthen the practice of keeping Saturday were punished" (Bishop Anjou, "Syenska Kirkans Historia after Motethiers, Upsala).

Lichenstein Family (estates in Austria, Bohemia, Morovia, Hungary, Lichenstein in the Rhine Valley wasn't their country until the end of the seventh century). "The Sabbatarians teach that the outward Sabbath, i. e, Saturday, still must be observed, They say that Sunday is the Pope's invention" (Refutation of Sabbath, by Wolfgang Capito, published 1599).

Bohemia (the Bohemian Brethren)

Dr. R. Cox says: "I find from a passage in Erasmus that at the early period of the Reformation when he wrote, there were Sabbatarians in Bohemia, who not only kept the seventh day, but were said to be ... scrupulous in resting on it" (Literature of the Sabbath Question, Cox, Vol. II, pp. 201, 202).

Historian's List of Churches (16th Century)

"Sabbatarians, so called because they reject the observance of the Lord's day as not commanded in Scripture, they consider the Sabbath alone to be holy, as God rested on that day and commanded to keep it holy and to rest on it" (A. Ross).[313]

Germany

-Dr. Eck (while refuting the Reformers) "However, the church has transferred the observance from Saturday to Sunday by virtue of her own power, without Scripture" (Dr. Eck's "Enchiridion," 1533, pp. 78, 79).

Princes of Lichtenstein (Europe)

About the year 1520 many of these Sabbath-keepers found shelter on the estate of Lord Leonhardt of Lichtensein held to the observance of the true Sabbath" (J. N. Andrews, History of the Sabbath, p. 649, ed).

India

"The famous Jesuit, Francis Xavier, called for the Inquisition, which was set up in Goa, India, in 1560, to check the 'Jewish wickedness' (Sabbath-keeping)" (Adency, "The Greek and Eastern Churches," p. 527, 528).

Norway -1544

"Some of you, contrary to the warning, keep Saturday. You ought to be severely punished. Whoever shall be found keeping Saturday, must pay a fine of ten marks" (History of King Christian the Third," Niels Krag and S. Stephanius).

Austria

"Sabatarians now exist in Austria." Luther, "Lectures on Genesis" (AD 1523–27).

Abyssinia - AD 1534

(Abyssinian legate at court of Lisbon) "It is not therefore, in imitation of the Jews, but in obedience to Christ and His holy apostles, that we observe the day" (Gedde's Church History of Ethiopia," pp. 87,8).

Martin Luther

"God blessed the Sabbath and sanctified it to Himself. God willed that this command concerning the Sabbath should remain. He willed that on the seventh day the word should be preached" (Commentary on Genesis, Vol. 1, pp. 138–140).

Baptists

"Some have suffered torture because they would not rest when others kept Sunday, for the declared it to be the holiday and law of Antichrist" (Sebastian Frank, AD 1536).

Finland - Dec 6, 1554

King Gustavus Vasa I, of Sweden's letter to the people of Finland: "Some time ago we heard that some people in Finland had fallen into a great error and observed the seventh day, called Saturday" (State Library at Helsingfors, Reichsregister, Vom J., 1554, Teil B.B. leaf 1120, pp. 175–180a).

Switzerland

"The observance of the Sabbath is a part of the moral law. I has been kept holy since the beginning of the world" (Rev. Noted Swiss writer, R Hospinian, 1592).

Holland And Germany

Barbara of Thiers, who was executed in 1529, declared: "God has commanded us to rest on the seventh day." Another martyr, Christina Tollingerin, is mentioned thus: "Concerning holy days and Sundays, she said: "In six days the Lord made the world, on the seventh day he rested. The other holy days have been instituted by popes, cardinals, and archbishops" (Martyrology of the Churches of Christ, commonly called Baptists, during the era of the Reformation, from the Dutch of T. J. Van

Bright, London, 1850, 1, pp. 113–4). [314]

The English reformation was a series of events in 16th century England by which the church of England broke away from the authority of the pope and the Roman Catholic Church.[315]

The following sections are lifted from *Wikipedia (Protestant Reformation)*

The Protestant Reformation, often referred to simply as the Reformation (… other language), was a schism from the Roman Catholic Church initiated by Martin Luther and continued by the early Protestant Reformers in 16th- century Europe.

Although there had been significant earlier attempts to reform the Roman Catholic church before Luther—such as Jan Hus, Peter Waldo, and John Wycliffe—Martin Luther is widely acknowledged to have started the Reformation with his 1517 work, the ninety-five theses. Luther began by criticizing the selling of indulgences, insisting that the pope had no authority over purgatory and that the Catholic doctrine of the merits of the saints had no foundation in the gospel. The Protestant position, however, would come to incorporate doctrinal changes such as sola scriptura and sola fide. The core motivation behind these changes was theological, though many other factors played a part, including the rise of nationalism, the Western Schism which eroded people's faith in the Papacy, the perceived corruption of the Roman Curia, the impact of humanism and the new learning of the Renaissance which questioned much of the traditional thought.[316]

On 15 March 1517, the Fifth Council of the Lateran closed its activities with a number of reform proposals (on the selection of bishops taxation, censorship and preaching) but not on the major problems that confronted the Church in Germany and other parts of Europe. A few months later, on 31 October 1517, Martin Luther issued his 95 theses in Wittenberg.

A general, free council in Germany

Luther's position on ecumenical councils shifted over time, but in 1520, he appealed to the German princes to oppose the papal Church, if necessary with a council in Germany, open and free of the Papacy. After the pope condemned in Esurge Domine fifty-two of Luther's these as heresy, Berman opinion considered a council the best method to reconcile existing differences. German Catholics, diminished in number, hoped for a council to clarify matter. It took a generation for the council to materialize, partly because of papal reluctance, five that a Lutheran demand was the exclusion of the papacy from the Council, and partly because of ongoing political rivalries between France and Germany and the Turkish dangers in the Mediterranean.[317]

The following sections are lifted from *www.markbeast.org/mark-beast-who.html*

MANY FAMOUS PEOPLE KNEW WHO IS THE BEAST

All these brilliant people knew that the Roman Catholic Papal Church is the little horn of Daniel 7 which is synonymous with the first beast of Revelation 13 that enforces 666 and the mark of the beast, and some that died by the hand of the Roman Catholic Church. See also the identity of the antichrist. "John Wycliffe, William Tyndale (translated the Bible – Tyndale Bible), Martin Luther, John Calvin, Thomas Cranmer, in the seventeenth century. Bunyan, the translators of the KING JAMES BIBLE and the men who published the Westminster and Baptist confessions of Faith; Sir Isaac Newton, John Wesley, Whitfield, Jonathan Edwards; and more recently Spurgeon, Bishop J. C. Ryle, and Dr. Martin Lloyd-Jones; these men among countless others, all saw the office of the Papacy as the antichrist" (All Roads Lead to Rome, by Michael de Semlyen. Dorchestor House Publications, p. 205, 1991).[318]

The following sections are lifted from *http://theopedia.com/protestant-reformation*

Protestant Reformation

The Protestant Reformation was a major 16th century European movement aimed initially at reforming the beliefs and practices of the Roman Catholic Church. The Reformation ended the unity imposed by medievaol Christianity and, in the eyes of many historians, signaled the beginning of the modern era A weakening of the old order was already under way in Northern Europe, as evidenced by the emergence of thriving new cities and a determined middle class.

In 1517, in one of the signal events of western history, Martin Luther, a German Augustinian monk, posted 95 theses on a church door in the university town of Wittenberg. That act was common academic practice of the day and served as an invitation to debate. Luther's propositions challenged some portions of Roman Catholic doctrine and a number of specific practices.

"The movement quickly gained adherents in the German states, the Netherlands, Sandinavia, Scotland and portions of France. Support came from sincere religious reformers, while others manipulated the movement to gain control of valuable church property.

"The term Protestant was not initially applied to the reformers, but later was used to describe all groups protesting Roman Catholic orthodoxy."

As the hope of reforming the Roman church faded the "protestants" were forced to separate from Roman Catholicism resulting in Lutheran churches in Germany, Scandinavia and some eastern European countries, the Reformed churches in Switzerland and the Netherlands, Presbyterian churches in Scotland, and the Anglican church in England, and other diverse elements all of which have evolved into the Protestant denominations of today.

Precursors to the Reformation John Wycliffe

John Wycliffe (1330–84) attacked what he saw as corruptions within the church, including the sale of indulgences, pilgrimages, the excessive veneration of saints, and the low moral and intellectual standards of ordained priests.

Wycliffe also repudiated the doctrine of transubstantiation, held that the Bible was the sole standard of Christian doctrine, and argued that the authority of the Pope was not grounded in Scripture. Some of Wycliffe's early followers translated the Bible into English, while later followers, known as Lollards, held that the Bible was the sole authority and that Christians were called upon to interpret the Bible for themselves. The Lollards also argued against clerical celibacy, transubstantiation, mandatory oral confession, pilgrimages, and indulgences.

John Huss

John Huss (1360–1415) was a Bohemian priest, excommunicated in 1410, and burned at the stake for heresy in 1415. His death lead to Hussite Wars in Bohemia. Huss followed Wycliffe's teaching closely, translating Wycliffe's Trialogus into Czechoslovakian, and modeling the first ten chapters of his own De Ecclesia after Wycliffe's writings. He believed in predestination, regarded the Bible as the ultimate religious authority, and argued that Christ, rather than any ecclesiastical official, is the true head of the church.

Prominent figures in the Reformation

Martin Luther

Martin Luther (1483–1546) – In 1517, nails his 95 Theses onto a Wittenberg Church door. These theses were Latin propositions opposing the manner in which indulgences (release from the temporal penalties for sin through the payment of money) were being sold in order to raise money for the building of Saint Peter's in Rome.

Huldreich Zwingli

Huldreich Zwingli (1484–1531) – Swiss theologian and leader of early Reformation Movements in Switzerland. Vigorously denounces the sale of indulgences in 1518.

John Calvin

John Calvin (1509–64) – Calvin was a French theologian and reformer who fled religious persecution in France and settled in Geneva in 1536. He instituted a form of Church government in Geneva which has become known as the Presbyterian church. He insisted on reforms including: the congregational singing of the Psalms as part of church worship, the teaching of a catechism and confession of faith to children, and the enforcement of a strict moral discipline in the community by the pastors and members of the church. Geneva was, under Calvin, essentially a theocracy.

John Knox

John Knoxs (1513–1572) was an ardent disciple of Calvin, Knox established Calvinistic Protestatism as the national religion of Scotland. He left a powerful political legacy within the Calvinist or Reformed branch of Protestantism, a political legacy known as Presbyterianism.

Henry VIII

Henry VIII (1491–1547) – In 1533, Henry was excommunicated by the pope for marrying Anne Boleyn and having the archbishop of Canterbury sanction the divorce from his first wife, Catherine. In 1534, Henry had Parliament pass an act appointing the king and his successors supreme head of the Church of England, thus establishing an independent national Anglican church.

Theological Issues of the Reformation

The theology of the Reformers departed from the Roman Catholic Church primarily on the basis of three great principles:

1. Sole authority of Scripture
2. Justification by faith alone, and
3. Priesthood of the believer.

Solo Scriptura

Sola Scriptura (by Scripture Alone) was one of the watchwords of the Reformation. This doctrine maintains that Scripture, as contained in the Bible, is the only authority for the Christian in matters of faith, life and conduct. The teachings and traditions of the church are to be completely subordinate to the Scriptures. Roman Catholicism, on the other hand, holds Scripture and the Tradition to be of the same inspired

Deposit of Faith.
Sola Fide

Sola Fide (by faith alone) was another watchword of the Reformation. This doctrine maintains that we are justified before God (and thus saved) by faith alone, not by anything we do, not by anything the church does for us, and not by faith plus anything else. It was also recognized by the early Reformers that *Sola Fide* is not rightly understood until it is seen as anchored in the broader principles of Sola Gratia, by grace alone. Hence the Reformers were calling the church back to the basic teaching of Scripture where the apostle Paul states that we are "saved by grace through faith and that not of ourselves, it is the gift of God" (Eph. 2:8).
Priesthood of all believers

The third great principle of the Reformation was the priesthood of all believers. The Scriptures teach that believers are a "holy priesthood" (1 Pet. 2:5). All believers are priests before God through our great high priest Jesus Christ. "There is one God and one mediator between God and man, the man Christ Jesus" (1 Tim. 2:5). As believers, we all have direct access to God through Christ, there is no necessity for an earthly mediator. The Roman Catholic and Eastern Orthodox concept of the priesthood was seen as having no warrant in Scripture, viewed as a perversion and misappliciation of the Old Testament Aaronic or Levitical priesthood which was clearly fulfilled in Christ and done away with by the New Testament.

As a result of these principles, the Reformers rejected the authority of the Pope, the merit of good works, indulgences, the mediation of Mary and the Saints, all but two sacraments instituted by Christ (Baptism and the Lord's Supper) the doctrine of transubstantiaition, the mass as a sacrifice, purgatory, prayers for the dead, confessions to a priest, the use of Latin in the services and all the paraphernalia that expressed these ideas.

Even though the Roman Catholic and Eastern Orthodox churches fall within Orthodoxy as most would define it, much of their teaching beyond the basic tenets is regarded as erroneous by conservative Protestants. In fact, they would say much of it is clearly to be regarded as false teaching which has perverted the gospel of God's grace in Jesus Christ. In general evangelical Protestants see the Reformation as simply a call back to biblical Christianity. [319]

"The governor of Bithynia, in rendering his report to the emperor, revealed the irresistible advances of the gospel. Pliny complains that the people are leaving the old gods and their heathen worship to go in throngs to the worship of Christ. He laments because the sale of heathen sacrifices has fallen off. Paying splendid tribute to the virtues of the Christians, he describes how they meet regularly once a week on 'a stated day' for worship, which was undoubtedly the seventh-day Sabbath.'[320]

It would be difficult to imagine that the apostle Paul, laboring in regions all the way from Babylon to the western borders of Asia Minor, would organize the churches upon any other mode. His congregations also were but repetitions of the original Christian communions in the province of Judea, particularly of the churches in Jerusalem. For some time, groups of Christian believers continued to meet in the synagogues on the Sabbath day with the Jews. This fact indicates that the apostolic church, in it primitive organization, did not cast away everything connected with the synagogue.[321]

"Hoever, Newman failed to add the facts admitted by *The Catholic Encyclopedia*, that 'for a long time Jews must have formed the vast majority of members in the infant Church.' Since the majority of believers in the East wer for a long time Jewish converts, it can easily be seen that the custom was general in the eastern church of observing Saturday as the Sabbath. It could hardly have been otherwise. The noble Christianity of converted Jews was second to none. Centuries of training under the prophets had endowed Jewish believers in Christ with ablity to propagate the truths of the Scriptures. They felt, as the heathen world did not, the force of such terms as God, sin, righteousness, and atonement.

Lucian, though he was a Gentile, is belittled by Cardinal Newman as a Judaizer. Why? Those who sanctified Saturday by abstaining from labor were stigmatized as Judaizers. Why should Lucian observe Saturday as sacred? It was the general custom. The church historian Socrates writes a century after Lucian: 'For although almost all churches throughout the world celebrate the sacred mysteries on the Sabbath of every week, yet the Christians of Alexandria and at Rome, on account of some ancient tradition, have ceased to do this.' Here we note the union between the church at Rome and at Alexandria, and their common antagonism to the seventh-day Sabbath.

Sozomen, a contemporary of Socrates, and also a church historian, writes likewise, 'The people of Constantinople, and almost everywhere, assemble together on the Sabbath, as well as on the first day of the week, which custom is never observed in Rome or at Alexandria.'

At the Synod of Laodicea (c. A.D.365) the Roman Catholics passed a decree that 'Christians must not Judaize by resting on the Sabbath, but must work on that day… But if any shall be found to be Judaizers, let them be anathema from Christ.' Thus this church law not only forbade its folowers to sanctify Saturday, but also stigmatized as Judaizers those who did."

A long list of early church writers could be given to show that for centuries the Christian churches generally observed Saturday for the Sabbath and rested from labor on that day. Many churches also celebrated the day of Christ's resurrection by having a religious meeting on Sunday, but they did not recognize that day as the holy day of the fourth commandment.[323]

The Sabbath. The majority of the churches of Syria and of the East continued to Saturday, the Sabbath of the fourth commandment from the daysof the apostles and throughout the centuries. Hence the attempt to stigmatize them as Judaizer.

The Papacy has always endeavored to substitute the observance of Sunday for the sanctification of Saturday, the Sabbath of the fourth commandment. Pope Gregory I, in 603, declared that when antichrist should come, he would keep Saturday as the Sabbath.[324]

The question of Sabbath and Sunday was particularly contested. As shown previously in quotations from Drs. Flick and Barnett, the traditional practice of the Celtic church was to observe Saturday instead of Sunday as the day of rest. This position is supported by a host of authors. The Roman Catholic historian, Bellesheim, gives the claim of the queen and describes the practice of the Scots as follows:

The queen further protested against the prevailing abuse of Sunday desecration. 'Let us,' she said, 'venerate the Lord's day, in as much as upon it our Savior rose from the dead: let us do not servile work on that day. . . The Scots in this matter had no doubt kept up the traditional practice of the ancient monastic Church of Ireland which observed Saturday rather than Sunday as a day of rest.'

Andrew Lang writing upon the general practice of the Celtic church says: 'They worked on Sunday, but kept Saturday in a sabbatical manner.'.

DANIEL 11:33

33. And they that understand among the people shall instruct many: yet they shall fall by the sword, and by flame, by captivity, and by spoil, many days.

by the sword,

The following sections are lifted from *http://haymakercrusades. wikispaces.com/Weapons+Of+the+Crusades*

One of the best-known weapons of the Middle Ages and of the Crusades is the sword. Most swords were customized to the user, such as the size, shape, and hand guard of the sword. For more rich men jewels and other gemstones were engraved into the pommel and cross guard. The sword was primary used for slashing and cutting technique with a weighted point at the top of the blade to use for thrusting to pierce armor. The tip of the sword became more weighted to pierce the new plate armor.

The dagger was used as a backup weapon for the knight in case his sword got lost or broken in battle. The dagger was also used to kill an enemy who was knocked on the ground. During the 16th century, a new fighting style developed and used the dagger as a parry weapon.

The Lance or Kissem was used in a variety of ways. First, infantry used this weapon against cavalry, the infantry men would get together to create a team of people to block the cavalry. Cavalry also made use of this weapon. The cavalryman would throw his lance from his horse to pierce the plate armor of another cavalryman or an infantryman.

The mace or morning star was a weapon to deliver crushing and blunting blows to the enemy. This weapon was the most common weapon in the Crusades. With the invention of plate armor, the mace and flail became more popular because it was difficult to cut through the armor with a sword and the crushing damage with a mace was a lot easier to hack through armor.

The war hammer is similar to the mace, the war hammer can deliver blunt damage to plate armor and is a lot easier to use than a sword.

The axe, a simple weapon used again for cutting and the spike on top and back of the axe was used for thrusting. The axe was used by infantryman as a primary weapon or as a backup to the sword. The front blade and the spike on the top of the axe would make to piece plate armor.

The crossbow was used as a range weapon of the crusades. The crossbow could be fired from horseback or fired from an infantry man. With the invention of plate armor, the arrowheads of the crossbow bolts became more needlepoint and were short and thick compared to the longbow's arrow.[326]

The following sections are lifted from *http://en.wikipedia.org/wiki/ Peter_the_Hermit*

Alexius—worried at the growing disorder and fearful of his standing before the coming armed Crusader armies—quickly concluded negotiations and shipped them across the Bosporus to the Asiatic shore in the beginning of August, with promises of guards and passage through the Turkish lines. He warned the People's Crusade to await his orders, but in spite of his warnings, the paupers entered Turkish territory. The Turks began skirmishing with the largely unarmed host. Peter (the Hermit) returned in desperation to Constantinople, seeking the Emperor's help.

In Peter's absence, the pilgrims were ambushed and cut to pieces in detail by the Turks, who were more disciplined, at the Battle of Civetot. Despite Peter's pronunciations of divine protection, the vast majority of the pilgrims were slaughtered by the swords and arrows of the Turks, or were enslaved. Left in Constantinople with the small number of surviving followers, during the winter of 1096–1097, with little hope of securing Byzantine support, the People's Crusade awaited the coming of the armed crusaders as their sole source of protection to complete the pilgrimage.[327]

and by flame,

I. John Huss (c. 1369 - 6 July 1415)

    A. When he had been fastened to the stake, and all was ready for the fire be lighted, the martyr was once more exhorted to save himself renouncing his errors. "What errors," said Huss, "shall I renounce? know myself guilty of none. I call God to witness that all that I had written and preached has been with the view of rescuing souls from s and perdition; and, therefore, most joyfully will I confirm with my bloo that truth which I have written and preached" (Wylie, b. 3, ch. 7). Whe the flames kindled about him, he began to sing, "Jesus, Thou Son David, have mercy on me," and so continued till his voice was silenc forever.[328]

The following sections are lifted from *http://wikipedia.org/wiki/JanHus*

1. After John Wycliffe, the theorist of ecclesiastical Reformation, Hu considered the first church reformer, as he lived before Luther, Cal and Zwingli. He was burned at the stake for heresy against doctrine the Roman Catholic Church. [329]

II. Jerome (1379-30 May 1416)

His last words, uttered as the flames rose about him, were a praye "Lord, Almighty Father," he cried, "have pity on me, and pardon me m sins; for Thou knowest that I have always loved Thy trut (Bonnerchose, vol. 2. 168). His voice ceased, but his lips continued move in prayer. When the fire had done its work, the ashes of the marty with the earth upon which they rested, were gathered up, and like tho of Huss, were thrown into the Rhine.[330]

The following sections are lifted from *http://en.wikipedia.org/wiki/ JeromeOfPrague*

B. His condemnation was predetermined in consequence of his gener acceptance of the views of Wyclif and his open admiration for Hu Consequently he did not have a fair hearing. The conditions of his imprisonment were so horrid that he fell seriously ill and so was induc to recant at public sessions of the council held on 11 and 23 September 1415. The words put into his mouth on these occasions made hi renounce both Wyclif and Hus. The physical weakness made him wri in Bohemian letters to the king of Bohemia and to the University Prague, which were declared to be entirely voluntary and to state his ow opinions, in which he announced that had become convinced that H had been rightfully burned for heresy. (Hus, had been burned at the sta while Jerome was imprisoned.) However, the Council of Constance ke him imprisoned as they doubted his sincerity and wanted a mo incriminating confession. On 23 May 1416, and on 26 May he was put trial by the Council. On the second day he withdrew his recantation, an on Juden (Leipzig, 1873), pp. 1117 – 30 May he was condemned and burned. [citation needed] In this w Jerome became the first official martyr for the Hussite reform cause. [331]

The following sections are lifted from *http://ecclesia.org/truth/sabbath-history.html*

Russia: "The accused [Sabbathkeepers] were summoned; they openly acknowledged the new faith, and defended the same. The most eminent of them, the secretary of state, Kuritzyn, Ivan Maximow, Kassian, archimandrite of the Jury Monastery of Novgorod, were condemned to death, and burned publicly in cages, at Moscow, Dec. 27, 1503" (Council, Moscow, 1503). H. Sternberf, Geschichte der Juden (Leipzig, 1873), pp. 1117–122.[332]

by captivity,

I. Martin Luther (10 November 1483–18 February 1546)

A. God had provided a way of escape for His servant in this hour of peril. A vigilant eye had followed Luther's movements, and a true and noble heart had resolved upon his rescue. It was plain that Rome would be satisfied with nothing short of his death; only by concealment could he be preserved from the jaws of the lion. God gave wisdom to Frederick of Saxony to devise a plan for the Reformer's preservation. With the cooperation of true friends the elector's purpose was carried out, and Luther was effectually hidden from friends and foes. Upon his homeward journey he was seized, separated from his attendants, and hurriedly conveyed through the forest to the castle of Wartburg, an isolated mountain fortress. Both his seizure and his concealment were so involved in mystery that even Frederick himself for a long time knew not whither he had been conducted. This ignorance was not without design; so long as the elector knew nothing of Luther's whereabouts, he could reveal nothing. He satisfied himself that the Reformer was safe, and with this knowledge he was content.

Spring, summer, and autumn passed, and winter came, and Luther still remained a prisoner. Alexander (papal legate) and his partisans exulted as the light of the gospel seemed about to be extinguished. But instead of this, the Reformer was filling his lamp from the storehouse of truth; and its light was to shine forth with brighter radiance. (p. 168)

In the solitude and obscurity of his mountain retreat, Luther was removed from earthly supports and shut out from human praise. He was thus saved from the pride and self-confidence that are so often caused by success. (p. 169)

and by spoil,

The following sections are lifted from _http://en.wikipedia.org/wiki/Rhineland_massacres_

On top of the general Catholic suspicion of Jews at the time, when the thousands of French members of the People's Crusade (April–October 1096) arrived at the Rhine, they had run out of provisions. To restock their supplies, they began to plunder Jewish food and property while attempting to force them to convert to Catholicism.

Not all crusaders who had fun out of supplies resorted to murder, some, like Peter the Hermit, used extortion instead. While nor sources claim he preached against the Jews, he carried a letter with him from the Jews of France to the community at Trier. The letter urged them to supply provisions to Peter and his men. The Solomon bar Chronicle records that they were so terrified by Peter's appearance at the gates that they readily agreed to supply his needs. Whatever Peter's own position on the Jews was, men claiming to follow after him felt free to massacre Jews on their own initiative, to pillage their possessions. Sometimes Jews survived by being subjected to involuntary baptism, such as Regensburg, where a crusading mob rounded up the Jewish community, forced them into the Danube, and performed a mass baptism. After the crusaders had left the region these Jews returned to practicing Judaism.[334]

34. Now when they shall fall (#3782) kaw-shal, they shall be holpen with a little help: but many shall
cleave to them by flatteries.
Now when they shall fall, (#3782 kaw-shal)

#3782 kaw-shal: a prim. root. To totter or waver (through weakness of the legs, spec. the ankle); by implic. To falter, stumble, faint or fall; bereave [from marg,] cast down, be decayed (cause to), make to) fall (-down, -ing) feeble be (the) ruin [-ed, of], (be) overthrown, (cause to) stumble x utterly, beware. Strongs, 1979

#3782 ka-sal v. [Q] to stumble, falter, fail; [N] be caused to stumble, be brought down; [H] to cause to stumble, overthrow, bring to ruin; [Ho] to be overthrown: Strongs, 2001

They

I. Huss and Jerome[335]
shall be holpen (#5826 aw-zar)

#5826 aw-zar: a prim. root; to surrender. i.e. protect or aid: help, succor. Strongs, 1979.

#5826 a-zar v. {Q] to help, support: [Qp] to be helped; [N to be helped Strongs 2001.

with a little (#4592 meh- at)

#4592 meh-at from 4591; a little or few (often adv. or compar.):--almost, (some, very) few (e-r, est), lightly, little (while), (very) small (matter, thing), some, soon, x very. Strongs, 1979

#4592 me 'at subst. little (of size), few (of quantity, short (of time) Strongs, 2001

help (#5828 ay-zer)

#5828 ay-zer; from 5826. aid:-help Strongs, 1979

#5828 e-zer n.m. n. m. (also used with compound proper names), help, helper. Strongs, 2001

I. Lord! I am with you always even unto the end of the world. (Mt. 28:20

II. Therefore say, Thus saith the Lord God; Although I have cast them fa among the heathen, and although I have scattered them among the coun yet will I be to them as a little sanctuary in the countries where they come. (Ezek. 11:16)

III. And let them make me a sanctuary that I may dwell among them. (Ex. 20)

IV. And the woman fled into the wilderness, where she hath a place prepare her of God, that they should feed her there a thousand two hundred threescore days. (Rev. 12:6)

V. And when they bring you unto the synagogues, and unto magistrates powers, take ye no thought how or what thing ye shall answer, or what shall say; For the Holy Ghost shall teach you in the same hour what ye o to say. (Lk. 12:11, 12)

But beware of men; for they will deliver you up to the councils, and they will scourge you in their synagogues; And ye shall be brought before governors and kings for my sake, for a testimony against them and the Gentiles. But when they deliver you up, take no thought how or what ye shall speak: for it shall be given you in that same hour what ye shall speak. For it is not ye that speak, but the Spirit of your Father which speaketh in you. (Mt.10:17–20)

Praying always with all prayer and supplication in the Spirit, and watching thereunto with all perseverance and supplication for all saints; And for me, that utterance may be given unto me, that I may open my mouth boldly, to make known the mystery of the gospel. (Eph. 6:18, 20)

VI. Reciting Scripture, prayer, and singing Like Paul and Silas sang in prison Acts 16:25 so John Huss (A.D. 1369-1415) and Jerome sang at the stake,

When the flames rose, they began to sing hymns; and scarce could the vehemency of the fire stop their singing.[336] transcending the temporal death they were about to experience, having the hope in the resurrection like Martha had for her brother Lazarus (Jn. 11:24, 32), they would take comfort in the promises of God, like Psalms 23:1-6.

The Lord is my shepherd I shall not want. He maketh me to lie down in green pastures, He leadeth me beside the still waters, he restoreth my soul, he leadeth me in the path of righteousness for his name sake, yea though I walk through the valley of the shadow of death I will fear no evil for thou art with me thy rod and thy staff they comfort me thou preparest a table before me

in the presence of mine enemies, my cup runneth over, surely
goodness and mercy shall follow me all the days of my life and
I shall dwell in the house of the Lord forever.

And thine ears shall hear a word behind thee saying, This is the way,
walk ye in it, when ye turn to the right hand, and when ye turn to the
left. (Isaiah 30:21)

but many shall cleave (#3867) to them

#3867 law-vaw; a prim. root; prop to twine, i.e. (by impl.) to unite, to
remain; also to borrow (as a form of obligation) or (caus.) to lend: -
abide with, borrow (-er), cleave, join (self), lender (-er) *Strongs,* 1979

#3867 la-wa v. [Q] to accompany; to borrow; [N] to be joined, be
attached, be bound to; [H]to lend *Strongs,* 2001

by flatteries. (#2519 khal-ak-kaw

#2519 khal-ak-lak-kaw; by redup. From 2505; prop. something
very smooth; i.e. a treacherous spot; fig. blandishment;-flattery, slippery.
Strongs, 1979

#2519 halaqlaq n.f.abst. slippery, slick and hard to walk on; by
extension: slippery words. Strongs, 2001

I. Yea, the time cometh, that whosoever killeth you will think that he
doeth God service. (John 16:2, last part) flatteries

II. Not everyone that saith unto me, Lord, Lord, shall enter the
kingdom heaven; but he that doeth the will of my father which is in
heaven. Many say to me on that day, Lord, Lord, have we not
prophesied in thy name in thy name cast out devils? and in thy name
done many wonderful w… And everyone who heareth these sayings
of mine and doeth them shall be likened unto a foolish man, which
built his house upon the sand. the rain descended, and the floods
came, and the winds blew, and beat that house; and it fell and great
was the fall of it. (Mt. 7:21, 22, 26. 27)

III. For when we were in the flesh, the motions of sin, which were by
the law work in our members to bring forth fruit unto death. (Rom. 7:5)

IV. Behold, I will make them of the synagogue of Satan, which say
the Jews, and are not, but do lie. (Rev. 3:9, first part)

V. And for this cause God shall send them strong delusion that they sh
believe a lie; That they might be damned who believe not the truth,
but pleasure in unrighteousness. (2 Thes. 2:11–12)

To the law and to the testimony; if they speak not according to this
word, it is because there is no light in them. (Isa. 8:20)

Where is boasting then? It is excluded. By what law? of works?
Nay: but by the law of faith. (Rom. 3:27)

But I, the cream of a sandwich cream cookie, see another law, the "law of sin and death" (Rom. 8:2) on the tails side of the love coin, or black side of a sandwich cream cookie, in my members, the cream of a sandwich cookie, like as is in Oreo cookies, warring against the law of my mind, the Ten commandment law (Ex. 20) and "law of faith" (Rom. 3:27) on the heads side of the love coin, the white side of a sandwich cream cookie, and bringing me, the cream in a sandwich cookie, into captivity to the law of sin, the tails side of the love coin, or black side of a sandwich cream cookie, which is in my members. (Rom. 7:23)

For the law of the Spirit of life in Christ Jesus hath made me free from the law of sin and death. (Rom. 8:2)

And it come to And it come to pass, when he heareth the words of this curse, that he bless himself in his heart, saying, I shall have peace, though I walk in the in the imaginations of mine heart, to add drunkenness to thirst. The Lord will not spare him, but then the anger of the Lord and his jealousy shall smoke against that man, and all the curses that are written in, this book shall lie upon him, and the Lord shall blot out his name from under heaven. (Dt. 29:19, 20)

Building on sand is building on flatteries

A. When you walk up a sand dune or hill, it is like two steps foreword an one step back, it's slippery.

And every one that heareth these sayings of mine, and doeth them not, shall be likened unto a foolish man, which built his house upon the sand. (Matthew 7:26)

DANIEL 11:35

35. And *some* of them of understanding shall fall, to try them, and to purge, and to make *them* white. even to the time of the end: because it is yet for a time appointed.

And *some* of them of understanding (#7919 sa-kal)

#7919 saw-kal': a prim. root; to be (cause. make or act) circumspect and hence intelligent:-consider, expert, instruct, prosper, (deak) prudent (-ly), (give) skill (=ful), have good success, teach, (have, make to) understand (- ing), wisdom, (be, behave self, consider, make) wise(-ly), guide wittingly. *Strongs*, 1979

#7919 sa-kal v. [Q] to have success; [P] to cross (the hands and arms in an extended motion); [H] to have insight, wisdom, understanding, to prosper, successful; the potent capacity to understand and to exercise skill in life, a state caused by proper training and teaching, enhanced by careful observation, *Strongs Concordance 2001*

I. Waldenses

A. Before the Reformation there were at times but very few copies of the Bible in existence, but God had not suffered His word to be whole destroyed. Its truths were not to be forever hidden. He could as easi open prison doors and unbolt iron gates to set His servants free. In the different countries of Europe men were moved by the spirit of God search for the truth as for hid treasures. Providentially guided to the Ho Scriptures, they studied the sacred pages with intense interest. They we willing to accept the light at any cost to themselves. Though they did n see all things clearly, they were enabled to perceive many long-burie truths. As Heaven- sent messengers they went forth, rendering asund the chains of error and superstition, and calling upon those who had be so long enslaved, to arise and assert their liberty.

Except among the Waldenses, the word of God had for ages been locked up in languages known only to the learned; but the time had come for the Scriptures to be translated and given to the people of different lands in their native tongue. The hours of darkness were wearing away, and in many lands appeared tokens of the coming dawn.[337]

II. John Wycliffe (1324-c. 1386)

    A. Wycliffe received a liberal education, and with him the fear of the Lo was the beginning of wisdom ...

    While Wycliffe was still at college, he entered upon the study of the Scriptures ... (p. 80)

Like after Reformers, Wycliffe did not, at the opening of his work foresee whither it would lead him. He did not set himself deliberately in opposition to Rome. But devotion to truth could not but bring him in conflict with falsehood. The more clearly he discerned the errors of the papacy, the more earnestly he presented the teachings of the Bible. He saw that Rome had forsaken the word of God for human tradition; he fearlessly accused the priesthood of having banished the Scriptures, and demanded that the Bible be restored to the people and that its authority be again established in the church. He was an able and earnest teacher and an eloquent preacher, and his daily life was a demonstration of the truths he preached. (p. 81)

At last the work was completed-the first English translation of the Bible ever made. (p.88)[388]

shall fall, (#3782 kaw-shal')

#3782 kaw-shal'; a prim. root; to totter or waver (through weakness of the legs, espec. the ankle); by impl. to falter, stumble, faint or fall:-bereave [from the marg.]., cast down, be decayed, (cause to) fail, (cause, make to) fall (down, -ing), feeble, be (the) ruin (-ed, of), (be) overthrown, (cause to) stumble, X utterly, be weak. Strongs, 1979

#3782 ka-sal v. [Q] to stumble, falter, fail; [N] be caused to stumble, be brought down; [H] to cause to stumble, overthrow, bring to ruin; [Ho] to be overthrown. Strongs, 2001

to try (#6884 sa-rap) them,

#6884 tsaw-raf'; a prim. root: to fuse (metal), i. e. refine (lit. or fig.):-cast, (re-) fine (-er), founder, goldsmith, melt, pure, purge away, try. Strongs, 1979 #6884 sa-rap v. [Q] to smelt, refine [metals]; (n.) (gold- or silver-) smith. Strongs 2001

The following sections are lifted from *http://sentientchristian.com/catholic-Inquisition:/*

'The Inquisition was a group of institutions within the judicial system of the Roman Catholic Church whose aim is to combat heresy. It started in 12th-century France to combat the spread of religious sectarianism, in particular the Cathars and the Waldensians.

This Medieval Inquisition persisted into the 14th century, and from the 1250s was associated with the Dominican Order. In the early 14th century, two other movementsattracted the attention of the Inquisition, the Knights Templar and the Beguines.

At the end of the Middle Ages, the concept and scope of the Inquisition was significantly expanded in response to the Protestant Reformation and the Catholic counter-Reformation. Its geographic scope was expanded to other European countries, [1] as well as throughout the Spanish and Portugues empires in the Americas, Asia and Africa. [2] Its focus now came to include the persecution of sorcery (an Inquisition), making it one of the agents in the Early Modern witch-hunts.

The institution persisted after the end of the witch-trial period in the 18th century, but was abolished outside of the Papal States after the Napoleonic wars. The institution survives as part of the Roman Curia, but it was renamed to Supreme Sacred Congregation of the Holy Office in 1904.[339]

I. Before three tribunals he (John Wycliffe 1324–1386) was successively summoned for trial, but to no avail.[340]

and to purge, (#1305 baw-rar)

#1305 baw-rar'; a prim. root; to clarify (i. e. brighten), examine, select:- make bright, choice, shosen, cleanse (beclean), clearly, polished, (shew self) pure (-ify), purge (out). Strong, 1979 #1305 ba-rar v. [Q] to be chosen, be choice; to be sharpened, polished, [N] to keep clean, be pure; [P] purify; [H] to cleanse; to sharpen; [Ht] to show oneself pure. Strongs, 2001

I. "A third time he [Wycliffe (1324–1386)] was brought to trial, and now before the highest ecclesiastical tribunal in the kingdom ... But Wycliffe would not retract."[341]

It was the express object and purpose of the trials and inquisitions to which the reformers, like Martin Luther at the diet of Worms were summoned, to recant his teachings and thus purge the land of his perceived heretical teachings, although they were in fact truth, and the traditions of the Catholic Church were false. They were much like the object and purpose of the priests and religious leaders at the time of Christ, who thought that by ridding the land of Israel of Jesus by crucifixion, they would preserve their leadership role in Israel, for they saw many people going away from themselves and their teachings of traditions and going over to become followers of Christ, following his way.

make them white (#3538 law-ban)

#3538 law-ban. a prim. root; to be (or become) white; also as denon. From3843) to make bricks, make brick, to (made, make) white (-r) Strongs, 1979

#3538 la-ban v. [Q] to make bricks [H] to make white, be whitened [Ht] to show self spotless. purified. Strongs, 2001

And one of the elders answered, unto me. What are these which are arrayed in white (#3022 lyoo-kos) robes? and whence came they?

And I said unto him, Sir, thou knowest. And he said to me, These are they which came out of great tribulation, and have washed their robes, and {[made (them) white] 3021 lyoo-kah-ee-no} in the blood of the Lamb. Rev. 7:13, 14.

#3021 lyoo-kah-ee-no from 3022: to whiten:-make white, whiten Strongs, 1979

#3021 leu-kai-no v. to bleach, whiten Strongs, 2001 #3022 lyoo-kos from lu ke ("light): white Strongs, 1979

#3022 leu-kos a. white; bright, gleaming Strongs, 2001

And they made coats of fine linen of woven work for Aaron and his sons. (Ex. 39:27)

Thou hast a few names even in Sardis which have not defiled their garments; and they shall walk with me in white (3022 lyoo-kos): for they are worthy.

He that overcometh, the same shall be clothed in white (3022 lyoo-kos) raiment; and I will not blot out his name out of the book of life, but I will confess his name before my Father, and before his angels. (Rev. 3:4, 5)

Because thou sayest, I am rich, and increased with goods, and have need of nothing; and knowest not that thou art wretched, and miserable, and poor, blind and naked:

I counsel thee to buy of me gold tried in the fire, that thou mayest be rich; and white (3022 lyoo-kos) raiment, that thou mayest be clothed, and *that* the shame of thy nakedness do not appear: and anoint thine eyes with eyesalve, that thou mayest see. (Rev. 3:17, 18)

"But we are all as an unclean thing, and all our righteousness are as filthy rags. . ." (Isa. 64:4).

And to her was granted that she should be arrayed in fine linen, clean and white (#3022 lyoo-kos): for the fine linen is the righteousness (#1345 dik- ah-'-yo-mah) of saints (Rev. 19:8).

As it is written, There is none righteous (#1342 dik'-ah-yos), no, not one (Rom. 3:10).

My little children, these things write I unto you, that ye sin not. And if any man sin, we have an advocate with the Father, Jesus Christ, the righteous (#1342 dik'-ah-yos) (1 Jn. 2:1).

And after that I looked, and behold, the temple of the tabernacle of the testimony in heaven was opened:

And the seven angels came out of the temple having the seven plagues clothed in pure and white (2986 lam-pros) linen, and having breasts girded with golden girdles (Rev. 15:5, 6).

Let us be glad and rejoice and give honour to him: for the marriage of the lamb is come (2064 er-cho-mai lit. fig.), and his wife has made herself ready.

And to her was granted that she should be clothed in fine linen, clean and white (#3022 lyoo-kos): for the fine linen is the righteousness of the saints (Rev. 19:7, 8).

And they made coats of fine linen of woven work for Aaron, and for his sons, And a mitre of fine linen, and goodly bonnets of fine linen, and linen breeches of fine twined linen, And a girdle of fine twined linen, and blue, and purple, and scarlet, of needlework; as the Lord commanded Moses (Ex. 39:27–29).

Let thy garments be always white (#3836); and let thy head lack no ointment (Eccl. 9:8).

While the skin of the animal which God used to cover the nakedness of Adam and Eve is not known to be white, like lamb's wool, there is an allusion that it could be by the text "though your sins be as scarlet, they shall be white as snow, though they be red like crimson, they shall be as wool." With some animal's skin or plant-based woven fabric humanity was called to provide covering for their nakedness. With the sacrifices on the altar, there was created the implication that someone, or something, would have to die to atone for the original sin of Adam and Eve of breaking faith in God, causing them to be transformed and transported from the original heads side of the love coin where they had been created and experienced face to face communication with God, clothed with the garment of light, to the tails side of the love coin where they needed something to cover their nakedness. While skins formed the clothing prepared to cover the original pairs nakedness, God designed that humanity should be clothed with the linen of Christ's righteousness, like the priests wore linen garments. Even after the sanctuary services were inaugurated, almost one year after the exodus, the priests performed their ministries, dressed in linen, in the tabernacle which had three coverings: the inner being goats hair, the middle being rams skins died red, and the outer being badger skins or some interpretations hides of sea cows.

For three months, after slaying the lamb or goat in Egypt, illustrating that their enslavement to the bondage experienced was placed on the head of the sacrifice, entitling them to go free in a journey toward Canaan, a symbol of heaven, there would be some time, several months, actually, a year before they would find out what they were to become after their deliverance from Egypt, i.e., a kingdom of priests and then at the end of that year actually become priests, having received the instructions from God through Moses, after he had spent two forty-day periods (Ex. 24:18–31:18, 34:4–28) a total of eighty days on Mount Sinai, how to become priests. While the whole nation of Israel was to become a "kingdom of priests" (Ex. 19:6), only a subset of that nation, the tribe of Levi, and even a subset of that tribe, Aaron and his sons were to literally minister as priests. As literal high priest Aaron and his sons, as priests, they were to "put upon (#3847 law-bash) on" lit. or fig., the linen garments, a symbol of believers in the future, after the antitypical life, death, resurrection, and ascension of the future incarnate Lamb of God, Christ Jesus, were to "put (ye) on #1746 en-doo-o lit. or fig. the Lord Jesus Christ" (Rom. 13:14) which symbolizes putting on the wedding garment (Mt. 22:11, 12) of Christ's righteousness.

The "making white" until the "time of the end" involves the process or journey in the "inner man" of being antitypically taken figuratively from sin, outside the Garden of Eden/outside a faith relationship to God to an inside faith relationship to God. Like Adam and Eve started their created existence inside the Garden of Eden, where they experienced face to face communion with God, so Jacob started his experience inside Canaan, a symbol of heaven. Because of broken faith, called sin, God provided skins, presumably from a slain animal, accomplished by Himself or Adam and Eve through His instruction regarding how to slay an animal, to cover their nakedness, indicating that something, or a future someone, would die to restore their faith relationship to God, albeit it was unlike the original relationship to God, in which they were

141

covered with a garment of light, for they now knew experientially the consequences of broken faith. While the skin of presumably animals initially covered their nakedness after the fall, God desired them to be clothed with the plant-based linen of righteousness, symbolized by the priestly garments worn as the priests ministered in the wilderness sanctuary.

The process of being "made white" in the priestly linen of future promised seed of Christ's righteousness would take some time as portrayed in the journey from Egypt to the Promised land of Canaan. Yet, Scripture records "Abraham believed God and it was counted unto him as righteousness." This passage indicates that "belief" in God equals justification by faith. It also indicates by the word "counted" sanctification by faith. Hence when the thief on the cross believed in Christ, he was not only justified but counted as being sanctified, i.e., being clothed in the priestly garment symbol of the risen Christ's righteousness.

In anticipation of deliverance from Egypt, and its enslavement, by believing the words of Moses to slay the lamb, apply its blood, and enter into the dwelling with the blood on the doorposts, safe from God's midnight judgment, salvation from sin is typified. With belief in Calvary's sacrifice, application of Christ's shed blood to our hearts, and entrance into a new life, dwelling under the banner of the cross, humanity is free from sin's condemnation and thus safe from God's unfavorable judgment of them, like He was unfavorable to the Egyptians without the blood on their doorposts, even though they are living among sinners on this earth.

During the hours Israel was in Egypt under the blood applied to their doorposts, they ate the roasted lamb or goat of the sacrifice which guaranteed them freedom from the midnight judgment. This is parallel to the believer, who, having accepted Christ as personal Savior, signified by the blood on the doorpost, enters into a new relationship to God, having died to his old way of life, called self, being figuratively resurrected with in Christ, in his inner being, eating the Word, like the Israelites ate roasted lamb or goat, awaiting the midnight judgment or confirmation that he/she has elected Christ as his personal Savior from sin, electing Him, as their empowering entitlement to leave Egypt, a symbol of sin, beginning the literal journey from Egypt and its enslavement to the promised land of Canaan, through empowering grace of the lambs shed blood on their doorposts, or figuratively from sin on this earth to heaven, by the shed blood of Christ figuratively applied to the dwelling place of their being.

Having literally or figuratively applied the blood, it did not appear what they were to become, but they knew that when God would come for them, they would be acceptable to Him through the power of the shed lamb/goats blood in Egypt or calvary's bloodshed on their behalf. As the Israelites waited for the midnight judgment hour, they ate roasted lamb, in a similar manner in which post-calvary believers imbibed Christ's calvary sacrifice on their behalf before the final judgment which would precede the second coming.

The "making white" of Dan. 11:35 occurs when people enter into the experience of Rev. "make themselves white through the blood of the lamb." While "Abraham believed God and it was counted to him for righteousness," he did not literally experience the transformation from coming out of Egypt, just as you are, and putting on the priestly robes one year after the Exodus, although the Israelites heard three months after the Exodus that they were to become 'a nation of priests," only a subset of the Israelites, the Levites literally functioned as priests, although the whole nation was called to be a "kingdom of priests." Even though they were told what they were to become, they did not know what that really meant until after Moses spent eighty days on Mt. Sinai, then instructed them how they were to become priests and what priests were to look like, putting on linen garments, a symbol of putting on Christ's righteousness.

Just as there was instruction, three months after the Exodus, having applied the blood to the doorposts, at Mt. Sinai, the Israelite nation discovered what they were to become, a kingdom of priests. While they were told what they were to become, a kingdom of priests, they did not initially know how they were to become priests. It was almost ninety days after their arrival at Mt. Sinai, when Moses descended the mount for the second time, having been on the mount for two forty day spans, that the Israelite nation would begin to understand what priestly life would involve. It would take another roughly six months until, one year after the Exodus, that priestly ministry in the recently constructed sanctuary would begin.

That ministry would involve the tribe of Levi, a subset of the Israelite nation, putting on linen garments to minister on behalf of the Israelite nation, who had come out of Egypt, a symbol of humanity after accepting Christ's shed blood at Calvary, entering into a new life free from the condemnation of sin, eating the word, like the Israelites ate roasted lamb, then being led out of the enslavement of sin, having

143

accepted the justification judgment at Calvary, to begin their journey of sanctification to heaven, like the Israelites took a journey from Egypt to Canaan.

While humanity would be led on a path free from sin, like Israel was led from Egypt to Succoth, where the Israelites and for that matter humanity could say, something like, "all that we needed to be saved from the enslaving bondage of Egypt or sin was to apply the blood to the doorposts of our dwellings or hearts." They were still not in Canaan or heaven. God had some lessons He wanted to teach Israel or humanity after he saved them from the enslaving bondage of Egypt or sin before they reached Canaan or heaven. It's called "growth in grace." (see Second Peter 3:18) Like God knew that if the Israelites or humanity, having experienced the saving power of the slain lamb in Egypt or calvary's sacrifice on earth, they might turn back to Egypt for a life of sin, if they encountered warring nations or temptations, He needed to lead Israel or humanity on the path to Canaan or heaven, free from the many distracting allurements that might distract their allegiance from serving Him. Hence, Christ's prayer many years later "lead us not into temptation." In being led to the Red Sea, where they would undergo the baptism of the Red Sea, when they experienced the pursuing Egyptians or temptation, they could pray, "Deliver us from evil" and really behold by their baptism through the Red Sea, declared victory over every besetting sin that would pursue them.

When in the wilderness, having run out of water and food, in the wilderness, they could pray, "Give us this day our daily bread." At Mt. Sinai, after they disobeyed the spoken Ten Commandments spoken by God, by making a golden calf, succumbing to the temptation to break faith in God they could pray, "Forgive us our debts."

It took six months between the time Moses came down from Mt Sinai the second time and when work began to construct the sanctuary according the instructions given to Moses, after which the sanctuary was set up. All this time Moses was giving instruction to the Israelites as to how they were to live after the sanctuary was set up, a year after they had slain the lamb in Egypt and acceptingly applied its blood to their doorposts and entered in.

This is much like humanity after accepting calvary's sacrifice and entering into a new life in Christ, eating, or imbibing His ways, although sin is all around them, once they see and understand calvary's justification for them, through the grace shining from the empty tomb,

144

they are led out of a life of sin, even though others in humanity around them are living a life of sin. Thus they begin to live a life "not of this world."

During the first forty days Moses was in Mt. Sinai, God said, "Let them make me a sanctuary that I may dwell among them." This pointed out to the Israelite nation that while they left their homes in Egypt and encamped in tents in the wilderness, that God would leave heaven, in the person of Jesus Christ, and many years later, come to dwell among them as a tabernacle within the sanctuary.

Just as the literal Hebraic priests put on the white linen clothes to minister in the sanctuary on behalf of the Israelite nation, so everyone who accepts the lamb of God sacrifice for their sins is to rise and put on Christ, the linen of His righteousness, and thus "make themselves white in the blood of the lamb." This making of oneself white occurs in the church of Sardis (Rev. 3:4, 5) who walk with me in white, for they are worthy. Because they are overcomers." It is perceived that they are worthy and overcomers because they have "put on Christ" like the priests put on their linen garments.

The putting on of Christ's righteousness by every believing Israelite, or Gentile—like the priests put on their linen garments to serve in the sanctuary—involves a figurative/spiritual resurrection of the inner man yielding a life of service for God. In the Scripture which says of God, "I will be a little sanctuary to them in the lands to which I scatter them" means in part that a person wherever he lives can follow Christ by (1) acknowledging that Christ the lamb of God died for their sin, like the Israelite slew the lamb in preparation to leave Egypt; (2) after that acknowledgement, the Israelite must take the blood and apply it to the doorposts of his home or heart confessing that the Lambs blood is the only entitlement/personal Savior from sin, for him to pass the midnight, at first justification then latter sanctification judgment and come forth free from Egypt/sin in unbroken families, symbolizing he will still possess the capacity to participate in the outside faith fallen nature, although God wants him to partake with an undivided heart of the divine nature. (3) Once the blood of the sacrifice is applied to the doorpost/heart, the Israelite/believer enters into his dwelling/body with a new, inner man, relationship to the destroying angel/God, free from the unfavorable midnight judgment of the destroying angel/God, because he is in right relationship to God, having accepted the merits of the slain lambs blood as entitlement to favor from the midnight destroying angel/God. Whether the Israelite/believer continues a "faith to faith" (Rom. 1:17) journey toward Canaan/heaven, he/she will be credited with the white linen symbol of Christ's righteousness which the priests (put on lit or fig.), one year after the slaying of the lamb in Egypt/Calvary and subsequent grace filled, justifying entitlement to leave Egyptian bondage/sin, to live a life free from Egypt/sin's enslavement, like "Abraham (and the thief on the cross, Lk. 23:42) believed God and it was counted unto him for righteousness" (Ja. 2:23). Thus the disciple Peter said the jailor in response to the question, "What must I do to be saved?" replying, "Believe on the Lord Jesus Christ and thou shalt be saved" (Acts 16:31).

While the Israelites in Egypt, dwelling in their houses, under the blood of the slain lamb/goat, which was applied to their doorposts, illustrating their acceptance of that sacrifice as their only entitlement to leave Egypt in unbroken families, so the post Calvary believer, having claimed Calvary's shed blood merits as their empowering grace-filled merits to leave a life of sin (having their human nature, outside faith, linkage to the sinful nature, "Crucified with Christ") are empowered by pre and post Calvary grace to rise (lit. or fig.) and link their human nature to the divine nature.

For the Israelite in Egypt prior to the midnight judgment, this meant in part, eating roasted lamb over the fire in their dwelling, along with bitter herbs and unleavened bread. Along with eating roasted lamb, the Israelites would eat bitter herbs, remembering their bitter experience of Egyptian bondage and unleavened bread which would be with them prior to entering, and within their blood stained dwelling, and after they left Egypt after the justifying midnight hour judgment. In Egypt they would be able to say, "I am safe from the judgment of God by the blood of the lamb. After the midnight justifying judgment of the destroying angel/God, they would be able to say, "We were saved by the blood of the slain lamb in Egypt applied to our doorposts, whether in their journey from (1) Egypt to Succoth, (2) before the Red Sea facing the pursuing Egyptians symbol of temptations to sin, (3) passing through the baptism of the Red Sea on dry (4) watching the waters engulf the pursuing Egyptians/temptations (5) so they could sing the song of Moses and the Lamb, declaring that the power of lambs bloodshed in Egypt had entitled and empowered them while in Egypt to live safe from the midnight, justifying, judgment hour, eating roasted lamb, bitter herbs, and unleavened bread, before, during, and after the midnight justification judgment hour. (6) After declaring through the song of Moses' deliverance through the Red Sea rooted in the blood of the slain lamb in Egypt, the journey of the Israelites/believers under the blood of the lamb, they ran out of water and bread calling them to provide their needs after they'd claimed the blood by applying it to doorposts and entering in/accepting Christ's sacrifice at Calvary as the entitling grace power to live in dependence upon God for their provisions for water and food. (7) In the provision of manna God gave the test of the Sabbath as a sign of allegiance to and trust in Him. (8) At three months into their journey from Egypt/sin to the promised land of Canaan/heaven, God announced to the Israelite nation what they were to become, "a kingdom of priests, a holy nation, a peculiar people." To show how priests were to live and the boundaries that were to guard their lives, He gave the Ten Commandments. They, as a nation, had already experienced living by the "law of faith" (Rom. 3:27) in obeying Moses' command to slay the lamb/goat, apply its blood to doorposts, and enter in, demonstrating their acceptance of that shed blood as their entitlement to leave Egypt/sin. Now three months later, having discovered what they were to become "a kingdom of priests," God spoke to them from Mt. Sinai, the Ten Commandment boundary law, which was guard the initial "law of faith" (Rom. 3:27) which they had initially entered into by slaying the lamb in Egypt, applying its blood, and entering into that dwelling.

Rooted in the "law of faith" (Rom. 3:27) the Israelite nation had seen how God had led them "from faith unto faith," (Rom. 1:17) as God provided: (1) deliverance from Egypt, (2) deliverance from the pursuing Egyptians, (3) provision of water, and (4) food, (5) the Sabbath (6) a declaration of what they were to become, a kingdom of priests (7) the Ten Commandments which were to function as the boundary of their initial faith, as they grew from "faith to faith," (Rom. 1:17) as they grew in relationship to God on their way to Canaan or heaven, "first the blade, then the ear, then the full corn in the ear" (Mk. 4:28), as they would grow in grace (2 Pet. 3:18).

With Moses' commandment to the Israelite nation to prepare themselves three days (Ex. 19:11) coupled to the first forty days and forty nights (Ex. 24:18) and second forty days and forty nights (Ex. 34:28) making it almost a second three month span, almost six months after the exodus from Egypt. For the next six months, the Israelites gathered the materials and built the sanctuary and tabernacle therein, so that one year after the exodus they reared up (lit. or fig.) the sanctuary and tabernacle therein (Ex. 40:17). It was at that time that Moses and Aaron and his sons washed their hands and their feet (Ex. 40:13) to begin their ministry.

Originally, in the slaying of the lamb/goat, symbolizing the future Calvary event in Egypt, applying its blood, and entering into the dwelling, the Israelites did not know what they were to become, echoing "and it doth not appear what we shall be" (1 Jn. 3:2). But they discovered at Mt. Sinai, they were to be "a kingdom of priest, a holy nation" (Ex. 19:5, 6.). While they now knew what they were to be, it was not until after six months of gathering materials for construction of the tabernacle, sanctuary, and priestly garments that they could see literally what and how a priestly nation was to look like. Yet there was to be a figurative fulfillment of an end-time people, like the church of Sardis "who would walk (in the deportment of their lives) with God in white for they are worthy" (Rev. 3:4) which would be figuratively dressed in white, symbolizing the righteousness of Christ, with the follow-up statement" He that overcometh, the same shall be clothed in white raiment" (Rev. 3:5).

Thus the end-time people who "make themselves white" are the overcomers, even though throughout the ages there will be those who have claimed the merits of Christ, yet may not have yet attained to a priestly walk, although they have risen with Christ spiritually, having been crucified with Him, they will be "those which came out of the great tribulation, and have washed their robes, and made them white in the blood of the Lamb" (Rev. 7:14).

even to the time (#6256 ayth)

#6256 ayth; from "5703; time, espec. (adv. with prep.) now, when, etc.:- +after, [al-] ways, X certain,+continually, +evening, long, (due) season, so [long] as, [even-, evening-, noon-] tide, ([meal-], what) time, when. Strongs, 1979

#6256 et n.f. time (in general); a unit of time (of various lengths), season. Strongs, 2001

The aspect of the meaning for the word "time" which seem to be appropriate for the context of the flow of the prophecy seems to be "a unit of time (of various lengths), or seasons," which would occur before the end of the twenty-three hundred day prophecy of Daniel 8:14. Jesus said a lot of events would occur "but the end is not yet" Matthew 24:6. Some of these events which would occur were the arisal of false prophets, wars and rumors of wars, famines, earthquakes, pestilences, love of many growing cold, hatred, delivering up people to be killed, and iniquity abounding etc. Despite events physically around them, believers would potentially experience being "saved by grace" (Epheians 2:8) and "grow in grace and in the knowledge of our Lord and Savior Jesus Christ" (2 Peter 3:18). In this way they would advance in the "inner man," [see Ephesians 3:16] the "kingdom of God that is within you." Luke 17:21.

of the end (#7093 kates);

#7093 kates; contr. From 7112; an extremity; adv. (with prep. pref.) after:,+after, (utmost) border, end, [in-] finite, X process. See 6975. Strongs, 1979

#7093 qes n. m. end, limit, boundary Strongs, 2001 The following are a list of the historical time prophecies which were to occur before the twenty-three hundred day prophecy of Daniel 8:14, i.e. "cleansing of the sanctuary" would be investigated and understood.

1260 days A.D 538–A.D 1798 Daniel 7:25 time, times, and the dividing of times. Rev. 12:6 a thousand two hundred and threescore days. Rev. 13:5 forty and two months.

1290 days A.D. 508–A.D. 1798 Daniel 12:11

1335 days A.D. 508–A.D. 1843 Daniel 12:12

2300 days 457 B.C. – A.D. 1844 Daniel 8:14

because it is yet for a time appointed.(#4140 mo-ed)

#4150 mo-ade; or mo-ade; or (fem.) (2 Chron. 8:13), mo-aw-daw; from 3259; prop. An appointment, i.e., a fixed time or season; spec. a festival; conventionally a year; by implication, an assembly (as convened for a definite purpose); technically the congregation; by extension, the place of meeting; also a signal (as appointed beforehand):-appointed (sign, time), (place of, solemn) assembly, congregation, (set, solemn) feast, (appointed, due) season, solemn (-ity), synagogue, (set) time (appointed). Strongs, 1979

#4150 mo-ed n.m. (Tent of) Meeting; appointed time, designated time, season Strongs, 2001

The mo-ed, "time appointed', conclusion of the 1260, 1290, 1335, and 2300 days is referred to the historical flow of the prophetic verse of Daniel 11 occurs in Daniel 11:40 in the years 1798, 1843, and 1844.

The aspect of the meaning for the word "time appointed" which seem appropriate to the context of the historical flow of this prophecy is "a fixed time or season." This passage reflects on the reality that while life went on as usual for the Israelite community, daily bringing appropriate

149

sacrifices into the sanctuary and receiving "type' forgiveness of sin. This is analogous to the post calvary life of the believer sending in prayer their petitions to Christ, our high priest in the heavenly sanctuary and receiving antitypical forgiveness of sin. Just as the Israelite believer had their sins brought into the sanctuary on the blood of the sacrifice which was sprinkled on the veil, so the post-calvary vail, of the human heart, (see 2 Corinthians 3:15) "nevertheless when it (the heart) shall turn to the Lord, the vail shall be taken away" 2 Corinthians 3:16. In other words the body of Christ is the vail upon whom humanities sins are sprinkled, enabling them to see the reconciling goodness of God.

While the Israelite, priestly, believer knew their sins on the slain blood of the lamb were sprinkled on the vail of the sanctuary, completing the process of their reception of "type" forgiveness, the day of atonement judgment was coming. So with humanity after Calvary, life would go on as usual, with believers coming by faith to Christ in prayer as he ministered on their behalf as high priest in the heavenly sanctuary. Thus they would receive antitypical forgiveness for sin. Yet believers were to potentially grow in the knowledge that the day of judgment, called the day of atonement was coming. This reality is reflected in Scripture "And as it is appointed unto men once to die, but after this that the judgment" Hebrews 9:27. This judgement would begin at the close of the twenty-three hundred day prophecy recorded in Daniel 8:14, October 22, 1844.

At the "time of the end," which begins in the future in historical flow from the reformers, such as Wycliffe, Huss and Jerome, and Martin Luther along with many others, they will have come to acceptance of, or heading toward an understanding of, the fact that Christ is the lamb of God that "taketh away the sin of the world." He is the one who rebuilds humanity, like the Daniel 9: Command to restore and rebuild. Jerusalem. He is the one ordained/baptized to accomplish reconciliation to God. By His life he showed man how to live. By His death he took away their sins. His death and resurrection was the empowering grace that enabled His post-calvary followers to live figuratively/spiritually dead to sin and alive to God. They would give their lives in service for God, some even dying for Him. But no matter their lot in life, they were assured that upon investigation of their lives, having claimed Christ's sacrifice for their sins, empowering them to live dead to sin, that they would be given white raiment (Rev. 7:14) at the Investigative Judgment which would begin first with the dead October 22, 1844, the conclusion of the 2,300-day prophecy, because they had "washed their robes and made them white in the blood of the lamb" (Rev. 7:14), and someday passing to the living, that they would be given white robes as a symbol of Christ's righteousness. Thus, they would proclaim that they were like Him because of the covering of the white robe of His righteousness.

DANIEL 11:36-39

39. And the king shall do according to his will: and he shall exalt himself, and magnify himself above every god, and shall speak marvelous things against the God of gods, and shall prosper till the indignation be accomplished: for that that is determined shall be done.

Neither shall he regard the God of his fathers, nor the desire of women, nor regard any god: for he shall magnify himself above all.

But in his estate shall he honour the God of forces: and a god whom his fathers knew not shall he honour with gold, and silver, and with precious stones and pleasant things.

Thus shall he do in the most strong holds with a strange god, whom he shall acknowledge and increaser with glory:

Coupling "I am crucified with Christ, nevertheless, I live, yet not I but Christ liveth in me" discussed and articulated in Daniel 11:35 with Romans 7:15, "For that which I (the cream in a sandwich cookie) would do (partake of the white cover in the sandwich cookie symbol of righteousness), I (the cream of a sandwich cookie) allow not: i.e., don't allow the cream self to partake of the white cover symbol of righteousness. For what I (the cream in a sandwich cookie) would, (partake of the white cover symbol of righteousness by faith) that I (the cream in a sandwich cookie) do not: but what I (the cream in a sandwich cookie) hate (partaking since calvary of the black cover of the cookie symbol of the broken faith called unrighteousness) that I (the cream in a sandwich cookie) do."
Romans 7:16

If then I (the cream in a sandwich cookie) do, that which I would not (partake of the white cover on a cookie symbol of righteousness by faith, related to "allow not," in 7:15), I (the cream in the sandwich cookie) consent unto the law (the original law of faith Rom. 3:17 under which the original pair were commanded not to eat of the forbidden tree and the Ten Commandment law given at Mt. Sinai Ex. 20) that it is good. Romans 7:17

Now then it is no longer I (the cream in a sandwich cookie) that do it ("that which I would not" Rom. 7:16), but sin (the ways of the black cover of the cookie symbol of rebellion and unrighteousness) that dwelleth (that links in a bent toward allegiance to) in me (the cream in a sandwich cookie).

Romans 7:18

For I (the cream in a sandwich cookie) know that in me (that is, in my flesh,) [since the fall of Adam and Eve, being born on the tails side of the love coin rather that where they were created on the heads side of the love coin)] dwelleth no good thing. For to will (to do the right thing) is present with me (the cream in a sandwich cookie); but how to perform that which is good I (the cream in the sandwich cookie) find not (meaning there is some power outside the cream in the sandwich cookie which is to enable the cream to do right).

Romans 7:19

For the good that I (the cream in the sandwich cookie) would (desire to partake of the white cover in the sandwich cookie symbol of righteousness) I (the cream in the sandwich cookie) do not: but the evil which I (the cream in the sandwich cookie) would not (desire not to do), that I (the cream in the sandwich cookie) do.

Romans 7:20

Now if I (the cream in the sandwich cookie) do that I (the cream in the sandwich cookie) would not (partake of the black cover of a sandwich cookie), it is no longer I (the cream in the sandwich cookie, by myself) that do it, but sin (coming from the temptations of the black cover of the cookie) that dwelleth (links me to with a bent to perform) in me (the cream in the sandwich cookie.)

Romans 7:21

I find then a law (the law of sin and death Rom. 8:2 coming from the black cover of the sandwich cookie symbolizing rebellion and unrighteousness), that, when I (the cream in the sandwich cookie) would (desire to) do good (linking the cream self of the cookie to the white cover symbol of righteousness), evil (the black cover symbol of rebellion and unrighteousness) is present with me (the cream in a sandwich cookie). Romans 7:22 For I (the cream in a sandwich cookie) delight in the law (offaith Rom. 3:27 and Ten Commandments Ex. 20) after the inward man (the cream in a sandwich cookie):

Romans 7:23

But I (the cream in a sandwich cookie) see another law (the law of sin and death Rom. 8:2. Gen. 2:17 coming from the black cover in a sandwich cookie symbol of rebellion and unrighteousness, on the tails side of the love coin), warring against the law of my mind (law of faith Rom. 3:27, initially on the heads side of the love coin with a boundary marker of the tree of knowledge of good and evil and after sin entered joined by the Ten Commandments Ex. 20 on both the heads and the tails side of the love coin), and bring me into captivity to the law of sin (anything outside the fence of faith and the Ten Commandments) which is in my members.

Romans 7:24

O wretched man that I (the cream in a sandwich cookie) am! Who shall deliver me from the body of death?

Romans 7:25

I thank God, through Jesus Christ, our Lord. (Through the empowering grace streaming from calvary's cross and our risen Lord, humanity can experience an overcoming life, declaring sin is dead in his experience.) So then with the mind I myself (the cream in the cookie sandwich) serve the law (of faith (Rom. 3:27, Ten commandments Ex. 20) of God; but with the flesh (its degeneracy) the law of sin (on the tails side of the love coin.).

Since "faith came" (Gal. 3:25) in the person of Christ Jesus, i.e., "the faith of Jesus," Rev. 14:12, denying in his (cream in a sandwich cookie) the partaking of the black side, symbol of the fallen, sinful nature, to which human nature had been linked after the fall, simultaneously linked to the white side, although both sides were initially white, although one forbidden, in freedom after which the forbidden, once partaken of turned black, symbol of broken faith, called sin, of the cookie, He called all others to do the same, deny in their "cream" self, participation in the ways of the black side of the cookie, calling them to only partake in their "cream" self of the white side symbol of righteousness in the cookie. The power to deny self or the ways of sin in the black side of the cookie came through the type grace of the slain blood of the sacrificial lamb, or the antitypical slain lamb of Calvary, Christ Jesus. The power of this grace was accessed through faith, which is given in measure to every human being (Rom. 12:3).

And the king (#4428 meh-lek)

used of God (Ps. 48:2); "the: king of kings" is the supreme sovereign and is not used of God in the OT: Strongs, 2001

154

This term can be used for leaders in "a covenant agreement." Thus when Dan. 11:25 refers to "the king of the South," it is referring to Arius (320) of Alexandria who advocated Arianism. It could also refer to Athanasius, a prince for advocating orthodoxy. In Daniel 11:29 the king of the south in Egypt is Dioscorus, (430) of Alexandria who was an advocate of monophysitism. Now at this juncture in the High Middle Ages Thomas Aquinas (1225–1274) combines theological principals of faith to the philosophical principles of reason.

While Scripture councils us to "come let us reason together" and "give a reason for our hope," when we lose faith we are on dangerous ground. For Scripture says "the just shall live by faith" Then Petrarch (1300s) emphasizes only reason choosing to go a different direction than faith. Hence this sets the historical footing or root for the 1793 Age of Reason.

There would be a battle called the great controversy between the kingdom of God symbolized in the white side symbol of righteousness, accessed through God's Rom. 12:13 gift of faith in sacrificial type or calvaries antitype inside the cookie empowering faith in God and the black side of the cookie symbol of sin empowering faithlessness and rebellion against God. Those who would cast their allegiance toward belief in God's reconciling provision would find that they, like Christ, would echo "I have come to do thy will) (Heb. 10:7, 9), or "For I came down from heaven, not to do mine own will, but the will of him that sent me" (Jn. 6:38).

The following section is lifted from https://en.wikipedia.org/wiki/Avignon Papacy "Temporal role of the Roman Church The papacy in the Late Middle ages played a major temporal role in addition to its spiritual role. The conflict between the pope and the Holy roman Emperor was fundamentally a dispute over which of them was the leader of Christendom in secular matters. In the early 14th century, the papacy was well past the prime of its secular rule – its importance had peaked in the 12th and 13th centuries. The success of the early Crusdes added greatly to the prestige of the Popes as secular leaders of Christendom, with monarchs like those of England, France and even the Holy Roman Emperor merely acting as marshals for the popes and leading "their" armies. One exception was Frederick II, Holy Roman Emperor, who was twice excommunicated by the Pope during a Crusade. Frederick II ignored this and was moderately successful in the Holy Land.

This state of affairs culminiated in the unbridled declaration of papal supremacy, Unam sanctam, in November 1302. In the papal bull, Pope

155

Boniface VIII decreed that "it is necessary to salvation that every human creature be subject to the Roman pontiff." This was directed primarily to King Phillip IV of France who responded by saying, "Your venerable conceitedness may know that we are nobody's vassal in temporal matters." In 1303 AD, Pope Bonifice VIII followed up with a bull that would excommunicate the king of France and put the interdict over France, and depose the entire clergy of France. Before this was finalized, Italian allies of the King of France broke into the papal residence and beat Pope Boniface VIII. He died shortly thereafter. Nicholas Boccasini was elected as his successor and took the name Pope Benedict XI. He absolved King Phillip IV and his subjects of their actions against Pope Boniface VIII; though the culprits who assaulted Boniface were excommunicated and ordered to appear before a pontifical tribunal. However, Benedict XI died within eight months of being elected to the papacy. After eleven months, Bertrand de Got, a French man and a personal friend of King Phillip IV, was elected as pope and took the name Pope Clenent V.[342]

With Thomas Aquinas there was a combining of the theological principals of faith to the philosophical principles of reason. His parents thought he was rejecting faith, thus doing "according to his will." While we are to be able to give a "reason for our faith, we are not to give reasons for things outside faith. Thus was the seed thought which caused Petrach to give up faith"

The following sections are lifted from *http://en.wikipedia.org./wiki/High_Middle_Ages High Middle Ages* 11th, 12th, and 13th centuries (c. 1001–1300)[343]

The following sections are lifted from http: *www.biography.com/people/st- thomas-aquinas-9187231#aw*

Movement from theological faith to philosophical reason

Thomas Aquinas (c. 1225–1274)

Combine Theological principals of faith to philosophical principles of reason. [344]

The following sections are lifted from

http://www.stapriority.org/dominicans

http://www.biography.com/people/st-thomas-aquinas-918723#aw

Circa 1239, St. Thomas Aquinas began attending the University of Naples. In 1243, he secretly joined an order of Dominican monks founded 1216, strong academic grounding in faith,345 receiving the habit in 1244. When his family found out, they felt so betrayed that he had turned his back on the principles to which they subscribed that they decided to kidnap him. Thomas's family held him captive for an entire year, imprisoned in the fortress of San Giovanni at Rocca Secca. During this time, they attempted to deprogram Thomas of his new beliefs. Thomas held fast to the ideas he had learned at university, however and went back to the Dominican order following his release in 1245.[346]

In the Garden of Eden, both the tree of life and tree of knowledge of good and evil were at the center. Like a top with a north and south pole, the tree of life and tree of knowledge of good and evil were at their respective pole centers with Adam and Eve on the center disk which spun in freedom and allegiance to God, always looking, or bent in faith, to partake of the tree of life and shun the tree of knowledge of good and evil. The reason they were to eat of the tree of life was to experience a life of faith and allegiance to God. God had given them the reason why they were not to eat of the tree of knowledge of good and evil, for in the day they did, they would die. Thus their hope for life with God entailed an obedience springing from a life of faith. Dwelling on the disk of freedom in the Garden of Eden, they were to dwell in faith experiencing fellowship with God and enjoying the fruit of the tree of life.

When they lost faith and focused on the reason of Satan, apart from faith, at the south pole of the top, his having already toppled, Adam and Eve's spinning top of faithful allegiance to God toppled. It was only after Christ would come in the likeness of sinful man, spinning in allegiance to God, then dying to provide the reconciliation to God, that the toppled tops of fallen human nature would have hope to once again spin in allegiance to God.

As humanity would spin in allegiance to God after the death of Christ, their reason for spinning in allegiance to God lay in the death, resurrection, and ascension of Christ.

When Thomas Aquinas' parents pled with him to return to faith and give up his life of reason apart from faith, a 'doing according to his will,' they were acknowledging that God calls us to live a life of faith. The Old Testament records "The just shall live by faith." And the New Testament in Peters command to the jailor, "Believe in the Lord Jesus Christ" echoes the same reality.

The following sections are lifted from
http://en.wikipedia.org/wiki/middleages.
http://en.wikipedia.org/wiki/late middle ages

And the king shall do according to his will:

"Let no man deceive you by any means: for that day shall not come, except there come a falling away first, and that man of sin be revealed, the son of perdition; Who opposeth and exalteth himself above all that is called God, or that is worshiped; so that he as God, sitteth in the temple of God, shewing himelf that he is God." 2 Thessalonians 2:3, 4.

The following sections are lifted from Paschal II-pope-Brittanica. com https://www.brittanica.com/biography/Paschal-II

"Although Paschal [pope 1099-1118] fostered the First Crusade and followed Gregory's great policies of church reform, his pontificate was dominated by the Investiture Controversy-the long conflict between popes and secular rulers over control of ecclesiastical appointments."[348]

The following sections are lifted from Innocent III-pope-Britannica. com https://www.britannica.com/biography/Innocent-III-pope

"Innocent III [pope 1198-1216]. . . the most significant pope of the Middle Ages. Elected pope on January 8, 1198, Innocent III reformed the Roman Curia, reestablished and expanded the pope's authority over the Papal States, worked tirelessly to launch Crusades to recover the Holy Land, combated heresy in Italy and southern France, shaped a powerful and original doctrine of papal power within the church and in secular affairs, and in 12 15 presided over the fourth Latern Council, which reformed manyclerical and lay practices within the church."[349]

The following sections are lifted from Pope Boniface VIII- Wikipedia https://en.wikipedia.org/Pope_Boniface VIII

"Pope Boniface VIII. . . was Pope from 24 December 1294 to his death in 1303.

He organized the first Roman Catholic "jubilee" year to take place in Rome and declared that both spiritual and temporal power were under the pope's jurisdiction, and that kings were subordinate to the power of the Roman pontiff."[350]

The following sections are lifted from Avignon Papacy-Wikipedia *https://en.widipedia.org/wiki/Avignon_Papacy*

"Temporal role of the Roman church"

The papacy in the Late Middle Ages played a major role in addition to its spiritual role. The conflict between the pope and the was fundamentally a dispute over which of them was the leader of Christendom in secular matters. In the early 14th century, the papacy was was well past the prime of its secular rule- its importance had peaked in the 12th and

13th centuries. The success of the early Crusades added greatly to the prestige of the Popes as secular leaders of Christendom, with monarchs like those of England, France, and even the Holy Roman Emperor merely acting as marshals for the popes and leading "their" armies. One exception was Frederick II, [1194-1213] Holy Roman Emperor, who was twice excommunicated by the Pope during a Crusade. Frederick II ignored this and was moderately successful in the Holy Land.

Beginning with Clement V, elected 1305, all popes during the Avignon papacy were French. However, this makes French influence seem greater than it was. Southern France at that time had a culture quite independent from Northern France, where most of the advisers to the King of France were based. The Kingdom of Arles was still independent at the time, formally a part of the Holy Roman Empire. The literature produced by the troubadours in the Languedoc is unique and strongly distinct from the Royal circles in the north. Even in terms of religion, the South produced its own variety of Christianity, Catharism, which was ultimately declared heretical. The movement was fueled in no small part by the strong scense of independence in the South years before. By the time of the Avignon Papacy, the power of the French King in this region was uncontested, although still legally binding. A stronger impact was made by the move of the Roman Curia from Rome to Poitiers in France in 1305, and then to Avignon in 1309. Following the impasse during the previous conclave, and to escape from the infighting of the powerful Roman families that had produced earlier Popes, such as the Coloma and Orsini families, the Roman Church looked for a safer place and found it in Avignon, which was surrounded by the lands of the papal fief of Comtat Venaissin. Formally it was part of Arles, but in reality it was under the influence of the French king. During its time in Avignon, the papacy adopted many features of the Royal court: the life-style of its cardinals was more reminiscent of princes than clerics; more and more French cardinals, often relatives of the ruling pope, took key positions; and the proximity of French troops was a constant reminder of where secular power lay, with the memory of Pope Boniface VIII still fresh."[351]

The following is a summary of events which had recently occurred under pope Boniface VIII extending into the Avignon papacy With the pope declaring that all "human creatures be subject to the Roman pontiff," it is perceived that God historically put in place the Avignon papacy, "a residual of the spirit of" (compare Malachi 2:15) the Roman pontiffs in Rome. Under the leadership of the Avignon pope John XXII (1316-

1334), the pope was styled "Lord God the pope." This is reminiscent of God's leaving in Canaan, after Israel's settlement in the land, according to Judges 3, several nations which he could use as instruments to punish Israel if they disobeyed him. In the pope's decree that "it is necessary to salvation that every human creature be subject to the Roman pontiff," followed by King Phillip IV response "your venerable conceitedness may know that we are nobody's vassal in temporal matter," there is a fortaste of the endtime (after the 2300 days of Daniel 8:14) peoples response to the three angels message of Revelation 14. Those who refuse to receive "the mark of the beast" (Revelation 19:20), which is worshiping on Sunday instead of Saturday, will be "priests and kings." (see Revelation 1:6). They will not endorse on pain of death that beast system of belief which "thinks to change times and laws"(Daniel 7:25). Thus people reading history could choose if they wanted to regard God as the God of gods or some creature like the pope or some other created thing.

Even at the close of the 12th and 13th century of the Middle Ages, the testimony of the French king Philip IV [A.D. 1285-1313] echoed the charge of Joshua "Choose ye this day whom ye will serve and as for me and my house we will serve the Lord" (Joshua 24:15). This would be amplified years later by the Elijah message "how long halt ye between two opinions, if the Lord be God follow him, if baal then follow him" (1 Kings 18:21). Finally, the sounding of the three angels messages of Revelation 14:6-12 would be the climax ending in the judgment of the world. That judgement would begin October 22, 1844 and be known as the cleansing of the sancturary recorded in Daniel 8:14, concluding its 2300 day/year prophecy. Although the church in the Middle Ages occurs during "the era of the Church of Thyatira, the pagan church 538-1514 A. D."[352], the looking forward to judgment is implied by king Phlip IV's response, reflecting his power of choice, "your venerable conceitedness may know that we are nobody's, vassal in temporal matters." A lesson from this event indicates that each person must stand in allegiance for or against God. They would either follow God, in allegiance to their creator or a creature which God had made, in this case the pope. They all knew, or would be made aware of, that having lived their lives, they would face death "and after that the judgment" (see Hebrews 9:27) was an ever present reality. That judgement would be decided upon by whom an individual chose to place their allegiance, the creator or the creature, respectively giving loyalty to the one they chose. While that judgement would not begin until the close of the 2300 day prophecy of Daniel 8:14, nevertheless each individual during their lifespan would decide on whom they would place their allegiance, the creator or creature. The ages of the two other prophetic churches would occur before that judgment. Those ages are Sardis, the church of the reformation beginning possibly 1517 or possibly 1798. The age of Philadelphia possibly began in 1833 with the falling of the stars. [The last church phase, Laodicea (Revelation 3:14-33)] began in 1844.[353] It can and should be noted in all these ages, the kingdom of God could, and was to, begin within the inner man relationship to God, even though they had not experienced the expected second coming of Christ. This is because "the kingdom of God is within you" John 17:21. An understanding of the sanctuary message, or the figure,(see Hebrews 9:24, same word as parable) would aid the reader or listener of history as to how long before the actual second coming of Christ would occur. Christ had said referring to the parables, that in them the ways of the kingdom would be understood.

"Let no man deceive you by any means: for that day shall not come, except there come a falling away first, and that man of sin be revealed, the son of perdition; Who opposeth and exalteth himself above all that is called God, or that is worshiped; so that he as God, sitteth in the temple of God, shewing himelf that he is God." 2 Thessalonians 2:3, 4.

I. Humanism

The followorty and two m http://New Advent.org-humanism

A. Humanism is the name given to the intellectual, literary, and scientific movement of the fourteenth to the sixteenth centuries, a movement which aimed at basing every branch of learning on the literature an culture of classical antiquity.

"It is customary to begin the history of Humanism with Dante (1265–1321) and Petrarch (1304–74). Of the two Dante, by reason of his poetic sublimity, was undoubtedly the greater, but as regards Humanism Dante was merely its precursor while Petrarch initiated the movement and led it to success. Dante certainly shows traces of the coming change; in his great epic classical and Christian materials are found side by side, while poetic renown, an aim so characteristic of the pagan writers yet so foreign to the Christian ideal, is what he seeks. In matters of real importance, however, he takes the Scholastics as guides. Petrarch, on the other hand, is the first Humanist; he is interested only in the ancients and in poetry. He unearths long-lost manuscripts of the classics, and collects ancient medals and coins. If Dante ignored the monuments of Rome and regarded its ancient statues as idolatrous images, Petrarch views the Eternal City with the enthusiasm of a Humanist, not with that of a pious Christian."[354]

The following section is lifted from

https://www.coursehero.com/filep6k6b47/Humanism-in-action-o-Petrach-a-

Humanism in action

Petrach, a poet. Referred to as the first humanist. Facinated by ancient Greece and Rome. Tried to seek out the works of ancient writers that had been overlooked for many centuries. He found a book by Cicero, a Roman orator (106-43 BCE.) Petrach wanted to study his teachings and letters to see what he had to teach. Cicero and Ancient Rome were able to provice a guide in education. Could teach boys to speak well. Petrach rescued Cicero to say "here is a guy who can teach us how to behave in the Republic of Florence."[355]

The following section was lifted from

http://www.newadvent.org/cathen/07538b.htm

Pius II (1458–64) was a Humanist himself and had won fame as poet, orator, interpreter of antiquity, jurist, and statesman; after his election, however, he did not fulfill all the expectations of his earlier associates, although he showed himself in various ways a patron of literature and art. Sixtus IV (1471–84) reestablished the Vatican Library, neglected by his predecessors, and appointed Platina librarian, "Here reigns an incredible freedom of thought" was Filelfo's description of the Roman Academy of Pomponio Leto (d. 1498) an institute which was the boldest champion of antiquity in the capital of Christendom. Under Leo X (1513–21) Humanism and art enjoyed a second golden age. . .The pillaging of Rome 1527 gave the deathblow to Italian Humanism, the serious political and ecclesiastical complications that ensued prevented its recovery.[356]

The following section is lifted from

http://en.wikipedia.org/wiki/petrarch

(Petrarch) He spent much of his early life at Avignon. . . where his family moved to follow Pope Clement V (1305–1314) who moved there in 1309 to begin the Avignon papacy …

Petrarch was a prolific letter writer … After the death of their parents, Petrarch and his brother Gherardo went back to Avignon in 1326, where he worked in numerous clerical offices. This work gave him much time to devote to his writing … On April 6, 1327 after Petrarch gave up his vocation as a priest, the sight of a woman called "Laura," in the church of Sainte-clair, Avignon awoke in him a lasting passion.[358]

The following section is lifted from Avignon Papacy-Wikipedia *https:// en.wikipedia.org/wiki/Avignon Papacy*

"The period has been called the "Babylonian captivity" of the popes. When and where this term originated is uncertain although it may have sprung from Petrarch, who in a letter to a friend (1340-1353) written during his stay at Avignon, described Avignon of that time as the: Babylon of the west," referring to the worldly practices of the church hierarchy. The nickname is polemical, in referring to the claim by critics that the prosperity of the church at that time was accompanied by a profound compromise of the papacy's spiritual integrity, especially in the alleged subordination of the powers of the Church to the ambitions of the French kings. As noted, the "captivity" of the popes at Avignon lasted about the same amount of time as the exile of the Jews in Babylon, making the analogy convient andrhetorically potent. The Avignon papacy has been and is often today depicted as being totally dependent on the French kings, and sometimes as even being treacherous to its spiritual role and its heritage in Rome."

The following sections are lifted from *http:// http://people.opposingview. humanism-Cath.doc*

The Renaissance ... was a cultural movement that spanned the 14th–17th, beginning in Italy, in the late middle ages and later spreading to the rest of Europe. Through the availability of paper and the invention of metal, moveable type, sped the ideas of the later 15th century, the changes were not uniformly experienced across Europe.

As a cultural movement, it encompassed innovative flowering of Latin and vernacular literatures, beginning with the 14th-century resurgence of learning based on classical sources, which contemporaries credited to Petrarch, the development of linear perspective and other techniques of rendering a more natural reality in painting, and gradual but widespread educational reform.[359]

"Let no man deceive you by any means: for that day shall not come, except there come a falling away first, and that man of sin be revealed, the son of perdition; Who opposeth and exalteth himself above all that is called God, or that is worshiped; so that he as God, sitteth in the temple of God, shewing himelf that he is God." 2 Thessalonians 2:3, 4.

The following sections are lifted from *http://people.opposingview. humanism-*

II. Secular humanism

A. Secular humanism is, as its name suggests, non-theistic. The philosophy that humans are the basic measure of everything has its roots in the rational thinking of classical Greece and the teachings of Socrates and Plato. Secular humanism values science, reason, evidence and human intelligence and accepts the theory of evolution. In this philosophy there is no place for religion or a God, divine intervention, heaven, theocracies or dictatorships. Humanists value ethical behavior that benefits society, individual freedom, satisfaction and happiness, and responsibility for the protection of nature and human rights. They argue for the separation of church and state and abjure any form of discrimination, censorship, restrictions on individual freedom of choice and the death penalty. Devout Christians, including Roman Catholics, believe that secular humanists embrace a false belief system.

Papal Call for Humanism the head of the Roman Catholic Church, Pope Benedict XVI wants to end proliferating warfare by declaring a new age of humanism. The pope defined humanism as a moral and spiritual mission to create a culture of peace, to rededicate resources from military spending to solving global economic and environmental problems and to agree to universal disarmament. Personal development and the elimination of violence are essential components of this "new humanism," as are compassion and a widespread commitment to solidarity in working for peace and social justice. In a sense, Pope Benedict is doing what Erasmus attempted to do in the 16th century—finding a way to reconcile secular ethics and scientific knowledge with a belief in God and fidelity to the core teaching of the Church.[360]

The following sections are lifted from *http://wikpedia.org.humanism*

Secular humanism is a comprehensive life stance or world view which embraces human reason, metaphysical naturalism, altruistic morality and distributive justice, and consciously rejects supernatural claims, theistic faith and religiosity, pseudoscience and superstition. It is sometimes referred to a Humanism (with a capital H and no qualifying adjective).

The International Humanist and Ethical Union (IHEU) is the world union of 117 Humanist, rationalist, irreligious, atheistic, Bright, secular, Ethical Culture, and free thought organization in 38 countries. The "Happy Human" is the official symbol for secular humanism.

According to the IHEU's bylaw Humanism is a democratic and ethical life stance, which affirms that human beings have the right and responsibility to give meaning and shape to their own lives. It stands for building of a more humane society through an ethic based on human and other natural values in the spirit of reason and free inquiring through human capabilities. It is not theistic and it does not accept supernatural views of reality. Humanism is a democratic and ethical life stance, which affirms that human beings have the right and responsibility to give meaning and shape to their own lives. It stands for the building of a more humane society through an ethic based on human and other natural values in the spirit of reason and free inquiry through human capabilities. It is not theistic, and it does not accept supernatural views of reality.

Religious humanism is an integration of humanist ethical philosophy with religious rituals and beliefs that center on human needs, interests, and abilities. Though practitioners of religious humanism did not officiall organize under the name of "humanism" until the late 19th and early 20th centuries, non-theistic religions paired with human-centered ethical philosophy have a long history. The Cult of Reason (French. . .) Was a religion based on deism devised during the French Revolution by Jacques Hebert ... and their supporters. In 1793 during the French Revolution, the cathedral Notre Dame de Paris was turned into a "Temple of Reason and for a time Lady Liberty replaced the virgin Mary on several altars.[361]

The following sections are lifted from _http:// www.brittanica.com// avignonpapacy_

III. Avignon papacy, Roman Catholic

A. papacy during the period 1309–77, when popes took up residence Avignon instead of at Rome, primarily because the current politic conditions.

Distressed by factionalism in Rome and pressed to come to France by Philip IV, Pope Clement V moved the papal capital to Avignon, which at that time belonged to vassals of the pope. In 1348 it became direct papal property. Although the Avignon papacy was overwhelming French in complexion (all seven of the popes during the period were French, as were 111 of the 134 cardinals created, it was not so responsive to French pressure as contemporaries assumed or as latter critics insisted.[362]

Avignon Popes

The following sections are lifted from *http://en.wikipedia.org/wiki/avignonpapacy*

1. Pope Clement V 1305–1314 (Curia moved to Avignon March 9, 1309.
2. Pope John XXII 1316–1334 a. For the title "Lord God, the Pope" see a gloss on the *Extravagante* Pope John XXII. title 14, ch. 4, *Declaramus*. In an Antwerp editio the *Extravaganetes,* dated 1584, the words *"Dominum Deus nost Papam"* ("Our Lord God the Pope") occur in column 140. In s editions published since 1612 the word *"Deum"* ("God") has b omitted.[363]
3. Pope Benedict XII 1334–1342
4. Pope Clement VI 1342–1352
5. Pope Innocent VI 1352–1362
6. Pope Urban V 1362–1370 (in Rome 1367–1370, returned to Avignon
7. Pope Gregory XI 1370–1378 (left Avignon to return to Rome September 1376.)[364]

History of the Catholic Church in France-Wikipedia *https://en.wikipedia.org/wiki/History_Of_The_Catholic_Church_In_France* *http:// www.catholicity.com/encyclopedia/g/gregoryxi.pope.html*

a. Pope Gregory XI

1' On 13 January, 1377, he left Corneto, landed at Ostia on the following day, and sailed up the Tiber to the monastery of San Paolo, from where he solemnly made his entrance into Rome on 17 January. But his return to Rome did not put an end to the hostilities. The notorious massacre of Cesena, which was ordered by Cardinal Robert of Geneva (afterwards antipope Clement VII), embittered the Italians still more against the pope. The continuous riots in Rome induced Gregory XI to remove to Anagui towards the end of May, 1377. He gradually quelled the commotion and returned to Rome on 7 Nov., 1377, where he died while a congress of peace was in process at Sarzano. Gregory XI was the last pope of French nationality. He was learned and pious, though not free from nepotism. In 1374 he approved the Order of the Spanish Hermits of St. Jerome, and on 22 May, 1377, He issued five bulls in which the errors of Wyclif (1320–1384) 365 was condemned. He was so disgusted with the conditions at Rome that only death prevented him from returning to Avignon. The Great Schism began after his death,[366]

B. It is one of the leading doctrines of Romanism that the pope is the visible head of the universal church of Christ, invested with supreme authority over bishops and pastors in all parts of the world. More than this, the pope has been given the very titles of Deity, He has been styled "Lord God the Pope" (see Appendix), and has been declared infallible. He demands the homage of all men. The same claim urged by Satan in the wilderness of temptation is still urged by him through the Church.

Rome, and vast numbers are ready to yield him homage.[367]

1. For the title "Lord God, the Pope" see a gloss on the *Extravagante* Pope John XXII. title 14, ch. 4, *Declaramus*. In an Antwerp edition of the *Extravaganetes,* dated 1584, the words *"Dominum Deus nostrum Papam"* ("Our Lord God the Pope" occur in column 140. In sever editions published since 1612, the word *"Deum"* ("God") has been omitted.[368]

and he shall exalt himself

The following section is lifted from History of the Catholic Church in France-Wikipedia *https://en.wikipedia.org/wiki/ History_Of_The_ Catholic_Church_In_France*

"Divine right" and the weakening of the influence of the papacy in Christendom. Under Philip IV, the Fair (1285-1314), the royal house of France became very powerful. By means of alliances he extended his prestige as far as the Orient. His brother Charles of valois married Catherine de Courtney, an heiress of the Latin Empire of Constantinople. The kings of England and Minorca were his vassals, the King of Scotland his ally, the Kings of Naples and Hunungary connections by marriage. He aimed at sort of supremacy over the body politic of Europe. Pierr dubois, his jurisconsult, dreamed that the pope would hand over all his domains to Philip and receive in exchange an annual income, while Philip would thus have the spiritual head of Christendom under his influence. Philip IV labored to increase the royal prerogative and thereby the national unity of France. By sending magistrates in feudal territories, by defining certain cases (cas royaux) as reserved to the king's competency, he dealt a heavy blow to the feudalism of the Middle Ages. But on the other hand, under his rule many anti-Christian maxims began to creep into law and politics. Roman law was slowly re-introduced into social organization, and gradually the idea of a united Christendom disappeared from the national policy. Philip, the Fair, pretending to rule by Divine right, gave it to be understood that he rendered an account of his kingship to no one under heaven. He denied the pope's right to represent, as the papacy had always done in the past, the claims of morality and justice where kings were concerned. Hence arose in 1294-1303, his struggle with Pope Boniface VIII, but in that struggle he was cunning enough to secure the support of the States-General, which represented public opinion in France. In later times, after centuries of monarchial government, this same public opion rose against the abus of power committed by its kings in the name of their pretended divine right, and thus made an implicit amende honorable to what the Church had taught concerning the origin, the limits, and the responsibility of all power, which had been forgotten or misinterpreted by the lawyers of Philip IV when they set up their pagan State as the absolute source of power. The election of Pope Clemt V (1305) under Philip's influence, the removal of the papacy to Avignon, the nomination of seven French popes in succession, weakened the influence of the papacy in Christendom, though it has recently come to light that the Avignon popes did not always allow the independence of the Holy See to waver or disappear in the game of politics. Philip IV and his successors may have had the illusion that they were taking the place of German empors in European affairs. The papacy was imprisoned on their territory; the German empire was passing through a crisis, was, in fact, decaying and the kings of France might well immaginthemselves temporal vicars of God, side by side with, or even in opposition to, the spiritual vicar who lived at Avignon."[369]

The following sections are lifted from *https://en.wikipedia.org/wiki/Henry_VII_Holy_Roman_Emperor*

I. Pope Clement V (1305–1314), established at Avignon, confirmed Henry's [VII 1312–24 Aug. 1313] election and initially agreed to personally crown him emperor at Candlemas, 1312, the title having been vacant since the death of Frederick II (1220–1250).[370]

37. Neither shall he regard the God of his fathers, nor the desire of women, nor regard any god: for he shall magnify himself above all.

The following sections are lifted from *https://en.wikipedia.org/wiki/Donatism*

Donatists argued that Christian clergy must be faultless for their ministration to be effective, and for the prayers and sacraments they conduct to be valid. Donatism had it roots in the long-established Christian community of the Roman Africa province (now Algeria and Tunisia), in the persecutions of Christians under Diocletian. Named after the Berber Christian bishop Donatus Magnus, they flourished in the fourth and fifth centuries.

The govenor of Roman North Africa was lenient towards the Christian minority under his rule throughout the persecutions, and satisfied when Christians handed over their Scriptures as a token repudiation of their faith. Christians who acceded to this were, when the persecutions came to an end, branded *traditores*, "thoses who handed (holy things) over", by their critics, mostly from the poorer classes.

Like the Novatianist movement of the previous century, the donatists were rigorists, holding that the church must be a church of "saints", not "sinners", and that sacraments, such as baptism, administered by *traditores* were invalid. In 311, a new bishop of Carthage, Caecilian, was consecrated by someone who had allegedly been a *traditor*, Felix of Aptungi; his opponents consecrated a Mojorinus, a short-lived rival, who ws succeeded by Donatus, after whom the schism was named.

In 313, a commission appointed by Pope Miltiades condemned the Donatists, but they continued to exist, viewing themselves, and not other Christians, as the "true Church", the only one with "valid sacraments". Because of their association with the Circumcellions, they brought upon themselves repression by the imperial authorities, but they drew upon African sentiment, while their opponents had the support of Rome. They were still in force at the time of Saint Augustine of Hippo at the end of the fourth century, and disappeared only after the Muslim conquest of the 7th-8th century.[371] It is perceived that Donatism, with its belief that the clergy must be faultless, eventually produced the notion of the infallibility of the pope. Coupled to the notion that the church was for saints, not sinners yielded a foothold for humanism to grow and develop.

I. Secular humanism

The following sections are lifted from *https:// people.opposingview. humanism-cath.doc*

A. Secular humanism values science, reason, evidence, and hum intelligence and accepts the theory of evolution.

In this philosophy there is no place for religion or a God, divine intervention, heaven, theocracies or dictatorships.[377]

. . Devote Christians, including Roman Catholics, believe that secular humanists embrace a false belief system.[372]

II. John Wycliffe promotes Scripture hence the God of his fathers and the desire of women (the church) who desires a relationship with Christ Jesus.

The following sections are lifted from *http://www.fampeople.com/cat-john- wycliffe_10*

Wycliffe became deeply disillusioned both with Scholastic theology his day and also with the state of the church, at least as represented by the clergy. In the final phase of his life in the years before his death 1384, he increasingly argued for Scriptures as the authoritative centre for Christianity, that the claims of the papacy were unhistorical, the monasticism was irredeemably corrupt, and that the moral unworthine of priests invalidated their office and sacraments.[373]

for he shall magnify himself above all.

"Ruler of princes and kings

As Innocent III had before him, Innocent IV saw himself as the Vicar of Christ, whose power was above earthly kings."[374] "Innocent IV. . . one of the great pontiffs of the Middle Ages (reigned 1243-54).)[375] The following sections are lifted from *http://wikipedia.org/wiki/popeBonifaceVII*

Boniface (VIII 1294–1303) had no choice but to contest Philip's demands, informing Philip that:God has set popes over kings and kingdoms.[376]

nor regard any god

Secular humanism

The following sections are lifted from *https:// people.opposingview. humanism-cath.doc*

A. Secular humanism values science, reason, evidence, and hum intelligence and accepts the theory of evolution. In this philosophy the is no place for religion or a God, divine intervention, heaven, theocraci or dictatorships.[377]

38. But in his estate shall he honour the God of forces: and a god whom his fathers knew not shall he honour with gold, and silver, and with precious stones and pleasant things.

But in his estate shall he honour the God of forces;

During the Reformation and Counter-Reformation of the 16th century, historians saw the Crusades through the prism of their own religious beliefs. Protestants saw them as a manifestation of the evils of the Papacy, while Catholics viewed the movement as a force for good.[378]

and a god whom his father knew not

"Erasmus (1466-1536) Erasmus was a Catholic theologian who has also been called the 'Prince of the Humanists'. He was willing to raise questions about the teachings of the church and not to rely on blind dogma. Erasmus was critical of the abuses of the church and advocated reform from within the church. He was an early advocate of

170

religious tolerance and advocate a middle path between the Catholic and Protestant movements."[379]

Historically Thomas Aquinas [A. D. 1225-1274[380]] living in the [High Middle Ages comprised of the 11th, 12, and 13th centuries (c. A. D. 1001- 1301)[381] "in 1243 secretly joined an order of Dominican monks. His family had "felt so betrayed so betrayed that he had turned his back on the principles they subscribed."[382] "It is customary to begin the history of Humanism with Dante (1265-1321) and Petrarch (1304-74)."[384] "On April 6, 1327 after Petrarch gave up his vocation as a priest, the sight of a woman caulled "Laura," in the church of Sainte-clair, Avignon awoke in him a lasting passion." "Erasmus (1466-1536) Erasmus was a Catholic theologian who has also been called the 'Prince of the Humanists'[385]

shall he honour with gold, and silver, and with precious stones and pleasant things.

I. Pope John XXII (1316-1344)

Like his predecessor, Clement V [1305-1314[386]], Pope John centralized power and income in the Papacy and lived a princely life in Avignon.[387]

The following sections are lifted from *http://en.wikipedia.org/wiki/Pope_Boniface_VIII*

Philip [IV, king of France 1285–1314] retaliated against the bull by denying the exportation of money from France to Rome, funds that the Church required to operate. Boniface [VIII 1294–1303] had no choice but to contest Philip's demands, informing Philip that: God has set popes over kings and kingdoms.[388]

"Philip [IV, king of France A. D. 1285-1314] was convinced that the wealth of the Catholic Church in France should be used in part to support the state. He wanted to make war against the English. He countered the papul bull by decreeing laws prohibiting the export of gold, silver, precious stones, or food from France to the Papal States. These measures had the effect of blocking a main source of papal revenue. Philip also banished from France the papal agents who were raising funds for a new crusade in the Middle East. In the bull ineffabilis amor of September 1296, Boniface retreated. He sanctioned voluntary contributions from the clergy for the necessary defence of the state and gave the king the right to determine that necessity. Phillip rescinded his ordinances regarding the exports and even accepted Boniface as arbitrator in a dispute between himself and King Edward I of England.

Boniface decided most of those issues in Philip's favor"[389]
The following sections are lifted from Boniface VIII I pope I Brittanica. com *https://www.brittanica.com/biography/Boniface -VIII*

"The two principal international conflicts that existed from the beginning of Boniface's pontificate were that between France and England concerning Guyenne and Flanders, and that between the kingdom of Naples and Aragon concerning the island of Sicily, which, after much provocation, had broken away from the Neapolitan king, disregarding papal feudal overlordship. Boniface finally, though unwillingly, accepted the independence of the island kingdom under Frederic of Aragon. His attempts to stop hostilities between Edward I of England and Philit IV O France, however, became enmeshed with another important problem, the increasing tendency of these warring monarchs to tax the clergy without obtaining papal consent. Although the desire of the late-medieval rulers to tax the wealth of their clergy has been defended and can perhaps be understood, the practice was unquestionably contrary to the canon law (ecclesiastical law) of the time. That Boniface refuseed to look on inactively while the struggle between France and England, which he was trying to terminate, was being financed at the cost and to the prejudice of the church and the papacy is not suprising. In 1296 he issued the *bull Clerricis Laicos,* which forbade under the sanction of automatic excommunication any imposition of taxes on the clergy without express license by the pope. This bull had some effect in England, chiefly because of its support by the archbishop of Canterbury, Robert Winchelsey: but in France there was no strong defender of papal prerogative against the concerted action of the King and his civil lawyers. His bull *Unam Sanctam* (1302) proclaimed the primacy of the pope and insisted on the submission of the temporal to the spiritual power.

Conflicts With Philip IV of France

Philip IV countered or even forestalled the publication of *Clericis Laicos* with an order forbidding all export of money and valuable from France and with the expulsion of foreign merchants. Although these measures were a serious threat to papal revenues, they alone probably would not have forced Boniface to the far-reaching concessions that he had to grant the French king within the year, concessions that almost amounted to revocation of *Clericis Laicos*. The necessity of coming to terms was primarily the result of an insurrection against Boniface by a section of the Colonna family, a powerful anti-papal Roman family that included two cardinals, culminating in the armed robbery of a large amount of papal treasure in May 1297. A year of military action against the Colonna followed, which ended with their unconditional surrender. They were absolved from excommunication but were not reinstated in their offices and possessions: they therefore rebelled again and fled: some of them went to Philip, with whom they had conspired, perhaps even before the issue of *Clericis Laicos.*"[390]

The following sections are lifted from Avignon Papacy-Wikipedia *https://en.wikipedia.org/wiki/Avignon Papacy*

"Centralization of Church administration

The temporal role of the Catholic Church increased the pressure upon the papal court to emulate the governmental practices and procedures of secular courts. The Catholic Church successfully reorganised and centralized its administration under Clement V and John XXII. The papacy now directly controlled the appointments of benefices, abandoning the customary election process that traditionally allotted this considerable income. Many other forms of payment brought riches to the Holy See and its cardinals: tithes, a ten- percent tax on church property; annates, the income of the first year after filling a position such as a bishopric; special taxes for crusades that never took place; and many forms of dispensation, from the entering of benefices without basic qualifications like literacy for newly appointed priests to the request of a converted Jew to visit his unconverted parents. Popes such as John XXII, Benedict XII, and Clement VI reportedly spent fortunes on expensive wardrobes, and silver and gold plates were used at banquets.

Overall the public life of leading church members began to resemble the lives of princes rather than members of the clergy. This splendor and corruption at the head of the Church found its way to the lower ranks: when a bishop had to pay up to a year's income for gaining a benefice, he sought ways of raising this money from his new office. This was taken to extremes by the pardoners who sold absolutions for all kinds of sins to the poor. While pardoners were hated but needed to redeem one's soul, the friars who failed to follow the Church's moral commandments by failing their vows of chastity and poverty werer despised. This sentiment strengthned movements calling for a return to absolute poverty, relinquishment of all personal and ecclesiastical belongings, and preaching as the Lord and his disciples had.[391]

The following sections are lifted from *http://en.wikipedia.org//wiki/Pope Innocent VI*

173

Most of the wealth accumulated by John XXII [A.D. 1316-1334] and Benedict XII [A.D. 1334-1342] had been lost during the extravagant pontificate of Clement VI [A.D. 1342-1352]. Innocent VI [A.D. 1352-1362] economized by cutting the chapel staff (or the "capellani capelle") from twelve to eight. Works of art were sold rather than commissioned. His pontificate was dominated by the war in Italy and by Avignon's recovery from the plague, both of which made draining demands on his treasury. By 1357, he was complaining of poverty.[392]

The following sections are lifted from Pope Clement VI-Infogalactic: the planetary knowledge core, *https://Infogalactic.com/info/Pope_Clement_VI*

"Clement VI issued the bull Uniqenitus Dei filus on January 1343 to justify the power of the pope and the use of indulgences. This document would laber be used in the defence of indulgences after Martin Luther pinned his "95 Theses" to a church in Wittenberg on 31 October 1517."[393]

The following sections are lifted from *http://en.wikipedia.org/wiki/Pope_Clement_VI*

Clement VI issued the bull Unigenitus Dei filius on 27 January 1343, reducing the interval between one Great Jubilee and the next from 100 years to 50 years. In the document he elaborated for the first time the power of the pope in the use of indulgences. This document would later be used by Cardinal Cajetan in the examination of Martin Luther and his 95 Theses in his trial at Augsburg in 1518.[394]

The following sections are lifted from Martin Luther, Against the sale of Indulgences *http://courses.wcupa.edu/jones/his101/web37luther.htm*

"This reading contains the text of Luther's "95 Theses," which express his concerns about the sale of indulgences by the Catholic church.

Indulgence: a pardon for certain types of sin. The Catholic Church sold indulgences in the late medieval period, and their sale motivated Martin Luther to present his "95 Theses."

John Tetzel: monk who sold indulgences in Germany in 1517 for Albert of Hohenzollern (a German noble) and Pope Leo X. That triggered Martin Luther's posting of the "95 Theses" in Wittenburg.

Background

As we have seen in this course, understanding the metaphysical world with certainty is impossible. As a consequence, individuals have frequently expressed doubts about the teachings of their religious leaders. The teachings of the catholic popes, whose authority over religion resembled that of emperors over the physical world, were no exception. In the 14th century, after the Crusades, the Mongol invasions and various scandals, the pressure for reform increased. Most reform movements were unsuccessful, but in the early 16th century, several movements succeeded at the same time, leading to the an era in history called the Protestant Reformation. It became the last stage of reaction against Christianity's engagement in political affairs—a history that began with Constantine's declaration of Christianity as the Roman state religion in the 4th century. As a result of the Reformation, a substantial number of Europeans ceased to recognize the supremacy of the pope.

Although reformers had many complaints about the Catholic Church of the 16th century, the practice of selling "indulgences" raised the most opposition. An indulgence was a payment to the Catholic Church that purchased an exemption from punishment (penance) for some types of sins. You could not hget an indulgence to excuse a murder, but you could get one to excuse many lesser sins, such as thinking lustful thoughts about someone who was not your spouse. The customers for indulgences were Catholic believers who feared that if one of their sins went unoted or unconfessed, they would send extra time in purgatory before reaching heaven or worse, wind up in hell for failing to repent.

The sale of indulgences was a byproduct of the Crusades in the 12th and 13th centuries. Because they risked dying without the benefit of a priest to perform the appropriate ceremonies, Crusaders were promised immediate salvation if they die while fighting to "liberate the Christian holy city at Jerusalem. Church leaders justified this by arguing that good works earned salvation, and making Jerusalem accessible to Christians was an example of a good work. Over time, Church leaders decided that paying money to support good works was just as good as performing good works, and it evened things up for people who were physically incapapable of fighting a Crusade. Over several centuries, the practice expanded, and Church leaders justified it by arguing that they had inherited an unlimited amount of good works from Jesus, and the credit for these good works could be sold to believers in the form of indulgences. In other words, indulgences functioned like "confession insurance" against eternal damnation because, if you purchased an indulgence, they you wouldn't go to hell if you died suddenly or forgot to confess something.

In later years, the sale of indulgences spread to include forgiveness for sins of people who were already dead. This is evicent in this passage from asermon by John Tetzel, the monk who sold indulgences in Germany and inspired Martin Luther's protest in 1517.

> Don't you hear the voices of your dead parents and other relatives crying out, "Have mercy on us, for we suffer great punishment and pain. From this, you could release us with a few alms. . . we have created you, fed you, cared for you and left us our temporal goods. Why do you treat us so cruelly and leave us to suffer in the flames, when it takes only a little to save us? [Source: Die Reformation in augenzeugen berichten, edited by Helmar Junghaus (Dusseldorf: Karl Rauch Verlag, 1967), 44.]

Martin Luther was a monk who taught at a Catholic university in the German town of Wittenburg (located southwest of Berlin). Like many others, he feared that the Roman Catholic Church had become too corrupt to provide people with the guidance they needed to obtain salvation. Luther thought that individuals could seek salvation on their own, whithout relying on priests. On October 31, 1517, he attempted to provoke a debate on reform by nailing a list of 95 questions to the door of the Wittenburg university cathedral. The debate became public when some unknown person reprinted his ideas in a pamphlet which was eventually distributed throughout Germany.[395]

Abstract

New St. Peter's Basilica is the second largest church in the world and considered by many to be the most beautiful. Built mainly during the sixteenth century, it took over a century to complete, and withstood corruption, wars, the Reformation, the counter-Reformation, good popes and evil ones, and inched its way toward completion in 1626. The main funding for the early stages of building New St. Peter's came from the sale of indulgences. Indulgences did more than help pay for the basilica, however. The abusive means of selling indulgences, including lies from priests and the papacy about their efficacy, resulted in an uprising, led by Martin Luther of Germany, and the result was the Reformation and split in the Church. For those who were seduced away from the Church by the allure of the Renaissance and the secular aspects of humanism, Luther's protestations offered an alternative ideology and the Protestant Church was born. Indulgences also paid for some of the most exquisite art in the world. The project brought together some of the world's greatest minds and talent, including Michelangelo, Bramante, Bernini, and Raphael.

They worked in concert, along with many others, toward a common goal: creating the most spectacular and inspiring religious site of all time. Its artwork is unsurpassed, making it a pilgrimage even for non-believers. The work focuses on the period from Nicholas V(r.1447-1455) to the death of Michelangelo in 1564, chief architect of St. Peter's at the time and argues that in spite of the avarice and corruption that surrounded indulgences, building the basilica was worth the cost. With the enormous help of indulgences, New St. Peter's brought together the greatest visionaries, artists, and architects-possibly of all time-to build the greatest basilica to the glory of God. Indulgence sales, in spite of their abuses, left their mark on history in a positive way. To this day, the basilica inspires thousands of Christians who come to view its splendor and rejuvenate their faith.[396]

The following sections are lifted from "How did the Catholic Church use the money from indulgences?"

"Indulgences have been used for many purposes. One of the very earliest was to encourage participation in the Crusades and later to raise money for their success. They became a common method of alms-raising, which gradually gave way during much of the Middle Ages to the general enrichment of the Church.

Michaela Davey (Mastering Theology) says that at the beginning of the 16th century, Pope Leo X [A.D. 1513-1521] needed money to finalise the construction of St Peter's in Rome and planned to declare indulgences for all who contributed."[397]

The following sections are lifted from"Pope Leo X and indulgences," Bing *https://www.bing.com/search? q=pope20%leo20%x20%and20%i n=QBRE&sp=-1&pq=pope%20leo%20x%*

"In 1517, Pope Leo X issued indulgences for people to buy so he could raise money for the construction of St. Peter's Basilica. This indulgence was highly criticized by Martin Luther and partially was the reason for theProtestant Reformation."[398]

"Construction of the present basilica, which would replace Old St. Peter's Basillica from the 4th century CE, began on 18 April 1506 and was completedon 18 November 1626."[399]

The following sections are lifted from *http://humansarefree. com/2012/03/christian-church-is-the-biggest-*

"The Vatican's treasure of solid gold has been estimated by the United Nations World Magazine to amount to several billion dollars. A large bulk of this is stored in gold ingots with the U.S. Federal Reserve

Bank, while banks in England and Switzerland hold the rest.[400]

pleasant things

The following section is lifted from *http://en.wikipedia.org/wiki/Renaissance*

The Renaisance was a period in European history from the 14th to 17th century regarded as the cultural bridge between the Middle Ages and modern history. It started as a cultural movement in Italy in the Late Medieval period and later spread to the rest of Europe, making the beginning of the Early Modern Age.[401]

The following section is lifted from *http://en.wikipedia.org/wiki/Leonardo da Vinci*

"Leonardo's [1452-1519] most famous painting of the 1490s is The Last Supper, commissioned for the refectory of the Convent of Santa Maria della Grazi in Milan. It represents the last meal shared by Jesus with his disciples before his capture and death, and shows the moment when Jesus has just said "one of you will betray me", and the consternation that this statementcaused."[402]

The following section is lifted from *http://www.academia.org.michaelangelo*

'1508-1514 Rome

The commission for the tomb is interrupted: Pope Julius II [1503-1513] asks Michelngelo to switch from sculpting to painting to decorate the ceiling of the Sistine Chapel. Buonarroti completes the 65-foot ceiling alone, spending endless hours on his back and guarding the project jealously until revealing the finished work, on October 31, 1512. The breathtaking cycle of frescoes stretches over 500 square meters of ceiling and contains over 300 stuning figures."[403]

The following section is lifted from *http://en.wikipedia.org.raphael*

"By the end of 1508, Raphael had moved to Rome, where he lived for the rest of his life. He was invited by the new Pope Julius II, perhaps at the suggestion of his architect Donato Bramante, then engaged on St. Peter's Basillica, who came from just outside Urbino and was distantly related to Raphael. Unlike Michelangelo, who had been kept lingering in Rome for several months after his first summons, Raphael was immediately commishioned by Julius to fresco what was intended to become the Pope's private library at the Vatican Palace."[404]

39. Thus shall he do in the most strong holds with a strange god, whom he shall acknowledge and increase with glory: and he shall cause them to rule over many, and shall divide the land for gain.

I. Pope John XXII 1316–1334[405]

A. John XXII was maligned for his nepotism.

II. Pope Gregory XI 1370–1378 (left Avignon to return to Rome September 13, 1376

A. Gregory XI was the last pope of French nationality. He was learned an pious, though not free from nepotism.[408]

Rome, known worldwide as the center of the papacy, has been for many centuries ruled by the popes, who unified the spiritual power with the temporal power. The names of Pope Paul V Borghes (1552–1621) and Innocent X Pamphli (1574–1555) are the most prominent among all; both are known for sharing their temporal power with family members and with their illegitimate children. This practice was called nepotism.[409] The following sections are lifted from *http://en.wikipedia.org/wiki/Nepotism*

The term comes from Italian word "nepotismo," which is based on Latin root "nepos" meaning nephew. Since the Middle Ages and until the late 17th century, some Catholic popes and bishops, who had taken vows of chastity, and therefore, usually had not legitimate offspring of their own, gave their nephews such positions of preference as were often accorded by father to son. Several popes elevated nephews and other relatives to cardinalate. Often, such appointments were a means of continuing a papal "dynasty." For instance, Pope Callistus III, head of the Borgia family, made two of his nephews cardinals, one of them, Rodrigo, later used his position as cardinal as a stepping stone to the papacy, becoming Pope Alexander VI. Alexander then elevated Allessandro Farnes, his mistress's brother to cardinal; Farnes would later go on to become Pope Paul III.

Paul III also engaged in nepotism, appointing for instance, two nephews, aged 14 and 16, as cardinals. The practice was ended when Pope Innocent XII issued the bull Romanum decet Pontificem, in 1692. The papal bull prohibited popes in all times from bestowing estates, offices, or relative, with the exception that one qualified relative (at most) could be made a cardinal.[410]

DANIEL 11:40

40. And at the time of the end shall the king of the south shall push at him; and the king of the north shall come against him like a whirlwind, with chariots, and horsemen, and with many ships, and he shall enter into the countries, and shall overflow and pass over.

And at the time (#6256 ayth) of the end (#7093 kates)

The persecution of the church did not continue throughout the entire period of the 1260 years. God in his mercy to his people cut short the time of their fiery trial. In foretelling the "great tribulation: to befall the church, the Saviour Said: "Except those days should be shortened, there othshould no flesh be saved: for the elect's sake those days shall be shortened" (Matthew 24:22). Through the influence of the Reformation the persecution was brought to an end prior to 1798.[411]

The 1,260 days or years, terminated in 1798. A quarter of a century earlier, persecution had almost wholly ceased.[412]

The following is lifted from The Jesuits and the Inquisition, 1540-1556-The Protestant Reformation *https://bib site of history.com/the-jesuites-and-the- inquisition-1540-1556-the-protestant-reformation/*

"While the Society of Jesus was the chief instrument of the Catholic Reformation, and old instrument of the church was also employed-the Inquisition. This special ecclesiastical court in its papal form had been started in the thirteenth century to put down those days" ended. {August 12, 1886 the Albigensian heresy, and in its Spanish form in the fifteenth century to bolster the efforts of the new Spanish monarchy to force religious uniformity on its subjects. Both papal and Spanish inquisitions were medieval courts that used medieval methods of torture, and both were employed against the Protestants in the sixteenth century."[413]

The following sections are lifted from *http://media.prophesyagain.orge/wp-content/uploads/2015/05/Obama-andPope-urge-Jesuit-Principles.pdf*

"8. What significant event took place in 1773 that caused persecution against God's church to almost wholly cease?

As the Inquisition was the tribulum by which the Papacy inflicted such sore tribulation upon the church, and as the Order of the Jesuits was the strength of the Inquisition, therefor we believe that the abolition of the Order of the Jesuits is the event that marks the end of the tribulation. They had been expelled from Portugal in 1753, from France in 1761, and from Spain in 1767; but these decrees could not be permantly successful as long as the Jesuits retained their Order intact, and had the support of the Pope. But it is not long before the Pope was forced to turn against them and the final crash came. {August 12,1886 ATJ, SITI 487.10}

"At last came the final blow that was to shatter into pieces the great army of Loyola. For more than two centuries the Jesuits had been lighting the battles of Rome. To exalt the supremacy of the Pope, they had died by thousnads in English jails and Indian solitudes, had pierced land and sea to carry the strange story of the primacy to heathen millions, and build anew the medieval church in the heart of Oriental idolatry. And now it was the Pope and Rome that were to complete their destruction. By cruel ingratitude, the deity of earth whom they had worshiped with fidelity unequaled among men, was to hurt his anathemas against his most faithful disciples France and Spain elected Pope Clement XIV, upon his pledge that he would dissolve the Order. He issued his bull July 21, 1773, directing that for the welfare of the church and good of mankind, the institution of Loyola should be abolished. *Historical Studies, Id. {August 12, 1886 ATJ, SITI 487.11}* For these reasons we believe that the abolition of the Order of Jesuits is the event and July 21, 1773 is the date, when "the tribulation of those days" ended. {August 12, 1886 ATJ, SITI 487.12}"[414]

The following section has been lifted from *https://en.wikipedia.org/wiki/Pope_Clement XIV*

"Suppression of the Jesuits"

The Jesuits had been expelled from Brazil (1754), Portugal (1759), France (1764), Spain and its colonies (1767), and Parma (1768). Though he had to face strong pressure on the part of the ambassadors of the Bourbon courts, Clemt XIII always refused to yield to their demands to have the Society of Jesus suppressed. His successor Clement XIV tried to placate their enemies by treating the Jesuits harshly: he refused to meed the Superior Gener, Lorrenzo Ricci, ordered them not to receive novices etc.

The pressure kept building up to the point that Catholic countries were threatening to break away from the church. Clement XIV ultimately yielded *"In the name of peace of the Church and to avoid secession in Europe"* and suppressed the Society of Jesus by the brief Dominus ac Redemptor of 21 July 1773, However, in non-Catholic nations, particularly in Pressia and Russia, where papal authority was not recognized, the order was ignored. It was a result of a series of political moves rather than a theologic controversy.[415]

The following sections are copied from Smith, Uriah, Daniel and the Revelatiion, 1944, page 265, 266. And lifted from pagelifted from *http:// worldlastchance.com/end-time-prophecy/time_of_the_end-*

In 1773, Pope Clement IV disbanded the Jesuit Society under pressure from Catholic kings and princes who grew weary of Jesuits excessive political influence and meddling with their societies.[416]

The following sections are lifted from *http://w.ikipedia.org/wiki/Age_ Of_Enlightenment*

The Age of Enlightenment (or simply the Enlightenment or Age of Reason) is the era from the 1650s or a bit earlier to about the 1780s in which cultural and intellectual forces in Western Europe emphasized reason, analysis and individualism rather than tradition lines of authority. It was promoted by "philosophes" and local thinkers in urban coffeehouse, salons and masonic lodges. It challenged the authority of institutions that were deeply rooted in society, such as the Catholic Church; there was much talk of ways to reform society with toleration, science and skepticism.[417]

Immediately after the tribulation of those days shall the sun be darkened, and the moon shall not give her light, and the stars shall fall from heaven, and the powers of the heavens shall be shaken (Mt. 24:29).

Prophetically and historically this Matthew 24:29 prophecy was fulfilled at the following times and locations, before the conclusion of the twenty-three hundred day/year prophecy of Daniel 8:14. At that time the inauguration of the Day of Atonement, Investigative Judgement, cleansing phase of the sanctuary, known as "cleansing of the sanctuary" began on October 22, 1844. The following is a list of events which have historically and prophetically occurred in the parable [see Hebrews 9:24] prior to the beginning of the cleansing of the sancturary, October 22, 1844.

The powers of the heavens shall be shaken sixth seal (Rev. 6:12). Lisbon, Portugal

Saturday, Nov. 1, 1755[418]

Sun darkened, and the moon shall not give her light. Sixth seal (Rev. 6:12). May 19, 1780[419]

Stars shall fall from the heavens sixth seal (Rev.6:13).

Nov. 13, 1833[420]

And then shall appear the sign of the Son of Man in heaven: (Mt. 24:30).

The sign of the Son of Man was announced by the angels to the shepherds in Bethlehem: "And this shall be a sign unto you: You shall find the babe wrapped in swaddling clothes, lying in a manger" (Lk. 2:12). Not only was the incarnation a sign to the literal Bethlehem shepherds but also to the spiritual undershepherds, known a pastors (see Ephesians 4:11) of Christ in all ages to the people in the world.

This infants birth, was to be the antitypical fulfillment, motherboard, development of the tabernacle within the wilderness sanctuary (Ex. 25:8) into whom all Jews and Gentiles were to enter and find "in type," reconciling salvation to God. While the religious leaders asked for a sign from heaven, the sign had already been given to the literal shepherds, that the Christ-child would be born, fulfilling the promised seed to Eve (Gen. 3:15), with God desiring that the religious leaders, who were to figuratively be spiritual shepherds to the flocks of people they influenced would accept that Christ was the temple into whom they were to enter as they serve the people they were called t to be guides into how to have a relationship to God.

The sanctuary coupled to its reconciliation to God message is the sign of how God would dwell among his people Israel and for that matter the earth and all its inhabitants. (see Exodus 25:8)

Trumpets resumed: The series of seven trumpets is here again resumed. The second woe ended with the sixth trumpet, August 11, 1840, and the third woe occurs under the sounding of the seventh trumpet, which began in 1844.[421]

The temple is opened, and the second apartment of the sanctuary is entered. We know it is the holy of holies that is here opened, for the ark is seen; and in that apartment alone the ark is deposited. This took place at the end of the 2300 days, when the sanctuary was to be cleansed. (Daniel 8:14) At that time the prophetic periods ended and the seventh angel began to sound. Since 1844, the people of God have seen by faith the open door in heaven, and the ark of God's testament within.[422]

But like the stars in the vast circuit of their appointed path, God's purposes know no haste and no delay.[423]

Like the Israelites in Ex. 12 participating in the command of Moses to slay the lamb/goat and apply its blood to the doorposts then enter in to that dwelling and eat roasted lamb/goat, unleavened bread and bitter herbs, awaiting the midnight judgment hour, the experience of humanity who has claimed Calvary's sacrifice, entered into new life of a relationship to God through Jesus Christ since the resurrection and ascension of Christ which involves victory over sin through claiming the merits of the blood of Christ. Now after1810 years after the close of the seventy-week prophecy, just prior to the close of the 2,300-day prophecy of Daniel 8:14 ending in October 22, 1844, the 1,260-day prophecy had come to the end in 1798. It is perceived to be noteworthy that two of the signs, the 1755 Lisbon, Portugal, earthquake and the 1,780 dark day, which Christ referred to had already occurred by the close of the 1,260-day prophecy. With the discovery by William Miller of Daniel 8:14 and the upcoming of the cleansing of the sanctuary, study was given as to the meaning of the sanctuary. Was it the earth? Was it heaven? How would the sanctuary be cleansed? By the second coming of Christ or some other means? Many believed that it would be cleansed by the second coming. After the Great Disappointment of October 22, 1844, believers discovered that Christ was beginning the cleansing of the heavenly sanctuary. It was and is to be discovered that Christ is the antitpycal tabernacle/temple and that the linin curtain enclosing the Hebraic sanctuary symbolized that after the incarnation, God's arms antitypically enclosed fallen humanity with the hopes that they would respond to his reconciling love and be saved.

Thus judgment began in 1844, like it had for the Israelites in Egypt to see if the lambs' blood was literally on their doorposts or post Calvary figuratively/spiritually on their hearts. All who had the blood on their doorposts/hearts would be saved, literally from Egypt and figuratively/spiritually from sin. Or if their lives were found to be without the blood on their doorposts/hearts would be lost. Thus there would be a separation between the sheep and goats, wise and foolish virgins.

And then shall appear (#5316 phan-o) the sign of the son of man in heaven.
(Mt. 24:30)

5316 phan-o v. (act.) to shine, give light; -(mid./pass.) to appear, be visible:-*Strongs* 2001

5316 fah-ee-no" prol. For the base of 457; to lighten (shine), i.e. show (trans or intrans. lit. or fig.) appear, be seen. shine x think *Strongs* 1979 The aspect of the definition which seems to fit the historical-prophetic contest is "to shine x think." After all the signs Christ announced in Matthew 24:29 of the sun being darkened, the moon not giving her light and the stars falling from heaven, the mind and thoughts of William Miller and others were directed to figure out the meaning of the sanctuary and its cleansing in Daniel 8:14. Initially the sanctuary was thought to be this earth and that its cleansing would occur at the second coming of Christ. After the vision, or thoughts of Hiram Edson in the corn field were drawn to the heavenly sanctuary, the Adventists, looking forward to the second coming changed their view that the sanctuary to be cleansed was not the earth but the heavenly. This change of view in their thought process caused the whole world to mourn. Something else was to occur instead of the second coming. That event would become known as the Investagative Judgment, starting on October 22, 1844. While the earth would not be cleansed by the literal second coming of Christ, its occupants would undergo an investigation in the heavenly sanctuary. The onlooking court of the unfallen universe would see if the earthly penitent believer had accepted Christ as their personal Savior and as such would be fit to save at the second coming. While acceptance of Christ as personal Savior would be their title to heaven, like a grain of mustard seed, the investigation would also examine the penitent's growth in grace, experiencing the process of fitness for heaven. While Christ was not only the penitents title to heaven, he was also their fitness for heaven. As the penitent believer grew in an ongoing relationship to Christ, he would become a part of Christ's body, becoming a full mustard tree in which birds of the air could dwell. Although the penitent believer might not be regarded as a full-grown, mustard tree, in relationship to Christ he would credited as being mature.

Immediately after the end of the 1260, 538–1798, and 1290, 508–1798, day, the sanctuary message appeared in the mind of William Miller who began studying the Bible. Miller and his associates at first believed that the 2300 days would terminate in the spring of 1844. GC328 "He had devoted two years to the study of the Bible, when, in 1818, he reached the solemn conviction that in about twenty-five years Christ would appear for the redemption of His people."[424]

For nine years he (William Miller) waited, the burden still pressing upon his soul, until in 1831 he for the first time publicly gave the reasons of his faith.[425]

In 1833, Miller received a license to preach, from the Baptist Church, of which he was a member.[426] A large number of ministers of his denomination also approved his work, and it was their formal sanction that he continued his work... In 1833, two years after Miller began to present in public the evidences of Christ's soon coming, the last of the signs appeared which were promised by the Saviour as tokens of His second advent. Said Jesus: "The stars shall fall from heaven" (Matthew 24:29). This prophecy received a striking and impressive fulfillment in the great meteoric shower of November 13, 1833.[427]

It is interesting to note that the historical events which occurred in the Lisbon earthquake of 1755, dark day of 1780, -end of a 1,260-day prophecy in 1793, another end of a 1,260 and 1,290-day prophecy, 1798, falling of the stars 1833, -year, month, day prophecy 1840, end of another 1,290-day prophecy in 1843, all occurring before October 22, 1844, the conclusion of the 2,300-day prophecy of Daniel 8:14 were like historical arrows (Num. 24:8, Dt. 32:23) in God's quiver (Isaiah 49:2), inviting fallen humanity to believe in God and accept His provision for their salvation. Those historical event arrows shot at fallen, sinful humanity (Amos 9:8), invited them to believe in God and accept his provision for salvation, were like the nations God left in Canaan used by God as lesser vessels, to discipline Israel, the greater vessel, with respect to knowledge about God and capacity of witness for him, like gold is of greater value than silver, bronze or iron, if they rebelled against Him. These nations were "(1) the five lords of the Philistines, (2)and the all the Canaanites, and Sidonians, and the Hivites that dwell in Mount Lebanon from mount Baalhermon unto the entering in of Hamath. And they were to prove Israel by them, to know whether they would hearken unto the commandments of the Lord, which he commanded their fathers by the hand of Moses" (Jdg. 3:3–4).

Hence at the conclusion of all these sign predicted by Christ in Mt. 24, the sign of the Son of Man would appear. The sign of the Son of Man is the sanctuary of Daniel 8:14. Like the Israelites, having experienced 430 years of Egyptian bondage came out of Egypt, a symbol of enslaving bondage to sin, through the power of the blood on their doorposts, having spent close to five months in the wilderness before they received the command to "make a sanctuary that I may dwell among them (Ex. 25:8) so Christ would come to this earth from heaven, not an enslaved to Egyptian bondage, symbol of sin, after four thousand years of sin to be the "temple of the tabernacle," into whom all Israel and for that matter all humanity was invited to enter, the sanctuary and be reconciled to God. Thus when Dan. 8:14 says, "Unto two thousand three hundred days, then shall the sanctuary be cleansed," it referred the end of time Day of Atonement phase of God's reconciliation judgment of fallen, sinful, redeemed humanity to Himself, with every individual becoming in their belief, a judgment for or against Him.

These Day of Atonement phases are depicted in Mt 24:30–31.Verse 30 reads: "And then shall appear the sign of the Son of Man in heaven." In Daniel 8:14, the "sanctuary to be cleansed" was and is Christ who is the "temple of the tabernacle" (Rev. 15:5). Thus Christ will undergo through the process of investigation at the end of the 2,300 days, a cleansing of Himself, by creatures of human nature who desire to remain in a faith relationship to Him and be saved and those who desire to live apart from a faith relationship to Him and be eternally banished from Him. This is analogous to the parable of separating the sheep from the goats (Mt. 25:32).

The second phase of the Day of Atonement depicted in Mt. 24:30–31, "And then shall all of the tribes of the earth mourn." With the proclamation of the close of the 2,300 days of Daniel 8:14 that Christ would return a second time at that date, resulting in the Great Disappointment of October 22, 1844, "all the tribes of the earth mourned." That is to say, they expected Christ to return to the earth, suffering the Great Disappointment, but in reality He had begun the investigative judgment Day of Atonement, Lev. 16 phase of His coming, in which he would separate like sheep and goats, wise and foolish virgins, those who, having claimed the type or antitype sacrifice of Calvary would be (Rev. 6:11) or were, clothed with the priestly robe of Christ's righteousness depicted in the implied "wearing of the wedding garment" (Mt 22:11, 12), and those who did and did not want to be clothed with the priestly robe of Christ's righteousness in a relationship to Him and "had not on a wedding garment" (Mt. 22:11, 12).

Miller accepted the generally received view that in the Christian age the earth is the sanctuary, and he therefore understood that the cleansing of the sanctuary foretold in Daniel 8:14 represented the purification of the earth by fire at the second coming of Christ.[428]

Christ had come, not to the earth, as they expected, but, as foreshadowed[429] in the type, to the most holy place of the temple in heaven. According to Heb. 9: 8, 9 the first tabernacle was a figure (KJV), illustration (NIV), symbolic (Andrews study Bible - Harper Study Bible, RSV) translated from the word (#3850 par-ab-ol-lay), being the same word used when Jesus spoke in parable (Mt. 18:30). It is perceived that when God command the Israelites to make a tabernacle according to the pattern, that word for "pattern" #8403 stems from a literal or figurative roots meaning "to build." Thus it is perceived that God desired and desires His creatures of fallen humanity to live out the parable of the sanctuary in the process of being reconciled to God. As we have seen earlier, "But like the stars in the vast circuit of their appointed path, God's purposes know no haste and no delay."[430], so we are called align our lives, through the grace of Calvary to be votes in favor of allegiance to God. By becoming "a part of the body of Christ" (1 Cor. 12:25), "a living stone" (1 Pet. 2:4),with Christ Jesus being the first "one like the son of man to approach the ancient of days" (Dan. 7:13), we, as part of His body, clothed with Christ's righteousness, will also experience "in Him" an "approaching of the ancient of days." This reality is advocated by Christ in John 16:26, 27, "At that day ye shall ye shall ask in my name: and I say not unto you that I will pray the Father for you. For the Father himself loveth you, because ye have loved me, and have believed that I came out from God."

While the main temple and center of worship was in Jerusalem, Jesus proclaimed to the woman at the well that "the day is coming and now is that the true worshiper of God will worship him in spirit and truth." This echoed the historical reality recorded in Ezek. 11:16, "Wherever they were scattered he would be a little sanctuary to them." Thus when Christ would cleanse the sanctuary at the end of the 2,300 days, he would cleanse his people wherever they were scattered who would in their memory invite Him to be a "little sanctuary" to them.

Like the time span of nearly five months between the 14th day of the first month (symbolizing the type Passover lamb sacrifice fulfilled antitypically in Christ's sacrifice on calvary, then fifty days later in the type feast of weeks, in the second month, antitypically being the Pentecostal outpouring of the Holy Spirit, in which the disciples had exchanged their plant-based wood spirits for plant-based wick spirits to be ignited by hypostasis heat Father in the outpouring of the oil of the Holy Spirit in the golden, symbol of faith, seven-branch candelabra churches) and the sounding of the trumpets in the seventh month (Lev. 23:24) on the first day, depicting the 1810 years between AD 34, the close of the seventy-week prophecy, after which would occur the Day of Atonement on the tenth day of the seventh month Lev. 24:27 on the beginning of the antitypical Day of Atonement, October 22, 1844, so there would be sometime between the ascension and the second coming.

This "time" would be a time to develop character. The purpose of this would be to move from "faith unto faith" (Rom. 1:17). That is "grow in grace" (2 Peter 3:18). That is to say (1) once an individual sees that his sin caused the death of Christ, (2) he is to claim the merits of that sacrifice, (3) then enter into a new life under the blood stained banner of Christ, i.e., the blood on the doorposts. (4) While waiting for the midnight justification judgment, he is to eat figuratively roasted lamb, a symbol of Calvary's sacrifice, like the Israelites did as they waited for the midnight judgment. (5) After the midnight justification judgment, he would be led out of a life of sin, like Jesus said to the woman, "Go and sin no more" to a place called Succoth."

Although it would seem to the believer that heaven, like Canaan, was just a short distance away, God would lead them in another direction to develop their character, teaching them more about himself. (7) They would be led to the Red sea, experiencing temptation that God might not be able to deliver them from sin, like he was about to do from the pursuing Egyptians. (8) By passing through the baptism of the Red Sea they would declare antitypically that they desired to be dead to Egypt/sin.(9)Then they were to learn dependence upon God for water, (10) then food, being supplied with manna, then find out about the Sabbath, (12) discover God would deliver them from the Amalekites, through the outstretched hands of Moses, a symbol of calvary, just as He had from the pursuing Egyptians (13) that God had given them ability to judge prior to their discovery of the Ten Commandments, since the law was written on their hearts (14) their need for the spoken Ten Commandments (15) a time of testing their obedience as a fruit of faith with full knowledge that they were three months into their journey toward Canaan/heaven when God spoke His law, telling them what they were to become by the power of the blood of the slain lamb in Egypt (16) after forty days, into the fifth month from their Exodus/sin they broke the spoken law of God, demonstrated by Moses throwing down the two tablets. (17) Then new tablets were made, like a new heart, upon which God wrote his law, in the second forty days on the mountain, placing Israel still within the fifth month from the Exodus after which time Israel began (18) the construction of the tabernacle sanctuary. (19) The tabernacle and sanctuary were completed one year after they left Egypt, nine months after they discovered what they were delivered from Egypt to be, a kingdom of priests, like the gestation period of a baby from conception to birth (20). Once the sanctuary was set up, they could start living in type as a kingdom of priests. Not all Israelites would function as priests in sanctuary/temple, but all could figuratively/spiritually put on Christ's righteousness and be regarded as priests. In a similar manner, Christ was born a long time after sin originated in Eden. The intention of his life would be to show fallen humanity how to live. Then by his death, he "would remove the iniquity of the land in one day." Zechariah 3:9. Believers would then be empowered to spiritually rise with him in his resurrection and be clothed with the priestly garment of his righteousness.

After the sanctuary was set up, the Levitical priests, a subset of the Israelite, nation, who as a nation were called to be a kingdom of priest, were the only ones to function as priests. This arrangement is analougous to present dayl ministers, a subset of humanity are called to function as religious teachers to the whole world. Everyone after calvary, not just the Jews, whose seventy-week prophecy ended in AD 34 as a nation but not for individuals of that nation, in the whole world was to be invited to accept Jesus as Savior from sin. This joining of the "inner man" to a kingdom of allegiance to God, would be "not of this world." It would advocate the message of John 3:16, "For God so loved the world that he gave his only begotten son that whosoever believeth in him should not perish but have everlasting life."

The following time frames articulate the historical dates during which specific time prophecies were fulfilled.

I. End of the 1,260 days, A. D. 538-1798 = time times and a half Daniel 7:25,

= 42 months Revelation 11:2. = Revelation 13:5.

A. A.D. 533–A.D 1793

[—————1,260 days/years—————]

A.D.533 A.D.1793

Justinian, during his long reign, took the Catholic side. But his empress, Theodora, was a Monophysite, and in His old age the emperor leaned in the same direction. We still possess the acts of a conference, between six Severian and seven orthodox bishops, held by his order in 533. The Great controversy of his reign was the dispute about the three chapters.[420]

"In the Revolutionof 1793, the Bible was discarded, and the existence of deity denied, as the voice of the nation." Devotion turned to the homage of liberty, equality, virtue and morality.[421]

The following[431] sections are lifted[432] from *The New Catholic Encyclopedia, Vol. II, c. 1967*

The emperor's letter must have been sent before the 25th of March 533. For, in a letter of that date to Epiphanius He speaks of it having been already dispatched, and repeats his decision that all affairs touching the church shall be reffered to the pope, 'head of all bishops, and the true and effective corrector of heretics.

B. A[433].D. 538–A.D. 1798

[————1,260 days/years————]

A[434][435][436]. D. 538 A.D.[1798]

Little Horn

Papal Rome

"A power that takes away the daily sacrificial services and Tramples the sanctuary (Dan. 11:31–39). The armies of the Byzantine emperor Justinian drove out The Arian Ostrogoths from Italy in 538 thereby putting into Effect Justinians's decree of 533 which recognized the prima- Cy of the bishop of Rome over Christendom. Thus began the 1,260-yar period (538–1798) when papal Rome hid the atoning Power of Christ from the people of the covenant. (Dan. 11:31; Compare 8:11)."

"The Third Council of Orleans, A. D. 538 says in its twenty-ninth Cannon: 'The opinion is spreading amongst the people, that it is Wrong to ride, or drive, or cook food, or do anything to the house Or person on the Sunday. But such opinions are more Jewish than Christian shall be lawful in the future, which has been so to the present time. On the other hand agricultural labor ought to be laid aside, in order that the people may not be prevented from attending church. . .

Labor in the country (on Sunday) was not prohibited till the Council of Orleans, AD 538. It was thus an institution of the Church as Dr. Paley has remarked. The earlier Christians met in The morning of that day for prayer and singing of hymns in Commemoration of Christ's resurrection, and then went about Their usual duties.

Fall of Rome "French punitive expedition against Rome. General Louis Berthier en tered the city Feb. 10, proclaimed the establishment of the of the Roman Republic, and drove Out)Pope) Pius VII. The French made him captive and began (March, 1799) forcing him from city to city toward France. . . where (Pius VI) is held prisoner in Valence, France July 14, 1799 until his death August 28, 1799. This moment marked the nadir of Papal fortunes in Modern Times.

The following sections are lifted from en.wikipedia.org/wiki/ Napoleoni_Wars The Second Coalition was formed in 1798 by Austria, Great Britain, the Kingdom of Naples, the Ottoman empire, the Papal States, Portugal, Russia, Sweden and other states. During the War of the Second Coalition, the French Republic suffered from corruption and internal division under the Directory (five directeurs, holding executive power). France also lacked funds, and no longer had the services of the Lazare Carnot, the war minister who had guided it to successive victories following extensive reforms during the early 1790s. Bonaparte, the main architect of victory in the last years of the First Coalition, had gone to campaign in Egypt. Missing two of its most important military figures from the previous conflict, the Republic suffered successive defeats against revitalized enemies whom British financial support brought back into the war.[437]

End of the 1290 and 1335 days of Dan.

12:11,12 A. 1,290 days

A.D. 503–A.D. 1793

The following sections are lifted from *http://wikipedia.org/wiki/ Napoleonic_Wars*

News of the French Revolution of 1789 was received with great alarm by the rulers of the France's neighbors, which only increased with the arrest and eventual execution of King Louis XVI of France. The first attempt to crush the French Republic came in 1793 when Austria, the Kingdom of Sardinia, the Kingdom of Naples, Prussia, Spain and the Kingdom of Great Britain formed the first coalition. French measures, including general conscription (levee-en-masse), military reform, and total war, contributed to the defeat of the First Coalition, despite the civil war occurring in France. The war ended when General Napoleon Bonaparte forced the Austrians to accept his terms in the Treaty of Campo Formio. Only Great Britain remained opposed to the French Republic.[438]

2. A.D.508–A.D.1798

[————1,290 days/years————-]

A.D.508 A.D. 1798

T[439]h[440]e following sections are lifted from *http:/www.bibleexplained. com/revelation/r-seg11-12/r11f-Fr-rev.ht*

Actually the new belief system began with the cult of reason as noted by Aulard. Quickly actions were taken to remove the Old faith, Christianity. The term "dechristianization" may well Have been promoted by the actions centuries earlier when the Roman church and government had effectively "Christianized" them. The French ancestors, called Franks, were the first to Embrace the new religion under King Clovis. That was 30 years Before the 1260 year period began. 1008c. see on da1211. Daily mediatorial work of Christ in the heavenly sanctuary was originally taken away by mid-third century believers in Christ who professed to believe that he was the "Lamb of God that taketh away the sin of the world," Jn. 1:29 and "no one comes to the Father but by me." Jn.14:6 teaching of "intercession of saints." This belief took the focus of direct access to the Father through Christ Jesus, Our risen Lord, introducing "another gospel" (Gal. 1:6. 2, Cor. 11:4), placing it on another creature or belief. It was to this belief of "intercession of saints" practiced by Clovis's wife, a Roman Catholic, that this pagan king of France subscribed when he "ascribed his victory at this moment [1799] Voille to Saint Martin of Tours." Thus the pagan marked the nadir King combined the power of the state with the power [lowest point] of Fall of Rome French punitive expedition against Rome. General Louis Berthier entered the city Feb. 10, proclaimed the Establishment of the Roman Republic,and drove out pope Pius VII. Drove out Pope Pius VII. The French made him Captive and began (March 1799) forcing Him from city to city to ward France, where (Pius VI) is Held prisoner in Valence France Until his death August 28, 1799. This moment marked The nadir of Roman Catholic belief, "taking away the daily" mediatorial work of Christ. In the pagan king, Clovis's subscribal to Roman Catholic Times.430 of papal Fortunes in modern the church received power to rebel against God.Times.

The[441] following sections are lifted from *http://en.wikipedia.org/wiki/ Napoleonic_Wars*

The Second Coalition was formed in 1798 by Austria, Great Britain, the Kingdom of Naples, the Ottoman Empire, the Papal State, Portugal, Russia, Sweden, and other states. During the War of the Second Coalition, the French Republic suffered from corruption and internal division under the Directory (five directeurs holding executive power). France also lacked funds and no longer had the services of the Lazare Carnot, the war minister who had guided it to successive victories following extensive reforms during the early 1791s. Bonaparte, the main architect of victory in the last years of the First Coalition, had gone to campaign in Egypt. Missing two of its most important military figures from the previous conflict, the Republic suffered successive defeats against revitalized enemies whom British financial support brought back into the war.[442]

B. 1335 days

1. A.D.508–A.D.1843
[————————1,335 days/years————————]
A.D.508 A.D.1843

T[443]he[444] following sections are lifted from *http:/www.bibleexplained. com/revelation/r-seg11-12/r11f-Fr-rev.ht*

Actually the new belief system began with the cult of Reason As noted by Aulard. Quickly actions were taken to remove the Old faith, Christianity. The term "dechristianization" may well clean-Have been promoted by the actions centuries earlier when the Roman church and government had effectively "Christianized" Them. The French ancestors, called Franks, were the first to Embrace the new religion under King Clovis. That was 30 yearsBefore the 1260 year period began. 1008c. see on da1211.

Daily mediatorial work of Christ in the heavenly sanctuary was Originally taken away by mid-third century believers in Christ who Professed to believe that He was the Lamb of God that taketh Away the sin of the world," Jn. 1:29 and "no one comes to theFather but by me." Jn. 14:6 teaching of "intercession of saints." This belief took the focus of direct access to the Father through Christ Jesus, Our risen Lord, introducing "another gospel" Gal.1:6. 2 Cor. 11:4, placing it on another creature or belief. according It was to this belief of "intercession of saints" practiced by Clovis's wife, a Roman Catholic, that this pagan king of France subscribed when he "ascribed his victory at Voille to Saint Martin of Tours."433 Thus the pagan king combined the earth. Power of the state with the power of Roman Catholic belief, "taking away the daily" mediatorial work of Christ. In the pagan king, Clovis' subscribal to Roman Catholic The church received power to rebel against God. Proclamation of the Three angels message and Daniel 8:14's cleansing of the sanctuary which was thought to be Christs' second Coming to the earth at first in the spring of 1844 and then with that disappointment re calculating to the Fall of 1844 with the Final date set ting of of Oct. 22, 1844 when the heavenly Sanctuary, perceived to be the earth, would be cleansed by the second coming of Christ to this While the date was correct, the event was incorrect result-In the Great Disap- Appointment.

III. End of "an hour, and a day, and a month, and a year" (Rev. 9:15)
[5- months=150 years] + [391 years, 15 days]
July 27, 1299
First Woe

Rise of Mohametanism = Othman founded Ottoman empire which grew until it extended over all the principle Mohammedan tribes, consolidating them into one grand monarchy. Othman's first assault on the Greek empire occurred July 17, 1299.

Jan. 6, 1449
Second Woe

John Palaeogous reining Byzantine emperor (1425–1448) left no son as heir to Eastern Empire throne, so the lawful successor, his brother, Constantine, the last of the Greek emperors was was crowned Jan. 6, 1449. Constan tine would not venture to ascend the throne without the consent of the Turkish sultan … By the hand of two il lustrious deputies the the imperial crown was placed at Sparta on the head of Constantine. "Let this historical fact be carefully examined in connection with the prediction givenabove. This was not a violent assault made on the Greeks, by which their empire was over thrown and their independence taken away, simply a voluntary surrender.

Aug. 11, 1840

Mohammedan Independence in Constantinople endswhen Me hemet, pasha of Egypt, in battle with Turkish sultan – takesTurkish fleet into Egypt. Mehemet refused to return fleet to Turkish sultan, declaring if powers took it, he would burn it. In this posture affairs stood, when in 1840, England, Russia, Austria, and Prussia interposed, and determined on a settle ment of the difficulty. For it was evident, if left alone, Mehemet would soon become master of the sultan's throne. The sultan accepted this intervention of the great powers, and thus made a voluntary surrender of the question into their hands. Daniel and the Revelation, by Uriah Smith p. 513–514 c. 1944] render of that indepen dence into the hands of Turks, by saying "I cannot reign unless you permit." The four angels (sultanies sit updated at Aleppo, Iconium, Damascus and Bagdad) were loosed for an hour, a day, a month, and a year … This period, during which Ottoman supremacy was to exist amounts to three hundred ninety-one years and fifteen days.

The prophecy of the first angel's message, brought to view in Revelation 14, found its fulfillment in the Advent movement of 1840–44.[445]

IV. End of 2,300 days/years (Dan. 8:14)

And he said unto me, Unto two thousand and three hundred days; then shall the sanctuary be cleansed. (Dan. 8:14)

2,300 Days

B.C 457 A. D. October 22, 1844

When the Israelites came out of Egypt by the power of the blood of the slain lamb on their doorposts at the command of Moses, symbolizing believers coming out of sin by the power or calvary's blood sacrifice applied to their hearts at the invitational command of God, Israel camped in tents (Ex. 33:10). This camping in tents parallels post-calvary believers regarding their bodies as tabernacles (2 Pet. 1:13,14). God planned to meet them where they were, so whenever Moses desired to inquire of God, he went outside the camp where he had pitched a tabernacle in which he would meet with God (Ex.33:7). This occurrence of meeting with God followed Israel's breaking of the spoken law of God recorded in Ex. 20, identifying a breaking of the spoken first and second commandment of the now written on two tables of stone, hitherto unknown in writing to the Israelite nation, Ten Commandments, which delineated how a nation of priests, saved from the Egyptian bondage/ sin by faith in the blood of the sacrifice, applied to their doorposts/ hearts by faith in Calvary's sacrifice, were to live. Earlier in Ex. 25:8, God had commanded in the first forty days, about five months from the Exodus from Egypt/sin, of Moses' encounter with God on Mt. Sinai, "Let them make me a sanctuary that I may dwell among them." This was God's way of announcing that one day He, in the second person of the Godhead would incarnate Himself as the fulfilment to the promised seed given to Eve and dwell among men in a more elaborate tent within a sanctuary into which all Israel was to come out of their tents (Ex. 33:7, 8) and enter, eventually entering into the sanctuary, almost a year after the Exodus (Ex. 40:2), although at the time of this written account the Israelite nation was at the end of Moses's first forty days on Mt. Sinai, which was in the fifth month from the Exodus. While the temple was constructed in the reign of Solomon, 480 years after the Exodus (1 Kings 6:1 in AD 970, Christ, in His three-and-a-half-year ministry proclaimed Himself as the fulfilment of the Temple Jn. 2:21. In principle, a coming out of their tents and entering into the sanctuary is like Christ, symbolized by the Temple (Jn. 2:21) whose roots were in the Hebraic wilderness sanctuary, being the antitypical "Temple of the tabernacle of the testimony" (Rev. 15:5) saying, "Come unto me all ye who are

196

weary and heavy laden, and I will give you rest. Take my yoke upon you and learn of me for my yoke is easy and my burden is light and ye shall find rest unto your souls" (Mt. 11:28). Thus, in antitypical reality, Christ's body, the temple was nailed to cavalry's cross. Hence, when Christ was resurrected from the grave, so was the antitypical sanctuary resurrected. When Christ ascended into heaven, He went, according to Heb. 9:11 entered "a greater and more perfect tabernacle, not made with hands, that is to say, not of this building." Through the prophet Ezekiel God said, "Therefore say, 'Thus saith the Lord God; Although I have cast them far off among the heathen, and although I have them, among the countries, yet will I be to them as a little sanctuary in the countries where they shall come" (Ezek. 11:16.) Thus at the end of the 2,300 days of Daniel 8:14, when "the sanctuary shall be cleansed," in the midnight hour of earth's history, with night [#3915 lah-yil] often meaning "fig. adversity with implic. illicit, illegal, immoral," the night time at which might be fig adversity or implication. illicit, illegal, or immoral of this world's history.

This reconciliation to God had been depicted in the Old Testament with its resulting forgiveness recorded in Leviticus 4. The tabernacle of the sanctuary in the Old Testament was the place where the priests would splash against the veil the blood of slain animals, releasing the penitent from sins committed. Yet on the Day of Atonement the High Priest would transfer the sins in the sanctuary to the scapegoat, cleansing the sanctuary from sin. By John's confession, "Behold the lamb of God that taketh away the sin of the world," an acknowledgement was made that Christ was the antitypical fulfilment of the Ex. 25:8 sanctuary in which God was to dwell and live among men. Like the Israelite nation came out of the enslaving bondage of Egypt, depicting post calvary humanity coming out of sin, to camp in literal tents symbolizing post calvary body tents on their way to Canaan or heaven, so Christ had left heaven to dwell on this earth in an antitypical tabernacle/temple in His all- encompassing sanctuary arms of his righteous love, like the sanctuary courtyards were enclosed in linen, now since the incarnation, all humanity lived as it were on the laver/sea/earth/world. Humanity was to come out of this world to which they were born as fish, die to self, and be transformed through calvary's sacrifice as priests of God, entering into a life of service for God.

Like the Israelites, at the word spoken to Moses, were to make God a sanctuary that he might dwell among them, so the shepherds were told of this incarnate wonder in the words "you will find the babe wrapped in swaddling close and lying in a manger" (Lk 2:12 last part). The first part of this verse says, "And this shall be a sign unto you." Here is fulfilled (Ex. 25: 8), "Let them make me a sanctuary that I may dwell among them." Surrounded by His righteousness, like the Hebraic tabernacle was surrounded by the linen courtyard of the sanctuary, Christ now enclosed fallen humanity by His righteousness to see if they would accept his provision for them of reconciliation to God.

While Christ, the "temple of the tabernacle," took away the sins of the penitent believers, to which he had been born, John echoed this reality when he said, "Behold the lamb of God which taketh away the sin of the world."

#4638 sky'-no-mah; from 4637; an encampment, i.e., (fig.) the Temple ((as God's residence), the body (as the tenement for the soul):-tabernacle. Strongs, 1979

#4638 skenoma n. tent, dwelling place, lodging place:-tabernacle [3] Acts 7:46. 2 Pet. 1:13, 14 Strongs,2001

#6256 ayth: from 5703; time, espec. (adv. with prep) now, when, etc.: - + after, [al-] ways, X certain + continually, + evening, long, (due) season, so [long] as [even, evening-, noon-] tide, ([meal-], what) time, when. Strongs, 1979 time- #6256 et n. f. time (in general); a unit of time (of various lengths), season. Strongs, 2001

#7093 kates contr. From 7112 an extremity; adv. (with prep.) after, (utmost) border, end. [in-] finite, X process. See 6975 Strongs, 1974

#7093 qes n. m. end, limit, boundary Strongs, 2001

The following sections are lifted from *http://en.wikipedia.org/wiki/Napoleon_and_the_Catholic_Church*

In 1796, French Republican troops under the command of Napoleon Bonaparte, invaded Italy, defeated the papal troops and occupied Ancona and Loreto.

Pope Pius VI sued for peace, which was granted February 19, 1797, but on December 28 of that year in a riot blamed by papal forces on some Italian and French revolutionists, the popular brigadier general Matherin-Leonard Duphot was killed, who had gone to Rome with Joseph Bonaparte as part of the French embassy was killed and a new pretext for invasion was furnished. General Berthier marched to Rome on February 10, 1798, and proclaimed a Roman Republic, demanded of the pope the renunciation of his temporal power.

Upon his refusal, he was taken prisoner and on February 20 was escorted from the Vatican to Siena, and thence to Certosa near Florence.

The French declaration of war against Tuscany led to his removal. (He was escorted by the Spaniard Pedro Gomez of Labrador) by way of Parma, Placenza, Turin, and Grenoble to the citadel of Valence, the chief town of Drome where he died six weeks after his arrival on August 29, 1799, having reigned longer than any other pope.[446]

C. 1335 days

   1. A.D. 508–A.D. 1843

V. End of the 2,300 days Dan. 8:14 A. B.C.457 –A.D. October 22, 1844

That there should be time no longer (Rev. 10:6).

VI. Year, day, hour

A.D. July 27,1299–A.D August 11, 1840

Shall the king (#4428 meh'-lek)

#4428 meh'-lek; from 4427; a king: king, royal Strongs, 1979

#4428 me-lek n. m. (also used with compound proper names) king, royal, ruler, (human and divine); the great king 'is more prominent of a leader in a covenant agreement and is used of God (Ps. 48:2); The "king of kings" is the supreme sovereign and is not used of God in the OT. _Strongs_, 2001

#4427 maw-lak; a prim. root: to reign; incept. to ascend the throne: causat. to induct into royalty, hence by (impl.) to take counsel;- consult X indeed, be (make, set a, set up), king, be (make) queen, (begin to, make to) reign (-ing), rule, X surely _Strongs_, 1979

#4427 ma-lak v. den. [Q] to reign as a king [N] to ponder, consider carefully within oneself [H] to make one king, have a coronation: [Ho] be made a king _Strongs_, 2001

#4427 maw-lak; a prim. root: to reign; incept. to ascend the throne: causat. to induct into royalty, hence by (impl.) to take counsel;- consult X indeed, be (make, seta, set up), king, be (make) queen, (begin to, make to) reign (-ing), rule, X surely _Strongs_, 1979

#4427 ma-lak v. den. [Q] to reign as a king [N] to ponder, consider carefully within oneself [H] to make one king, have a coronation: [Ho] be made a king _Strongs_, 2001

"They had a king over them." From the death of Mohamed (570–632) until near the close of the thirteenth century, the Mohammedans were divided into various factions under several leaders, with no general civil government extending over them all. Near the close of the thirteenth century, Othman founded a government which was has since been known as the Ottoman government, or empire, which grew until it extended over all the principal Mohammedan tribes, consolidating them into on grand monarchy.

Their king is called "the angel of the bottomless pit." An angel signifies a messenger, a minister, either good or bad, and not always a spiritual being. "The angel of the bottomless pit" would be the chief minister of the religion which came from thence when it was opened. That religion is Mohammedanism, and the sultan was its chief minister.

His name in the Hebrew tongue is "Abaddon," the destroyer; in Greek, "Apollyon," one that exterminates or destroys. Having two different names in two languages, it is evident that the character rather than the name of the power is intended to be represented. If so, as expressed in both languages, he is a destroyer. Such has always been the character of the Ottoman government.

But when did Othman make his first assault on the Greek empire?[447]

According to Gibbon, "It was on the twenty-seventh of July, in the year twelve hundred and ninety-nine of the Christian Era, that Othman first invaded the territory of Nicomaedia; and the singular accuracy of the date seems to disclose some foresight of the rapid and destructive growth of the monster."[448]

shall the king of the south (#5045 neh-gheb) **push** (#5055 naw-gakh) **at him**;

#5045 neh-gheb; from an unused root mean. To be parched; the south (from its drought):

c. the negheb or southern district of Judah, occasionally Egypt (as south of Pal.): south (country, side,-ward) Strongs, 1979 #5045 negeb n. [pr. m.] the Negev. Strongs, 2001

#5055 naw-gakh a prim. root: to but with the horns; fig. to war against:- gore, push (down, -ing) Strongs, 1979

#5055 na-gah v. [Q] to gore (a bull into a person); [P] to gore, push back, butt; to engage in pushing back, butting, thrusting Strongs, 2001 The king of the south has its philosophical belief roots in Egypt grounded in Pharaoh's proclamation "who is the Lord that I should obey his voice to let Israel go? I know not the Lord, neither will I let Israel go" (Ex. 5:2). From *Strongs.* 2001, the word for king #4428 meh-lek stems from #4427 maw-law, one definition meaning "to ponder, consider carefully within oneself." Thus Pharaoh could probably say, "Who is God that I should obey him.? Although Pharaoh had ample opportunity to behold God's workings in the 400-year history of Israel in Egypt, he chose to discredit, devalue, and discount, who God really is. It is perceived that within himself, he pondered and considered that the God of the Hebrews was not a powerful God.

200

The word for "push" (#5055 naw-gakh) in Deut. 33:17, speaking of Joseph says, "He shall 'push' the people 'together.'" This is in a good sense. But it is perceived that when vile person, i.e., the system of Roman Catholicism "pushes" believers, along with its belief in worship on Sunday instead of the Biblical Sabbath, Saturday toward a belief in evolution, as it were, on the provided for in love yet not designed to be experienced tails side of the love coin, in contrast to belief in God, the creator, on the head's side of the love coin as it were, as advocated in the fourth commandment (Ex. 20:8–11) and first angels message (Rev. 14:7), that is a bad sense.

The following sections are lifted from *http:www.the-scientist. com>...>April_2010_Issue>Uncategorized*

Researchers and historians have collected approximately fifteen thousand letters written both to and by Charles Darwin an effort to better understand his life and science. One of his most frequent contacts was Joseph Dalton Hooker, a botanist who helped identify many of the plant specimens collected during Darwin's HMS Beagle journey, including his famed stop at the Galapagos Islands. Their discourse, which spanned more than 1,400 letters over four decades—including the one pictured here dated January 11, 1844—was one of the first places Darwin expressed his theory of natural selection as a driver of speciation and evolution.[449]

The following sections are lifted from *http://history1800s.about.com/ od/scienceculture/a/darwin-on-origin-of- species_published 1859 and*

This led to "Charles Darwin published On the Origin of Species on November 24, 1859,[450] so that by the time of Pope John Paul II (1978–2005), he advocated that "evolution is more than a theory."[451]

The following sections are lifted from *http://www.icr.org/article/ evolution-*

"Strong creationists (discussed later in this article) not only among lay Catholics, but among Catholic scientists as well 'oppose evolution.' We mention Dr. Guy Berthault of France, Dr. Roberto Fondi (paleontologist) and Dr. Giuseppe Sermont (geneticist), refute evolution. In this country, Dr. Wolfgang Smith has a 'devastating critique of evolution in general. He says that the doctrine of macroevolution 'is totally bereft of scientific sanction. . .

'It is too bad that Pope John Paul II (who is not a scientist) did not consult such real Catholic Scientists as Wolfgang Smith before glibly stating, as he did, that 'new knowledge leads us to recognize in the theory of evolution, more than a hypothesis.'"[452]

So it is perceived that God, working through His seven literal or figurative churches, located in Turkey, is the antitypical king of the north on, as it were, the heads side of the love coin, or on top of the vertical shank of a horizontally spinning top with inside faith creatures on the upper side of that top, spinning in allegiance to God. This is perceived to be different from outside faith belief, denying God's creatorship, expressed in evolution as the kingly force of the south, where Satan/ (outside faith science) dwells on the bottom point of the vertical shank in the horizontal spinning top, where creatures in rebellion against God live on the tails side of the love coin. Yet God in His mercy and love desires to draw people from the inherited since the fall, living as it were, on the tails side of the love coin, or bottom side of the horizontal spinning top to come out of their rebellion and figuratively/spiritually through the power of Calvary to be restored and once again live in allegiance to God, and "Fear Him" (Rev. 14:7) being "in the world but not of the world" (Rev. 15:19) overcoming sin.

****

The following sections are lifted from *http://en.wikipedia.org/wiki/Irreligion_In_France*

The French Revolution marked a turning point for the ascendancy of atheism to a preeminent position as a cognitive and cultural stance against the papal supremacy and the Holy Roman Empire across Europe and through the world. Now known as the atheist Cult of Reason ideology, established by Jacques Heber, Pierre Gaspard Chaumentte, and their supporters and intended as a replacement for Christianity, and was replete with ceremonious destruction of Christian relics, conversion of churches into Temples of Reason and the personification of Reason as a goddess, it also held such festivities as the Festival of Reason (or Festival of Liberty), dated on November 10 (20 Brumaire) 1793. The cult of Reason, which strongly advocated the destruction of Christian and theistic cultural influences by force, was opposed to Robespierre's Cult of the Supreme Being, which was considered a deistic cult which referred back to the theism of Christianity. The Cult of Reason was finally ended by Robespierre and the Committee of Public Safety through their execution of Hebert and several of his followers on March 24, 1794, having ascended just seven months earlier.[453]

The words "having ascended just seven months earlier" go along with the Strongs, 2001 definition for the #4427 maw-law, "to ponder, consider within oneself" which is the root word king.

The following sections are lifted from *http://en.wikipedia.org/wiki/ Dechristianization_of_France_during_the_F*

Dechristianization of France during the French Revolution *http:// dictionary.sensagent.com/Dechristianization%20 of % 20France %20 during%20the%20French%20 Revolution/en-en/*

I. Dechristianisation of France during the French Revolution.

    A. The dechristianization of France during the French Revolution is conventional description of the result of a number of separate policie conducted by various governments of France between the start of the French Revolution in 1789 and the Concordat of 1801, forming the bas of the later and less radical Laicite movement. The goal of the campaig was the destruction of Catholic religious practice and of the religio itself.[454]

II. The Church under the Ancient Regime

    A. In 18th-century France, ninety-five percent of the population were ad of the Catholic Church; most of the rest were Protestant Huguenot although greatly outnumbered by the Catholics, nonetheless retained powerful positions in French local governments. (A small population of amounting to around 40,000, also existed, and a very small community; in a country whose total population was at least 27 however, these groups remained numerically negligible.) The Ancien institutionalized the authority of the clergy in its status as the First Estate the realm. As the largest landowner in the country, the Catholic controlled properties which provided massive revenues from its tena Church also had an enormous income from.

    B. Constitution. For others the oath presented a grave matter of con eased only on 13 April 1791 when the pope, who had the collection tithes. Since the Church kept the registry of births, deaths, and marria was the only institution that provided primary and secondary educati hospitals, it influenced all citizens.

New policies of the Revolutionary authorities

The program of dechristianization waged against Catholicism and eventually against all forms of Christianity included:

- Confiscation of Church lands, which were to be the security for the new Assignant currency.
- Destruction of statues, plates and other iconography from places of worship

- Destruction of crosses, bells and other external signs of worship
- The institution of revolutionary and civic cults, including the Cult of Reason and subsequently the Cult of the Supreme Being.
- The enactment of a law on October 21, 1793, making all nonjuring priests and all persons who harboured them liable to death on sight.

The climax was reached with the celebration of the goddess "Reason" in Notre Dame Cathedral on 10 November 1793.

The dechristianization campaign can be seen as the logical extension of the materialist philosophies of some leaders of the enlightenment, while for others with more prosaic concerns it was an opportunity to unleash resentments against the Church and clergy.[455]

[The seeds of evolution advocated by Darwin in 1844 to in the "Vestages of Natural Selection" gave way to Darwin's "Survival of the fittest" which led many years latter to the pope advocating evolution.]

at him

The following section is lifted from *http://en/wikipedia.org/wiki/ Dechristianisation_of_France_during_the_French*

I. "The Revolution" and the Church

In August 1789, the State cancelled the taxing power of the Church. The issue of church property became central to the policies of the new revolutionary government. Declaring that all church property in France belonged to the nation, confiscations were ordered and church properties were sold at public auction. In July 1790, the National Constituent Assembly published the Civil Constitution of the Clergy that stripped clerics of their special rights—the clergy were to be made employees of the state, elected by their parish or bishopric, and the number of bishoprics was to be reduced—and required all priests and bishops to swear an oath of fidelity to the new order or face dismissal, deportation or death.

French priests had to receive Papal approval to sign such an oath, and Pius VI spent almost eight months deliberating on the issue. On April 13, 1791, the pope denounced the Constitution resulting in a split in French Catholic church. Abjuring priests ("jurors") became known as "constitutional clergy" and nonjuring priests as "refractory clergy."

In September 1792, the Legislative Assembly legalized divorce, contrary to Catholic doctrine. At the same time, the State took control of the birth, death, and marriage registers away from the Church. An ever-increasing view that the Church was a counterrevolutionary force exacerbated the social and economic grievances and violence erupted in towns and cities across France.

In Paris, over a forty-eight hour period beginning on September 2, 1792, as the legislative Assembly (successor to the National Constituent Assembly) dissolved into chaos, three Church bishops and more than two hundred priests were massacred by angry mobs; this constituted part of what would become known as the September Massacres. Priests were among those drowned in mass executions *(noyades)* for reason under the direction of Jean-Baptiste Carrier, priests and nuns were among the mass executions at Lyons, for separatism, on the orders of Joseph Fouche and Collot d'Herbois. Hundreds more priests were imprisoned and made to suffer in abominable conditions in the port of Rochefort.

Anti-church laws were passed by the legislative Assembly and its successor, the National Convention, as well as by department councils throught the country. Many of the acts of dechristianization in 1793 were motivated by the seizure of church gold and silver to finance the war effort. In November 1973, the departement council of Indre-et-Loir abolished the word dimanche (English: Sunday)[citation needed]. The Gregorian calendar, an instrument decreed by Pope Gregory in 1582, was replaced by the French Republican Calendar which abolished the Sabbath, saints' days and any references to the Church.

Anticlerical parades were held, and the Archbishop of Paris was forced to resign his duties and made to replace his mitre with the rod "Cap of Liberty." Street and place names with any sort of religious connotation were changed, such as the town of St. Tropez, which became Heraclee. Religious holidays were banned and replaced with holidays to celebrate the harvest and other non-religious symbols. Robespierre and his colleagues decided to support both Catholicism and the rival atheistic *Cult of reason* with the *Cult of the Supreme Being.* Just six weeks before his arrest, on June 8, 1794 the still-powerful Robespierre personally led a vast procession through Paris to the Tuileries garden in a ceremony to inaugurate the new faith…"

The dechristianisation of France reached its zenith around the middle of 1794 with the fall of Robespierre. By early 1795 a return some form of religion-based faith was beginning to take shape and a law passed on

February 21, 1795, legalized public worship, albeit with strict limitations. The ringing of church bells, religious processions and displays of the Christian cross were still forbidden.

As late as 1799, priests were still being imprisoned or deported to penal colonies and persecution only worsened after the French army led by General Louis Alexander Berthier captured Rome and imprisoned Pope Pius VI, who would die in captivity in Valence, France in August 1799. Ultimately, with Napoleon now in ascendancy in France, year-long negotiations between government officials and the new Pope, Pius VII, led to the Concordat of 1801, formally ending the dechristianization period and establishing the rules for a relationship between the Roman Church and the French State.

Victims of the Reign of Terror totaled somewhere between 20,000 and 40,000. According to one estimate, among those condemned by the revolutionary tribunals, about 8 percent were aristocrats, 6 percent clergy, 14 percent middle class, and 70 percent were workers or peasants accused of hoarding, evading the draft, desertion, rebellion, and other purported crimes. Of these social groupings, the clergy of the Roman Catholic Church suffered proportionately the greater loss.

While persecution of certain Roman Catholic clerics and monastic orders occurred during the Third Republic, the Concordat of 1801 endured for more than a century until it was abrogated by the government of the Third Republic, which established a policy of laicite on December 11, 1905.
Toll on the Church

Under threat of death, imprisonment, military conscription, and loss of income, about twenty thousand constitutional priests were forced to abdicate and hand over their letters of ordination, and six thousand to nine thousand of them were coerced to marry. Many abandoned their pastoral duties altogether. Nonetheless, some of those who had abdicated continued covertly to minister to the people.

By the end of the decade, approximately thirty thousand priests had been forced to leave France, and others who did not leave were executed. Most French parishes were left without the service of a priest and deprived of the sacraments. Any non-juring priest faced the guillotine or deportation to French Guianna. By Easter 1794, few of France's forty thousand churches remained open; many had been closed, sold, destroyed, or converted to other uses.

Victims of revolutionary violence, whether religious or not, were popularly treated as Christian martyrs, and the places where they were killed became pilgrimage destinations. Catechising in the home, folk religion, syncretic and heterodox practices all became more common. The long-term effects on religious practice in France were significant. Many who were dissuaded from their traditional religious practices never resumed them."[456]

The following sections are lifted from Cult of Reason-Wikipedia
http://en.wikipedia.org/wiki/Cult_of_Reason,
http://en.wikipedia.org/wiiki/Goddess_of Reason

"Cult of Reason"

From Wikipedia, the free encyclopedia

The **Cult of Reason** (////////French: Culte de la Raison)[note1] was a belief system established in France and intended as a replacement for Roman Catholicism during the French Revolution

Origins

Opposition to the Roman Catholic Church was integral among the causes of the French Revolution, and this anticlericalism solidified into official government policy in 1792 after the First French Republic was declared. Most of the dechristianisation of France was motivated by political and economic concerns, but philosophical alternatives to the Church developed gradually as well. Among the growing heterodoxy, the structural concepts of the Culte de la Raison became defined by Jacques Hebert, Antoine-Francois Momoro, Pierre Gaspard Chaumette, Joseph Fouche and other radical revolutionaries. Jacques Hebert gained a significant degree of popularity after being arrested for attacks on Girondists. Upon his release and with his newfound popularity, along with Pierre Gaspard Chaumette, Hebert founded the "worship of Reason." Unlike Robespierre's Cult of the Supreme Being, Hebert's cult rejected the existence of a deity. The cult was founded on the principles of the Enlightenment and anticlericalism.

Philosophy

The cult of reason was explicitly anthropocentric. Its goal was the perfection of mankind through the attainment of Truth and Liberty, and its guiding principle to this goal was the exercise of the human faculty of Reason. A careful distinction was always drawn between the rational respect of Reason and the veneration of an idol. There is one thing that one must not tire telling people," Momoro explained, "Liberty reason, truth are only abstract beings. They are not gods, for properly speaking they are part of ourselves."

The overarching theme of the Cult was summarized by Anacharsis Clootz, who declared at the Festival of Reason that henceforward there would be "one God only, Le Peuple." The Cult was intended as a civic religion— inspired by the works of Rousseau, Quatremere de Quincy and Jacques-Louis David, it presented "an explicit religion of man."

Revolutionary impact

Adherence to the Cult of Reason became a defining attribute of the Hebertist faction. It was also pervasive among the ranks of the *sans-culottes*. Numerous political factions, anticlerical groups and events only loosely connected to the cult have come to be amalgamated with its name. The earliest public demonstrations ranged from "wild masquerades" redolent of earlier spring festivals to outright persecutions, including ransackings of churches and synagogues in which religious and royal images were defaced.

Joseph Fouche

As a military commander dispatched by the Jacobins to enforce their new laws, Fouche led a particularly zealous campaign of dechristenisation. His methods were brutal but efficient, and helped spread the developing creed through many parts of France. In his jurisdiction, Fouche ordered all crosses and statues removed from graveyards, and he gave the cult one of its elemental tenets when he decreed that all cemetery gates must bear only one inscription—"Death is an eternal sleep." Fouche went so far as to declare a new civic religion of his own, virtually interchangeable with what would become known as the Cult of Reason, a ceremony he dubbed the "Feast of Brutus" on 22 September 1793.

Festival of Reason

The nationwide *Fete de la Raison*, supervised by Hebert and Momoro on 20 Brumaire, Year II (10 November 1793) came to epitomize the new republican way of religion. In ceremonies devised and organized by Chaumette, churches across France were transformed into modern Temples of Reason. The largest ceremony of all was at the cathedral of Notre Dame in Paris. The Christian altar was dismantled and an altar to Liberty was installed and the inscription "to Philosophy" was carved in stone over the cathedral's doors. Festive girls in white Roman dress and tricolor sashes milled around a costumned Goddess of Reason who "impersonated Liberty." To avoid statuary and idolatry the Goddess figures were portrayed by living women, and in Paris the role was played by Momoro's own wife Sophie, who is said to have dressed "provocatively" and according to Thomas Carlyle, "made one of the best Goddesses of Reason, though her teeth were a little defective."

Before his retirement, Georges Danton had warned against dechristianizers and their "rhetorical excesses" but support of the Cult only increased in the zealous early years of the First Republic. By late 1793, it was conceivable that the Convention might accept the invitation to attend the Paris festival en masse, but the unshakeable opposition of Maximillien Robespierre and others like him prevented it from becoming an official affair. Undeterred, Chaumette and Hebert proudly led a sizable delegation of deputies to Notre Dame.

Reaction

Many contemporary accounts reported the Festival of Reason as a "lurid," affair of scandalous "depravities" although some scholars have disputed their veracity. These accounts, real or embellished, galvanized anti-revolutionary forces and even caused many dedicated Jocobins like Robespierre to publicly separate themselves from the radical faction. Robespierre particularly scorned the Cult and denounced the festivals as "ridiculous farces."

In the spring of 1794, the Cult of Reason was faced with official repudiation when Robespirre, nearing complete dictatorial power during the Reign of Terror, announced his own establishment of a new deistic religion for the Republic, the Cult of the Supreme Being. Robesierre denounced the Hebertistes on various philosophical and political grounds, specifically rejecting their perceived atheism. When Hebert, Momoro, Ronsin, Vincent and others were sent to the guillotine on 4 Germinal, Year II (24 March 1794), the cult lost its most influential leadership; Chaumette and other Hebertistes followed them four days later, the Cult of Reason effectively ceased to exist. Both cults were officially banned by Napoleon Bonaparte with his Law on Cults of 18 Germinal, Year X.[457]

The following sections are lifted from _http://www.historytoday.com/gemma-_

In 1789, the year of the outbreak of the French Revolution, Catholicism was the official religion of the French State. The French Catholic Church, known as the Gallican Church, recognized the authority of the pope as head of the Roman Catholic church but had not negotiated certain liberties that privileged the authority of the French monarch, giving it a distinct national identity characterized by considerable autonomy. France's population of 28 million was almost entirely Catholic, with full membership of the state denied to Protestant

209

and Jewish minorities. Being French effectively meant being Catholic. Yet, by 1794, France's churches and religious orders were closed down and religious worship suppressed. How did it come to this? What did revolutionaries hope to achieve? And why did Napoleon set out to reverse the situation?

The Decline of Catholicism?

Historians are divided over the strength of Catholicism in late eighteenth-century France. Some suggest that it was still flourishing after the efforts of the Council of Trent (1545–63) to reform and revitalize the Church, as witnessed by its well-educated clergy, numerous and varied religious orders, and renewed forms of worship. Others trace a period of decline, with a small but noticeable decrease in religious observance in the decades before the Revolution. Region studies of religious belief and practice reveal significant differences between urban and provincial France, between elites and the rest of the population, and to a lesser degree, between men and women. What is clear, however, is that the eighteenth-century Church was attracting growing criticism from the philosophes, the intellectuals of the Enlightenment who systematically questioned every aspect of French government and society.

The Enlightenment quest to promote reason as the basis for legitimacy and progress found little to praise in the church. While the philosophes appreciated the value of religion in promoting moral and social order, the Church itself was condemned for its power and influence. The scandal surrounding the divisive theological movement of Jansenism, exacerbated by the heavy-handed treatment of its followers earlier in the century, furnished one reason for attacking the Church's authority and its close links with the monarchy. France's lack of toleration for religious minorities provided another. Although the philosopher Voltaire managed some praise for young nuns who devoted their lives to caring for the sick and poor, the clergy were seen as less useful. The writer Louis-Sebastien Mercier complained in 1782 that Paris was full of priests and tonsured clerics who serve neither the church nor the state' and who were occupied with nothing but 'useless and trifling' matters. Criticism was specifically directed at monasteries where monks and nuns spent their days in prayer, much to the ire of philosophes who though they should instead be reproducing for the good of the nation. The solemn vows taken by these men and women, binding them to the religious state for life, also led to concerns about individual liberty. Denis Diderot rallied against the lifelong nature of these vows, warning about decisions taken too young in life and, in his novel La Religieuse (The Nun), raising the spectre of young woman forced to be a nun against her will. Although most philosophes promoted reform rather than destruction, their comments gave encouragement to a growing anticlericalism whose spite was sharpened by resentment of the Church's wealth.

The Church's revenue in 1789 was estimated at an immense—and possibly exaggerated—150 million lives. It owned around six percent of land throughout France, and its abbeys, churches, monasteries and convents, as well as the schools, hospitals and other institutions it operated, formed a visible reminder of the Church's dominance in French society. The Church was also permitted to collect the tithe, worth a nominal on-tenth of agricultural production, and was exempt from direct taxation on its earnings. This prosperity caused considerable discontent, best illustrated in the cahiers de doleancesor or statement of, sent from throughout the kingdom to be discussed at the meeting of the Estates-General in May 1789. Calls for the reform or abolition of the tithe and for the limitation of Church property were joined by complaints from parish priests who, excluded from the wealth bestowed upon the upper echelons of the Church hierarchy, often struggled to get by. When crowds began to gather in Paris on 15 July 1789, the religious house of Saint-Lazare and its neighbouring convent were among the first places search for supplies and weapons. The Catholic Church may have been the church of the majority of the French people, but its wealth and perceived abuses meant that it did not always have their trust.

The Nationalisation of Property

On the eve of the Revolution, the French state was on the verge of bankruptcy. Repeated attempts at financial reform had floundered but the Revolution opened the way for a new approach that, from the beginning, involved the Church. On 4 August 1789, when the remains of France's feudal past were abolished in a night of sweeping reforms, the clergy agreed to give up the tithe and allow the state to take over its funding. The Declaration of the Rights of Man and Citizen, adopted on 26 August, made no recognition of the special position of the Catholic church. With all authority located henceforth within the nation, the Church now found itself open—and vulnerable—to further reform. On 2 November 1789, France's new National Assembly, known as the Constituent Assembly, passed a decree that placed all church property "at the disposition of the nation." Talleyrand, the bishop of Autun and one of the few clerics to support the measure, argued that all Church property rightfully belonged to the nation and that its return, by helping to bring about a better society, should therefore be viewed as a "religious act."

Despite clerical support for the Revolution itself, this decree became the first in a series that targeted the Church in a way that soon cast doubt on the revolution's motives. On 29 October 1789, just days before the nationalization of Church property, the Assembly heard that two women in a nearby convent were being forced into the religious life. A proposal was immediately made to halt the taking of solemn vows. Not only did this development associate the Church with the scheming and corruption featured in the anticlerical literature of the eighteenth century, but it prepared the way for the closure of France's monasteries and the departure of their inhabitants, decreed on 13 February 1790. It was hoped that the quick sale of monasteries and their contents would help stabilize the nation's finances. The announcement was met with thousands of letters of protest. The new French state had not only taken control of the Church's revenue and property, but, through such radical intervention, seemed to be redrawing the boundaries between church and state.

Growing Suspicion

Charged with the Church's financial administration, the Assembly now took the opportunity to reorganize it. On 12 July 1790 the Assembly approved the Civil Constitution of the Clergy, a constitution whose very name reflected the state's new control of Church affairs. Among acts the constitution's reforms, dioceses were redrawn in line with state administrative divisions, clergy were to be paid by the state according to a new salary scale, and priests and bishops ere to be elected by citizens. The pope's refusal to approve the Constitution, together with growing criticism from conservative members of the Assembly decreed on 27 November 1790 that all clergy must take a public oath of loyalty to the Constitution or surrender their salary and position.

As Nigel Aston has suggested, this oath became "a referendum on whether one's first loyalties were to Catholicism or the Revolution." Figures varied considerably between regions, but over 50 percent of parish clergy swore their loyalty to the better way than what Scripture advocated in Christ's saying, "No man cometh to the Father but by me." Endorsing this view often hesitating, issued his condemnation. Those who took the oath became known as "jurors" while those who refused were labeled "non-jurors" or "refractory priests." A growing number fled overseas, joining those nobles and clergy who had already emigrated rather that live under the revolutionary regime. The French population gradually split between those who supported the "Constitutional Church" and those who remained loyal to refractory priests, initially allowed to continue. Rather than confirming the allegiance of French clergy to a state operated church, the oath had put before them a decision that, by forcing them to choose between the Constitutional Church and Rome, would cause a schism among French Catholics for the next decade and generate hostility toward the Revolution and its aims.

Meanwhile, support for the refractory Church became increasingly associated with counter-revolution. Émigré priests and bishops preached against the Revolution from abroad, while the refractories that remained became a focal point for broader resentment of the Revolution. The suspicion with which many people viewed constitutional priests, especially in parts of regional France, helped create popular support for the counterrevolutionary cause. This association had immediate implications. In the first week of April 1791, the sisters of a Parisian religious congregation were attacked by crowds of women who accused them of teaching 'false principles' to children and plotting counter-revolution with refractory priests. Such sentiments found official expression in the debates of the 'Legislative Assembly,' formed in October 1791 and determined to carry through the policies of the early Revolution. In November it stopped the pensions of refractory priests and prohibited their use of religious buildings. On 6 April 1792 it banned all forms of religious dress, seeking to abolish this visible reminder of the ancient regime and force people to see priests as "citizens like any others."

France's declaration of war on Austria on 20 April 1792 and its early losses cast further suspicion on refractory clergy and their followers, now suspected of plotting with the enemy. The fall of the monarchy on 10 August provided added impetus for the destruction of anything connected with the ancient regime. The Assembly suppressed all remaining religious orders, including those staffing schools and hospitals, and ordered remaining non-jurors to leave or be arrested and deported. Concern peaked on 2 September when news arrived that the fortress-town of Verdun near Paris had fallen to the allied Prussian forces. Parisians, imaging that imprisoned counter- revolutionaries were preparing to break out and join the enemy, dispersed their own preventative justice when they descended on the city's prisons and, over the course of several days, slaughtered over 1,200 prisoners, including at least 200 priests. The September Massacres made clear the distrust that would prevent any accommodation between the Church and the new republic proclaimed on 22 September 1792.

The new Republican government, known as the Convention, responded to growing civil unrest and the ongoing overseas threat with the Reign of Terror. The Revolutionary Tribunal, established on 10 March 1793, aimed to demonstrate that persons of danger to the Republic were being identified and punished. Laws of September 1793 and June 1794 targeting "enemies of liberty" and enemies of the people saw mounting numbers of priests and nuns arrested and placed on trial. Their charges included not only counterrevolution but "fanaticism" and possession of items used in the celebration of mass, again demonstrating the suspicion now attached to religious worship. Only a small percentage were guillotined, but their trials—designed to set an example—instead garnered further support for counterrevolutionary forces in the Vendee and other parts of western France and drove religious practice underground.
Revolutionary Religion

Although the constitutional church had been permitted to continue its work, the Convention now considered Catholicism in any form suspicious. Its association with ancient regime France, its adherence to values not of the Revolution's making, and the private nature of worship seemed incompatible with the values of the Republic. From her spring a movement referred to as "dechristianisation," which aimed to excise religion from French society. Constitutional priests were advised to abandon the priesthood and were encouraged—or in some cases forced— to marry. Any priest that continued to practice, whether constitutional or refractory, now faced arrest and deportation. In October 1793, public worship was forbidden and over the next few months all visible signs of Christianity were removed, a policy pursued with particular enthusiasm by revolutionary armies eager to seek revenge on the institution that harboured so many counterrevolutionaries. Church bells were pulled down and melted, ostensibly to help the war effort, crosses were taken from churches and cemeteries, and statues, relics and works of art were seized and sometimes destroyed. Such iconoclasm caused considerable concern at official levels, not least because of the destruction wrought on France's artistic and cultural heritage. On 23 November 1793, churches were closed, to be converted into warehouses, manufacturing works or even stables. Streets and other public places bearing the names of saints were given new, often Republican themed names, and time itself was recast to further repudiate France's Christian past. The Revolutionary calendar started with the advent of the French Republic (Year 1). The names of its months reflected the seasons and its ten-day week eliminated Sunday as a day of rest and worship. Although such measures were unevenly applied, and in many cases met with considerable local opposition, they reinforced the message that Christianity had no place in the Republic.

The revolutionary government had learnt, however, that when destroying the past, it was wise to have something to put in its place. The creation of the Republic in 1792 had given rises to ceremonies and festivals that aimed that aimed to make a religion of the Revolution itself, commemorating revolutionary martyrs as its saints and venerating the tricolor cockade and red liberty cap as its sacred symbols. Prominent among such revolutionary "cults," as they were known, was the Cult of Reason which recognized no god but instead worshiped the goddess of reason in the former churches, now known as "temples of reason." Robespierre, wary of atheism and the political forces behind certain cults, introduced on 7 May 1794 the Cult of the Supreme Being, which he envisaged as a new state religion. Its recognition of a supreme deity would, it was hoped, attract and harness the persistent desire for religious belief and worship among Frenchmen and women while its proclamation of the soul's immortality would encourage moral behavior of the type that would ensure a stable and virtuous Republic. But the festival of the Supreme Being, held on 8 June 1794 throughout France and presided over in Paris by Robespierre, provided little beyond spectacle and, like other cults, it attracted minimal interest outside urban centres. Catholicism had been squeezed out of the Republic, but alternatives imposed from above failed to catch on. The fall of Robespierre in July 1794 brought a thaw toward religious practice. Dechristianisation had forced religious observance into the privacy of the home. With the emigration and abdication of so many priests, and the disruption of regular forms of worship, the laity had become accustomed to taking over services, even performing 'white masses' when there was no priest available. The convention, anxious to achieve some form of stability, recognized that somehow it would have to accommodate this private worship. It did so by announcing on 21 February 1795 the formal separation of Church and State. Churches were reopened, refractory priests were released from jail, and both constitutional and refractory priests were permitted to practice on the condition that they promised to respect the laws of the Republic.

Yet complete separation proved impossible. Religion was still considered a threat and subsequent decrees sought to monitor worship and ban outward signs of religion, such as statues or religious dress from the public eye. Royalist uprisings led to the reapplication of earlier laws concerning refractory priests, as did the coup of 18 Fructidor (4 September 1797), which saw thousands of refractory priests arrested yet again. Like earlier governments, the Directory (November 1795–99) tried introducing alternatives to Catholicism, noticeably in the new cult of Theophilanthropy. Yet again, these failed to gain popular support. The Directory instead witnessed a religious revival in which Catholic men— especially women— played an important role in reestablishing their faith around the wreckage left by the Revolution. Any new regime would have to acknowledge this revival and, if it wanted to ensure the loyalty of France's Catholics, make a place for a Church that could bridge the divisions, confusion, pain, and bitterness of the previous decade.[458]

The following sections are lifted from *www.napoleon- series.org/ research/napoleon/c_religion1.html*

Napoleon I, while continuously striving to influence French society and gain new backing from the believers of any faith that lived within his empire, devoted considerable time to his efforts of manipulating an institution almost as old as the Roman Empire. The relationship between the Catholic Church and the French state deeply concerned the emperor. Napoleon I greatly understood the power of a religious majority, as first evidenced by his actions during his military campaign to conquer Egypt from 1798 to 1799. The then General Bonaparte, who liked to compare himself to Julius Caesar, after crushing a violent uprising in Egypt, pardoned the imams and sheiks of the El-Azhar mosque, who had done nothing against the French, while ordering the beheading of the real rebels. Just as Alexander the Great and his army had marched through the desert to visit the shrine of Amon, Bonaparte treated Islamic sites with admiration and respect during his own desert odyssey. Bonaparte felt flattered by those Egyptians who called him Sultan Kebir, which literally means the "Breat" Sultan. Bonaparte even went so far as to outright state that the Koran predicted his defeat of the Mameluke caste that ruled Egypt and he also talked of the conversion of the French Army of the Orient to Islam. In the spring 1799, Bonaparte actually had the ulemas of El-Azhar proclaim that Sultan Kebir "loved the Muslims, cherished the Prophet, instructed himself by reading the Koran every day, and desired to build a mosque unrivalled in splendor and to embrace the Muslim faith.

When Napoleon Bonaparte returned to France in 1799, he made use of his past experiences with religion to gain support from the Catholic majority in France that had been disillusioned by revolutionary excesses. The activities of the various revolutionary regimes had created religious disunity, which Rene Remond sees as "a final religious war," evidenced by the police's recording of at least some violation of the laws restricting public worship in every one of the sixty-nine cantons of the department of Yonne between the fall of Robespierre and the coming of Bonaparte. In the aftermath of the left- wing coup d'etat of September 1797, France had endured a comprehensive two-year dechristianization campaign, which lasted until December 1799, when Bonaparte overthrew Barras' feeble government known as the Directory. In that year Bonaparte recognized what the directors did not: he understood that only the Catholic religion stirred the emotions of the people, could effectively mend the religious divisions of the revolution, provide a basis for morality, and support the authority of the new Consular regime. Within two months after the coup d'etat of brumaire an VIII Firs Consul Bonaparte allowed non-alienated churches to re-open and began to grant amnesty to deported priests. As generous as these efforts appear, Bonaparte only intended to restore Catholicism to a certain extent, without returning the Catholic Church's full *ancient regime* privileges. Evidence exists suggesting that although Bonaparte did not personally adhere to any definite faith he nonetheless wisely wanted to pour water on the fires of animosity that had erupted against the Catholic church, so that a united Catholic church in France could serve as a veritable fortress of order and social peace.

.[] From 1801 to 1802, Bonaparte and his diplomats negotiated and had passed into law this concordat with Pope Pius VII that reversed anticlerical revolutionary laws passed in the 1790s and reestablished Catholicism's preeminent religious position amongst the French. In some respects, the Concordat went back to the earlier concordat of Leo X and François I in 1516, which allowed the French government to supervise the appointment of the higher clergy and the payment of the lower ones. This new concordat of Bonaparte and Pius VII lasted until 1905, when the anticlerical backlash following the Dreyfus Affair made the separation of church and state palatable to French political-religious-taste-buds. Still, that concordat of 1801 endured for over on hundred years indicates that the Concordat can be justifiably regarded as Bonaparte's most durable civil achievement after the Napoleonic Code.

The Concordat contained many important components. Amusingly, Bonaparte allowed compulsory priestly celibacy to be reversed in his concordat with Rome, which shows Bonaparte's wish to determine even the sexual behavior of his subjects. The Concordat also significantly incorporated an agreement establishing special relations between France and the papacy that made Pius VII available to sanction Bonaparte's acceptance of a crown at a coronation. This arrangement foreshadowed an event that plays a key role in illustrating the power of religion in Bonaparte's propaganda efforts. This historic event occurred on December 2, 1804, when Pope Pius VII attended Napoleon I's coronation in Paris. Napoleon I's coronation did not include the traditional sacramental rites of other imperial or royal coronations, which meaningfully indicated a decrease in the papal role in consecrating the new emperor. Furthermore, although Pope Leo III had crowned Charlemagne in December 800, Napoleon I crowned himself during his coronation rather than allowing Pius VII to retain this millennium old honor. This groundbreaking act symbolically meant that Napoleon I did not owe his crown to any divine power that the pope correspondingly did not hold a position higher that the emperor. Subsequently, Napoleon I continued his attempts to supersede the pope's authority by publishing the Imperial Catechism in April 1806, summoning a nation council of French and Italian bishops in Paris in June 1811, and negotiating the Concordat of Fontainebleau on January 25, 1813.

Through these actions and through others, Napoleon I exploited the Church to glorify himself, more so that God. Three church feasts, Ascension Day, All Saints on November 1, and Christmas, became state festivals, while the Church sanctified two state occasions, July 14 and December 2, the anniversary of the coronation and the victory of Austerlitz. Perhaps the most poignant example of Napoleon I's efforts to aggrandize himself in the religious sense can be seen with how the Imperial Catechism proscribed the veneration of the emperor's name day. While the *ancient regime* attached the feast of St. Louis, the patron saint of every king from 1610 to 1792, to August 15, the feast of Assumption, Napoleon I replaced the royal saint with St. Napoleon. The catechism went further still by asserting that Napoleon I had been raised up by God in difficult circumstances that he was God's anointed, and that good Christians must love him, pay taxes, accept conscription or go to hell." Thus progressively, Catholicism had become a religion of imperial grandeur under Napoleon I.[459]

The following section was lifted from *http://en.wikipedia.org/wiki/Mamluk_Sultanate_(Cairo)*

Napoleon defeated Mamluk troops in the Battle of the Pyramids in 1798 and drove them to upper Egypt. The Mamluks used their cavalry charge tactics changed only by the use of muskets.[460]

The followingsection was lifted from *http://en.wikipedia.org/wiki/Napoleon_Wars*

War of the Seventh Coalition 1815

The Seventh Coalition (1815) pitted Britain, Russia, Prussia, Sweden, Austria, the Netherlands and a number of German states against France. The period known as the Hundred Days began after Napoleon escaped from Elba and landed at Cannes (March 1815). Travelling to Paris, picking up support as he went he eventually overthrew the restored Louis XVIII. The Allies rapidly gathered their armies to meet him again. Napoleon raised 280,000 men, whom he distributed among several armies. To add to the 90,000 strong standing army, he recalled well over a quarter of a million veterans from past campaigns and issued a decree for the eventual draft of 2.5 million new men into the French army. This faced an initial Coalition force of about 700,000 – although Coalition campaign plans provided for one million front-line soldiers, supported by around 200,000 garrison, logistics and other auxiliary personnel. The Coalition intended this force to have overwhelming numbers against the numerically inferior imperial French army-which in fact came close to reaching Napoleon's goal of more than 2.5 million under arms.

Political Effects

In most European countries, subjugation in the French Empire brought with it many liberal methods of the French Revolution including democracy, due process in courts, abolition of serfdom, reduction of the power of the Catholic Church, and a demand for constitutional limits on monarchs. The increasing voice of the middle classes with rising commerce and industry meant that restored European monarchs found it difficult to restore pre-revolutionary absolutism, and had to retain many of the reforms enacted during Napoleon/s rule. Institutional legacies remain to this day in the form of civil-law legal systems, which clearly redacted codes compiling their basic laws-an enduring legacy of the Napoleonic Code[461]

The following section was lifted from *www.bibleexplained.com/revelation/r-Background*

By 1789 King Louis XVI and his royalist party were losing power rapidly. A national assembly was proclaimed in June. In July the Bastille, which had held political prisoners, was taken. In October, martial law was decreed, and in November church (meaning Catholic) property was nationalized and sold to help a failing economy. Thus the revolt was against religious and civil traditional authority. Both had suppressed the people. Earlier event such as the St. Bartholomew Massacre 1315c had been tools in the hands of the state to fulfill the ends of the dominant church. This time the throne as well as the altar were objects of the developing disbelief and unrest.

Reign of Terror

The time historians call "the reign of terror" began in 1793. King Louis XVI was beheaded on January 21. Power was shifting among political factions and the guillotine often couldn't keep up with the demand to remove heads.

Rejection of Religion

On October 5, 1793, the law for a new calendar was passed replacing the seven-day week with a ten-day "decade." Also the months were renamed and days allocated differently. This meant that there was officially no longer a weekly day of worship. This was the major event that initiated the "dechristinization."

Many of the clergy, both Catholic and Protestant, resigned their posts to join the revolution. With excitement high, the local and regional governments proclaimed grand celebrations at the Notre cathedral. That was November 10, 1973 (20th of Brumaie, by the new calendar). A statue of Liberty would replace the image of the "Blessed Virgin." The Mayor of Paris called this ceremony the "Festival of Liberty and Reason."

The ceremony of the 20th Brumaire was very important. The insignia of the Catholic religion in the Church of Notre-Dame had been covered up, and a mound had been heaped up, on which stood a Greek temple, with an inscription "To Philosophy" and with four busts of philosophers. The "Torch of Truth" flamed upon an altar. Young girls defiled [marched] in procession, they were clade in white, with tricolor shashes. Wore wreaths of flowers and carried torches. Then there emerged from the temple a beautiful woman, dressed in a mantle of blue and wearing the red cap. As the personification of liberty she received the homage of the Republicans, who stretching their hands toward her, sang a hymn ...

"Come, holy Liberty, inhabit this temple, Become the goddess of the French people."

The whole scene was enacted artistically and tastefully by actresses from the Opera. Then the Department and the Commune assembled at the bar of the Convention, where Chaumette declared, in their name, that the people wanted no other priests of gods than those which nature offers us: "We, their magistrates, have gathered from their lips this expression of their wish, and we bring it to you from the Temple of Reason and he asked that henceforth Notre-Dame should be known as the Temple of Reason. A decree to this effect was immediately passed. The Worship of Reason was nearly everywhere deistic and not materialistic or atheistic" (Aulard, Ibic pp. 106,107, 111). In Deism, nature is worshiped. It was atheistic in the sense of replacing the creator of nature with nature itself as the object of worship. The Deism developed from the atheism.

Dechristianization (quotation begins)

"A dechristianization of France started in 1793. . . first with the Cult of Reason, then with that of the Supreme being. [The foremost aim was] to defend the country and the Revolution ... against the priests, who showed themselves hostile. It seemed as if the priesthood was indestructible except by the overthrow of its altars. That work was carried out by revolutionary patriotism, and supported by a movement of free-thought which had long been bred through the intolerance of the State religion, while philosophers like Voltaire stimulated and disseminated it. . . Supposing the success of the National Defense had been delayed, and a liberating victory. . . [had been delayed, too, allowing time for the masses to become more agitated] it is a question whether the protracted Terror, considered as a dechristianizing factor, would not have dealt the deathblow to the Catholic religion in particular, nay to Christianity in general. . . When I speak of Christianity, I refer chiefly to Catholicism, but the two French Protestant Churches, the Lutheran and the Calvinist, were also affected by the anti-religious movement of 1793. . . Preface (p. 13) of Christianity and the French Revolution. A. A. Aulard, translated by Lady Frazier, 1927 Emest Benn Limited, London.

Actually the new belief system began with the Cult of Reason as noted by Aulard. Quickly actions were taken to remove the old faith, Christianity. The term "dechristianization" may well have been promoted by the actions centuries earlier when the Roman church and the government had had effectively "christianized" them. The French ancestors, called Franks, were the first to embrace the new religion under King Clovis. That was 30 years before the 1260 year period began 1008c. See on da1211.[462]

Through the two great errors, the immortality of the soul and Sunday sacredness, Satan will bring the people under his deceptions. While the former lays the foundation of spiritualism, the latter creates a bond of sympathy with Rome.[463]

It was popery that had begun the work which atheism was completing.[464]

The "old faith, Christianity" was belief in Christ Jesus as personal Savior from sin. With Christianity's endorsement of the "mid-third century intercession of the saints"[465] the "daily mediatorial work of our risen High Priest was taken away by placing faith in dead saints, who being "dead, know not anything" (Eccl. 9:5). Ellen White states that the belief in the mediatorial work of dead saints on behalf of the living is the foundation of spiritualism. This was the Christianity to which Clovis, a pagan king, subscribed, thirty years before the 1,260-year period began. History records that in 507 with Clovis' victory at Voille, the source of power for that victory was ascribed to St. Martin of Tours. With this ascribal of victory to a creature rather than the risen High Priest, Christ Jesus, God-man, it is perceived that Clovis, crowned as king in 508 in his "inner man" being, "pondered, considered carefully within himself" #4427 maw-lak (*Strongs*, 2001), endorsed the Roman Catholic view that "dead saints intercede before God on their behalf. This is in marked contrast to Christ "who is their Advocate before the Father" (1 John 2:1). With Clovis' A.D. 507-508 endorsement of his Catholic wife's belief of "intercession of the saints" began the "dechristianization" for 1,290 years. When the pagan state, under the leadership of Clovis endorsed the Roman Catholic view of "intercession of the saints" rather than the Scriptural teaching of Christ, who is the advocate before the Father," from whom believers receive all power in life, dechristianization begins. By adopting the midthird century of intercession of saints, Roman Catholicism had already dechristianized the source of their power, although they may have believed in Christ, they thought they had to go to Him through dead saints, another gospel, (see Galations 1:6,7). This was something different than the old faith, Christianity, which advocated direct access to God through Christ. Instead they subscribed to the seeds of reason dechristianizing their belief, not adhering to the "old faith Christianity."

The following sections are lifted from *en.wikipedia.org/wiki/Cult_Of_Reason*

Origins

Opposition to the Roman Catholic Church was integral among the causes of the French Revolution, and this anticlericalism solidified into official government policy in 1792 after the First French Republic was declared. Most of the dechristianisation of France was motivated by political and economic concerns, but philosophical alternatives to the Church developed gradually as well. Among the growing hererodoxy, the structural concepts of the Culte de la Raison became defined by Jacques Hebert, Antoine-Francois Momoro, Pierre Gaspard Chaumette, Joseph Fouch, and other radical revolutionaries. Jacques Hebert gained a significant degree of popularity after being arrested for attacks on Girondists. Upon his release and with his newfound popularity along with Pierre Gaspard Chaumette, Hebert founded the "worship of Reason." Unlike Robespirre's Cult of the Supreme Being, Hebert's cult rejected the existence of a deity. The cult was founded on the principles of the Enlightenment and anticlericalism.

Philosophy

The Cult of Reason was explicitly anthropocentric. Its goal was the perfection of mankind through the attainment of Truth and Liberty, and its guiding principle to this goal was the exercise of the human faculty of Reason. In the manner of conventional religion, it encouraged acts of congregation worship and devotional displays to the ideal of Reason. A careful distinction was always drawn between the ration respect of Reason and the veneration of an idol: "There is one thing that one must not tire telling people," Momoro explained, "Liberty, reason, truth are only abstract beings. They are not gods, for properly speaking they are part of ourselves."

The overarching theme of the Cult was summarized by Anacharis Clootz, who declared at the Festival of Reason that henceforward there would be "one God only, Le-Peuple." The Cult was intended as a civic religion- inspired by the works of Rousseau, Quatremere de Quincy, and Jacques- Louis David, it presented "an explicit religion of man."[466]

The following sections are lifted from _em/.Wikipedia.org/wiki/High_ Middle_Ages_

With the High Middle Ages of the 11th, 12th, and 13th centuries (c. 1001–1300)[467] there was a movement from theological faith to philosophical reason. With Thomas Aquinas (1225–1274) there was a combining of the Theological principles of faith to philosophical principles of reason. When St Thomas Aquinas began attending the University of Naples in 1243 he secretly joined an order of Dominican monks founded 1216 who had strong academic grounding faith … ., himself receiving the habit in 1244. When his family found out, they felt so betrayed that he had turned his back on the principles to which they subscribed that they decided to kidnap him.

A few years later Petrach gave up faith for the new ideas. Thus the fruit of giving homage to dead saints in 507–508 by Clovis who subscribed to the Catholic faith of his wife, seeking intercession of dead saints on behalf of the living, was different from the New Testament faith, the faith of Jesus.

The following sections were lifted *https://en.wikipedia.org/wiki/Petrarch*

(Petrarch) He spent much of his early life at Avignon ... where his family moved to follow Pope Clement V (1305–1314) who moved there in 1309 to begin the Avignon papacy ...

Petrarch was a prolific letter writer. . . After the death of their parents, Petrarch and his brother Gherardo went back to Avignon in 1326, where he worked in numerous clerical offices. This work gave him much time to devote to his writing ... On April 6, 1327 after Petrarch gave up his vocation as a priest, the sight of a woman called "Laura," in the church of Sainte-clair, Avignon awoke in him a lasting passion.[468]

The following sections were lifted https://en.wikipedia.org/wiki/Petrarch

(Petrarch) He spent much of his early life at Avignon. . . where his family moved to follow Pope Clement V (1305–1314) who moved there in 1309 to begin the Avignon papacy. . .

Petrarch was a prolific letter writer. . . After the death of their parents, Petrarch and his brother Gherardo went back to Avignon in 1326, where he worked in numerous clerical offices. This work gave him much time to devote to his writing. . . On April 6, 1327 after Petrarch gave up his vocation as a priest, the sight of a woman called "Laura," in the church of Sainte-clair, Avignon awoke in him a lasting passion.[469]

These are some of the roots of atheism that crept into the Catholic Church and influenced the 1793 age of reason.

In reality, both St. Thomas Aquinas and Petrarch, their inner beings had allowed cultivation of the intercession of saint, contrary to Christ's intercession, setting up those ideas to rule as king of their lives. Like Strongs, 2001, 4427, maw-lak to ponder consider, within oneself, they took the view that dead saints intercede on their behalf before God rather than accept the reality that Christ ever liveth to make intercession on their behalf before God.

And the king (#4428 meh-lek) **of the north** (#6828 tsaw-fone) #4428 meh'-lek; from 4427; a king: king, royal *Strongs.* 1979

#4428 me-lek n. m. (also used with compound proper names) king, royal, ruler, (human and divine); the great king 'is more prominent of a leader in a covenant agreement and is used of God (Ps. 48:2); The "king of kings" is the supreme sovereign and is not used of God in the OT. *Strongs*, 2001

#4427 maw-lak; a prim. root: to reign; incept. to ascend the throne: causat. to induct into royalty, hence by (impl.) to take counsel;- consult X indeed, be (make, set a, set up), king, be (make) queen, (begin to, make to) reign (-ing), rule, X surely *Strongs*, 1979

#4427 ma-lak v. den. [Q] to reign as a king [N] to ponder, consider carefully within oneself [H] to make one king, have a coronation: [Ho] be made a king *Strongs*, 2001

#6828 tsaw-fone; from 6845: prop. Hidden, i.e. dark; used only of the north as a quarter (gloomy and unknown): north (-ern, side, -ward, wind) *Strongs*, 1979

#6828 na-pon n. f. north, northern Strongs, 2001

Since the word *meh-lek*, the word for "king" is used in Ps. 48:2, "the city of the great King" #4428 meh-lek) of God, it is perceived that at the close of salvation history, it would be referring to God, following his sanctuary timetable, after the close of the 1,260, forty-two months, 1,290-, 1,335-, and 2,300-day prophecy, come against those creatures of humanity who are opposed to Him, simultaneously coming for those who are in favorable allegiance to Him, a separation of the sheep and the goats. In the sanctuary timetable this reality is yearly demonstrated in the "daily" and once a year, "day of atonement" Hebraic ministries. The literal Hebraic wilderness sanctuary was according to Hebrews 9:9 a figure (KJV), par-a-bo-lay (Gr), illustration (NIV) for the present kairos time. The following sections are lifted/copied from Early Writings *"End of the 2300 days"*

I saw a throne, and on it sate the Father and the Son. I gazed on Jesus'countenance and admired His lovely person. The Father's person I could not behold, for a clould of glorious light covered Him. I asked Jesus if His Father had a form like Himself. He said He had, but I could not behold it, for said He, "If you should behold the glory of His person you would cease to exist.' Before the throne I saw the Advent people-the church and the world. I saw two companies, one bowed down before the throne, deeply interested, while the other stood uninterested and careless. Those who were bowed before the throne would offer up their prayers and look to Jesus; then He would look to His Father, and appear to be pleading with Him. A light would come from the Father to the Son and from the Son to the praying company. Then I saw an exceeding bright light come from the Father to the Son, and from the Son it waved over the people who were before the throne. But few would receive this great light. Many came out from under it and immediately resisted it; others were careless and did not cherish the light, and it moved off from them. Some cherished it, and went and bowed down with the little praying company. This company all received the light and rejoiced in it, and their countenances shone with its glory.

I saw the Father rise from the thone, and in a flaming chariot go into the holy of holies within the veil and sit down. Then Jesus rose up from the throne, and most of those who were bowed down atose with Him. I did not see one ray of light pass from Jesus to the careless multitude after He arose, and they were left in perfect darkness. Those who arose when Jesus did, kept their eyes fixed on Him as He left the throne and led them out a little way. Then He raised His right arm and we heard His lovely voice saying, "Wait here; I am going to my Father to receive the kingdom; keep your garments spotless, and in a little while I will return from the wedding and receive you to Myself." The a cloudy chariot, with wheels like flaming fire, surrounded by angels came to where Jesus was. He stepped into the chariot and was borne to the holiest, where the Father sat. Ghere I beheld Jesus, a great High Priest, standing before the Father. On the hem of His garment was a bell and a pomegranate. Those who rose up with Jesus would send up their faith to Him in the hoiest, and pray, "My father, give us Thy Spirit." Then Jesus would breathe upon them the Holy Ghost. In that breath was light, power, and much love, joy, and peace.

I turned to look at the company who were still bowed before the throne; they did not know that Jesus had left it. Satan appeared to be by the throne, trying to carry on the work of God. I saw them look up to the throne and pray, "Father, give us thy spirit." Satan would breath upon them an unholy influence; in it was light and power, but no sweet love, joy, and peace. Satan's object was to keep them deceived and to draw back and deceive God's children.[470]

Thus when the Israelites obeyed from faith in Moses' the command to slay the type lamb, apply its blood to the doorposts, enter into that bloodstained dwelling, awaiting the type midnight judgment and Exodus from Egypt to follow God, discovering, three months into the journey, that they were to become a kingdom of priests, but really not able to enter into that experience until a year after the Exodus, so Christ had come as the lamb of God, been slain at calvary, subsequently resurrected and ascended to heaven, where He ministers as Our High Priest, teaching us how to become priests, carrying out on our behalf the antitypical daily service. And when the king came to see the guests. (Mt. 22:11)

At the "time of the end" of the 2,300-day prophecy, October 22, 1844, Christ, Our High Priest moved from, the antitypical "daily" phase which involved the believer claiming Christ's blood as their entitlement to heaven, then rising to walk in newness of life, putting on the priestly robe of Christ's righteousness and ministering in His body the church, to the antitypical "day of atonement" phase called the Investigative Judgment. This phase examined whether or not an individual desired to be saved or lost, a sheep or goat, a wise virgin or a foolish virgin, a wise man or a foolish man, one who from faith put into practice what he had learned or with unbelieving faithlessness did not put, or put, into practice what he had heard.

Time of the end. Here the king of the north and the king of the south are mentioned as such for the first time since vs. 14, 15. Seventh-day Adventist expositors who find the career of France during the Revolution the subject of vs. 36–39 hold that Turkey is the king of the north of vs. 40–45. Those who apply vs. 36–39 to the papacy here find a prophetic picture of the climax of its career. Some of the latter group identify the papacy as the king of the north, while others distinguish between the two. A few consider that vs. 40–met their fulfilment in the collapse of the Ottoman Empire in 1922. See on v. 45.[471]

Perceiving that the "king of the north," at this juncture in the prophetic flow is God, which can be substantiated by Strongs, 2001 definition #4428 me-lek which can mean "king ... (human or divine); the great king is more prominent of a leader in a covenant agreement and is used of God (Ps. 48:2), toward the close and after the conclusion of the 1,260-, 1,290-, 1,335-, and 2,300-day prophecies, God has in His quiver, an arsenal of country/nation arrows which He will use as lesser vessels, like silver, bronze, and iron in comparison to gold with Jews or Christian nations, called out to have the greatest knowledge of Him in contrast to Gentile or heathen nations symbolized by silver, bronze, or iron vessels, not having as much light about God as the "chosen, set apart" people, being used to chastise the chosen when they are outside of God's will and thus to accomplish His prophetic purposes.

The following is lifted from *http://www.mazzaroth.com/Chapter_six/ sevenHistoricalChurchAges*

It is perceived that Turkey is the "type" king of the north at this historical juncture, for in that country are located the actual, literal, geographical seven churches (Rev. 2–3); Ephesus, Symrna, Pergummum, Thyatira, Sardis, Philadelphia, Laodicia, with their "historical age Ephesus (33–100), Symrna (100–312), Pergammum (312–590), Thyatira (590–1517), Sardis (1517–1750), Philadelphia (1750–1925) and Laodicia (1925— the tribulation and apostate world)"[472] through whom God, "the antitypical" king of the north, as it were on the heads side of the love coin, would communicate his literal/figurative-spiritual messages to the world, as it were on the tails side of the love coin. The tails side of the love coin is perceived to be the place where Satan, the ultimate antitypical "king of the south," also known as "the prince of this world" temps creatures of fallen human nature to break and maintain a broken faith relationship to God. The last part of this section is lifted from *www.the-scientist.com/? articles.view/articleNo28870/title/Darwin-Joseph-Hooker—1844/*

At the end of the 2,300-day prophecy of Daniel 8:14 which ended October 22, 1844, with the Great Disappointment, then a resurgence of the proclamation of the three-angels message (Rev. 14:6–12), by the churches of "the north," in fulfillment of Rev. 10:11 prophecy "you must prophecy again" (Revelation 10:11), Darwinism of the "south" pushed at belief in God in a discourse between Charles Darwin and Joseph Hooker "which spanned more than 1,400 letters over four decades— including the one pictured here, dated January 11, 1844–was one of the first places Darwin expressed his theory of natural selection as a driver of speciation and evolution."[473]

The following section is lifted from *www.icr.org/article/evolution-pope/*

"According to the Vatican Information Service in a news release on October 23, Pope John Paul II was reported as saying that evolution is "more than just a theory." This seems to mean, despite the tenuous wording, that he now considers evolution a scientific fact. His written message to his science advisers, the Pontifical Academy of Sciences, speaks of "a series of discoveries made in different spheres of knowledge: which have convinced him to make this bold statement supporting evolution and suggesting that his millions of followers do the same.

. . .

Now comes the pope with his "surprise" announcement that it is acceptable for Catholics to believe and teach evolutionism. He did include the small proviso that they should still allow God to create each human soul. Atheism thus remains inappropriate for Catholics, and that's a relief to know!

As a matter of fact, this public papal evolutionism is hardly a surprise to anyone who has followed the pronouncements of the last four popes, or who is familiar with the teachings of the various Catholic colleges and seminaries in this country. Even the last true conservative pope, Pius XII, in his famous 1950 encyclical, "humani Generis," while not promoting evolutionism and still seeming to lean toward special creation, did make a point of allowing Catholics to study and accept evolution as a scientific theory of origins, again with the limitation that God created the soul, and that all men are descendants of Adam, along with the doctrine of original sin as inherited from Adam.

The freedom to study and teach evolution with this constraint seemed very quickly to result in the widespread acceptance of theistic evolutionism in Catholic institutions and churches everywhere. As far as the present pope, John Paul II, is concerned, he has been an evolutionsit in this sense probably since his youth. Despite this sudden supposed surprising pontificating, it is nothing new to his personal beliefs.

Pope John Paul II was Karol wojtyla, Cardinal of Krakow when he was name pope in 1978 (-2005).[474] He had earlier been an actor and was apparently quite comfortable as a government-approved ecclesiastic in Communist Poland. When he was elected pope, his election was enthusiastically endorsed by Poland's Communist Party and by World communism in general. Since his election, he has seemingly been promoting a syncretistic agenda, not only with Protestants but also with Hindus, Lamaists, and others. In any event, he is not a recent convert to evolutionism, as the media have implied.

Perhaps the most influential evolutionist among Catholic theologians was the Jesuit priest, Teilhard de Chardin, now considered in effect to be almost the "patron saint" of the New Age movement with his strong pantheistic evolutionism. Teilhard was involved in the controversial discoveries of both Piltdown Man and Pekin Man and vigorously promoted total evolutionism all his life, greatly influencing such leading secular evolutionists as Theodosius Dobzhansky, George Gaylord Simpson, and Sir Julian Huxley. His books were banned at one time by the Catholic church but have apparently become respectable, and even very influential among Catholics during the reigns of the recent more liberal popes.

There have been many other leading evolutionary scientists in the domain of Catholicism, and this description would ceretainly apply to most of the scientists of the Pontifical Academy. On the other hand, we need to recognize that there are many strong creationsits, not only among lay Catholics, but also among Catholic scientists as well. We could mention Dr. Guy Berthault of France, for example, whose studies on sedimentation have been profoundly significant in refuting geological uniformitarianism. Two Italian creationists, Dr. Roberto Fondi (paleontologist) and Dr. Giuseppe Sermonti (geneticist) have published important scientific books and papers refuting evolution. There are many others.

In this country, Dr. Wolfgang Smith, born in Austria but educated in this country (at Cornell, Purdue, and Columbia, in physics and mathematics) and having served since 1968 as Professor of Mathematics at Oregon State, after previous faculty positions at M.I.T. and U.C.L.A., has written a devastating critique of de Chardin's teachings and evolutionism in general. In this book, he says that the doctrine of macroevolution *"is totally bereft of scientific sanction"* (Teilhardism and the New Religion. Tan Books, 1988, p. 5; emphasis his.) He then adds that "there exists to this day not a shred of bona fide scientific evidence in support of the thesis that macroevolutionary transformations have ever occurred" (Ibid., p. 6.).

It is too bad that Pope John Paul II (who is not a scientist) did not consult such real Catholic scientists as Wolfgang Smith before glibly stating, as he did, that "new knowledge leads us to recognize in the theory of evolution more than a hypothesis." Just what new knowledge would that be Pope John Paul II? Possibly the Mars rock? Or the fantasy of a walking whale?

One wonders whether he might be thinking of Teilhard's famous definition of evolution when he says it is more than a hypothesis. Here is what Teilhard said:

Is evolution a theory, a system, or a hypothesis? It is much more: it is a general condition to which all theories, all systems, all hypotheses must bow.

. . Evolution is a light illuminating all facts, a curve that all lines must follow (The Phenomenon of Man Harper and Row 1965, p. 219.)

Evolution was, to all intents and purposes, Teilhard's "god," and his goal was globalism, a unified world government, culture, and religion, with all religions merged into one.

There are more and more signs that such globalism is also the aim of Pope John Paul II and other modern liberal Catholics. If so, this publicized commitment to evolutionism would contribute substantially to such a goal. All world religions-including most of mainline Protestantism, as well

230

as Hinduism, Buddhism, and the rest—except for Biblical Christianity, Orthodox Judaism, and Fundamentalist Islam, have embraced some form of evolutionism (either theistic, deistic, or pantheistic) and rejected or allegorized the true record of origins in Genesis. The pope has participated in important meetings with leaders of communism, Zen Buddhism, Hinduism, Taoism, Lamaism, and others, as well as the world Council of Churches, the Trilater Commission, the B'nar B'rith of Liberal Judaism, and a wide assortment of still others. He has traveled to India, Australia, the United States, and all over the world in his bullet-proof "popemobile," speaking to immense crowds everywhere.

All cults and movements associated with the "new world order" of the so-called New Age Movement have two things in common-evolutionism as their base and globalism as their goal. It is disturbing now to see even many large evangelical movements (e.g., Promise Keepers, charismatic ecumenism) inadvertently drifting into the same orbit while eulogizing this evolutionist pope.

The pope insists, of course, that Catholic evolutionists must still believe that God started the universe with its Big Bang and still creates each human soul.

The scientific establishment, however, will never be content ultimately with anything less than total evolutionism.

The man who is believed by many to be the world's greatest living scientist, Stephen W. Hawking, has an insightful comment regarding his own audience with the pope, in his best-selling book, *A Brief History of Time* (Bantam Books, 1988). He had been a speaker at a high-level papal scientific conference on cosmology. After which he describes his encounter thus:

> At the end of the conference the participants were granted an audience with the pope. He told us it was all right to study the evolution of the universe after the Big Bang, but we should not inquire into the Big Bang itself because that was the moment of creation and therefore the work of God. I was glad then that he did not know the subject of the talk I had just given at the conference— the possibility that space—time was finite but had no boundary, which means that it had no beginning, no moment of Creation. (p. 116)

That being the case, according to his cosmological mathematics, he concludes: "What place, then, for a Creator?" (p. 140). Hawking's book refers frequently to God, but he ends up concluding in his heart: "There is no god." And such must inevitably be the ultimate logical conclusion of any consistent evolutionism.

Among the most poignant verses in the Bible, with its reality coming more and more into focus these days, are the words of the Lord Jesus in Luke 18:8:

When the Son of man cometh, will He find faith on the earth?[475]
The following section is lifted from www.realclearscience.com/lists/
four_book_on_evolution_before_Darwin's_1

In 1844, a book on evolution was published that would outsell Charles Darwin's *On the Origin of Species*. Written by Scottish journalist Robert Chambers, *Vestiges of the Natural History of Creation* was a well-written and understandable account of the groundbreaking, contemporary ideas on the evolution of the solar system and the evolution of species. In the book, Chambers used the term "transmutation" to suggest that everything in existence—from rocks and plants to fish and mammals—developed from earlier forms, describing a universe where a "Divine Being" created everything, then let it all play out based on natural laws.

Thus is seen that the papacy exhibits a double-minded, undivided heart which Christ and the rest of Scripture cautions against in creation. On the one hand the pope, i.e., John Paul II (1978–2005), advocates that God is the creator of the soul of a person and on the other he advocates evolution of the rest of the universe, stating that it is acceptable to teach and believe . In the fourth commandment (Ex. 20:8–11), acknowledgement is made that "God created the heavens and earth. This acknowledgement is also made in the first angel's message (Rev. 14:7 "Worship him that made heaven, and earth, and the seas, and the fountains of waters"). Romans 1:20 also talks of "the creation of the world." It is perceived that God is love. This love has two sides to the coin. For example, the whole universe is/was created as it were, on the head's side of the coin, to enjoy face-to-face communion with God. Yet in freedom, God also provided for in love, a not desired to be experienced tails side of the love coin, in which one could not see God face to face. It was on this tails side of the love coin that every outside faith imagination could take place. Since humanity since the fall is on the tails side of the love coin, that is where thoughts of evolution could occur. Yet God, on the head's side of the love coin as it were, through the first angel's message would call humanity, on the tail's side of the love coin as it were, to come out of this false belief to worship, from faith, God the creator.

Since the days of Thomas Aquinas (1225–1274)[477], his parents wanted him to return to faith in God, but he chose to reject the priesthood and side with the Dominican philosophy. Petrarch (1304–1374)[478] also sided with philosophy. Rather than maintain the faith the choice was made to follow philosophy.[479,480,481]

Utilizing the prophetic model of horses and chariots depicted in Zechariah 6 as the spirits before God with red horses with a chariot along with black horses with chariot and white horses with a chariot and finally bay and grizeled horses with a chariot. The black horses with chariot went north, the white horses with chariot followed them. The bay horses went to and fro on the earth. The grizeld horses went south.

It is perceived that unfallen beings ride in the chariots pulled by black horses going north where God is. It is perceived that fallen redeemed beings ride in the chariots pulled by white horses who follow the black horses as they go to where God is. It is perceived that fallen redeemed or those who have not accepted that redemption ride on the disk plane of the spinning horses top in the valley of indecision, while the grizzled horses have decided to rebel against God by heading south. Nowhere in this passage does it mention where the red horse and his chariot are or go.

Thus it is perceived that God in his love and mercy hid from view where the red horse and chariot would go. Only after the seven seals of Revelation were opened would it be discovered that Satan and his angels would be in the second seal (Rev. 6:3, 4) of the red horse.

So free creatures, as it were, were originally created on disk of a spinning top, symbolized by the Garden of Eden. The two trees in the center of the Garden were the tree of life and the tree of knowledge of good and evil. Riding on the power of choice bay horse, they were created with a bent to also desire to follow God on white horses which followed the black horses, ultimately eating of the tree of life.

A window into understanding that Lucifer, who became Satan, rode on his bay horse of the power of choice. Mysteriously and unexplainably, because of his created bent of faith, he decided to rebel against God. He chose not to ride on the white horse in the created bent of faith. He chose mysteriously and unexplainably to ride on the provided in freedom but not designed to be ex[erienced grizled horse. He entertained rebellion against God, not knowing what that outcome would be. Despite the pleadings of God to return to riding the chariot with white horses which went north following the black horses, there developed war in heaven. In this war Michael and his angels riding on chariots drawn by white and black horses were against chariots heading south led by grizzled horses.

When Satan and his angels, riding on the bay, power of choice, and grizzled horses with chariots after being cast out of heaven was summoned by God to heaven, still did not know in mystery his ultimate fate of riding of the red horse of the second seal (Rev. 6:3, 4). A knowledge of that fate would only be disclosed to him after calvary Before calvary God asked him, "From whence comest thou? And Satan answered the Lord and said, From going to and fro on the earth, and from walking up and down in it" Job 2:2. Thus before Satan and his angels were sealed by the red horse second seal (Rev. 6: 3, 4) after calvary, they would still be riding in spirit on bay and grizeled horses and chariot. It was from this spirit position of riding on bay and grizeled horses that Satan spoke through the serpent to Eve, saying, "You shall not surely die."

Created to spin, as a top, on the disk of life, partaking of the tree of life, located at the top, north center of their lives symbolized in the tree of life in the midst of the garden, as long as they stayed away, on the disk of their lives, symbol of the Garden of Eden, in the obedience of faith from the tree of knowledge of good and evil at the south center of Eden, they were to live in allegiance to God. If they partook of the tree of the knowledge of good and evil at the south center midst of Eden, their faith life would topple and they would be expelled from Eden and a face-to-face allegiance to God.

Christ, possessing inner faith, clothed with a body of degenerate sinful humanity would come to this earth, demonstrate how to live by faith, then die as the lamb of God substitute sacrifice for sin. Three days later, he would rise from the dead, live among them for forty days and then ascend to heaven to be the high priest for fallen humanity. All who claimed the merits of his blood sacrifice at calvary as their own would be empowered to journey in thr wilderness of this world to the conditional place where they put on the righteousness of Christ. This would be figuratively/ spiritually in their "inner man" like the priests who literally put on their robes, becoming priests in a kingdom of priests, a holy nation.

Then would be fulfilled the scripture, "It doth not yet appear what we are to become, but when he comes we shall be like him" (1 Jn. 3:2). We will be like him in that we are all clothed with the righteousness of Christ which is the wedding garment.

shall come (#935)

#935 bo, bow; A prim. root; to Go or come (in a wide variety of applications):-abide, apply, attain, x be, befall, + besiege, bring (forth, in, into, to pass), depart x doubtless, again, + eat, +employ, (cause to) enter (in, into, ing, -trance,-try), fallen, fetch, + follow, get, give, go (down, in, toward), grant, + have x indeed, [-in] vade, lead, lift [-up] mention, pull in, put, resort, run (down), send, set, x (well) stricken [in age] x surely, take (-in) way <u>Strongs</u>, 1974

#935 bo v. [Q] to come. go [H] to bring. Tale; [Ho] to be brought:- <u>Strongs</u>, 2001

The aspect of the meaning of the word (#935 bo) continues to be "a besiegement, or a befalling, or bringing upon humanity on this earth the investigative judgement in the heavenly sanctuary which began October 22, 1844. This reality at the close of the twenty-three hundred day prophecy of Daniel 8:14 seems to fit the historical-prophetic context.

That investigative judgment, day of atonement phase, comes after all the signs Christ announced in Matthew 24:29 of the sun being darkened, the moon not giving her light and the stars falling from heaven.

This investigative judgment phase[482] would precede the retributive phase of God's judgment. That retributive phase of judgment would be spread out over one thousand years (see Revelation 20:2). "Christ saw in Jerusalem a symbol of the world hardended in unbelief and rebellion and hastening on to meet the retributive judgemts of God."[483]

The investigative phase would begin October 22, 1844 with the 'time to judge the dead' (see Revelation 20:2). The first part of that judgment would culminate in the second coming of Christ, who would as a reward take home to heaven those who "love me and keep my commandments" Exodus 20:6. At that time "many of those who sleep in the dust of the earth, shall awake, some to everlastingl life" Daniel 12:2. Both the resurrected dead, and translated living would be taken to heaven (see 1 Thessalonians 4:16, 17). The second part of the that judgment would occur at the end of the thousand years when the devil, his angel, and human followers are cast into the lake of fire which is the second death. (see Revelation 20:10, 13-14).

Hence, the mind and thoughts of William Miller and others were directed to figure out the meaning of the sanctuary and its cleansing in Daniel 8:14.

When Hiram Edson was walking across the cornfield field,[484] the day after the great disappointment of October 22, 1844 and had a vision in his mind that it was the heavenly sanctuary to be cleansed, it was as if standing on earth, he held a kite string connected to the heavenly sanctuary kite.

"Both the prophecy of Daniel 8:14, "Unto two thousand and three hundred days; then shall the sanctuary be cleansed," and the first angel's message, "fear God, and give glory to Him; for the hour of His judgment is come," pointed to Christ's ministration in the most holy place, to the investigative judgment, and not to the coming of Christ for the redemption of His people and the destruction of the wicked. The mistake had not been in the reckoning of the prophetic periods, but in the event to take place at the end of the 2300 days."[485]

And when the king came in (#1525 eis-er-cho-mai lit. or fig.) to see (#2300 the-a-o-mai lit. or fig.) the guests, he saw (#1492 i-do lit. or fig.) there a man which had not on a wedding garment. Matthew 22:11

#2525 ice-er-khom-ahee, from1519 and 2064; to enter (lit. orfig.): arise, come (in, into) enter in (-to), go in (through) Strongs, 1979

And then shall appear (#5316 phain-o) the sign of the Son of man in heaven: and then shall all the tribes of the earth mourn, and they shall see the Son of man coming in the clouds of heaven with power and great glory. (Mt. 24:30)This word (#5316 phain-o, trans. or intrans. lit. or fig.) translated "appear" is significant in that it can mean according to Strongs, 2010 "seem, be seen, shine x think." After the great disappointment of October 22, 1844, Christ did not come, according to their Matthew 24;27 expectation. "For as the lightning cometh out of the east and shineth even unto the west; so shall also the coming of the son of man be." Hiram Edson had a vision486 while walking in the cornfield. In this vision his mind was drawn to the meaning of the sanctuary. This was like, as already discussed in Daniel 11:31 under "sanctuary of strength," a man, standing on earth, tethered by the string of righteousness by faith, flying the kite of the heavenly sanctuary message.

Originally people had thought this earth was the sanctuary and it would be cleansed according to Daniel 8:14 by the second coming of Christ to the earth. In that walk through the cornfield, Hiram Edson's thoughts were drawn from earth to heaven. Thus it began to dawn on his consciousness, helping him to think, enabling the events of the great disappointment of October 22, 1844, to seem that the sanctuary to be cleansed was not the earthly but the heavenly sanctuary.

Because of the transitive (requiring a direct object) or intransitive (not requiring a direct object) plus the literal or figurative/spiritual nature of this word phain-o, all humanity will be required to accept or reject the provisions of Christ for salvation from sin. This acceptance or rejection will be manifested by the individual response to the Revelation 3:20 call,

"Behold, I stand at the door and knock: if any man hear my voice, and open the door, I will come in (#1525 eis-er-cho-mai lit. or fig.) to him, and will sup with him, and he with me."

While the earth was not the sanctuary to be cleansed, its occupants did have a part in the cleansing of the heavenly. This reality is reflected in the parable of the wedding feast, highlighting the king in Matthew 22:11 coming (1525 eis-er-cho-mai lit. or fig.) to see the guests. Thus the Investigative judgment in the sanctuary is a figure (KJV) illustration (NIV) (#3850 par-ab-o-lay) of what is beginning to occur in October 22, 1844 as the antitypical Day of Atonment. This word par-ab-o-lay is the same word Christ uses when he says, "I speak to them in parables" Matthew 13:13.

"Christ had come, not to the earth, as they expected, but, as foreshadowed in the type, to the most holy place of the temple of God in heaven. He is represented by the prophet Daniel as coming at this time to the Ancient of Days: "I saw in the night visions, and, behold, one like the Son of man came with the clouds of heaven, and came"-not to the earth, but- "to the Ancient of Days, and they brought Him near before Him." Daniel 7:13."[487]

"The coming of Christ as our high priest to the most holy place, for the cleansing of the sanctuary, brought to view in Daniel 8:14; the coming of the son of man to the Ancient of Days, as presented in Daniel 7:13; and the coming of the Lord to His temple, foretold by Malachi, are descriptions of the same event; and this is also represented by the coming of the bridegroom to the marriage, described by Christ in the parable of the ten virgins of Matthew 25."[488]

And let them make me a sanctuary that I may dwell among them. According to all that I shall shew thee, after the pattern of the tabernacle, and the pattern of all the instruments thereof, even so shall ye make it. (Ex. 25:8, 9) dwell #7931tab-neeth lit.or fig. pattern #8403 tab-neeth. from #1129 baw-naw, to build. lit. or fig.

And Moses took the tabernacle, and pitched it without the camp, afar off from the camp, and called it the Tabernacle of the congregation. And it came to pass, that everyone which sought the Lord unto the tabernacle of the congregation which was without the camp. (Ex. 33:7)

And it came to pass when Mosesunto the tabernacle, that all the people rose up, and stood every man at his tent door, and looked after Moses, until he was gone into the tabernacle. (Ex. 33:8)

Yet the Lord hath not given you an heart to perceive, and eyes to see and ears to hear, unto this day. (Deut. 29:4)

Thy way, O God, is in the sanctuary: who is so great a God as our God? (Ps. 77:13)

"The Scripture which above all others had been both the foundation and the central pillar of the advent faith was the declaration: "Unto two thousand and three hundred days; then shall the sanctuary be cleansed" (Daniel 8:14). These prophetic days had been shown to terminate in the autumn of 1844. In common with the rest of the Christian world, Adventists then held that the earth, or some portion of it, was the sanctuary. They understood that the cleansing of the sanctuary was the purification of the earth by the fires of the last great day, and that this would take place at the second advent. Hence the conclusion that Christ would return to the earth in 1844.

But the appointed time and passed, and the Lord had not appeared."[489]

"The cleansing of the sanctuary therefore involves a work of investigation—a work of judgment ...

Thus those who followed in the light of the prophetic word saw that, instead of coming to the earth at the termination of the end of the 2,300 days in 1844, Christ had entered the most holy place of the heavenly sanctuary to perform he closing work of atonement preparatory to His coming."[490]

Investigative Judgment

"And he saith unto him, Friend, how hither not having a wedding garment? And he was speechless." (Mt. 22:12)

"After a long time the lord of those servants cometh, and reckoneth with them." (Mt. 25:19) **against** (#5921 al) **him**

#5921 al; prop. the same as 5920 used as a prep.) in the sing. or plur., often with pref., or as conj. with a particle following); above, over, upon, or against (yet always in this last relation with a downward aspect) in a great variety of applications (as follows). . . Strongs, 1979

#5920 al; from 5927; prop. The top; spec. the Highest (i. e. God); also (adv.) aloft, to Jehovah:-above, high, most High. Strongs, 1979

#5927 aw-law; a prim. root; to ascend, intrans (be high) or act. (mount); used in a great variety of senses, primary and secondary, lit. and fig. Strongs, 1979 #5921 al; pp. & c. marker of relationship: spatial: on, upon, over, against, toward; logical: because of, according to; temporal: on, when, during. Strongs, 2001

Thus at the beginning of the antitypical Day Of Atonement, Investigative Judgement parable (see Hebrews 9:9) phase in the heavenly sanctuary time table which began October 22, 1844, Christ would come (#2064 er-cho-mai, lit. or fig. Mt. 24:30 not #3952 par-oo-see-ah Mt. 24:27) in the clouds. Like the Israelites had followed "in type" the cloud from Egypt to Sinai, so now post-calvary believers were to follow "antitypically" from the cross to acknowledging that the risen Christ is the "temple of the tabernacle of the testimony" Revelation 15:5 into whom all believers are to enter and serve.

They were to acknowledge that wherever they went, the post-calvary, risen Christ had been "to them a little sanctuary in the countries they have been" (Ezek. 11:15), for He their God had come (#2064 er-cho-mai lit. or fig.) to them. These believers would be the saved, wise men, sheep, and wise virgins.

Those people to whom God, the king of the north (see Ps. 48: 2) would come against include the foolish man, foolish virgins, and goats.

It is perceived to be acknowledged that there exist in all religious faith groups both wise and foolish, sheep and goats, people who do and don't put into practice from an attitude of faith things that they know. That's why God, the ultimate king of the north (See Ps. 48:2) investigates, as a demonstration to the unfallen universe that some people by their works springing from an attitude of faith in Jesus, or what pointed to Jesus, namely the sacrifice, are fit to save and some people by their works springing from an attitude of faithlessness in Jesus or what pointed to Him were unfit to save.

Historically the Roman Catholic church belief system with regard to worship on Sunday—the first day of the week verses worshiping on Saturday—the seventh-day Sabbath will be a belief that God will come against as the king of the north in the Investigative Judgement. While there will be people who find favor with God and are saved in the judgment [Catholic or otherwise, who do not know of the seventh-day Sabbath, because their "growth in grace" has only journeyed to (1) acceptance of Christ as personal Savior, (2) applied His blood to the doorposts of their heart, (3) entered into a relationship with Christ, like the Israelites entered into their dwellings with the blood on their doorposts,(4) ate the Word, like the Israelites ate roasted lamb or goat, unleavened bread, and bitter herbs as they waited, in an abiding faith relationship to God, under the banner of the blood on their doorposts, for the midnight justification judgment, in which the destroying angel would pass over the homes, or lives, declaring them fit to save because of their faith in the blood of the slain lamb in Egypt, (5) through the midnight justification judgment to life outside Egypt, a symbol of sin, hence outside sin, to freedom from sin before they experience the baptism of the Red sea, where they declared they wanted no part of sin, believing God had cleansed them from sin and its temptations, like he drowned the pursing Egyptians, (6) discover that God would supply their need for water, like the Israelites ran out of water and then their need was supplied (7) discover that God would supply their need for food with the manna, which they gathered enough for one day, yet on Friday, gathered twice as much so they could rest on the Sabbath] (8)receive water from the rock which gushes out from within them, (9) realize that the power of the cross, depicted days earlier in the slain lamb in Egypt, symbolized by Moses' outstretched arms which were held up by Aaron and Hur, finally putting a stone under them, in the victory over the Amalekites/symbol of sin-temptation after the future calvary event, illustrating the powerful grace of God after initial acceptance of Him in Egypt/sin into their lives to be victorious over temptation and sin (10) and education so that one can judge things rightly, like Moses set up the judges over thousands, hundreds, fifties, and tens. All of these experiences can and are to potentially occur prior to an encounter with the Ten Commandment law at Sinai. Prior to the Sinai encounter, the Israelites, and for that matter, people who have no knowledge about the Ten Commandments, do the things required in the Ten Commandments because the "law is written on their hearts." Yet, at the end time, people just before the second coming, who are trophies of his grace, and most probably will be those who are translated, will be keeping the seventh-day Sabbath.

It is interesting to note that the country of Turkey literally contains the cities to which the letters to the seven churches are addressed. Geographically Turkey is north of Israel. Since God dwells in the two altars, the altar of burnt offering symbol of calvary and altar of incense upon which the golden censer rests and the bronze censers of the priests who are a symbol churches as the consuming fire, "one God," King of the north, comprised of first person of the Godhead, hypostasis essence, heat, Father, second person of the Godhead hypostasis essence plant-based wood/fuel Son, and third person of the Godhead possessing two hypostasis essences of plant-based oil/fuel and elemental atmosphere, like air, He would give counsel, admonition, and reprimands to the seven churches of Revelation 2–3 after He ascended to heaven. Like the country Turkey is in a different location than the land of Israel, so the heaven to which Christ ascended is in a different location than the earth.

"Great is the Lord, and greatly to be praised in the city of our God, in the mountain of his holiness. Beautiful for situation, the joy of the whole earth, is Mount Zion, on the sides of the north" (#6828 meh-lek) (Ps. 48:1, 2).

"Ps48:2 north. The Canaanites had the mythological concept of a pantheon of gods, whose chief deity El had a palace on Mount Zaphon (the Hebrew word for "north"). Similarly, it was believed that Baal dwelleth on the north.

However, the psalmist firmly confesses that not Mount Zaphon or Olympus (the sacred citadel of Zeus for the Greeks), but Mount Zion is the true North (Zaphon), the holy mountain of the living God from where the world is controlled (see also Job 37:22; Is. 14:13; Ezek. 1:4)."[491]

"Fair weather cometh out of the north: with God is terrible majesty." (Job 37:22)

'For thou hast said in thine heart, I will ascend into heaven, I will exalt my throne above the stars of God: I will sit also upon the mount of the congregation, in the sides of the north." (Isaiah 14: 13, 14)

"And I looked, and, behold, a whirlwind came out of the north, a great cloud, and a fire infolding itself, and a brightness was about it, and out of the midst thereof as the color of amber, out of the midst of the fire." (Ezek. 1:4)

"Ezek. 1:4 note north. The direction from which judgment often came upon Israel (e.g., Jer. 1:14)."[492] like a whirlwind, (#8175 saw-ar) with {chariots, (#7393 reh-keb) and horsemen, (#6571 paw-rash) like a whirlwind, (#8175 saw-ar)

#8175 saw-ar: a prim. root: to storm; by impl. To shiver, i.e. fear:-be (horribly) afraid, fear, hurl as a storm, be tempestuous, come like (take away as with) a whirlwind. Strongs, 1979

#8175 sa-ar v. [Q] to shudder, bristle with horror; to sweep away (by the wind); to know about, be acquainted with; [N]to be in a storm; [Ht] to storm against. Strongs, 2001 with chariots, (#7393 reh-keb)

#7393 reh-keb; from 7392: a vehicle; a vehicle: by impl. A team: by exten. cavalry, by analogy a rider, i.e. the upper millstone, multitude [from the marg.] wagon Strongs, 1979

#7393 re-keb n. m. chariot, large upper millstone Strongs, 2001

The following section was lifted/copied from the chapter entitled "End of the 2300 Days" Early Writings by Ellen G. White page 55

"I saw the Father rise from the throne, and in a flaming chariot go into the holy of holies within the veil and sit down. Then Jesus rose up

241

from the throne, and the most of those who were bowed down arose with Him. I did not see one ray of light pass from Jesus to the careless multitude after He arose, and thy were left in perfect darkness. Those who arose when Jesus did, kept their eyes fixed on Him as He left the throne and led them out a little way. Then he raised hHis right arm, and we heard His lovely voice saying, "Wait here; I am going to My Father to receive the kingdom; keep your garments spotless, and in a little while I will return from the wedding and receive you to Myself." Then a cloudy chariot, with wheels like flaming fire, surrounded by angels, came to where Jesus was. He stepped into the chariot and was borne to the holiest, where the Father sat. There I beheld Jesus, a great High Priest standing before the Father.[493]

And I turned, and lifted up mine eyes, and looked, and behold, there came four chariots (#4818 mer-kaw-baw) out from between two mountains; and the mountains were mountains of brass.

In first chariot (#4818) were red horses (#5483); and in the second chariot (#4818) black horses (#5483); And in the third chariot(#4818) white horses (#5483);

And in the fourth chariot (#4818) grisled and bay horses (#5483).

Then I answered and said unto the angel that talked with me, What are these my Lord?

And the angel answered and said unto me, These are the four spirits of the heavens, which go forth from standing before the Lord of all the earth.

The black horses (#5483) which are therein go forth into the north country; and the white go forth after them; and the grisled go forth toward the south country.

And the bay went forth, and sought to go that they might walk to and fro through the earth: and he said, Get you hence, walk to and fro through the earth. So they walked to and fro through the earth.

The cried he upon me, and spake unto me, saying, Behold, these that go toward the north country have quieted my spirit in the north country. (Zech. 6)

#4818 mer-kaw-baw; fem. of 4817; a chariot:-chariot. See also 1024 Strongs, 1979

#4818 mer-ka-ba n. f. chariot:- Strongs, 2001

#5483 soos; from an unused root. mean. to skip (prop. for joy); a horse (as leaping); also a swallow (from its rapid flight);-crane, horse ([-back, --hoof]). comp 6571. Strongs, 1979

#5483 sus n. m. (male) horse, stallion; swallow, swift:- <u>Strongs</u>, 2001

It is perceived that this passage of Zechariah 6 proclaims how free creatures, being reproduced from the brass loins of the image in Daniel 2, or disk surrounding the poll which has both north and south realities were created. Symbolically God is represented as the black horse who dwells in the north, or at the top tip of the center poll, and Satan dwells on the bottom, or south end of the center pole. Thus it is possible to conceive that Adam and Eve, and for that matter, all creatures were created as it were on the top side of the disk, in the northern hemisphere as it were of the earth or whatever location. Being created on the top side of the disk meant that they possessed a created bent of faith to partake of the tree of life, at the north center of the Garden of Eden. They were commanded from their spinning in allegiance to God position on the top side of the disk, not to wander to the bottom side of the disk, toward the tree of knowledge of good and evil. That forbidden tree was located in the in the south center of their experience of a spinning in allegiance relationship to God top From their created position on the top side of the disk relationship to God, they were warned not to entertain or enter into the ways or desires of the bottom side of the disk which would constitute rebellion. If rebellion was entertained and they entered into life on the bottom side of the spinning top, their faith relationship to God would topple. Only by something God would do typified by the slain lamb would they be reinstated to spin in the allegiance of a faith relationship to God.

Hence at creation, they were to ride on the spirit of the white horse as it followed the black horse, continually discovering God as he revealed His mysteries to them as they headed toward the north country. Yet there was the spirit of the grizzled and bay horses reflecting the power of choice to remain faithful to God, with the bay horse weighing whether or not he would follow God and the griseled one deciding to rebel against God and go for eating the forbidden fruit of the tree of knowledge of good and evil.

It is perceived that Adam and Eve upon creation rode on the white horses, having a bent to follow God. Yet in all their choices, they simultaneously rode in their "inner man" on the bay horse. With God's declaration and subsequent command, "You are free to eat of all the trees in the garden, but of the tree knowledge of good and evil you shall not eat, for in the day you eat, you shall surely die," Eve when she left the side of Adam and wandered toward the tree of knowledge of good and evil. Although created to ride on the bay horse, she decided to investigate the tree of knowledge of good and transferred to the griseled horse That horse took her from her original created position on the top side of the disk, called the Garden of Eden, to the bottom side of the disk, still in the Garden of Eden. Now Eve was not headed in the right direction. She was now headed toward investigation of the tree of knowledge of good and evil, in the south center pole of the spinning top. At that position she was tempted to entertain more knowledge of the tree of knowledge of good and evil which God had commanded them not to eat. While Eve had not sinned, in freedom, by transferring (in her inner being) to riding on the grisled horse, she was nevertheless more susceptible to be tempted by Satan outside faith temptations. Heading south toward the forbidden tree, she now (with her outer being coupled to her inner being) placed herself in a position where her original bent of faith in God could potentially be tempted to be broken. Originally created to ride in her inner being on the bay horse, known as the power of choice, simultaneously she rode, like all free beings in the universe of God's love, on the white horse toward the north, where God lives. In the Hebraic wilderness sanctuary, God the Father and God the Son are depicted as the two stacks of bread on the table of showbread. This table is also perceived to be God's north side throne in the holy place. From this bread priests, entering from the east, would eat once a week on Sabbath as it would be replaced by new six loaf stacks of bread.

Since the fall of Adam and Eve, it is perceived that believers in God simultaneously rode in their inner creature being on the on the bay horse power of choice, coupled to riding on the black horse who followed the white horse in allegiance to God. Riding on the black horse of their outer creature being, they would be tempted, while the rode simultaneously on their inner creature being bay horse powere of choice to disbelieve God. These temptations by the enticement of the devil, dragon, who dwelt in the tree of knowledge of good and evil, would come from the south center pole of the spinning top, through the vehicle of the spoken word of the serpent. Although this passage of Zech 6 does not tell in which direction the red horse and its rider went, it is perceived from the description of the red horse in Rev. 6:3, 4 that this is describing Lucifer's decision to rebel against God and enter into the experience of the originator of sin. Although provided for in freedom, evil, on the tails side of the love coin was not designed to be experienced. When he became Satan, the father of lies and the rider of the red horse, Lucifer was cast out of heaven to the south center of spinning top, tree of knowledge of good and evil in the Garden of Eden.

It is perceived that in Lucifer's unfallen state, he originally rode simultaneously on the bay and white horse spirit in his inner being. Mysteriously and unexplainably, because of his inner creature nature heart bent on the heads side of the love coin, he conceived that it did not matter to God what his relationship to the Creator was. This second person of the Godhead also rode on the white horse inner spirit as He omnipresently yoked himself to unfallen angelic beings also riding with bay horse inner spirit, on the white horse spirits. As such these unfallen angelic creatures were in pursuit of the things of God.

When the broken faith of sin occurred, Satan and his angels were cast out of heaven to the south center pole of the spinning top in the Garden of Eden with Adam and Eve originally on the upper horizontal plain of that top called Eden. From that position Satan, the dragon, through the medium of the serpent on the south center pole tempted Adam and Eve on the upper horizontal plain, to break faith in God and join them on the lower, south, underside horizontal plain.

After the fall of broken faith, the only way Adam and Eve, and for that matter fallen human nature, could be reinstated to the original upper side of the spinning top plain, called Eden, was to accept the type and antitypical lamb sacrifice. Once that sacrifice was accepted in their inner creature nature, bay horse, power of choice, their redeemed outer creature nature would be placed on the black horses which followed the white horses. In this explanation of the white, black, bay, red horse relationships to each other lies a parable, illustration, window, about provisional reconciliation available to God.

Herein lies a partial understanding of the window of freedom in which all unfallen creatures are created. God gives unfallen, moral, creatures the choice in their inner being as they ride on the inner spirit bay horse to decide to remain faithful and follow after God on the black horse spirit as they simultaneously ride with inner bay spirits on the white horses headed north toward the black horse symbol of God's spirit.

It was Lucifer's inner bay spirit, questioning outside a faith relationship to God, that led him to transfer from riding in his inner bay spirit on the white horse which heads north to the grisled horse spirit which heads south. While there is no description as to the direction that the red horse headed, it is perceived that God, in mystery, would hid from the rebellious what their end would be. Only after rebellion had occurred, despite God's pleading with them to return to a right relationship to God, transferring back to a bay horse spirit riding on white horse spirits, would Lucifer, who became Satan, know what his ultimate fate of rebellion, that is, banishment from God in a red horse experience.

While all free creatures, riding as bay spirit horses after white spirit horses had, had the capacity in their freedom of choice of choosing to ride, as bay spirit horses on grisled spirit horses, if followed to its end, despite the pleadings of God to return to their original bent of riding on white horse spirits, they, the followers of, or he, Lucifer, would become the red horse spirit, originator of sin, father of lies. This red horse would emerge in the second seal (Rev. 6:3, 4).

It is perceived that when Satan, speaking through the serpent, at the tree of knowledge of good and evil spoke to Eve, he may have been still riding in spirit on the bay horse spirit that runs to and fro, having not yet been sentenced to ride on the red horse spirit which would occur after calvary. The reason this perception is considered is because in the account of Job, God asks him in heaven where have you been and what are you doing when Satan answers "running to and fro" on the earth.

And it came to pass, as they still went on, and talked, that, behold, *there appeared* of [fire #784 aysh lit or fig], and [horses #5483 soos] of [fire #784 aysh lit. or fig.], and parted them both asunder; and Elijah [went up #5927 aw-law prim. sec. lit. or fig] by a whirlwind into heaven. (2 Kings 2:11)

And when the servant of the man of God was risen early, and gone forth, behold, an host compassed the city both with horses and chariots, And his servant said unto him, Alas, my master! How shall we do?

#5483 soos from an unused root; mean. to skip (prop. for joy): a horse (as leaping); also a swallow (from rapid flight); crane, horse [-back,-hoof] comp. 6571. Strongs, 1979

#5437 saw-bab'; a prim root ; to revolve, surround, border; used in various applications,) lit. and fig. (as follows): Strongs, 1979

#7393 reh-keb; from 7392; a vehicle; by imply. a team; by ext. calvary, by anal. A rider, i.e., The upper millstone, multitude [from the marg.] wagon Strongs, 19.

And he answered, Fear not: for they that be with us are more than they that be with them. And Elisha prayed, and said, I pray thee, open his eyes, that he may see. And the Lord opened the eyes of the young man; and he saw: and,: beheold, the mountain was full of horses (#5483 soos) and chariots (#7393 reh-keb) of fire (#784 aysh lit. or fig.) round about Elisha 2 Kings 6:16-17

#784 aysh. a prim. word; fire (lit. or fig.) burning, fiery, fire flaming, hot; _Strong_s, 1979. and horsemen, (#6571 paw-rash)

#6571 paw-rash; from 6567; a steed (as stretched out to, a vehicle, not single or for mounting [comp. 5488]; also by impl. A driver (in a chariot), i.e. (collect.) cavalry:-horseman, Strongs, 1979

#6571 pa-ras n.m. horse; horseman Strongs, 2001

And it came to pass, as they still went on, and talked, that _behold, there appeared_ a chariot (#7393 reh-keb) of fire (#784 aysh lit. or fig.), and (horses #5483 soos) of (fire, #784 aysh lit. or fig.) and parted them both asunder, and Elijah (went up #5927 aw-law prim. sec. lit or fig.) by a (whirlwind #5591 sah-ar) into heaven. (2 Kings 2:11)

And when the days of mourning were past, Joseph spake unto the house of pharaoh, saying, If how I have found grace in yours eyes, speak, I pray you in the ears of Pharaoh, saying,

If now I have found grace in your eyes, speak I pray you, in the ears of Pharaoh saying; My father made me swear, saying, Lo, I die in my grave which I have digged for me in the land of Canaan, there shall thou bury me. Now therefore let me go up, I pray thee, and bury my father, and I will come again. And Pharaoh said, Go up, and bury they father, according as he made thee swear.

And Pharaoh said, "Go up, and bury thy father, according as he made thee swear. And Joseph went up to bury his father: and with him went up all the servants of Pharaoh, the elders of his house, and all the elders of the land of Egypt. And all the house of Joseph, and his brethren and his father's house: only their little one, and their flocks, and their herds, they left in the land of Goshen. And there went up with him both chariots (#7393 reh-keb) and horsemen: and it was a very great company." (Gen. 50:4–9)

I. Four horses of the apocalypse Rev. 6:1–8

And I saw when the Lamb opened on of the seals, and I heard, as it were the noise of thunder, one of the four beasts saying, "Come and see."

And I saw, and behold a white horse: and he tat sat on him had a bow; and a crown was given unto him: and he went forth conquering, and to conquer.

And when he had opened the second seal, I heard the second beast say, "Come and see."

And there went out another horse that was red: and power was given to him that sat thereon to take peace from the earth, and that they should kill one another: and there was given unto him a great sword.

And when he had opened the third seal, I heard the third beast say, "Come and see." And I beheld a black horse: and he that sat on him had a pair of balances in his hand

And I heard a voice in the midst of the four beasts say, A measure of wheat for a penny, and three measures of barley for a penny; and see thou hurt not the oil and the wine.

And when he had opened the fourth seal, I heard the voice of the fourth beast say, "Come and see."

And I looked, and behold a pale horse: and his name that sat on him was Death, and Hell followed him. And power was given unto them over the fourth part of the earth, to kill with sword and with hunger, and with death, and with the beasts of the earth.

White horse with rider followed by an army clothed in fine linen on white horses.

And I saw heaven opened, and behold a white horse; and he that sat upon him was called Faithful and True, and in righteousness he doth judge and make war. (Rev. 20:11)

And the armies *which were* in heaven followed him upon white horses, clothed in fine linen, white and clean. (Rev. 19:14) and with many ships;

For in one hour so great riches is come to nought. And every shipmaster, and all the company in ships, and sailors, and as many as trade by sea, stood afar off. (Rev. 18:17)

And they cast dust on their heads, and cried, weeping and wailing, saying, Alas, alas, that great city, wherein were made rich all that had ships in the sea by reason of her costliness! For in one hour is she made desolate. (Rev. 18:19)

And he shall enter into the countries

And the Lord said unto Moses, Speak unto Aaron thy brother, that he come not at all times into the holy place within the vail, before the mercy seat, which is upon the ark; that he die not: for I will appear in the cloud upon the mercy seat. (Lev. 16:2)

Thus shall Aaron come into the holy place, with a young bullock for a sin offering, and a ram for a burnt offering. (Lev. 16:3)

And Aaron shall offer his bullock of the sin offering, which is for himself, and make an atonement for himself and for his house. (Lev. 16.6)

This is a reiteration of the comment at the beginning of Daniel 11:40. Prophetically and historically these prophecies were fulfilled at the following times and locations, before the conclusion of the twenty-three hundred day/year prophecy of Daniel 8:14.

"Immediately after the tribulation [A.D. 538–A.D. 1798][494] of those days shall the sun be darkened. [A.D May 19, 1780] and the moon shall not give her light and the stars shall fall from heaven [Nov. 13, 1833][495], and the powers of the heavens shall be shaken [A.D. Nov. 1, 1755 Lisbon, Portugal earthquake][496]. And then shall appear the sign of the Son of man in heaven" (Mt. 24:30).

Sign of the Son of Man

Let them make me a sanctuary that I may dwell among them. — Exodus 25:8

"The mistake had not been in the reckoning of the prophetic periods but in the event to take place at the end of the 2,300 days. Through this error, the believers had suffered disappointment, yet all that was foretold by the prophecy and all that they had any Scripture warrant to expect had been accomplished. At the very time when they were lamenting the failure of their hopes, the event had taken place which was foretold by the message and which must be fulfilled before the Lord could appear to give reward to His servants.

Christ had come not to the earth as they expected, but as foreshadowed in the type, to the most holy place of the temple of God in heaven. He represented by the prophet Daniel as coming at this time to the Ancient of Days: "I saw in the night visions, and, behold, one like the Son of man came with the clouds of heaven, and came"—not to the earth, but—"to the Ancient of Days, and they brought Him near before Him" (Daniel 7:13")[497]

"The coming is foretold also by the prophet Malachi: "The Lord, who ye seek, shall suddenly come to His temple, even the Messenger of the covenant, whom ye delight in: behold, He shall come, saith the Lord of hosts" (Malachi 3:1). The coming of the Lord to His temple was sudden, unexpected, to His people. They were not looking for Him *there*. They expected Him to come to earth, "in flaming fire taking vengeance on them that know not God, and that obey not the gospel" (2 Thessalonians 1:8)"

"The coming of Christ as our high priest to the most holy place, for the cleansing of the sanctuary, brought to view in Daniel 8:14; the coming of the son of man to the Ancient of Days, as presented in Daniel

7:13; and the coming of the Lord to His temple, foretold by Malachi, are descriptions of the same event; and this is also represented by the coming of the bridegroom to the marriage, described by Christ in the parable of the ten virgins of Matthew 25."[499]

"I saw the Father rise from the throne, and in a flaming chariot go into the holy of holies within the veil, and sit down. Then Jesus rose up from the throne, and most of those who were bowed down arose with Him. I did not see one ray of light pass from Jesus to the careless Multitude after He arose, and they were left in perfect darkness. Those who arose when Jesus did kept their eyes fixed on Him as He left the throne and led them out a little way. Then He raised His right arm, and we heard His lovely voice saying, "Wait here; I am going to My Father to receive the kingdom; keep your garments spotless, and in a little while I will return from the wedding and receive you to Myself." Then a cloudy chariot, with wheels like flaming fire, surrounded by angels, came to where Jesus was. He stepped into the chariot and was borne into the holiest where the Father sat. There I beheld, Jesus, a great high priest standing before the Father."[500]

Therefore say, Thus saith the Lord God; Although I have (#7368 raw-khar) cast them far off among the heathen, and although I have scattered them among the [countries, (776 eh-rets)] yet will I be to them as a little sanctuary in the (#776 eh-rets countries) where they shall come. (Ezek. 11:16)

776 eh-rets from an unused root prob. Mean. to be firm. The earth (at large or partitively a land)):- -x common, country, earth, field, ground, land x nations, way, wilderness, world Strongs, 1979

776 'eres n. f. & m, world, earth, all inhabited lands; parts of the earth (in contrast to water), ground, soil, country, region, territory; "heaven and earth" means the totality of creation. "the ends of the earth" means "a very distant place." Strongs, 2001

7368 raw-khak: a prim. root; to widen (in any direction) i.e. (intrans.) recede, (or) (trans.) remove (lit. or fig. of place or relation):- [a-, be, cast, drive, get, go, keep (self), put, remove, be too, (wander), withdraw] far (away, off), loose, x refrain, very, (be) a good way (off) Strongs, 1979

This passage is analogous to the truth Christ spoke to the Samaritan woman at the well, "The time and has now come when the true worshipers will worship the Father in spirit and in truth, for they are the kind of worshipers the Father seeks. God is spirit, and his worshipers must worship in spirit and in truth (Jn. 4:23).

Like the Old Testament recorded after the deliverance from Egypt by the blood of the lamb on their doorposts, the Israelites experienced the baptism of the Red Sea. In that experience, they declared that they longed to be dead to the ways of Egyptian slavery/sin. With the center of their experience was the sanctuary which goverenered their wanderings in the wilderness for forty years. Then crossing the Jordan into the promised land, they experienced the age of the judges, building Solomon's temple. In Jerusalem being destroyed by the Babylonians, the Israelited nation was scattered to places like Babylon, Medo-Persia, Greece, and being ruled by those nations including Rome. All during the time of their captivity, the Israelite nation was unable to worship in Jerusalem. Yet during these years of exile they were able to worship God figuratively/spiritual in their inner being as a little sanctuary wherever they were, since they had been "cast off"[see Ezekiel 11:16]out of literal Jerusalem, Just as their worship was "literal or figurative/ [spiritual] of place or relation,"501 now they could literally be with Christ, the antitypical fulfillment of the temple, experiencing how He walked with God, themselves following him in their deportment of life In their minds they would litterally remember the calvary scene when all their sins were placed on him the Lamb of God For them the antitypical daily provisional forgiveness of sin, was instituted. In their minds eye seeing their Savior Christ Jesus rise from the dead, victorious over sin and the grave, and death, so the believer would be invited to enter into the heavenly sanctuary. That heavenly sanctuary was enclosed with Christ's righteousness, even as the linen curtain enclosed the earthly sanctuary. The believer would be invited to accept Christ's atoning sacrifice as his substitute sacrifice for sin, then rise in newness of life, to be like their risen Savior, Christ Jesus.

and shall over flow(#7857 shaw-taf)

#7857 shaw-taf; a prim root: to gush: by impl. to inundate, cleanse; by anal.

to conquer: drown, (over-) flow (-whelm), rinse, run, rush, (thoroughly) wash (away) Strongs Concordance, 1979

Same word used in Dan. 11:22 "And with the arms of a flood #7858 shall they be [overflown #7857 shaw-taf]

and pass over(#5674 aw-bar)

#5674 aw-bar: a prim. root; to crossover; used very widely of transition (lit. fig.; trans. intrans., intens. or causat.). spec. to cover in (copulation):-alienate, alter, x at all, beyond, bring (over, through), carry over, (over-) come, (on, over), conduct (over), convey over, current, deliver, do away, enter, escape, fail, gender, get over (make) go (away, beyond, by, forth, his way, in, on, over, through), (cause to, make) + proclaim (-ation), perish, provoke to anger, put away, put away, rage, + raiser of taxes, remove, send over, set apart + shave, cause to (make), sound x speedily, x sweet smelling, take (away), (make to) transgress (-or), translate, + turn away, [way-] faring man, beneath. Strongs 1979

Same word as used in Ex. 12:23, "When the Lord will [pass #5674] through the land to smite.

For the Lord will [pass [#5674 aw-bar)] through to [smite #5062 nah-gaf] the Egyptians; and when he [seeth #7200 raw-aw lit. or fig, direct and impl., trans, intran. and causat.] l the blood upon the lintel, and on the two side posts, the Lord will {pass over #6452 naw-gaf [fig.] to skip over (or spare)} the door, and will not suffer the destroyer to come in unto your houses to smite [#5062 naw-gaf] you."

(#5062 naw-gaf) the Egyptians; and when he seeth the blood upon the lintel, and on the two side posts, the Lord will pass over (#6452 pan-sakh) the door, and will not suffer the destroyer to come in unto your houses to [smite #5062 naw-gaf)] you.

#6452 pan-sakh a prim. root; to hop, i.e. (fig) to skip over (or spare); by impl. To hesitate: also lit. to limp, dance, halt, become lame, leap, passover. Strongs, 1979

#6452 pa-sah, v. [Q] to pass over; to be limp; [N] to become crippled; to worship in a limping dance:- Strongs, 2001

Same word as used in Ex 12:12. "For I will pass through (#5674 aw-bar)the land of Egypt this night, and will smite (#5221 naw-kaw) all the firstborn in the land of Egypt, both man and beast; and against all the gods of Egypt I will execute judgment: I am the Lord."

#5221 naw-kaw: a prim. root: to strike (lightly or severely, lit. or fig):- beat, cast forth, clap, give [wound], X go forward, slaughter, slay (-er, -ing) smite (-r, -ing) strike, be striken, (give) stripes, X surely, wound Strongs, 1979

#5521 na-ka v. [N] to be struck; [Pu] to be destroyed: [H] to kill, slaughter, destroy, defeat, [Ho] be struck, be wounded, be killed Strongs, 2001

Thus at the time of the end of the 2,300-day prophecy of Daniel 8:14, the investigative judgment begins the Day of Atonement coming of God to this earth. He investigates the lives of all who have experienced the sleep of death to see if they were or were not in a right relationship to

God. In the initial judgment of the dead, God marks those who were in a favorable relationship to Him as fit to experience the first resurrection of Daniel 12. Those who were not in a favorable relationship to Him would resurrection at the end of the millennium to experience the fate of Satan and his fallen angels, banishment from the presence of God in the lake of fire.

Thus the judgment of the dead would overflow the whole earth, with some being found fit to live with God forever, and experience "everlasting life" (Dan. 12:2),being passed over with that mark while others would be found unfit, not having the mark and be unfit for the first resurrection, only fit for the second resurrection to experience "everlasting contempt" (Dan. 12:2) and suffer the ultimate fate of eternal banishment from God's presence, prepared only for the devil and his angels.

This would be like the parable of the sheep and the goats, wise or foolish virgins, or the wise contrasted to the foolish builder. If the sheep, wise virgins, or wise builder experienced the sleep of death, they would await the first resurrection and awake to "everlasting life." If the goats, foolish virgins, or foolish builder experienced the sleep of death, they would awake at the second resurrection at the end of the millennium to everlasting contempt.

It was this investigative judgment arrow in God's quiver that would determine who would be part of the first or second resurrection.

DANIEL 11:41

41. He shall enter also into the glorious land, and many countries shall be overthrown: but these shall escape out of his hand, even Edom, and Moab, and the chief of the children of Ammon.
He shall enter also into the glorious land

I. Paul 1963–1978

The following section was lifted from *http://www.times-of-Israel.com/ pope-paul-vi-first-pontiff-to-first-visit-israel*

Paul VI, who reigned from 1963 to 1978, visited Jerusalem in Janua 1964 on a brief trip to Israel and Jordan. It was the first time a reignin pope had visited the Holy Land. At the time, the Vatican did n recognize Israel as a state. – Israel and the Holy See established fu diplomatic relations in 1993. Also, his trip came before the landma Nostra Aetate declaration of 1965 which opened .the way to Catholi Jewish dialogue.

Pope Francis will visit Israel, Jordan, and the Palestinian Authority at the end of May, in part to mark the 50th anniversary of Pau VI's trip. Both Francis's predecessors, Benedict XVI and John Paul II visited Israel.[502]

The following section was lifted from *www.Jewishvirtuallibrary.org/ source/anti-semitism/jp.html*

II. John Paul II (1978–2005)

Pope John Paul II arrive in Israel March 21, 200, for a historic five-day visit during which he visited the holy sites of the three major religions and met with Israel's political leaders and Chief Rabbis.[503]

The following sections were lifted from *http://en.wikipedia.org/wiki/ list_of_Journeys_of-Pope_Benedict_xvi*

III. Benedict XVI (2005–2013)

    A. Jordan, Israel, and the Palestinian territories (May 8 to May 15, 2009)

    B. The pope (Benedict XVI) arrived in Amman, Jordan on 8 May, embar his tour of Jordan, Israel, and the Palestinian Territories.[504]

And many countries shall be overthrown:

The following sections were lifted from *http://en.wikipedia.org/wiki/list_of_Journeys_of-Pope_Benedict_xvi*

With an average of three foreign journeys per year from 2006 to 2009, Pope Benedict was as active in visiting other countries as his predecessor John Paul II was at the same age from 1999 to 2002. Pope Benedict was more active since then, however making five foreign journeys each in both 2010 and 2011, significantly more than the six total trips made by Pope John Paul at the same age in 2003 and 2994. As of the 2012 apostolic journey to Mexico and Cuba, Pope Benedict XVI is older than Pope John Paul II was at the time of his death and is now the oldest pope to travel outside Europe as well as being the oldest pope to travel to Africa, Asia (including the Middle East), Australia, or the Americas.[505]

But these shall escape out of his hand,

The perceived reason Edom, Moab, and the chief of the children of Ammon escape out of the hand of the religio-politico vile person [i.e., the influential system of Roman Catholicism, who maintains belief in the intercession of saints, going against the state of the dead and the fourth commandment of the Decalogue] is that these countries have a new name Jordan by the time the Roman Catholic pope travels in them.

Even Edom and Moab and chief of the children of Ammon.

The following sections were lifted from *http://en.wikipedia.org/wiki/Jordan*

In antiquity, the present-day Jordan became a home for several Semitic Canaanite-speaking ancient kingdoms, including the kingdom of Edom, the kingdom of Moab, and kingdom of Ammon, the kingdom of Israel, and also the Amalekites.[506]

Today the land of Edom is part of Jordan.[507]

The following sections were lifted from *www.ancient_hebrew.org/21_edom.html*

In biblical lore, Edom was the implacable adversary and menacing neighbor of the Israelites. The Edomites lived south of the Dead Sea and east of the desolate rift valley known as Wadi Arabah, and from time to time, they had to be dealt with by force, notably by the likes of Kings David and Solomon.

An international team of archaeologists has recorded radiocarbon dates that they say show the tribes of Edom may have indeed come together in a cohesive society at early as the 12th century BC, certainly by the 10th. The evidence was found in the ruins of a large copper processing center and fortress at Khirbat en Nahas in the lowlands of what was Edom and is now part of Jordan.[508]

Today the country known as Moab does not exist, the area that was Moab during Biblical times is now part of Jordan.

The following sections were lifted from *http:// englishdictionary. education/en/ammon*

Ammon, also referred to as the Amonites and children of Ammon, was an ancient nation best known from the Old Testament which describes Ammon as located east of the Jordan River, Gilead, and the Dead Sea, in present-day Jordan. The chief city of the country was Rabbah or Rabboth. Ammon, site of the modern city of Amman, Jordan's capital Milcom and Molech (who may be one and the same) as named in the Bible as the gods of Ammon.[510]

DANIEL 11:42

42. He shall stretch forth his hand also upon the countries: and the land of Egypt shall not escape.

He shall stretch forth his hand also upon the countries;

Pope Paul VI June 21, 1963– Aug. 6, 1978

The following section is lifted, although not quoted, from _en.wikipedia/ wiki/list_of_pastoral_visits_of_Pope_Paul_VI_

1964 Jan. 4–6 Jordan and Israel

Dec. 2-5 Lebanon, and India

1965 Oct. 4 Unites States

1967 May 13 Portugal July 25–26 Turkey

1968 August 21–25 Columbia and Bermuda

1969 June 10 Switzerland

July 31–August 2 Uganda

1970 November 25–December 5, 1970—Iran, East Pakistan (now Bangladesh) (stopped over in Dacca), Philippines, America Samoa (Stopped over in Pago Pago) Samoa, Australia, Indonesia, Hong Kong, and Celone. The pope's last international trip took him to nine countries. He met several heads of state including shah Mohammad Reza Pahlavi of Iran, President Ferdinand Marcos of the Philippines, the o-le-Ao-o-le-Malo of Samoa Malietoa tanumaffi, Governor General Paul Hasluch of Australia, and Present Shuarto of Indonesia. On November 27, 1970, the pope was the target of an assignation attempt by Benjamin Mendoza amor of Flores at Manila International airport in the Philippines.[512]

And the land of Egypt shall not escape.

On April 8, 2013, Botros Fahim Awad Hanna was appointed bishop of Miya Egypt by Pope Francis.[513]

The following sections were lifted, although not quoted, from _http:// huffingpost.com.//2013/05/10/pope-tawados-ii-ppe_

Vatican City – Two popes prayed together Friday at the Vatican, one Catholic and one Orthodox, in a sign of improving ties following the election of new leaders for both churches.

Pope Francis welcomed the head of the Coptic Orthodox Church of Egypt, Pope Tawadro II, in the first such meeting at the Vatican in 40 years, saying his visit "strengthens the bonds of Friendship and brotherhood" between the two churches.

The Coptic and Catholic churches split in the fifth century over theocratic differences.

The occasion was to mark the 40th anniversary of a declaration improving ties signed in 1973 at the Vatican by pope Paul VI and Tawadros' predecessor, pope Shenouda III who died last year. The late pope John Paul II visited

Shenouda in Cairo in 2000.

The following sections were lifted from en.wikipedia.org/wiki/Pope_ Paul_VI. In May 1973, the Coptic Patriarch Shenouda III of Alexandria visited the Vatican where he met three times with Pope Paul VI. A common declaration and joint Creed issued after the visit demonstrated that there are virtually no more theological discrepancies between the Coptic and Roman Catholic Churches.[515]

The following sections were lifted from *http://en.wikipedia/wiki/pope_ Shendouda_III_of_Alexandria*

"In 1973 Pope Shenouda II became the first Coptic Orthodox Pope of Alexandria to meet the Pope of Rome in over 1,500 years. In this visit Pope Shenouda III and Pope Paul VI singed a common declaration on the issue of Christology and agreed to further discussions on Christianity. There were also dialogues with various Protestant churches worldwide."[516]

The following sections were lifted from *http://en.wikipedia.orge/wiki/ pope_shenouda_III_Of_Alexandria*

In a message of condolence to Copts, the Roman Catholic Pope Benedict XVI said, "I recall with gratitude his commitment to Christian Unity, his memorable visit to my predecessor Pope Paul VI, and their signing of the Joint Declaration of Faith in the Incarnation of the Son of God together in Rome on 10 May 1973 as well as his Cairo meeting with Pope John Paul II during the Great Jubilee of the Incarnation on 24 February 2000[517]. I can say how the Catholic Church as a whole shares the grief that afflicts the Orthodox Copts, and how she stands in fervent prayer asking that He, who is the Resurrection and the Life, might welcome his faithful servant."

He offered prayers for Shenouda on the day of his death and was said to share the point of Copts over Shenouda's death.

Director of the Holy See Press Office Federico Lombardi said that He, Benedict XVI desired that "the Lord welcomes this great pastor" and added that "we will never forget the meeting between Pope Shenoudda III and Pope John Paul II in Cairo on the occasion of his pilgrimage to Mount Sanai [in 2000]." A statement attributed to him read: "The Catholic Church shares in the grief and prayers of Coptic Christians in mourning the loss of their spiritual leader ... May the Lord welcome this great shepherd and give him the reward he deserves for his service. In a message of condolence to Copts, the Roman Catholic Pope Benedict XVI said: "I recall with gratitude his commitment to Christian Unity, his memorable visit to my predecessor Pope Paul VI, and their signing of the Joint Declaration of Faith in the Incarnation of the son of God together in Rome on 10 May 1973, as well as his Cairo meeting with Pope John Paul II during the great Jubilee of the Incarnation on 24 February 2000 (Feb. 13, 2015). I can say how the Catholic Church as a whole shares the grief that afflicts the Orthodox Copts, and how she stands in fervent prayer asking the he, who is the Resurrection and the Life, might welcome his faithful servant." He offered prayers for Shenouda on the day of his death and was said to share the pain of Copts over Shenouda's death.

Director of the Holy See Press Office federico Lombardi said that He, Benedict XVI desired that "the Lord welcomes this great pastor" and added that "we will never forget the meeting between Pope Shenouda III and Pope John Paul II in Cairo on the occasion of his pilgrimage to Mount Sinai [in 2000... A statement attributed to him read: "The Catholic Church shares in the grief and prayers of Coptic Christians in mourning the loss of their spiritual leader. . . May the Lord welcome this great shepherd and give him the reward he deserves for his service."

In a message of condolence to Copts, the Roman Catholic Pope Benedict XVI said:. . . I recall with gratitude his commitment to Christian Unity, his memorable visit to my predecessor Pope Paul VI and their signing of the Joint Declaration of Faith in the Incarnation of the son of God together in Rome on 10 May 1973, as well as his Cairo meeting with Pope John Paul II during the Great Jubilee of the Incarnation on 24 Feb 2000.]

DANIEL 11:43

43. But he shall have power over the treasures of gold and of silver, and over all the precious things of Egypt: and the Libyans and the Ethiopians shall be at his steps.

Have power over the treasures of gold and of silver

"A growing source of precious metal came from Nazi concentration camps and death camps, where all property was taken from the victims, and included personal effects such as wedding rings, eye glasses, pocket watches, cigarette cases, jewelry and gold teeth. (All other substantial property, such as houses, paintings, shares, and bonds, were stolen from the victims before they entered camps.) The gold was collected at the camps and sent to the Reichsbank under the false-name Max Heilger accounts for melting down for bullion".[518]

The following sections are lifted from _http://www.archives.gov/ publications/prologue/1999/spring/nazi-gold-_

"Nazi Gold: The Merkers Mine Treasure"

Late on the evening of March 22, 1945, elements of Lt. Gen. George Patton's Third Army crossed the Rhine, and soon thereafter his whole army crossed the river and drove into the heart of Germany. Advncing noreast from Frankfurt, elements of the Third Army cut into the future Soviet Zone and advanced on Gotha. Just before noon on April 4, the village of Merkers fell to the Third Batalion of the 358th Infantry Regiment, Ninetieth Infantry Division, Third Army. During that day the next ninetieth Infantry Division, with its command post at Keiselbach, consolidated its holdings in the Merkers area. (1) During April 4 and 5, displaced persons in the vicinity interrogated by the Counter Intelligence Corps (CIC) personnel of the Ninetieth Infantry Division mentioned a recent movement of German Reichsbank gold from Berlin to the Wintershal AG's Kaiseroda potassium mine at Merkers. In all of these instances

they quoted rumors, but none stated their own knowledge that gold was present in the mine. But just before noon on April 5, a member of Military Intelligence Team 404-G, attached to the 358th Infantry Regiment, who was in Bad Salzungen, about six miles from Merkers, interviewed French displaced persons who had worked in the mine at Merkers. They told him they had heard that gold had been stored in the mine. The information was passed on to the G-2 (intelligence section) of the Ninetieth Infantry Division, and orders issued prohibiting all civilians from circulating in the area of the mine. (2)

Early the next morning, two military policemen guardig the road entering Keiselbach from Merkers saw two women approaching and promply challenged and stopped them. Upon questioning, the women stated that they were French displaced persons. One of the women was pregnant and said she was being accompanied by the other to see a midwife in Keiselbach. After being questioned at XII Corps Provost Marshal Office, they were driven back into Merkers. Upon entering merkers, their driver saw the Kaiseroda mine and asked the woen what sort of mine it was. They said it was the mine in which the German gold reserve and valuable artworks had been deposited several weeks before and added that local civilians and displaced persons had been used for labor in unloading and storing the treasure in the mine. (3)

By noon on April 6 the women's story had reached Lt. Col. William A. Russell the Ninetieth Infantry Division G-5 (cilvian affairs) officer. He proceeded to the mine, where interviews whith displaced persons in the area confirmed the women's story. They told him that works of art were also stored in the mine and that Dr. Paul Ortwin Rave, curator of the German State Museum in Berlin as well an assistant director of the National Galleries in Berlin, was present to care for the paintings. Russell then confronted mine officials with this information, and they stated they knew that gold and valuable art were stored in the mine and that other mines in the area were likewise used for storing valuables. Russel also questioned werner Veick, the head cashier of the Reichsbank's Foreign Notes department who was also in the mine, and Rave. The latter informed Russell that he was in Merkers to care for paintings stored in the mine. Veick indicated that the gold in the mine constituted the entire reserve of the Reichsbank in Berlin. (4)

Russell also that afternoon told a XII Corps G-5 officer what was going on at the mine site, and word was passed on to the Corps Commander Maj. Gen. Manton S. Eddy. He immediately called Patton and informed him of the capture of the German gold reserves at Merkers. Patton, who had been burned on so many rumors, told him not to mention the capture of the gold until they definitely confirmed it. (6)

Throughout most of the war, the bulk of the German gold reserves was held at the Reichsbank in Berlin. In 1943, however, some gold bars were shipped to numerous branches of the Reichsbank. During late 1944 and early 1945, as American bombing of Berlin increased and the Allies pushed towar the city from the east and west, more of the gold reserve was dispersed to branch banks in central and southern Germany. Also, early in 1945, a large quantity of Reichsmarks were dispatched from Berlin to branch banks. (8)

Following the bombing [February 3, 1945], Walter Funk, president of the Reichsbank and Reich minister of economics, decided to send most of the gold reserves, worth som $238 million, and a larhge quantity of the monetary reserves to a mine at Merkers, about two hundred miles southwest of Berlin, for safekeeping. Space in that mine, like all of the other salt and potassium mines in Germany, had been requisitioned by the government because firms found it necessary to store materialsa and continue armament production underground because of the bombings. (9)

On February 11 most of the gold reserves, including gold brought back from the branch banks to Berlin for shipment to Merkers, currency reserves totaling a billion Reichsmarks bundled in one thousand bags, and a considerable quanty of foreign currency, were transported by rail to Merkers. Once the train reached merkers, the treasure was unloaded and placed in a special vault area in designated Room No. 8. (10)

In addition to the shipment to Merkers, it was decided to send a substantial quantity of currency and staff to the Reichsbank branch in Erfurt in early February. The currency and upwards of ten employees were sent packing to Erfurt. Among them were Veick and Otto Reimer, chief cashier in the Reichsmarks Department. Once there they began circulating money to other branch banks as well as sending some of it back to Berlin when the need arose. Currency was also taken out of the Merkers mine and redistributed to branch banks and to the Reichsband in Berlin as needed. (11)

The Schutzstaffen's (ZZ) Office for Economy and Administration, which operated the concentration camps, also wanted their loot held by the Reichsbank to be sent to Merkers for safekeeping. From August 26, 1942. Until January 27, 1945, the SS made seventy-six deliveries to the Reichsbank of property seized from concentration camp victims.

This stolen property was received for a holding account in the name of "Meimer," named for SS Capt. Bruno Melmer, who made most of the deliveries. Gold jewelry was sold abroad, gold of some fineness was sold either to the Prussian Mint or to Dequssa, a large Berman industrial firm that engaged in the refinement of precious metals. Securities, foreign currency, and similar items were purchased by the reichsbank. Much of the miscellaneous jewelry was sold through the Berlin Municipal Pawn Shop. Once the transactions took place, the proceeds were credited to the account of "Max Heiliger," codeword for Heinrich Himmler and his SS. By early 1945, much of the loot had been processed, but a significant amount still remained with the Reichsbank. (12)

The confiscated property on hand in March 1945 consisted of all kinds of gold and silver items ranging from dental work to cigarette cases, diamonds, gold and silver coins, foreign currencies, and gold and silver bars. The gold and silver bars were placed in 18 bags, and the remainder of the loot was placed in 189 suitcases, trunks and boxes and, along with other items, were sent by rail to Merkers on March 18. The Shipment was under the control of Albert Thoms, head of the Reichsbank's Precious Metals Department. Once the SS loot arrived, it was stored in Room No. 8 along with the gold and currency. (13)"[519]
The following section is lifted from _http://www.archives.gov/publications/prologue/1999/spring/nazi-gold-merkers-mine-treasure.html_

"Nazi gold (German Raubgold, "stolen gold") is the rumored gold allegedly transferred by Nazi Germany to overseas banks during World War II, The regime is believed to have executed a policy of looting the assets of its victims to finance the war, collecting the looted assets in central depositories. The occasional transfer of gold in return for currency took place in collusion with many individual collaborative institutions. The precise identities of those institutions, as well as the exact extent of the transactions, remain unclear.

The present whereabouts of Nazi gold that disappeared into the European banking institutions in 1945 has been the subject of several books, conspiracy theories, and a failed civil suit brought in July 2000 against the Vatican Bank the Franciscan Order, and other defendants."
"U.S. Document Links Vatican, Nazi Gold"
July 23, 1997-Tyler Marshall-Times Staff Writer

Washington—Two months after a comprehensive U.S. study severely criticized Switzerland and several other neutral countries for dealing in gold plundered by Nazis during World War II, a U.S. government document came to light for the first time Tuesday containing evidence that links the Vatican with such dealings.

The 1946 Treasury Department document states that the Nazi puppet regime in Croatia, the Ustashe, smuggled about 350 million Swis francs (about $295 million at today's prices) out of Yugoslavia 'where Jew and Serbs were plundered to support the Ustashe organization in exile,' apparently during the Third Reich's final months. The document said that 'approximately 200 million [francs, valued today at $170 million] was original held in the Vatican for safekeeping.'

The document goes on to cite a rumor that much of this money was latter funneled to Spain and Argentina through what it termed the "Vatican's pipeline" to finance the lifestyles of fleeing Nazis.

In Rome chief Vatican spokesman Joaquin Navarro-Valls dismissed the document's validity. "There is no basis in reality to the report," he said, adding that the account was based on an anonymous source "whose reliability is more than dubious."[521]

The following is lifted from en.wikipedia.org/wikiNazi_goldVatican

"On October 21, 1946, the U.S. State Department received a Top Secret report from US Treasury Agent Emerson Bigelow. The report released by the U.S. government finally in 1997, established that Bigelow received reliable information on the matter from the American Office of Strategic Services (OSS) or CIC intelligence officials of the US Army. The document referred to as the "Bigelo Report" was declassified on December 31, 1996, and released in 1997.

The report asserted that in 1945, the Vatican had confiscated 250 million Swiss francs in Nazi gold for "safekeeping," of which 150 million Swiss francs had been impounded by British authorities at the Austro-Swiss border. The report also stated that the balance of the gold was held in one of the Vatican's numbered Swiss bank accounts. Intelligence reports, which corroborated the Bigelo Report, also suggested that more than200 million Swiss francs, a sum largely in gold coins, were eventually transferred to Vatican City of to the Institute for Works of religion (a.k.a. the Vatican Bank), with the assistance of Roman Catholic clergy and the Franciscan Order.

Such claims, however, are denied by the Vatican Bank. "There is no basis in reality to the [Bigelow] report," said Vatican spokesman Joaquin Navarro-Valls, as reported in Time magazine."[522]

The following section is lifted from *http//www.msn.com/encyclopedia/world/Vatican-city-the-palaces-vatican-treasure.html*

Vatican City
The Palaces and the Vatican's Treasures

The Vatican palaces are an irregular mass of three-story and four story buildings, built on long plain lines and broken by additions and alterations. The papal residence and offices occupy the portion near the colonnade, and the rest is given over to museums and the Vatican Library...The Vatican museums are among the most important in the world; they are the Museo- Pio-Clementino, founded in the 18th century. And containing one of the world's great collections of antiquities; the Chiaramont Museum, founded in the early 19th cent and holding a collection of Greek sculptures and Renaissance imitations; the Braccio Nuovo, considered by many to be the most beautiful of all the museums; The Egyptian Museum and the Etruscan Museum, opposite the Braccio Nuovo; and the Pinacoteca Vaticana (opened in 1932), which contains paintings by Giotto, Guercino, Caravaggio, Poussin and others.

The museums, however, house only part of the Vatican's treasure, for many of the Renaissance and modern paintings are found in the galleries surrounding the various courtyards, such as the Cortile del Belvedere and the Cortile San Damasco. Adjoining the Cortile San Damasco is the building containing the Borgia apartments on the first floor and the Raphael rooms on the second. The works of Raphael and his followers in the building make it one of the most famous artistic monuments in the world. The Vatican Library lies all along the western side of the Giardino della Pigna and Cortile del Bevedere. It is one of the world's richest repositories of ancient and medieval manuscripts in many languages. The principal chapel in the Vatican is the Sistine Chapel, the ceiling of which was painted (1508–12) by Michelangelo.[523]

and over all the precious things of Egypt

The following sections were lifted from *http//www.msn.com/ encyclopedia/world/Vatican-city-the-palaces-vatican-*

Egyptian Museum

The museum was founded by Gregory XVI (1831–1846). In the lateran palace in 1884 and John XXIII had it relocated in the Vatican in 1970. It contains Greek original works, Roman copies and sculptures dating from the 1st to the third c. A.D. The most famous group is Athena and Marsyas, a copy of a Greek original by Myron (c450 B. C.) Inaugurated by Pius XI in 1926 this museum was also moved from the Lateran Palace. The collection consists of artworks and historical vestiges from missions all over the world. There are some interesting models of non-Catholic places of worship, such as Beijing's Temple of the Sky (originally from the 15th century but re-done in the 18th century), the altar of Confucius and the Shinoist Temple of Nara, Japan's ancient capital city. The Buddhist devotional statues are testimonies of spiritual life in Tibet, Indonesia, India and the Far East: the findings of Islamic and Central African culture are also interesting and so are objects and works of art, especially from Mexico, Guatemala and Nicaragua.[524]

The following sections were lifted from *www.viator.com/Rome-*

The Vatican Egyptian Obelisk, often simply called the Vatican Obellisk, is situated in the middle of St Peter's square and standing 84 feet (25.5 meters) high, it's the second largest of the 13 remaining obelisks in Rome. It has survived two millennia of world history and was brought from Heliopolis to Rome on the order of Caligula in 37 A. D. as a demonstration of power in ancient times, it was located in the center of Circus of Nero, but was moved in 1588 to the famous St Peter's Square which was built around it later on.[525]

The following sections were lifted from *http://voanews.com/ mediaassets2/learningenglish/2012_04/se-exp-vatican-*

Pope Gregory the Sixteenth established the Etruscan Museum in 1837. The collections include vases and objects made of bronze and gold. It also includes statues of full human bodies and sculptures representing heads. In addition you can see objects that added beauty to the Etruscan temples or religious centers.[526]

and the Libyans

Pope Benedict (XVI elected April 19, 2005, inaugurated April 24, 2005, until resignation Feb. 28, 2013527) calls for suspension of arms in Libya crisis. March 27, 2011 Lissacaldena[528]

Benghazi Cathedral is a former Roman Catholic cathedral in the city of Benghazi, Libya [529]

and the Ethiopians

Vatican City May 12, 2014 03:55 am (CNA.EWTN.News). Addressing the bishops of the northeast African nations Ethiopia and Eritrea at their ad limina visit to Rome on May 9, Pope Francis thanked them for their witness to Christian unity. [530]

Saturday 10 May, 2014

Pope receives unified Catholic hierarchy of Ethiopian and Eritrean bishops.

-Latin and Ge'ez rites Ethiopian church rites

2014-05-09

Pope Francis met with the bishops of Ethiopia and Eritrea, in Rome for their 'ad limina apostolorum' visit. The bishops gave the Pope four Ethiopian crosses as well as liturgical vestments hoping they made the right choice. "I think it will be your size."[531]

DANIEL 11:44

44. But tidings out of the east and out of the north shall trouble him: therefore he shall go forth with great fury to destroy, and utterly make away many.

But tidings

#8052 shem-oo-aw, fem. pass. part. of 8074; something heard, i.e. announcement: bruit, doctrine, fame, mentioned, news, report, rumor, tidings. <u>Strongs</u>, 1979

#8052 S e–mu-a n. f. message, rumor, report Strongs, 2001

He shall not be afraid of evil tidings (#8052 shem-oo-aw): his heart is fixed, trusting in the Lord. (Ps.112:7)

Concerning Damascus. Hamath is confounded, and Arpad: for they have heard evil tidings (#8052 shem-oo-aw): they are fainthearted; there is sorrow on the sea; it cannot be quiet. (Jer. 49:23)

But tidings (#8052 shem-oo-aw) out of the east and out of the north shall trouble him. (Dan. 11:44)

Whom shall he teach knowledge? And whom shall he make to understand doctrine (#8052 shem-oo-aw)? *them that are* weaned from milk, and drawn from the breasts. (Isa. 28:9)

For thy sister Sodom was not mentioned (#8052 shem-oo-aw) by thy mouth in the day of thy pride. (Ezek. 16:56)

As cold waters to a thirsty soul, so is good news (#8052 shem-oo-aw) from a far country. (Prov. 25:25)

out of the east

#4217 mis-rawkh: from 2224: sunrise, i.e. the east: east (side, -ward), (sun) rising (of the sun) Strongs, 1979.

#4217 miz-rah n. [m] direction of the sunrise, east, eastern: The east was the direction of orientation in the ancient near east. Strongs, 2001

"And after these things I saw four angels standing on the four corners of the earth, holding the four winds of the earth, that the wind should not blow on the earth, nor on the sea, nor on any tree. And I saw another angel ascending from the east {#395 an-at-o-lay)+2246 (he-li-os), having the seal of the living God: and he cried with a loud voice to the four angels, to whom it was given to hurt the earth and the sea, Saying, Hurt not the earth, neither the sea, nor the trees, till we have sealed the servants of our God in their foreheads. And I heard the number of them which were sealed: and there were sealed an hundred and forty and four thousand of all the tribes of the children of Israel. (Rev. 7:1–4)

#395 an-at-ol-ay. From 393; arising of light i. e. dawn (fig.) by impl. The east (also in plur.), dayspring, east, rising. Strongs, 1979

#395 an-at-ol-ay. East rising of the sun; note that the east is the compass direction of orientation in the ancient near east, just as north is in the modern western world. Strongs, 2001

#2246 hay-lee-os from hele (array perh. Akin to alt. of 138); the sun; by impl. Light:- + east, sun. Strongs, 1979

#2246 he-li-os n. sun Strongs, 2001

Who raised up (#5782 oor lit. or fig.) a righteous (#6664 se-deq nat. mor. or legal) man from the east (#4217 mis-rawkh), called him to his foot, gave the nations before him, and made him rule over kings? He gave *them* as the dust to his sword, and as driven stubble to his bow. Isaiah 41:2.

#5782 oor. A prim. root [rather ident. with 5783] through the idea of opening the eyes]; to wake (lit. or fig.):- (a-) waken (up), lift up (self), X master, raise (up), stir up (self). Strongs, 1979

#5782 ur v. [Q] to awaken; [N] to be aroused, stirred up, wakened; [Pol] awaken, arouse, raise up; [Pil] to raise, keep up; [H] to stir up, rouse, waken; [Htpol] to rouse oneself. Strongs, 2001

(Isa) 41:1ff The "one from the east" is Cyrus II of Persia, who would be king within a century and a half (he is also mentioned by name in 44:28) He conquered Babylon in 539 B.C. and was responsible for the decree releasing the exiled Jews to return to Jerusalem. God could even use a pagan ruler to protect and care for Israel, because God is in control of all world empires and politics. (Life Application Bible New International Version, 1991)

"Cyrus, he is my shepherd, [#7462 raw-aw intrans. to graze (lit. or fig.) gen. to rule] and will perform all my pleasure: even saying unto Jerusalem

"Thou shalt be [built; (#1129 baw-naw lit.or fig.)] and to the temple, "Thy foundation shall be laid." "I have (raised him up #5782 oor lit.

or. fig.) in (righteousness #6664 tseh-dek, nat. mor. or legal) and I will direct all his ways: he, and he, shall (build #1129 baw-naw lit. or fig.) my city, and he shall let go My captives (#1546 gaw-looth.), not for price or reward, saith the Lord of hosts" (Isa. 44:28; 45:13. *Prophets and Kings*, p. 552).

#1546 gaw-looth; fem from 1540; captivity; concr. exiles (collect.): -(they that are carried away) captives (-ity). Strongs, 1979

#1546 ga-lut n. f. exile, captive Strongs 2001

#1540 gaw-law: a prim root: to denude (espec. in a disgraceful sense); by implic. To exile (captives being usually stripped): fig. to reveal: + advertise, appear, be wray, bring. (carry, lead, go) captive (into captivity, depart, disclose, discover, exile, be gone, open, X plainly, publish, remove, reveal X shamelessly, shew X surely tell, uncover Strongs, 1979

#1540 ga-la v. [Q] to tell, uncover, reveal; depart, leave, be exiled, banished [Qp] to be opened, unseal; be make known; [N] to be revealed, be exposed,; to reveal, expose (nakedness) = sexual relations: [Pu] to be opened, exiled; [H} to deport, exile Strongs, 2001

Then he said, Knowest thou wherefore I come unto thee? And now will return (#7725 shoob lit. or fig. not necessarily with the idea of returning to the original starting point) to fight with the prince of Persia: and when I am {gone forth, (#3318 yaw-tsaw) lit. or fig. direct and proxim} lo, the prince of Grecia shall come. (Dan. 10:20)

#7725 shoob: a prim. root: to turn back (hence away)) trans. or intrans.. lit. or fig. (not necessarily with the idea of returning to the original starting point.); gen. to retreat; often adv., again. [(break, build, circumcise, dig, do anything, do evil, feed, lay down, lie down, lodge, make, rejoice, send, take, weep)] X again, (cause to) answer (+again), X in any case (wise), X at all, averse, bring (again, back, home again), call [to mind], carry again (back), cease X certainly, come again (back) X consider, + continually, convert, deliver (again), + deny, draw back, fetch home again, X fro, get [oneself] (back) again, X give (a, again), go again, put (again, up again), recall, recompense, recover, refresh, relieve, render (again), X repent, requite, rescue, restore, retrieve cause to, make to), return, reverse, reward, + saynay, send back, set again, turn (again, self again, away, back, back again, back, backward, from, off0, withdraw. Strongs, 1979

I am the good shepherd {#4166 poi-mane (lit. or fig.) shepherd, pastor}: the good shepherd giveth his life for his sheep. John 10:11.

Historically, Cyrus was the literal prince of Persia, a non-Jew, who God prophesied about and chose to shepherd his chosen people, Israel from Babylon to Jerusalem and the promised land of Canaan in 539 BC. This was followed some years later by another exodus from Babylon to Canaan under another Persian king, Darius. Finally the last journey from Babylon to the Promised Land occurred under the rule of Artaxerxes also a Persian king in 457 B. C. with the command to restore Jerusalem. That command marked the beginning of the 70 week prophecy of Daniel 9:24–27.

God desired to prophetically show "in type" how he designed to rescue his chosen people, the children of Israel, literally, from Babylon. A symbol of theworld to Jerusalem, in the promised land symbol of heaven. He would accomplish "in type" by Cyrus, who was not of Jewish descent, yet calling him to shepherd (see Isaiah 44:28) his people, the Israelite nation in their journey back to Canaan. This is analogous figureatively/spiritually to Christ, who although he was a Jew 'in the world but not of this world' (see John 17:13-16) was set aside to shepherd humanity to heaven. In an abiding, saving faith relationship to Christ, God desires to demonstrate "antitypically" how humanity is to be provisionally reconciled to Himself, through Christ Jesus, the Good Shepherd (see John 10:14).

Rooted in Israel, Joseph, a shepherd and son of Jacob held special distinction among his eleven brothers, is parallel to Christ Jesus relationship with the Father, who is the Lord, my shepherd Ps. 23. This reality is portrayed in the scriptural account of Joseph:

Joseph is a fruitful bough, even a fruitful bough by a well; whose branches run over the wall: The archers have sorely grieved him, and shot at him, and hated him: But his bow abode in strength, and the arms of his hands were made strong by the hands of the mighty God of Jacob; (from thence is the shepherd, the stone of Israel). (Gen. 49:22– 24)

In Israel's journey from the enslavement of Egypt, a symbol of sin's bondage to ultimate freedom and restoration in the promised land of Caanan, a symbol of heaven, although the nation was free inside dwellings with the blood on their doorposts in Egypt, a symbol of sin, they were not at their ultimate destination. There was still "growth in grace," a maturing process of dependence upon God to be experienced prior to an entrance into the promised land of Canaan/heaven.

While God delivered them from Egypt by the blood on their doorposts, accepting them "just as they were," He did not want them

271

to remain "just delivered," but longed for, and desired them to be "transformed" into a nation of priests.

The first awareness of this desired transformation occurred three months after the Exodus at Mt. Sinai just prior to receiving the spoken Ten Commandments.

It was not until forty-plus days later that the Israelites were to have received the written Ten Commandments but broke the law of God by worshiping the golden calf, being demonstrated by Moses throwing down the two tables of stone (Ex. 32) at time which he—their leader who God was working through —manifested anger that they had broken the spoken law of God forty days given forty days earlier.

This experience of Israel is perceived to demonstrate the weakness of fallen human creature nature's cream filling, originally encased by fluid faith shield of faith, inside the two top and bottom covers of the sandwich cookie, like an Oreo cookie.—The black side of an oreo cookie symbolizes the fallen, outside the fluid of faiths shield of the sinful nature to which the cream filling of the human nature can partake. The white side of the oreo cookie symbolizes the inside the fluid of faith shield of the divine nature to which the cream fill of the human nature was originally bent to partake. Originally, it is perceived that creature nature cream fillings throughout the universe of God's love were in righteousness created with a freedom, fluid of faith bent of allegiance to God between two white covers of the sandwich cookie. In that freedom fluid of faith bent of allegiance to God, cream fillings of creature natures were given instruction what was appropriate and inappropriate to do in guarding their shield of fluid faith relationship to God. For Adam and Eve's creature nature, filling in the sandwich cookie of their lives, the appropriate thing to do in the fluid shield of faith bent of allegiance to God was to eat of all the trees in the Garden of Eden, except the tree of knowledge of good and evil. Eating of that tree was inappropriate and, if eaten, would demonstrate rebellion against the spoken word of God. If Adam or Eve ate of the forbidden tree, the white cookie cover in God's righteousness, which contained the forbidden tree of knowledge of good and evil, that white cover would turn black, symbolizing rebellion against God. If rebellion occurred, the cream filling offspring of Adam and Eve would possess an inherited since the fall bent in their cream filling creature nature to partake of the black cover, sinful nature in which Satan dwelt. Simultaneously they would feel the wooing's of God's Holy Spirit, the third person of the Godhead, beckoning them, from the white cookie cover, to return to a life of faithful allegiance to God. Thus they would be double minded. They would need a Savior to reconcile them back to a right relationship to God.

At creation, Adam and Eve stood naked before each other and God, not being ashamed. It is perceived that later God covered them with a garment of light (Ps. 103) to hide their nakedness. This caused them after the sin of broken faith occurred in the Garden of Eden, to loose the garment of light. The couple now stood naked before God, resulting in their exclamation when God called them, "Where are you?" We were afraid because we were naked.

God provided skins of an animal, presumably a lamb, to cover the nakedness of Adam and Eve, thus restoring them "in type," to himself., although it was not like the original face-to-face communion they had originally enjoyed prior to the fall. Through patriarchs and prophets, God would now communicate with the fallen human race until finally the promised incarnate, second person of the Godhead, deliverer, would come as a cream filling of human nature and provide a rescue from the enslavement to sin and victory over it. Adam and Eve in their cream filling, degenerate since the fall human nature, possessed a, duel linkage to the white cookie cover, inside a measure of faith symbol of the divine nature, as well as the outside faith black cookie cover. Christ also possessed in his degenerate since the fall cream filling of human nature this same linkage to the white cover symbol of the divine nature as well as the fully developed since the fall linkage to the black cookie cover of the sinful nature. A fluid film of faith covered the cream filling of the human nature of Adam and Eve before the fall. After the fall they lost that film of faith, although they were given a "measure of faith" Romans 12:3. Although Christ's degenerate since the fall cream filling of the human nature was like fallen humanity's, it was ulike theirs in that his cream filling of human nature was shielded by the film of faith. This fluid film encasement of faith covered the cream filling of Christ's human nature and was bombarded with the fully developed temptations of the devil coming from his domain of the black, symbol of sin, cookie cover. Thus Christ "was tempted in all points (not in Greek)as we are yet without sin." Hebrew 4:15

From fruit trees in nature, a similar contrast/analogy can be made in at least two fruits, the walnut and apple. Like the sandwich cookie has two cover, so the walnut shell possesses two halves. Both halves are designed by God to produce a shield of faith bent for the nut to develop.

One of the halves symbolized allegiance to God while the other half symbolized the provisional possibility in freedom to rebel against God. The nut meat inside the walnut is analogous to the cream personhood in a sandwich cookie. Throughout the inner nut meat is a less hard material sectioning off the different areas of the nut meat symbolizing the shield of faith. It is perceived that Lucifer in his inner nut meat unexplainably in freedom became jealous of God, breaking several of the less hard material sections of faith in his life. In the nut meatof his life, he broke the outer, hard shell of the nut shield of faith, manifesting rebellion against God. Over time this rebellion became visible to the unfallen angels. One-third of the unfallen angels yielded to Lucifer's temptations to break faith in God. Like Lucifer one-third of the angels broke their inner less hard material of faith which sectioned off aspects of their lives. Finally one third of the angels broke their outer shell shield of faith that protected their allegiance to God They joined Lucifer, fighting against Michael and his angels. Since there is no room in heaven for those who maintain broken faith relationships to God, Lucifer, who became the dragon, devil, Satan and his angels were cast out of heaven.

This is an analogy of an apple as it relates to a life of faith. The apple tree produces apples. Each apple possesses several seeds in their core center, surrounded by some meat of the apple, indicating what they have potential to become, more apples. The apple core is supported by a stiffer material analogous to faith. This indicates the design in their inner core being (inner man) of what they are to produce more apples with their seeds representing truth. In reality apple fruit-meat in the core surrounds the apple seed with the core structures of faith. Usually the core is not eaten, but only the meat of the apple surrounding the core, within the apple skin. The skin of the apple symbolizes what the creature looks like to the viewer. It is perceived that all creatures in their inner nature (inner man, in the case of humanity, or inner being) throughout the universe of God's love were to experience life, being all they were meant to be in a faithful relationship to God.

Yet there was a provision in freedom that the creature could break their faith relationship to God. This is what Lucifer did, unexplainably thinking that the meat of his angelic skin should be equal to God. Having broken his inner faith in God, he wormed, in his inner self, his way out of his apple, standing on the skin of his beauty and tempted one-third of the angels to also do the same thing. Consequently they all became rotten apples and were cast out of heaven to the earth.

274

Now Lucifer's worm being became the snake in the tree of knowledge of good and evil and tempted Eve to break her faith in God, rebelling against Him resulting of her and her husband being cast out of the Garden of Eden. [This experience on earth] was] parallel to the one that occurred in celestial realms, regarding faith and allegiance to God, within the inner man (Eph. 3:6) in the case of human nature and in the case of angelic natures], just like Satan and his angels being cast out of heaven.

While this understanding is perceived to be a window giving a picture as to what happened in the great controversy which started in heaven with Lucifer, then coming to this earth, there is never a reason why it happened, only to say that in freedom, it could happen and did happen. Because all creatures in God's universe are created, as it were, on the head's side of the love coin experiencing face-to-face communion with God with a faith bent to always obey Him. They were like walnuts, whose meat beneath the hard shell of the shield of faith permeated the nut meat with softer material of faith, dividing all areas of the soft nut, just like the human brain is divided into many sections, all of which were designed to have faith in God.

This reality is also perceived in the outer appearance of an apple. It has meat beneath the skin just like a person has inner man/creature values beneath his covering of skin which are deeper in meaning within the biological/physiological and sociological factors which comprise his being. Those values/beliefs go to the center core of his being which surrounds the seed/beliefs with a tougher texture, inner man/creature, symbol of faith, woven through the apple meat from top to bottom forming its core, surrounding the seed. From the seed within the core is programed the production of the apple essence/texture of the fruit enclosed by the fruit's skin. Once the skin/faith of the apple is broken by the teeth in a bite—the creature nature, in this case humanity—can enjoy the reality of his being. In the case of Eve, acknowledging to the serpent, who was in an "outside faith" relationship to God that obedience to God by not eating of the tree of knowledge of good and evil, she proclaimed the boundaries of their freedom which was to protect their "inside faith" relationship to God, yielding allegiance to Him.

It is perceived that the angel Lucifer, prior to his fall was like an apple/walnut, whose inner meat being essence, was under the angelic skin/shell of "the law of faith" (see Rom. 1:17). They possessed the unwritten law, written on the heart (the seed in the core of his being) according to Rom. This yielded a bent of allegiance to God as it were on the head's side of the love coin, where he enjoyed face-to-face relationship to God. Unknown to Lucifer, like a veil, in mystery, was the hidden reality of the tail's side of the love coin. If he broke the "law of faith" which yielded, in freedom, allegiance to God, he would be cast out of heaven, which was on the head's side of the love coin to dwell on the tail's side of the love coin until his obliteration from the universe of God's love.

While Lucifer and Michael were both morning stars in heaven, Lucifer was a creature and Michael was God, the creator. Both had the status of being archangels. Lucifer was created in freedom, shielded by faith, on the head's side of the love coin, as it were, to yield allegiance to his Maker, Michael, the archangel, creator of the universe. He ecame unexplainably jealous, entertaining in freedom, the outside faith provision that was provided for but not designed to be experienced. Lucifer in his created bent of faith, was a creature "morning star" look alike to the creator "morning star" Michael.

From his creature relationship to God, Lucifer, also a "morning star," could not comprehend in mystery why Michael, an archangel, his look-alike, was invited by the Father into a special relationship and he was not. Thinking "more highly of himself than he ought to think," he, in freedom—in his inside faith relationship to God on the head's side of the love coin—began to entertain outside faith in God notions. In his inner angelic apple core being. also described as the inner angelic walnut soft divisions of faith in the nut meat of his brain he unexplainably, due to the shield of faith that guarded his live, began to think that he deserved to be invited into the consults with the Father for advice into future prospective creation plans just as much as Michael, the archangel. Thus he broke faith in God.

When angelic being, Lucifer—broke the softer material of faith that formed grooves in the nut meet of his mind, there was pleading, from Michael, who is God, in love to return to his original faith relationship to God In the meat of the apple, or walnut meat, being analogy, between the core of stiffer substance of faith and the skin which also confessed faith in God, or walnut nut meat, under the hard outer shell of faith— Lucifer unexplainably chose to breakfaith in God. In Lucifer's softer material of faith that formed grooves in the nut meat, there was pleading, from Michael, who is God, in love to return to his original faith relationship to God.

When that did not occur, Lucifer's inner angelic apple/ nut meat was transformed into a rebellious worm/serpent on the apple/walnut of his life. From this outside-faith relationship to Michael and God, Lucifer tempted the angels to follow him, one-third of them breaking their faith in God, rebelling against Him just as Lucifer had done.

Consequently there was war in heaven between Michael and His angels, and Lucifer, who was called the dragon, and his angels. Michael and his angels maintained the shield of faith which was demonstrated outwardly by behavior. Lucifer and his angels also demonstrated their behavior. Michaels followers because of the semihard fibrous faith material in the core/hard and soft material of their apple/walnut being demonstrated allegiance to God. Lucifer and his angels broke the shield of faith in the apple/walnut semi-hard fibrous faith material created to be present in the core/hard and soft material, of their inner angelic being. That reality parallels human nature's inner man (Eph. 3:16) being prior to and after the fall.

There was no place found in heaven for rebellious creatures in an outside- faith relationship to God. Hence, Lucifer, who became Satan, the dragon with his angels were cast out of heaven. Choosing to go to the earth, the only place they were allowed to live was in the forbidden tree of knowledge of good and evil, at the south center as it were of a spinning top in the Garden of Eden while the north center of the spinning top, as it were, was located the tree of life from which they were encouraged to freely eat from and live, along with all the other trees in Eden.

Eden was located, as it were, on the upper side of the spinning disk top which contained the garden. Adam and Eve were free to go toward the center of the Garden of Eden and go north toward the tree of life, partaking of its fruit, while they were forbidden to go south and partake of the tree of knowledge of good and evil. On the disk which contained the Garden of Eden, they continued to enjoy face to face fellowship with God as long as they turned north and partook of the tree of life on the spinning top.

When Eve left the side of Adam and journeyed toward the south center of the Garden of Eden, toward the tree of knowledge of good and evil, she possessed in the inner core of her being, the shield of faith. The tough fibrous strands of faith surrounding an apple seed and forming its core are analougos to the shield of faith which surrounds the inner man. When the serpent at the tree of knowledge of good and evil spoke to her inviting her to take and eat of the forbidden fruit, her inner fibrous faith response, forming the fibrous core of faith surrounding the seed of truth, was, "God hath said 'don't partake of that fruit' or you will die." As she lingered around the forbidden tree, Satan, using the medium of the serpent, said, "You shall not surely die, for in the days you eat it you will be as gods, knowing good and evil."

While what the serpent said was partly true, "you shall be as gods knowing good and evil," it was not part of God's plan that creatures were to know evil, in freedom on the tail's side as it were of the love coin. If they did come to know evil, they would die.

To be truly free, it is perceived that there are boundaries to that freedom. Hence God restricted their behavior stemming, in free love, from an inner bent or core shield of faith relationship to God. Because there exists in reality, two sides to the coin of love—a head's side, and a tails side. The heads side of the love coin is that upon which all creatures are created, designed to give allegiance to God stemming from a shield of faith bent The tails side of the love coin is provisional. It can be experienced, demonstrating rebellion outwardly which indicates inner broken faith but is not designed from a faith bent to be experienced.

Scripture records, for as many as have sinned without law shall also perish without law: and as many as have sinned in the law shall be judged by the law; (For not the hearers of the law are just before God, but the doers of the law shall be justified. For when the Gentiles which have not the law, do by nature the things contained in the law, these, having not the law, are a law unto themselves: Which shew the work of the law written on their hearts. Their conscience also bearing witness, and their thoughts the mean while accusing or else excusing one another;). In this way God shall judge the secrets of men by Jesus Christ according to my gospel (Rom. 2:12–16).

While the Israelites left Egypt symbolizing sin under the blood banner of the slain lamb or goat to dwell in tents on their way to Canaan, so the post Calvary believer would be empowered by grace coming from Calvary's Lamb of God sacrifice. the subsequent resurrection, resulting in the empty tomb and ascension. Between Calvary and resurrection or translation, the believer was to regard himself as living in a tent in the wilderness of this world on his way to heaven. While on the earthly journey, having believed in Christ as his personal Savior from sin, where he ministered on behalf of the believers as he, in his inner man spirit, was invited to regard himself as being "made to sit together in heavenly places in Christ" Ephesian 2:6" In this abiding relationship to God through Jesus Christ, he was to live a life of expectancy as he awaits the resurrection or translation to heaven. During this journey, his inner man spirit could go, from the tent body of his life to Christ, the risen temple of the tabernacle, for forgiveness and strength, and meet all their needs, even as the Israelites went into the sanctuary one year after they left Egypt. That temple of the tabernacle, Christ Jesus would be the safe "place prepared of God that they should feed here" (Rev. 12:6) in the wilderness of this world.

The following passages of scripture at the end of the twenty three hundred day prophecy of Daniel 8:14 are to be understood in a figurative/spiritural sense. When Jesus looked at the temple and said "Destroy this temple, and in three days I will raise it up," John 2:19 he "spake of the temple of his body." John 2:21. Jesus is the foundation stone of the spiritual temple upon which all believers, as stones, are to be figuratively/spiritually be built. Believers "arethe body of Christ." 1 Corinthians 12:27. This occurs as people put into practice, or confirm, like the wise man who built his house on a rock, [see Matthew 7:24, 25] from an attitude of faith, the principles that Christ taught. Believers will be "living stones,"[1 Peter 2:4] like Peter, who make up the church built spiritually on the foundation rock Christ Jesus.

Jesus saith unto them, "Did ye never read in the scriptures, The stone (#3037 lee-thos) which the builders [(#3618 oy-kod-om-eh-o) to construct, or (fig.) confirm] rejected, the same is become the head of the corner: this is the Lord's doing, and it is marvelous in our eyes? Therefore say I unto you, The kingdom of heaven shall be taken from you, and given, to a nation bringing forth the fruits thereof. And whosoever shall fall on this stone (#3037 lee- thos) shall be broken: but on whosoever it shall fall, it will grind him to powder (Mt. 21:43–44).

#3037 lee'-thos; apar. A prim. word; a stone (lit. or fig.):- (mill-, stumbling-) stone. Strongs, 1979

#3037 lith-os n. stone, boulder, this can refer to stone as a material or substance, and to a stone as a piece of rock. A "precious stone" is a "gem." Strongs, 2001

#4073 pet-ra; fem. Of the same as 4074; a (mass of) rock (lit. or fig.):-rock Strongs, 1979

#4073 pet-ra n. rock, bedrock, rocky crag, or other large rock formation, in contrast to individual stones. Strongs, 2001

The aspect of the definition for the word "stone," that seems to fit the historical/figurative-spiritual flow is that Jesus is the rock upon whom believers, as "living stones" (1 Peter 2:4) in their inner man (see Ephesians 3:16) are to be spiritually built. They will literally construct belief systems upon Jesus which confirm his teachings.

And I say unto thee 'Thou art Peter, and upon this rock (#4073) petr-ra I will [build (#3618 oy-kod-om-eh-o)] my church (#1577)]; and the gates of hell shall not prevail against it. Mt. 16:18

#1577 ek-klay-see'-ah; from a comp of 1537 and a der. Of 2564; a calling out i.e. (concr.) a popular meeting, espec. a religious congregation (Jewish synagogue, or Chr. Community of members on earth or saints in heaven or both):- assembly, church. Strongs, 1979

#1577 ek-kle-si-a. n. church, congregation, assembly; a group of people gathered together. It can refer to the OT assembly of believers (Acts 7:38), or a riotous mob (Acts 19:32), but usually to a Christian assembly, a church: as a totality (Eph. 3:10), or in a specific locale (Col. 4:15). In the NT a church is never a building or meeting place. Strongs, 2001

#3618 oy-kod-om-eh-o from the same as 3619; to be a house builder, i.e. construct or (fig.) confirm: - (be in) build (-er, -ing, up), edify, embolden Strongs 1979

#3618 oi-kod–o-me-o v. to build up, rebuild, a physical edifice, by extension: to edify, strengthen, develop another person's life through acts and words of encouragement. Strongs, 2001

And I turned to see the voice that spake with me. And being turned, I saw seven golden candlesticks; And in the midst of the seven candlesticks one like unto the Son of man, clothed with a garment down to the foot, and girt about the paps with a golden girdle. His head and his hairs were white like wool, as white as snow; and his eyes were as a flame of fire; And his feet like unto fine brass, as if they burned in a furnace; and his voice as the sound of many waters. (Rev. 1:12–15)

This image's head was of fine gold, his breast and his arms of silver, his belly and his thighs of brass. (Daniel 2:32)

And after thee shall arise another kingdom inferior to thee, and another third kingdom of brass, which shall bear rule over all the earth. (Daniel 2:39)

For behold, the day cometh, that shall burn as an oven; and all the proud, yea, and all that do wickedly, shall be stubble: and that day that cometh shall burn them up, saith the Lord of hosts, that it shall leave them neither root nor branch. But unto you that fear my name shall the Sun [#8121 sheh'-mesh] - of righteousness (#6666 sedaqa) arise with healing in his wings: and ye shall go forth, and grow up as calves of the stall. (Mal. 4:1–2)

#8121 sheh'-mesh; from an unused root mean. to be brilliant; the sun; by impl. The east; fig. aray, i.e., (arch.) a notched battlement: - + east side (-ward), sun ([rising]), + west (-ward), window. See also 1053 Strongs, 1979 #8121 seme n. f & m. sun Strongs, 2001

#6664 tseh-dek; from 6663; the right (nat. mor. or legal); also (abstr.) equity or (fig.) prosperity: - X even, (that which is altogether) just (-ice), ([un-]) righ (-eous) (cause, -ly. –ness). Strongs, 1979.

#6664 sedeq n.m. righteousness, justice, rightness, acting according to a proper (God's) standard, doing what is right being in the right. Strongs, 2001

#6666 tsed-aw-kaw'; from 6663; righteous (abstr.), subj. (rectitude), obj. (justice), mor. (virtue) or fig. (prosperity);- justice, moderately, right (-eous) (aact, -ly, -ness). Strongs, 1979

#6666 sedaqa righteousness. Acting according to a proper (God) standard, doing what is right, being in the right, being in the right. Strongs, 2001

#6663 tsaw-dak'; a prim. root; to be (causat. make) right (in a moral or forensic sense):- cleanse, clear self, (be, do) just (-ice, -ify, self), (be, turn to) righteous(-ness). Strongs, 1979.

#6663 sa-daq v. den, [Q] to be righteous, be innocent, be vindicated; in accordance with a proper (God's) standard, and so implying innocence. Strongs, 2001

With a tree symbol of God that produces seeds, as it were on the head's side of the coin, they enjoy face-to-face communion with him. This is because they possess a created bent to produce righteous trees with righteous fruit. The Sun of righteousness arises from the east, the east being the compass direction of the near east, suggesting a new day when righteousness, according to God's standard reigns. This is in contrast to life, as it were, on the tail's side of the coin where the darkness of rebellious wickedness reigns. Even then there are occasional rays from the sun of righteousness on the heads side of the coin that pierce the darkness of the gloom of wickedness on the tails side of the coin. The following section is lifted from *en.wicipedia.org/wiki/Iran*

Iran—formerly known as Persia, officially known as the Islamic Republic of Iran—is a country in western Asia. Iran reached the pinnacle of its power during the Achaemenid Empire (first Persian Empire) founded by Cyrus the Great 550 B.C.[532]

The suggested reality that "God could even use a pagan ruler to protect and care for Israel, because God is in control of all world empires and politics," is perceived to stem from Judges 3:1-4:

Now these are the nations which the Lord left, to prove Israel by them, even as many of Israel as had not known all the wars of Canaan; Only that the generation of the children of Israel might know, to teach them war, at the least such as before knew nothing thereof; Namely, five lords of the Philistines, and all the Canaanites, and the Sidonians, and the Hivites that dwelt in Mount Lebanon, from mount Baalhermon unto the entering in of Hamath. And they were to prove Israel by them, to know whether they would hearken unto the commandments of the Lord, which he commanded their fathers by the hand of Moses.

Christ said, "For as the lightening cometh (#1831 ex-er-cho-mai, lit, or fig.) out of the east, and shineth even unto the west; so shall also the coming (#3952 par-ou-see-a) of the Son of man be" Mt. 24: 27. It is perceived that there will be a people just prior to Christ's second coming who will herald/advocate the sanctuary messagewhich is "the sign of the Son of Man" Mt. 24:30. In William Millers study of Daniel 8:14 he and many others thought the sanctuary to be cleansed was the earth. It was not discovered until the vision in the cornfield by Hiram Edson that the sanctuary to be cleansed was the heavenly sanctuary. Since Christ is the foundation stone on which the believer/living stones are to be built, the cleansing of the heavenly sanctuary is the weeding out of professed believers who do not follow Christ wholeheartedly. The wise builders put into practice what they know. This response is contrasted to the foolish builders who do not put into practice what they know. These believers, may not be at the same maturity level. Some will be at the blade, ear, or full corn in the ear level of understanding. Nevertheless they all believe in Christ as their Savior from sin, not necessarily understanding every thing about him, yet, desiring to grow in relationship to him. When Christ cleanses the heavenly sanctuary, of which he himself is the "temple of the tabernacle of the testimony" Revelation 15:5, he will separate the sheep from the goats. The sheep are those wise builders [see Matthew 7:24] who put into practice what they know. The goats are the foolish builders [see Matthew 7:26] who do not put into practice what they know.

Since his ascension, all penitent believers could and are invited to antitypically come to the foot of Calvary's cross in the midst of the outer court of the heavenly sanctuary. Along with themselves, they are to bring their elder brother, Christ Jesus as their substitute, lamb of God, sacrifice for sin. At the foot of the Cross, Christ would explain to the believer that he had taken away their sins at calvary. He would then invite them to rise in newness of life and live victorious over their besetting sins, through his gift of faith. While they may occasionally fall, he would be their advocate to the Father. As they grew in grace and in a knowledge of him and what he had done for them, they would discover that he wanted them to live as priests before him, their high priest, wearing the robe of his righteousness. They would also grow to discover that he was symbolized not only in the sacrificial lamb of the wilderness sanctuary services, but also as the tabernacle into which the priests would minister, completing the "daily" service. Thus clothed in his righteousness, they were to minister as priests in relationship to him, the risen Lamb of God. This risen Lamb of God had become the tabernacle into whom they were to relationally enter, [see John 10:9] and go out to witness.

Thus the antitypical judgement would "begin in heavenly the sanctuary" [see Ezekiel 9:6]. This Day of Atonement phase of the parable [See Hebrews 9:9] of the sanctuary would begin with the judgment of the dead beginning with Abel. He had died a martyers death, believing that the slain lamb was God's appointed way of reconciling fallen mankind to himself. He probably did not understand that the lamb symbolized God sending himself in the future, in the person of Jesus Christ. He nonetheless had the promise, given to his parents that one of their seed would bruise the serpents head.

Thus, when the time to judge the dead [see Daniel 7:10, Revelation 11:18] began in October 22, 1844, at the close of the twenty-three hundred day prophecy of Daniel 8:14, Abel, would the first to be judged and found fit to save. He had followed God's prescribed way, by faith [see Hebrews 11:4], not being under the Ten Commandment law [see Romans 2:12] but under the "law of faith"[see Hebrews 3:27]. He had followed God by faith even in fallen humanities condition, after Adam and Eve sinned, of being "under the law of sin and death" Romans 8:2.

This "law of faith" in God's spoken word is the same law operative with Adam and Eve prior to eating the forbidden fruit. That "law of faith" was manifested in Eve's exclaimation to the serpent that God had said they may eat of all the trees except the tree of knowledge of good and evil or they would die [see Genesis 3:2, 3]. This same "law of faith" in the spoken, now coupled to written word of God was evidenced in Christ's response to Satan's temptation by "It is written."[Matthew 4:4, 7, 10. Thus Christ could say "I have overcome the world" John 16:33.

It is perceived that in overcoming the world, Christ meant that "the world" is any belief that is outside an abiding faith relationship to God. He had "overcome the world" in that he always had been in a faith relationship to his father. Adam and Eve were both created under the "law of faith" Romans 3:27 when God gave them the command not to eat of the tree of knowledge of good and evil [See Genesis 2:17]. While the command was initially given to Adam, he was to pass the information down to his future wife Eve [see Genesis 2:23]. When Eve wandered from the side of Adam to the tree of knowledge of good and evil, listened to the serpent, partook of the fruit, eating it then giving some to Adam which he did eat, the "outside faith in God world" began to develop. Evidence that Adam and Eve were created under the "law of faith" Romans 3:27 is seen in Eve's response to the serpent "We may eat of every tree in the garden: but of the fruit of the tree in the midst of the garden, God hath said, 'Ye shall not eat of it, neither shall ye touch it, lest ye die." Genesis 3:2-3.

Like Eve was tempted by Satan speaking through the medium vessel of the serpent to break faith in God, which if entered into is sin, [see Romans 14:23] so Christ was tempted "in all" Hebrew 4:15 [the word "points" is not in the original Greek] of faith "as we are yet without sin" Hebrews 4:15. For Christ to have sinned, it would mean in part, to break faith in his fathers spoken, and now written, since the prophets, word. Scripture records that "whatsoever is not of faith is sin" Romans 14:23.

In Gethsemane, Christ had prayed to his father "not my will but thine be done." Luke 22:42. It was God's will that Christ, the second person of the Godhead, would be the righteous one, who would substitutionally be, the atoning sacrifice for sin. Type would meet antitype.

The temple at Jerusalem, having its roots in the wilderness sanctuary and its services would be done away with, evidenced by "the veil of the temple was rent in twain from top to bottom." (Matthew 27:51. Mark 15:38). Christs' death on calvary would inaugurate the sacrificial aspect/ phase of the upcoming ministry of Christ Jesus, our elder brother, high priest (see Hebrew 9:11) in the heavenly sanctuary.

In that atoning sacrifice Christ would be "wounded for our transgressions, bruised for our iniquities: the chastisement of our peace

284

was upon him; and with his stripes we are healed." Isaiah 53:5. Like the penitent Israelite, "in type" had laid their hands upon the heads [see Leviticus 4:4, 15, 24, 29, 33,] of the sacrifices they brought, confessing their sins, transferring the guilt of thier sins to the animal, so "the Lord hath," antitypicaly "laid on him"(Christ) "the iniquity of us all." Isaiah 53:6. In like manner the whole Israelite community, Leviticus 4:13, rulers Leviticus 4:22, common people Leviticus 4:22, if they followed the prescribed process, of the priest making an atonement, they would be forgiven [see Leviticus 4:20, 26, 32].

Now, at the "end of time," i.e. after the close of the 2300-day prophecy of Daniel 8:14 was fulfilled in October 22, 1844, potential believers or non-believers on earth, hold or are invited to hold, as it were, the kite string which begins Christ's righteousness. That kite string, as it were righteousness is connected to the kite of the heavenly sanctuary. In that heavenly sanctuary, Christ, our high priest, stands before the father, between the believer and the father, pleading with the believer, or non-believer to fully accept his merits at calvary. With the measure of faith [see Romans 12:3] given to all, everyone [see John 3:16] is invited to believe in Jesus Christ and be reconciled to God.

Believers or non-believers will be called to accept the heavenly sanctuary message, first advocated by Hiram Edson,[533] following the great disappointment of October 22, 1844. That view had been preceded by William Miller's preaching on Daniel 8:14 that the sanctuary to be cleansed was this earth, by the second coming of Christ on that date. Out of this disappointment, there was to be a new proclaimation identified in Revelation 10:11 "Thou must prophecy again before many peoples, and nations, and tongues, and kings." It would be discovered that "Christ had come in the fulfillment of the prophecy, but not to the earth as expected. He had come to the Day of Atonement, Investigative Judgemnt phase of the parable of the heavenly sanctuary.

"Christ had come, not to the earth, as they expected, but, as foreshadowed in the type, to the most holy place of the temple of God in heaven. He represented by the prophet Daniel as coming at this time to the Ancient of Days: "I saw in the night visions, and, behold, one like the Son of man came with the clouds of heaven, and came"- not to the earth, but- "to the Ancient of Days, and they brought Him near before Him." Daniel 7:13[534] GC424

So just before Christ's second coming during the Investigative Judgment of the living, believers who advocate the sanctuary message will be like the Israelites in Ezekiel 11:16 where God says, "Yet will I be to them a little sanctuary in the countries they have come." They will be like people, as it were, on earth holding the kite string of Christ's righteousness which is connected to the heavenly kite sanctuary where Christ is ministering before the father on their behalf. Sometimes they will reel in the string connected to the kite to see what Christ is doing for them in heaven. Nevertheless, they would have access to the book of Hebrews which records:

"Now of the things which we have spoken this is the sum: We have such an high priest, who is set on the right hand of the throne of the Majesty in the heavens; A minister of the sanctuary, and of the true tabernacle, which the Lord pitched, and not man." Hebrews 8:1, 2.

"Then verily the first covenant had also ordinances of divine service, and a worldly sanctuary. For there was the tabernacle made; the first, wherein was the candlestick, and the table, and the shewbread; which is called the sanctuary. And after the second veil, the tabernacle which is called the Holiest of all; which had the golden censer, and the ark of the covenant overlaid round about with gold, wherein was the golden pot of manna, and Aaron's rod that budded, and the tables of the covenant. And over it the cherubims of glory shadowing the mercy seat; of which we cannot now speak particularly." Hebrews 9:1-5.

To better understand, or gain insight into what Christ was doing in the heavenly sanctuary, believers could study the model of the earthly wilderness sanctuary, with the subsequent temple, and its services. Every believer was to see according to Philippians 1:6 God, through the grace of calvary had begun a good work in them. Not only would the believer be able to to die to the outside faith atmosphere called self, but through the quickening power of the Holy Spirit, experience God within him, performing how to live a priestly life.

This is because according to 1 John 5:4 "faith is the victory that overcomes the world." According to John 16:33 Jesus said "I have overcome the world." So the end time people of whom it is said, "here are they who keep the commandments of God and have the faith of Jesus" (Revelation 14:12) will be believers who "as one body in Christ" (Romans 12:5) will by faith in his grace, be victorious over sin [see Revelation 2:7,11, 17. 26. 3:5, 12, 21].

The blood of the sacrifices had been splashed against the veil that separated the holy from the most holy place, poured out at the base of the altar of burnt offerings, or rubbed on the altar horns. These places where the blood was found symbolized penitent Israelites acceptance of the substitute sacrifice on their behalf providing "type" forgiveness for specific or general sins and subsequent reconciliation to God.

On the Day of Atonement, with the High Priest went behind the veil. The stones on the breastplate symbolized in type that the whole nation whose individual sins had been atoned for by pouring out, splashing against the veil, the blood so that they were cleansed, "in type" from sin.

Now, post-calvary believers who had come, figuratively/spirituall, at the wooing of the Holy Spirit, to the foot of the cross would discover that, Christ Jesus, their elder brother, had died as their substitute, atoning for their, outside faith, sins. Now in the antitypical Day of Atonement, parable [see Hebrews 9:25] phase of the sanctuary, Christ, their elder brother, High Priest, took their name, as a penitent believer, behind the veil. Investigation would be made as to whether or not they had claimed his atonement, then walked, deporting their lives, as "first the blade, then the ear, then the full corn in the ear,"(Mark 4:28) according to his empowering grace. This walk is analogous to the layers on an onion, making their witness flavorable and savory, to the taste of others. If they had, they would be safe to save. Regardless of their maturity level of "growth in grace"[see 2 Peter 3:18], they would be given white robes. [see Revelation 6:11]

#3952 par-oo-see-ah: from the pres. Part. Of 3918; a being near, i.e. advent(often, return; spec. of Christ to punish Jerusalem, or finally the wicked): (by impl) phys. Aspect: - coming presence. Strongs, 1979.

#3952 par-ou-si-a n. presence; coming, advent,; in the NT usually of the second coming of the Son of Man, arriving as a conquering king. Strongs, 2001

#1831 ex-er-khom-ahee, from 1537 and 2064; to issue (lit. or fig.) come (forth, out), depart (out of), escape, get out, go (abroad, away, forth, out, thence), proceed (forth), spread abroad. Strongs, 1979

#1831 ex-er-cho-mai v. to go out, leave Strongs, 2001

At this juncture in the prophetic flow of salvation history, it is perceived that wherever righteousness occurs, it comes from the east. Just like the righteousness attributed to Cyrus's work in the release of the Israelites from Babylon came from the east or Persia (modern-day, Iran), so the righteousness of Christ, claimed by believers, brings about figuratively/spiritually a new day. This was depicted literally-figuratively/spiritually by the priest, in the experiential act of putting on the white linen garments. Having died figuratively/spiritually to the outside-faith ways of the sinful nature, on the tail's side of the love coin, experienced in the inner man (Eph. 3:16), the believer "puts on the righteousness of Christ" (Rom. 13:12, 14). This experience parallels the priest putting on (Ex. 29:8) the linen garments before he enters the "tabernacle of the sanctuary" (Ex. 25:8,. Rev. 15:5). Christ Jesus, humanity's elder brother, high priest in the heavenly sanctuary is the person into whom all priestly believers covered by the linen symbol of His righteousness are to figuratively/spiritually enter. In relationship to Christ, "'the temple [see John 2:21] 'of the tabernacle of the testimony'" (Revelation 15:5) all priestly believers were to figuratively/spiritually enter and serve as part of the "body of Christ" (Eph. 5:30).

and out of the north

"He cried also in my ears with a loud voice, saying, "'Cause them that have charge over the city to draw near, even every man with his destroying weapon in his hand.' And, behold six men came from the way of the higher gate, which lieth toward the north [#6828 tsaw-fone], and every man a slaughter weapon in his hand; and one man among them was clothed with linen, with a writer's inkhorn by his side: and they went in, and stood beside the brazen altar. And the glory of the God of Israel was gone up from the cherub, whereupon he was, to the threshold of the house. And he called to the man clothed with linen, which had the writer's inkhorn by his side: and they went in. and stood beside the brazen altar. And the glory of the God of Israel was gone up from the cherub, whereupon he was, to the threshold of the house. And He called to the man clothed with linen, which had the writer's inkhorn by his side; And the Lord said unto him, 'Go through the midst of Jerusalem, and set a mark upon the foreheads of the men that sigh and cry for all the abominations that be done in the midst thereof.' And to the others he said in mine hearing, 'Go ye after him through the city, and smite: let not your eye spare, neither have ye pity: Slay utterly old and young, both maids and little children, and women: but come not near any man upon whom is the mark; and begin at the ancient men which were before the house.' And he said unto me, 'Defile the house, and fill the courts with the slain: go ye forth.' And they went forth. And they went for and slew in the city. And it came to pass, while they were slaying them and I was left, that I fell upon my face, and cried, and said, 'Ah Lord God! wilt thou destroy all the residue of Israel in thy pouring out of thy fury upon Jerusalem?'" (Ezek. 9:1–8).

288

#6828 tsaw-fone; from 6845: prop. Hidden, i.e. dark; used only of the north as a quarter (gloomy and unknown): north (-ern, side, -ward, wind) Strongs, 1979

#6828 sa-pon n. f. north, northern Strongs, 2001

Since the word *meh-lek*, the word for "king" is used in Ps. 48:2, "the city of the great King' #4428 meh-lek) of God, it is perceived that at the close of salvation history, it would be referring to God, following his sanctuary timetable, after the close of the 1260, forty-two months, 1290, 1335, and 2300-day prophecy, come against those creatures of humanity who are opposed to Him, simultaneously coming for those who are in favorable allegiance to Him.

It is perceived, that God literally-figuratively-spiritually stands in favor with his creation. They, as it were, have been created on the upper horizontal top side of a spinning top. This top has a center pole whose top symbolizes the north pole from which they were to eat of the tree of life. i The bottom center of that spinning top symbolizes the south pole in the Garden of Eden which contained the tree of knowledge of good and evil from which they were forbidden to eat. That tree was provided for in freedom but not designed by God to be experienced.

Utilizing this analogy, Adam and Eve, and for that matter, all freethinking creatures throughout the universe of God's love were created to live on the upper side of the spinning top. There they would be shielded by faith which is symbolized by the raised ridge surrounding a coin. In that relationship to God, they were free to partake of all the trees in the garden. This freedom included partaking the tree of life, which was on the top/center/pole of their existence. That freedom also forbad them to eate of the provided for but not designed to be partaken of tree of knowledge of good and evil located at the south center pole of their existence. If this relationship to God was maintained in the case of Adam and Eve, they would be entitled to live forever in the Garden of Eden.

On this plain, they experienced the garment of light (Ps. 103) which covered their nakedness, although at creation, they were allowed to see each other's nakedness and not be ashamed. It is perceived that once they viewed each other's physical differences, God turned up his light like a rheostat lamp, increasing the intensity of the brightness of light as a cover hiding their nakedness.

Once Adam and Eve broke the ridge of faith in God which originally surrounded their lives, like the raised ridge surrounding the circumference of a coin and partook of the fruit of the forbidden tree of knowledge of good and evil in the south center of the garden, they lost their garment of light. This event caused them to be afraid of God, who turned down the rheostat light exposing their nakedness. After acquiring skins, presumed to be a lamb's, perceived to be God showing them how to kill the lamb, God made clothing for them which was acceptable to hide their nakedness. Anything they did to cover their nakedness with fig leaves was not acceptable. Only a slain lamb symbolizing the future incarnation, life, death, resurrection, and ascension of the second person of the Godhead, Christ Jesus, would be acceptable. Until then their life would be spent on lower horizontal side of the top, outside Eden, unable to live in face-to-face communion with God like they had in Eden. It would only be through Christ, taking on a degenerate body of sinful humanity, that fallen humanity, who claimed his that merits, could hope to be restored to face to face communion with God as they had enjoyed in Eden. Christ possessed an an inner faith heart and spirit bent, which yielded or produced a life of faithfulness to God. That inner faith was continually bombarded by the temptations common to fallen man. Hence Scripture in Hebrews 4:15 records "He was in all *points* tempted as we *are*, yet without sin." Christ was victorious over sin, then died as human nature's substitute sacrifice for sin. In an abiding, saving faith relationship to Christ, fallen humanity who claimed His merits as their own, could hope to be restored to face-to-face communion with God as they had enjoyed in Eden. This restoration would be, as it were, from the tails side of the love coin otherwise known as the bottom side of the disk on a top, to the heads side of the love coin, or upper side of a disk on a spinning top. This restoration to God was different from their original relationship to God which had not known sin. Now they had known sin, but through Christ's blood sacrifice, they could be restored to God, even though they had known sin.

While the birth, life, death, resurrection, and ascension had historically occurred at this juncture of the prophecy it would always be until the second coming, a struggle for humanity to die to self. Each individuals personhood would be invited through the grace of Christ provided at calvary to die to outside faith life, called self. That atmospheric, outside faith life called self is the, inner allegiance, divided heart life on the underside of the spinning top disk. With death to outside faith life, called self, the believer is to rise figuratively/spiritually with Christ in his ressurrectionwalking by faith in Christ on the upper side of the spinning top. That is what it means to live "in the world but not of the world."[see John 15:19. A life "in the world but not of the world" is depicted by the Pen Of Inspiration:

"I turned to look for the Advent people in the world, but could not find them, when a voice said to me, 'Look a litter higher.' At this I raised my eyes, and saw a straight and narrow path, cast up high above the world. On the path the Advent people were traveling to the city, which was at the farther end of the path. They had a bright light set up behind them at the beginning of the path, which an angel told me was the midnight cry. This light shown shone all along the path and gave light for their feet so that they might not stumble."[535]

Since the fall of mankind, performing sacrifices for sin was an outward demonstration of an inward faith that someday according to Gen. 3:15, God would send His son, as the Lamb of God, to provisionally take away the sin of the world, to all who would accept His substitute sacrifice for sin. The acceptance of this substitute sacrifice would yield an empowerment of grace to live free from sin.

There would be a lifestyle illustrating growth in grace. This living by grace through faith was reflected in their journey from Egypt to Canaan. First, there was a need to slay the lamb and apply its blood to their doorposts which antitypically means they confessed that it was because of their sins that Christ had to die. Second by taking the blood and applying it to their doorposts indicated an acceptance of Christ as personal Savior from sin. This was and can continue figuratively/spiritually for all believers in Christ as they celebrate the Passover. Prior to and following the Passover was the feast of unleavened bread, meaning that for three-and-one-half "type" days, symbolizing the three-and-a-half literal years before his crucifixion, on Passover, people could get to know about God and what he was going to do for them. Then for another three-and-one-half days symbolizing another three-and-one-half literal years, the Israelites/believers would proclaim what he had done by eating unleavened bread.

Since Christ had been raised from the dead after three literal days, Israel and for that manner humanity would acknowledge that He is the First Fruit of the dead, consequently celebrating the feast of firstfruits. Following this feast of Firstfruits was the Feast of Weeks called Pentecost. Then in the seventh month, they would celebrate the Feast of Trumpets, and at the beginning of the tenth month which proclaimed more fully what God had done and a judgment day was coming. Then the tenth day of the seventh month was the Day of Atonement, the Day of Judgment. All who passed the judgment would then celebrate several days later the feast of tabernacles, commemorating what God had done, making them tabernacles, like himself, the more elaborate Tabernacle of the congregation.

These seven feasts: (1) Passover, (2) Unleavened bread, (3) Firstfruits, (4) Feast of Weeks/Pentecost (5) Trumpets, (6) Day of Atonement, and (7) Tabernacles are perceived to be the seven thunders of Rev. 10:3, 4. These seven thunderous truths describe the walk or journey in the "inner man" (Eph. 3:16) which will be typically and antitypically experienced, acknowledged, and proclaimed by believers until Christ comes the second time.

A practical celebration of the seven thunderous truths in a creature of sinful nature could look something like this. Daily they could look to Jesus and study the way he lived and desire to become like Him. This could occur even before they accepted Him as their personal Savior from sin. This studying of His life would be like the Feast of Unleavened Bread. The more they studied His life, the more they wanted to live like He did. This would be analogous to the tenth day of the first month which began what would be known as the "Feast of Unleavened bread." That is when the Israelite was to set aside a lamb to be sacrificed on the fourteenth day symbolizing Calvary. So prior to accepting Christ as personal Savior, an individual could study His life, desire to be like Him, and discover that Christ was, the lamb of God, who was set aside to take away the sin of the world. This reality was parallel to the skins that clothed Adam and Eve's nakedness once they broke faith and sinned by eating of the forbidden tree. Those skins, a symbol of Christ's righteousness, made them once again acceptable to God, although not at the same level of acceptance they had experienced with their original garment of light because they now knew what sin was experientially, while before sin entered they did not know, other than what God said, "They will die."

When the believer comes to understand that Christ is the lamb of God who was slain because his sins were laid on Him, he experiences the first part of the Feast of the Passover, He realizes that Christ died for his sins, to set him free from those sins, like the Israelites were provisionally set free from the enslavement of Egypt by the blood of the slain lamb on their doorposts. In the application of the blood to the doorpost, one acknowledges that something or someone outside himself sets him free. Thus Christ would say, "You shall know the truth and the truth shall set you free" (Mk. 7:11). In like manner, after eating or imbibing the word of God into their lives, like the Israelites in type and the believer in antitype under the bloodstained banner of their dwelling they would continue to eat roasted lamb, unleavened bread along with bitter herbs. Eating the roasted lamb was a symbol of ingesting/imbibing the power of God/calvary's sacrifice which got them out of Egypt/sin. The eating of bitter herbs commemorated the bitter experience of slavery in Egypt/sin from which they were delivered. Still in their dwelling in Egypt/the land of earth where sin continued to exist that dwelling had blood on the doorposts. They would be free from the Egyptian taskmasters/enslavement to sin because of the powerful grace of God shining from the animal/Lamb of God type/antitype sacrifice in Egypt/Calvary (Ex. 12:6; Rev. 11:8).

After the midnight/justification judgment, the power of the slain lamb was symbolically raised. This reality symbolized the Feast of the Firstfruits, pointing forward to the resurrected Christ. Because of "type" slain lamb in Egypt blood on the doorposts, pointing forward to Calvary's blood sacrifice "antitypically" claimed by believers on their hearts, God would now be empowered by grace to justifiably rescue Isarelite-belivers from Egypt/sin.

The 'type/anti-type" reality is that those who had the blood on their doorposts/hearts would be delivered in unbroken families from Egypt/sin. It is possible that some in Egypt who had lost their first born, also joined theIsraelites forming what would be known as the mixed multitude[see Exodus 12:38]. Yet even that mixed multitude had to be circumcised [see Exodus 12:44], symbolizing heart circumcision[see Deuteronomy 10:16, Romans 3:29], acknowledging that it was the blood of the slain lamb that was the power to get them out of Egypt/sin.

It was not until three months into their journey, that the redeemed Israelite-mixed multitude/believer would discover for what purpose God wanted them to be, "a kingdom of priests, and an holy nation" [Exodus 19:6]. This time lapse between antitypically accepting the merits of Christ as savior from sin and discovering what God wants a person to be, a priest/king might take some time. During this initial time from their deliverance from Egypt/sin, the delivered Israelite/believer, it is perceived, would be heard to exclaim, "All we needed to be delivered from Egypt's/sin's enslavement was the blood of the slain lamb to be applied to our doorposts/accept Christ as personal Savior from sin."

God wanted them to be a kingdom of priests (Ex. 19:6). The Israelites had no idea how priests were to live and behave themselves. For starters God gave them the Ten Commandments, first spoken from Mt. Sinai, then forty days later, during which God gave Moses the command, "Let them make me a sanctuary that I may dwell among them,"(Ex. 25:8), which announced His future incarnation in "type," when God would become man, and having written on two tables of stone, the original spoken law, which were broken because they worshipped a golden calf. Then new tablets were made and engraved with God's finger after another forty days.

Finally into the sixth month, they began to construct the sanctuary where God was to dwell among them. This symbolized that one day he would leave heaven at the incarnation, unlike their leaving Egypt, and dwell among them. It took the Israelites one year from the Exodus before the sanctuary was set up (Ex. 40:17). The nine months from the giving of the Ten Commandments on Mt. Sinai is similar for the gestation period of a baby. It took some time for materials had to be gathered and construction for the sanctuary to begin. Just like it takes some time from the conception of a baby to be born, so some time had to occur in order for the Israelites and humanity to understand in part what the tent God, in the person of Christ, was to live in was like [see Hebrews 10:5]. While discovering how it was to be different from the tents they lived, in other respects it would be like theirs. For starters, it was a tent/tabernacle into which only those who were clothed with linen, a symbol of Christ's righteousness could enter and serve. Yet it had a courtyard surrounding it, into which everyone could come with their sacrifices. So the invitation of Christ, symbolized by the sanctuary and tabernacle, was "Come unto me all ye who labor and are heavy laden and I will give you rest." This was fulfilled in type prior to the incarnation.

After the setting up of the sanctuary, the penitent Israelite could bring their sacrifice to the altar of burnt offering in the midst of the outer court Prior to the setting up of the sanctuary people brought sacrifices to altars from Abel, Abraham, Jacob and many others. The practice of bringing animal sacrifices to the altar of burnt offering continuedup until the veil separating the Holy from the Most Holy was rent from top to bottom by Christ's death on calvary. Only the altar of burnt offering had a more elaborate surrounding of the linen courtyard symbolizing the future righteousness of Christ which would encircle after His incarnation fallen humanity. The "type" sacrifices were still in effect for the three-

and-a-half years ministry of Christ up until His death. This reality was evident when Christ cleansed the ten lepers who went to the priests for verification of their healing, just as today the sick go to doctors after treatment to verify their healing. Yet only one returned to Jesus to say thank you. Unlike their tents in which only their families could live, all Israel could enter the courtyard with the priests going into the temple on their behalf, although the whole nation was to be a kingdom of priests. The antitypical reality is that all believers are invited after accepting Him as their Saviour to rise with Him and put on the robe of His righteousness, like the priests put on their priestly robes to minister in the tabernacle.

For seven months into the second year after the Exodus under the banner of the bloodshed in Egypt and put on their doorposts entitled Israel to leave Egyptian enslavement/sin.Israel/believers were to experience what it was like to live as a kingdom of priests. Only a pre-calvary subset of the Israelite nation, the Levites, were called to minister as priests, even though the whole nation was called to be a kingdom of priests. Now the post Calvary parallel believer provisionally redeemed by Calvary's blood is invited to rise up with Christ from the tomb and put on the robe of His righteousness and minister in Him, the "temple of the tabernacle" (Rev. 15:5) as a priesthood of believers. In the seventh month, they held the fifth feast, the Feast of Trumpets celebrating what God had done for them through the blood of the slain "type" lamb in Egypt or "antitypical" lamb of God, Christ Jesus at Calvary.

The Feast of Trumpets following the deliverance from Egypt by the blood of the lamb on their doorposts and subsequent Incarnation with its three-and- a-half-year ministry of Christ is echoed by His command, "Go tell what God has done for you" (Mk. 5:19). For Israel the seven trumpets (Josh 6:4) used in marching around Jericho resulting in its fall, parallel the seven trumpets of Revelation (Rev. 8:6–11:19). Those prophetic trumpets sound historically sound up to and including the Day of Atonement/Investigative Judgment phase of the sanctuary parable [see Hebrews 9:25 (KJV) figure (NIV) illustration. Greek word "par-ab-o-lay] which begins October 22, 1844.

The beginning of this Day Of Atonement/Investagative Judgemt phase of the parable of the sanctuary is portrayed in the parable of the king coming to the wedding banquet to see who are guests [see Matthew 22:11] This coming was prior to the expected October 22, 1844 coming announced in Matthew 24:27 "as the lightening cometh out of the east and shineth unto the west; so shall also the coming of the Son of man be."

At the triumphal entry, when the Israelite nation expected, as Christ rode into Jerusalem to set up his kingdom, they were to be disappointed at the end of the week with his death on Calvary's cross. So at the close of the twenty-three hundred day prophecy of Daniel 8:14, the Millerites and other other believers, expected the second coming to be the cleansing of the sanctuary. They experienced the Great Disappointment of October 22, 1844. This was according to the sanctuary-parable plan.

Like the parable of the king coming to the wedding banquet [see Matthew 22:1-14], he found one person without the wedding garment. In his final week before his crucifixion, Christ literally came to the temple [see Matthew 21:12-17. Mark 11:12-19. Luke 19:45-48] with a judgment message, throwing out the buyers and sellers, allowing the praying ones to remain. That was a judgment message for and against some people.

Hence, Christ came at the close of the twenty-three hundred days of the Daniel 8:14 prophecy to the "sign of the son of man" [see Matthew 24:30], to begin the Day of Atonement/Judgment phase of his coming. He had previously come to every human hearts door saying "Behold I stand at the door and knock. If any man hear my voice and open the door, I will come into him, and sup with him." Revelation 3:20. This knocking is a coming into a relationship with the person prior to the second coming referred to Matthew 24:27 as" lighting coming out of the east and shineth also unto the west." in the "clouds where every eye shall see him" refered to in Revelation 1:7. Now he would confirm with the onlooking court of the universe that people who had died in a saving relationship to him, or if they would have known of that relationship, were safe to save. This would be called the Investigative Judgment or Day of Atonement in the parable of the sanctuary.

This coming was prior to His expected Parousia #3952 (Mt. 24:27, 1 Thes. 4:15) coming (# 2064 er-cho-mai lit. or fig.) in the clouds to this earth when every eye shall see (#3700 op-tan-om-ahee mid.) Him. (Rev. 1:7).

The following is lifted from *http://en.wikipedia.org/wiki/Voice_(grammar)*

In classical Greek, the middle voice often has a reflexive sense: the subject acts on or for itself, such as "the boy washes himself" or "the boy washes." It can be transitive or intransitive. It can occasionally be

296

used in a causative sense, such as "The father causes his son to be set free," or "the father ransoms his son."[536]

Hence during the Feast of Trumpets, in its proclamation of the gospel, the eye of the individual will come to see in his mind that Christ, the second person of the Godhead came from heaven in the incarnation as a sanctuary, to dwell as a tabernacle/tent among men, parallel to the Israelites/believers coming from Egypt/sin, both to dwell in the wilderness in tents, a symbol of this earth before an entrance into Canaan/heaven. In that Feast of Trumpets, they would proclaim that not only had God redeemed them from Egypt/sin by the blood of the slain lamb on their doorposts/hearts, but He had told them what they were to become before they entered Canaan/heaven. They were to become a kingdom of priests.

Although the tribe of Levites were priests, they were still part of fallen human nature. If they sinned, there were literal appropriate "type" sacrifices that could be brought to the altar of burnt offering and they would receive forgiveness. If a leader, or a member of the community, sinned unintentionally, there were different specific animal sacrifices which were to be brought to that same altar according to Leviticus 4, and the penitent would be forgiven.

Now after Calvary's sacrifice, Christ, "the Lamb of God which taketh away the sin of the world" (Jn. 1:29) was the only figurative/spiritual appropriate "antitypical" sacrifice that could be brought by all penitent believers. In n their minds' eye, praying to the risen Christ in heaven, who is humanity's elder brother, substitute lamb of God sacrifice for sin, risen High Priest in the heavenly sanctuary was the only one who could forgive their sins. [see 1 John 1:9] This heavenly sanctuary high priestly ministry of Christ occurs in heaven according to Hebrews 9:9. The word translated as a "figure" (KJV), "illustration" (NIV) of the sanctuary This is the same word Jesus used when He spoke in parables.

Following the Feast of Trumpets which began on the first day of the seventh month, the Day of Atonement began on the tenth day of the seventh month. Literally the High Priest on that day went from the Holy to the Most Holy Place behind the veil with the golden censer whose smoke shielded a view of the mercy seat. Antitypically October 22, 1844, is the conclusion of the 2,300-day prophecy of Daniel 8:14. That is the time when Christ, fallen human nature's High Priest went into the Most Holy Place and began the work of judging the dead (#3498 nekros lit. or fig. see Rev. 11:18). Literally dead people had ceased to breath and are usually buried in the earth, or the remains are disposed of in some other fashion. So from the time of Abel to the present time, those people would be judged to see whether or not they were fit candidates for heaven. Since Mt. Sinai the Jews and other believers like them would be judged under the Ten Commandment law. All others prior to and following Mt. Sinai encounter would not be judged by the Ten Commandment law, but the law, according to the Romans 2:15, says that is "written on their hearts, their consciences also bearing witness, and their thoughts now accusing, (now even defending them." This was the "law of faith" (Rom. 3:27).

On the Day of Atonement, the High Priest went alone into the Most Holy Place with the golden censor from the altar of incense in the Holy Place to make an atonement for the children of Israel. Leading up to this occasion, all Israel had confessed their sins upon the head of a sacrifice, transferring the sins from themselves to the sacrifice, who were killed and some of its blood taken into the holy place and sprinkled on the veil. Consequently the sins had been transferred from the believer to the head of the sacrifice, to the holy place. In like manner, the post-Calvary sins of believers—past, present, and future—were laid at Calvary, on Christ, the lamb of God, Sin bearer.

Since the risen Christ is depicted as the encircling arms of God's love which surround the Hebraic sanctuary with linen curtains, His physical, incarnate self is depicted as the tabernacle/tent similar to Israel's wilderness tent dwellings. To the wilderness tent dwellers, Christ, as it were, invited all those encamped around the tabernacle symbol of God dwelling among them in a more elaborate tent so that all could be extended an invitation to come unto Him. Since fallen humanity since Calvary, the resurrection and ascension are depicted as fish in the laver/sea symbol of the earth, to be caught in the nets of His resurrection, dying to self, their old way of life, they are to rise to be transformed into priests ministering in Christ's body, the church.

With all of the sins of the nation of Israel transferred from the penitent believer to the sacrifice with some of the blood being poured out on the earth and some of the blood being transferred to the tabernacle to be sprinkled on the veil or placed on the horns of the altar of incense, it was only the holy place, a symbol of Christ's body, the church, that needed to be cleansed from sin. Every sin confessed at the altar of burnt offering by placing the penitents hands on the head of the sacrifice was represented by the blood on the veil, a symbol of Christ's slain body at Calvary. Hence the only thing needed to be cleansed on the Day of Atonement was the Holy Place. Every Israelite, with all their confessions, was represented by the blood on the veil.

Hence, when Christ began the Investigative Judgment on the Day Of Atonement phase, according to the parable [figure KJV, illustration NIV, par-ab-o-lay Hebrews 9:9] of the sanctuary, in the heavenly sanctuary October 22, 1844, with the knowledge that he would have died for the sins if only one person of the human race could be saved as illustrated by the parable of the lost sheep or lost coin, it is as if each individual was the provisional recipient of the matchless substitute merits of His grace. Each individual would be called to appropriate Christ's merits on Calvary, the resurrection, and ascension as his entitlement and fitness to new life in the journey from Egypt/sin toward Canaan/heaven. While corporate Israel/humanity was to individually bring sacrifices to the altar of burnt offering, symbol of Calvary, confess their sins upon the lambs/ Christ's head, they were immediately forgiven, being able to walk away free from sin, yet their sin, while not being counted against them, was noted on the veil, separating the holy from the most holy place in the tabernacle.

When the judgment for an individual came up, all the times he committed sin and asked for forgiveness came up, being coalesced together, so that Christ could say to the Father, "See this person has believed on Me and is covered by my blood and therefore is safe to save." Thus the person, having claimed the merits of Christ's blood would be a judgment in favor of God. That person would agree with God that He was right in granting him salvation because he had accepted the provisions of Calvary. This experience would be replicated until the whole world would pass favorable or unfavorable judgment on God regarding His dealing with sin.

Some believers would proclaim that the only thing necessary for salvation was to accept Christ and His sacrifice as personal Savior from sin, being at the blade level of belief, others, while not negating Calvary's sacrifice would go on from faith unto faith, maturing into the ear and the full corn in the ear in their relationship to God. So in the judgment there would be people at varying levels of growth in grace, all having the same reward of eternal life, but at different stages of development in their relationship to God. These people would be sheep followers of the Good shepherd. They were on a course that would enable them to become like their leader.

Our professed believers would profess that Calvary's sacrifice was not necessary, for why does someone have to die? Isn't God a God of love? They forgot or deliberately denied that God set the boundaries of what was acceptable, declaring that if those boundaries were violated the person doing the infraction would die. So God set the rules of love, and if a creature decided to live outside those rules, although the capacity was provided in freedom, it would result in death. This group believed that really the only thing necessary is to do good works, or ascent to certain beliefs about God. This group would choose a path to God other than faith. They would negate the Scripture that said, "When the Son of Man comes, will he find faith."

Thus they would follow some shepherd other than the Good shepherd. They follow some other course that would not enable them to become like the Good shepherd.

After the Day of Atonement came the Feast of Tabernacles. While Christ was the tabernacle in the midst of the Israelite encampment, having learned to become like Him, they would be living stone, tabernacles, built on Christ the solid rock in the Feast of Tabernacles.

While the believer could accept the teaching of Jesus, symbolized in eating unleavened bread, prior to Calvary, he would continue eating that bread after acceptance of Christ as personal savior from sin typified lamb/goat type slain in Egypt, antitypically experienced at Calvary, continuing to eat the unleavened bread symbol after Calvary. He would acknowledge that Christ, the risen lamb was the first fruits, having had ascended to heaven and was their High Priest who desired to outpour the Holy Spirit at the Feast of Weeks also known later as the day of Pentecost. On the day of atonement, His followers, confessing their sins, would proclaim a judgment in favor of the way God had reconciled them to Himself through belief in His Son as their sin bearer, who had taken away their sin in His method to save them.

In the present/future Feast of Tabernacles, his followers would become living stone witness tabernacles for Him, because they are like Him, being clothed as priests in the garments of His righteousness.

shall trouble (#926 baw- hal) him

#926 baw-hal: a prim. root to trouble inwardly (or palpitate), fig. be (cause, make) (suddenly) alarmed or agitated: by impl. to hasten anxiously: be make affrighted (afraid, amazed, dismayed, rash), (be, get, make), haste (-n,-y, -fly, give) (-ily), thrust out, trouble, vex. Strongs,1979

#926 ba-hal v. [N] to be terrified, alarmed, dismayed, bewildered; [P] to make afraid, terrify; to make haste; [Pu] to be hastened, made to hurry, to cause terror; to cause to hurry:- Strongs, 2001

Therefore he shall (#3318 yaw-tsaw go forth)

#3318 yaw-tsaw; a prim. root; to go (causat. bring) out, In a great variety of appl. lit. and fig. direct and proxim. – x after, appear, x assuredly, bear out x begotten, break out, bring forth (out, up), carry out, come (abroad), out, thereat, without), + be condemned, depart (-ing,-ure), draw forth, in the end, escape, exact, fall, fall (out), fetch forth (out) get away (forth, hence, out), (able to, cause to, let) go abroad (forth, on, out) going out, grow, have forth (out), issue out, lay (lie) out, pluck out, proceed, pull out, put away, be risen, x scarce, send with, command, bent, shoot forth, spread, spring out, stand out, x still, x surely, take forth (out), any time, x to (and fro), utter Strongs, 1979

#3318 a-sa v.[Q] to go out, come out [H} to bring out, lead forth; produce: [Ho] to be brought out; emptied; by extension; to grow (of plants), to have offspring. Strongs, 2001 with great (#1419 gaw-dole) fury (#2534 khsy-may), great(#1419 gaw-dole)

#1419 gaw-dol (or short) gaw-dole; from 14

31; great; great (in any sense); hence older also insolent:-+ aloud, elder (- est) + exceeding (-ly)+ (far man) great (man, matter, thing, -er,-ness) high, long, loud, mighty, more, mercy, noble, proud thing x sore, very Strongs, 1979

#1419 ga-dol a. great, large (great king, high priest, much, more; this can refer to physical size, quantity, degree, and social status (great king, high priest) Strongs, 2001

fury (#2534 khay-may)

#2534 khay-may; or (Dan. 11:44) from 3179; heat; fig. anger, poison (from its fevor):- anger, bottles, hot displeasure, furious (-ly, -ry) heat, indignation, poison, rage, wrath (-ful). See 3529.

#2534 he-ma n.f. anger, wrath, fury, rage, from the base meaning of heat (as in "hot-headed"); by extension: venom (poison that causes a burning sensation). Strongs, 2001

to destroy (#8045 shaw-mad)

#8045 shaw-mad: a prim. root; to desolate:- destroy(-uction), bring to nought, overthrow, perish, pluck down, x utterly Strongs, 1979

#8045 sa-mad, v. [N] to be destroyed; [H] to destroy, demolish, annihilate Strongs, 2001

and utterly to make away (#2763 khaw-ram) many.

#2763 khaw-ram: a prim. root; to seclude: spec. by a ban) to devote to relig. Uses (espec. destruction): phys. and reflex to be blunt as the nose:- make accursed, consecrate, (utterly destroy, devote, forfeit, have a flat nose, utterly (slay, make away). Strongs, 1979

#2763 ha-ram v. [Qp] to be disfigured, mutilated, any split portion of the face, possibly a cleft palate; [H] to completely destroy, devote to destruction, exterminate, annihilate [Ho] to be destroyed, be devoted to destruction; this can refer to anything which is under the ban from common use, some things are set apart for use by the priests, other things are destroyed utterly as devoted to the Lord. Strongs, 2001

"Therefore, rejoice, ye heavens, and ye that dwell in them. Woe to the inhibiters of the earth and of the sea! For the devil is come down (#2597 kat- a-bai-no) unto you, having great wrath, because he knoweth that he hath but a short [time #2540 kai-ros]. And the dragon (saw #1492 i-do lit. or fig.) that he was cast unto the earth, he persecuted the woman which brought forth the man child. And to the woman were given two wings of a great eagle, that she might fly into the wilderness, into her place, where she is nourished for a time and times, and half a time, from the face of the serpent." Revelation 12:12, 13. #2597 kat-ab-ah-ee-no; from 2596 and the base of 939; to descend (lit.or fig.): -come (get, go, step) down, descend, fall (down). Strongs, 1979

#2597 kat-a-bai-no v. to go down, descend. Strongs, 2001

The aspect of the definition for the word "come down" (#2597 kat-a-bai- no) portrays not only literal but the figurative-spiritual assault battle of the devil on the heart of the"inner man" [see Ephesians 3:16] who is referred to as a "living stone," [see 1 Peter 2:4] in the "holy place, sanctuary, a saint."[537]

The aspect of the definity for the word "time" (#2540 kairos) portrays the short, opportune time during which the Investagative Judgement, Day of Atonement ministry in the parable [see Hebrews 9:24 of the heavenly sanctuary will occur.

#2540 kai-ros; of uncertain affin; an occasion i.e. set or proper time: x always, opportunity, (convenient, due) season (due, short, while) time, awhile. Comp. 5550 Strongs, 1979

#2540 kairos n. time (particular and general): right time, opportune time, proper time, appointed time. Strongs, 2001

#1492 i-do. a prim. verb used only in certain tenses. The others being borrowed from the equiv. 3700 and 3708; prop. to see (lit. or fig.);

by imply. (in the perf. only) to know:- be aware, behold, x can (+ not tell), consider, (have) know (-ledge), look (on), perceive, see, be sure, tell, understand, wist, wot. Comp. 3700. Strongs, 1979.

#1492 ei-do v. to know, to possess information, recognize, realize, to come to know; to be able to use knowledge. Strong, 2001

And the serpent cast out of his mouth water as a flood after the woman, that he might cause her to be carried away of the flood.

And the earth helped the woman, and the earth opened her mouth, and swallowed up the flood which the dragon cast out of his mouth.

And the dragon was wroth with the woman, and went to make war with the remnant of her seed, which keep the commandments of God, and have the testimony of Jesus. (Rev. 12:12–17)

And he said unto me, thou must prophecy again before many peoples, and nations, and tongues, and kings. (Rev. 10:11)

After the great disappointment of October 22, 1844, experienced by the Millerite movement, at which time they had expected Christ to come to this earth in fulfilment of the 2,300-day prophecy of Daniel 8:14, Hiram Edson had a vision in the cornfield of the heavenly sanctuary. The Pen of Inspiration records:

The following section is lifted/copied from White, Ellen G. Early Writings, 1945, page XVIII

Hiram Edson, one of this group, lived in central New York State at Port Gibson. He was the leader of the Adventists in that area. The believers met in his home on October 22, 1844, to await the coming of the Lord. Calmly and patiently the awaited the great event. But as the hour of midnight came and they realized the day of expectation had passed, it became clear that Jesus would not come as soon as they had thought. It was a time of bitter disappointment. In the early morning hours Hiram Edson and a few others went out to his barn to pray, and as they prayed, he felt assured that light would come.

A little later, as Edson and a friend were crossing a cornfield to visit fellow Adventists, it seemed as if a hand touched his shoulder. He looked up to see- as if in a vision-the heavens opened, and Christ in the heavenly sanctuary entering into the most holy place, there to begin a work of ministry in behalf of His people, instead of coming forth from the most holy place to cleans the world with fire, as they had taught.[538]

In this interpretation, it is leaned to the perception, that William Miller's study of the 2,300-day prophecy of Daniel 8:14 with its subsequent cleansing of the sanctuary is a direct fulfillment of Matthew 24:30 (first part), "And then shall appear the sign of the Son of man in heaven." Just as the Israelites/ came out of the bondage of Egypt, so believers are to come out of enslavement to sin under the power of the blood of the slain lambat calvary. It took Israel three months until they came to Mt. Sinai where they first discovered what they were redeemed from Egypt/sin to become, i.e., a kingdom of priests. So it could potentially take believers some time after accepting calvaries sacrifice to discover what they are to become. Like the Levites, a subset, of the Israelite nation were set apart to eventually minister in the tabernacle.. so ministers, a subset of humanity, would be called to shepherd believers. That literal "type" tabernacle within the earthly sanctuary into which priests were to minister was set up a year after their exodus by the power of the blood/ calvary on their doorposts. Post calvary humanity was to discover that the risen Christ was the figurative/spiritual tabernacle within the linen curtains/arms symbol of Christ's righteousness into whom they were to enter. So like Israel, all humanity would discover that God in the person of Jesus Christ was the tabernacle within the sanctuary arms of His righteousness who dwelt among them While all Israel was invited to come into the sanctuary with their sacrifices, all humanity enclosed within the arms of Christ's righteousness on the laver/sea/earth/world were to come out of the world to the foot of Calvary. The altar of burnt offering in the midst of the outer court is a symbol of Calvary. While the literal Israelites brought lambs, other animal sacrifices, and grain offerings to this altar, post-calvary believers would bring their risen, elder brother, Christ Jesus figuratively/spiritually to that altar symbol of Calvary. There the post calvary believer would have explained to him/her by the risen Christ that he was the Lamb of God who took away the sin of the world at Calvary. Then the risen Christ would plead with the believer to accept Him as the Lamb of God that taketh away the sin of the world. Realizing that their sin had been atoned for, the believer, by the powerful grace shining from Calvary's empty tomb, would separate himself, by choice, dying to the outside faith atmosphere called self or sin. With this death to sin, also known as outside faith atmosphere, self, the believer was to rise with Christ and put on the garments of His righteousness. and serve as priests in his body, the tabernacle "temple of the tabernacle" (Rev. 15:5). That garment of His righteousness was the priestly wedding garment prepared for them to accept. See Matthew 22:11, 12.

The layout of the sanctuary, is the motherboard, as it were, describing the phases, in a parable (see Hebrews 9:9, of Christ's coming to bring reconciliation of fallen mankind to God. The first phase was the type promise of the slain lamb in Eden practiced prior to and through the Hebraic sanctuary with its temple replacement which culminated in the death of Christ. Once the birth life, death, and resurrection of Christ occurred the "antitypical" phase of the heavenly sanctuary was simultaneously obserevable along side the "type" Hebraic sanctuary with its temple replacement. Christ's death on Calvary demonstrated that lamb of God had been slain and with the veil between the holy and most holy place torn proved that the "type" sacrifice had been replaced by the "antytipical." When Christ cried out from the cross "It is finished," he was saying that the "antitypical" fulfilment of the daily "type" sacrificial lamb coupled to the provisional holy place phase ministry of the sanctuary parable was finished by his death. As their risen and ascended elder brother, high priest, tabernacle/temple, Christ would provisionally cloth believers who were in relationship to him with the priestly robe of his righteousness. In this relationship to Christ, who had taken away humanity's naked standing before God, redeemed humanity would serve him as priests. This experience would be parallel and more advanced to the skins that covered Adam and Eve's nakedness after they sinned in Eden. Thus the tabernacle/temple risen Christ was the "place prepared by God where she might be taken care of" (Rev 12:6) "out of the serpent's reach" (Rev. 12:14).

The second phase of Christ's coming was the type promise of believers being clothed with the righteousness of Christ, like the Levitical priests who lived in the Israelite community put on linen garments to serve in the sanctuary. This is portrayed in Christ's parable of the wedding banquet (Mt. 22:3–12) when the king came to see if all of the guests were wearing the provided for, appropriate attire, which is the righteousness of Christ. When Christ did not come to this earth, in the "second coming," at the close of the twenty-three day prophecy of Daniel 8:14 to cleanse the earth as expected, the great disappointment of October 22, 1844 occurred. This disappointment resulted in believers "mourning" (Mt. 24:30, last part) as predicted by Christ.

Prior to the October 22, 1844 disappointment, starting with his ascension in A.D. 31, Christ, our high priest, had been carrying out the "daily" antitypical ministry in the heavenly sanctuary. This was according Hebrew 9:9 Greek word par-ab-o-lay translated as figure (KJV), and illustration (NIV). With believers who figuratively/spiritually accepted his atoning sacrifice at Calvary, laying their sins on him, dying to self, which is a denial of breathing outside faith life, Christ would raise to life since they were dead to sin. Under the powerful grace of the banner of his shed blood, they would live in relationship to their risen lord for forty days, similar to the Israelites who lived in dwellings with the blood on their doorposts up until the midnight judgment. God was justified in leading the Israelites who had the blood on their doorposts, just as God is justified in leading believers out of sin whose blood is on their hearts. God's justification to save both Israelites or believers lay in the fact that both had accepted something which pointed to someone, Christ, outside themselves as personal savior from Egyptian bondage or sin. Just as there was much to be learned by Israel in the year from slaughtering the lamb and putting its blood on their doorposts to functioning as priests, so there are many things to be learned after a person accepts Christ as personal savior from sin until a believer puts on, figuratively/spiritually, the righteousness of Christ. This garment of the righteousness of Christ is to be "put on," [see Galations 3:27, Col. 3:10] figuratively/spiritually by post calvary priestly believers.

If a pre or post-calvary believer, like Abraham, believed God, not knowing about the sanctuary and priestly ministry therein, it would be "counted to him for righteousness." Genesis 15:6. Under the fifth seal "souls were slain for the word of God, and for the testimony which they held... And white robes were given unto every one of them." [see Revelation 7:9-11]. Just as Abraham did not have the ten commandment law as given to Moses and consequently would not be judged under the law, he like all unbelievers would be judged by the law that was "written on their hearts" Romans 2:15.

The following section is lifted/copied from *White, Ellen G. The Great Controversy, 1950 The Pacific Press page 489.*

The intercession of Christ in man's behalf in the sanctuary above is as essential to the plan of salvation as was His death on the cross. By His death He began that work which after His resurrection He ascended to complete in heaven. GC489[539]

Christ is the "foundation," [1 Corinthians 3:10] chief corner (stone), [Ephesians 2;20. 1 Peter 2:6] of the "temple of the tabernacle of the testimony" {Revelation 15:5.] Upon that foundation believers lay the ["foundation of 1) repentance from dead works and of 2) faith toward God, 3) of the doctrine of baptisms 4) and of laying on of hands, 5) and of the resurrection of the dead, 6) and of eternal judgment.] Hebrews 6:1,2. The next layer of foundation is "foundation of the apostles" Ephesians 2:20. Peter is one of the apostles and of him Christ says, "Though art Peter, and upon this rock, I will build my church" Matthew 16:18. Peter, like all other apostles and believers were to be "living stones." 1 Peter 2:4.

DANIEL 11:45

45. And he shall plant the tabernacles of his palace between the seas in the glorious holy mountain; yet he shall come to his end, and none shall help him.

And he shall plant (#5193 naw-tah)

#5193 naw-tah; a prim. root: prop. to strike in, i.e. fix. spec. to plant. (lit. or fig.):- fastened, plant (-er) Strongs, 1979

#5193 na-ta v. [Q] to plant (seed or stock); by extension: to place, set, set up, (only object on any surface. Strongs, 2001.

The tabernacles (#168 o-hel)

#168 o-hel; a tent, (as clearly conspicuous from a distance)-covering, (dwelling), (place), home, tabernacle, tent. Strongs, 1979

#168 o-hel n. m. (also used with compound proper names). tent, tent-dwelling; by extension; home, dwelling place, a permanent dwelling; family group. "The Tent Of The Meeting" was the worship tent built before the Temple. Strongs, 2001

of his palace (#643 ap-peh-den)

#643 ap-peh-den; appar. of for. der.; a pavilion or palace-tent:- palace. Strongs, 1979

#643 ap-pe-den n. (m.) palace tent, royal tent. Strongs, 2001

and none(#369 'ay-in) shall help (#5826 aw-zar) him

This is in contrast to Daniel 10:13 which states "Then Michael, one of the chief princes, came to help (#5826 aw-zar) me. . ." and Daniel 11:34 "And when they shall fall they will be holpen (#5826 aw-zar) with a little help (#5828 ay-zer).

#369 'ay-in subst neg. there is no, not, none, without Strongs, 2001

#5826 aw-zar; a prim. root; to surrender, i.e. protect or aid: help, succor. Strongs, 1979.

#5826 a-zar v. [Q] to help, support [Qp] to be helped; [N] to be helped Strong, 2001

#5828 ay-zer; from 5826; aid – help Strongs, 1979.

#5828 'e-zer n. m. (also used with compound names) help, helper. Strongs, 2001

This Michael in Daniel 10:13 is the same as the Michael depicted in Revelation 12:7.

> And there was war in heaven: Michael and his angels fought against the dragon; and the dragon fought and his angels. And prevailed not; neither was there place found anymore in heaven. And the great dragon was cast out, that old serpent, called the Devil and Satan, which deceiveth the whole world: he was cast out into the earth, and his angels with him.

He is portrayed as the tabernacle in Exodus 25:8 who, at His incarnation, came from heaven to earth to dwell among the Israelites in the wilderness, in their tent (Ex. 33:4) dwellings, having put off, or left their Egyptian dwellings on their way from Egypt/sin to Canaan/heaven. While the Israelites lived in tent/tabernacle dwellings for nearly a year after the Exodus, discovering what they were to become, three months into the journey, a kingdom of priests who were to live according to the spoken Ten Commandment law at Sinai, although they had been living by faith under the blood which they had placed on their doorposts in Egypt up to that time in tent/tabernacles, a symbol of the future, as yet unknown, feast of tabernacles.

I. If one does not obey Moses and the prophets from an attitude of faith in God, "he will come to an end and none shall help him."

A. And there was a certain beggar named Lazarus, which was laid at his gate, full of sores, And desiring to be fed with the crumbs which fell from the rich man's table: moreover the dogs came and licked his sores. And it came to pass, that the beggar died, and was carried by the angels into Abraham's bosom: the rich man also died, and was buried; And in hell he lift up his eyes, being in torments, and seeth Abraham afar off, and Lazarus in his bosom. And he cried and said, Father Abraham, have mercy on me, and send Lazarus, that he may dip the tip of his finger in water, and cool my tongue; for I am tormented in this flame. But Abraham said, Son, remember that thou in thy lifetime receivedst thy good things, and likewise Lazarus evil things: but now he is comforted, and thou art tormented. And beside all this, between us and you there is a great gulf fixed: so that they which would pass from hence to you cannot; neither can they pass to us, that would come from thence. Then he said, I pray thee therefore, father, that thou wouldest send him to my father's house: For I have five brethren; that he may testify unto them, lest they also come into this place of torment. Abraham saith unto him, They have Moses and the prophets; let them hear them. And he said, Nay, father Abraham: but if one went unto them from the dead, they will repent. And he said unto him, If they hear not Moses and the prophets, neither will they be persuaded, though one rose from the dead.

II. If one does not have the oil of the Holy Spirit, he will come to an end and none shall help him.

A. Then shall the kingdom of heaven be likened unto ten virgins, which took their lamps, and went forth to meet the bridegroom. And five them were wise, and five were foolish. They that were foolish took the lamps, and took no oil with them: But the wise took oil in their vesse with their lamps. While the bridegroom tarried, they all slumbered an slept. And at midnight there was a cry made, Behold, the bridegroo cometh; go you out to meet him. Then all those virgins arose, an trimmed their lamps. And the foolish said unto the wise, Give us of yo oil; for our lamps are gone out. But the wise answered, saying, Not s lest there be not enough for us and you: but go ye rather to them that se and buy for yourselves. And while they went to buy, the bridegroo came; and they that were ready went in with him to the marriage; and t door was shut. Afterward came also the other virgins, saying, Lor Lord, open to us. But he answered and said, Verily I say unto you, know you not. Watch therefore, for ye know neither the day nor the ho wherein the Son of man cometh. (Mt. 25:1–13)

III. Babylon will fall and none will help her.

A. And the kings of the earth, who have committed fornication and lived deliciously with her, shall bewail her, and lament for her, when they shall see the smoke of her burning, standing afar off for the fear of her torment, saying, Alas, alas, that great city Babylon, that mighty city! for in one hour is thy judgment come. And the merchants of the earth shall weep and mourn over her; for no man buyeth their merchandise any more: the merchandise of gold, and silver, and precious stones, and of pearls, and fine linen, and purple, and silk, and scarlet, and all thyine wood, and all manner vessels of ivory, and all manner vessels of most precious wood, and of brass, and iron, and marble, and cinnamon, and odours, and ointments, and frankincense, and wine, and oil, and fine flour, and wheat, and beasts, and sheep, and horses, and chariots, and slaves, and souls of men.

And the fruits that thy soul lusted after are departed from thee, ad all things which were dainty and goodly are departed from thee, and thou shalt find them no more at all.

The merchants of these things, which were made rich by her, shall stand afar off for the fear of here torment, weeping and wailing, And saying, Alas, alas, that great city, that was clothed in fine linen, and purple, and scarlet, and decked with gold, and precious stones, and pearls!

For in one hour so great riches is come to nought. And every shipmaster, and all the company in ships, and sailors, and as many as trade by sea, stood afar off, And cried when they saw the smoke of her burning, saying, What city is like unto this great city!

And they cast dust on their heads, and cried, weeping and wailing, saying, Alas, alas, that great city, wherein were made rich all that had ships in the sea by reason of here costliness! For in one hour is she made desolate.

Rejoice over here, thou heaven, and ye holy apostles and prophets; for God hath avenged you on her. And a mighty angel too up a stone like a great millstone, and cast it into the sea, saying, Thus with violence shall that great city Babylon be thrown down, and shall be found no more at all. And the voice of harpers, and musicians, and of pipers, and trumpeters, shall be heard nor more at all in thee; and no craftsman, of whatsoever craft he be, shall be found any more in thee; and the sound of a millstone shall be heard no more at all in thee; And the light of a candle shall shine no more at all in thee; and the voice of the bridegroom and of the bride shall be heard no more at all in thee: for thy merchants were the great men of earth; for by thy sorceries were all nations deceived. And in here was found the blood of prophets, and of saints, and of all that were slain upon the earth. (Rev. 18:9–24)

IV. The dragon, beast, and false prophet "will come to an end and none shall help them."

A. And I saw the beast, the kings of the earth, and their armies, gathered together to make war against Him who sat on the horse and against His army. 20 Then the beast was captured, and with him the false prophet who worked signs in his presence, by which he deceived those who received the mark of the beast and those who worshiped his image. These two were cast alive into the lake of fire burning with brimstone. (Rev. 19:19–20)

    a. And the devil, who deceived them, was thrown into the lake of burning sulfur, where the beast and the false prophet had been thrown. They will be tormented day and night for ever and ever.

    b. But the fearful, and unbelieving, and the abominable, and murderers, and whoremongers, and sorcerers, and idolaters, and all liars, shall have their part in the lake which burneth with fire and brimstone: which is the second death.

    c. He answered and said unto them, He that soweth the good seed is the man; The field is the world; the good seed are the children of the but the tares are the children of the wicked one; The enemy that so is the devil; the harvest is the end of the world; and the reapers are t As therefore the tares are gathered and burned in the fire; so shall it end of this world. The Son of man shall send forth his angels, and t gather out of his kingdom all things that offend, and them which do And shall cast them into a furnace of fire; there shall be wailing and of teeth. Then shall the righteous shine forth as the sun in the ki their Father. Who hath ears to hear let him hear. (Mt. 13:37–43)

1.) Again, the kingdom of heaven is like unto a net, that was cast into sea; and gathered of every kind: Which, when it was full, they drew shore, and sat down, and gathered the good into vessels, but cast the b away. So shall it be at the end of the world: The angels shall come for and sever the wicked from among the just. And shall cast them into furnace of fire; there shall be wailing and gnashing of teeth. (Mt. 13:4 50)

V. Death and hell "will come to an end and none shall help them."

    A. And death and hell were cast into the lake of fire. This is the second death. And whosoever was not found written in the book of life was ca into the lake of fire. (Rev. 20:14, 15)

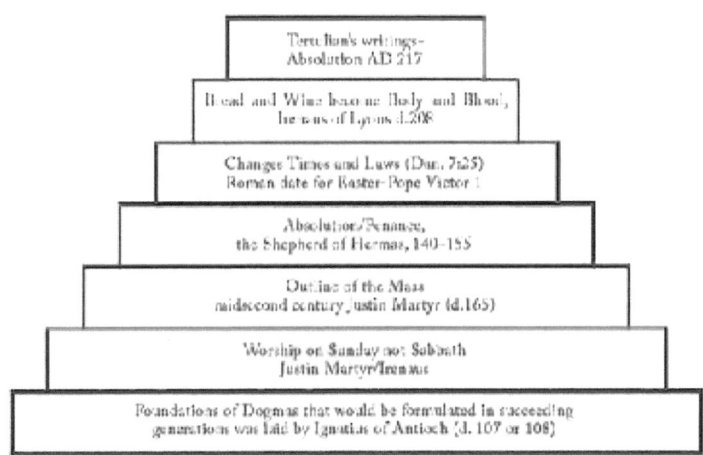

The first and bottom step being the foundations for dogmas that would be formulated in succeeding generations laid by Ignatius of Antioch (d. 107 or 108).[10] The second ascending circular stair step in this tower is "worship on Sunday not Sabbath" as advocated by Justin Martyr (d. 165)[11] and Irenaus (d. 208). [Note:Mark 15:42ff]"The Sabbath began at sundown on Friday and ended at sundown on Saturday. Jesus died just a few hours before sundown on Friday. It was against Jewish law to do physical work or to travel on Sabbath. It was also against Jewish law to let a dead body remain exposed overnight (Deuteronmy 21:23). Joseph came to bury Jesus body before the Sabbath began. If Jesus had died on the Sabbath when Joseph was unavailable, his body would have been taken down by the Romans. Had the Romans taken Jesus'body, no Jews could have confirmed his death, and opponents could have disputed his resurrection." [Note: Luke 6:1, 2]

313

DANIEL 11:22

22. And with the arms of a flood shall they be overflown from before his, and shall be broken; yea, also the prince of the covenant.

And with the arms of a flood

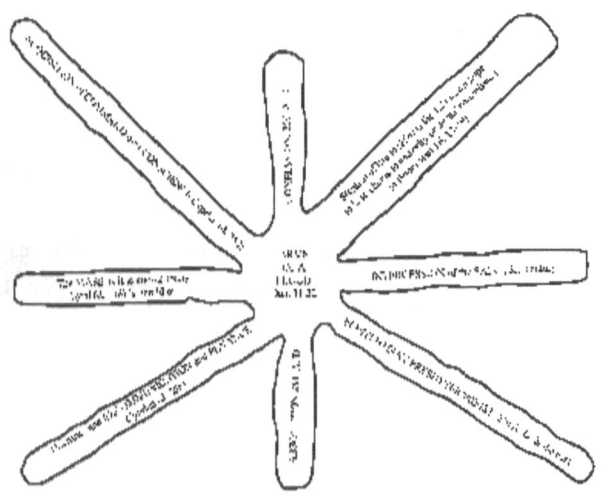

www.ingramcontent.com/pod-product-compliance
Lightning Source LLC
Chambersburg PA
CBHW020918140626
46545CB00015B/160